REED ILLUSTRATED HISTORY OF NEW ZEALAND

BY THE SAME AUTHOR

Hawke's Bay: Lifestyle Province

Wonderful Wairarapa

Wellington/Kapiti Coast

Hawke's Bay: The History of a Province

Havelock North: The History of a Village

Napier: City of Style

Kiwi Air Power: The History of the RNZAF

New Zealand's Engineering Heritage

Working Together: The History of Carter Oji-Kokusaku Pan Pacific Ltd 1971–1993

Battle for Crete: New Zealand's Near-run Affair, 1941

Quake: Hawke's Bay 1931

Town and Country: The History of Hastings and District

Blue Water Kiwis: New Zealand's Naval Story

Desert Duel: New Zealand's North African War 1940–43

Wings Over New Zealand: A Social History of Aviation in New Zealand

Italian Odyssey: New Zealanders in the Battle for Italy, 1943–45

Pacific War: New Zealand and Japan 1941–45

Rails Across New Zealand: A History of Rail Travel

REED ILLUSTRATED HISTORY OF NEW ZEALAND

MATTHEW WRIGHT

Illustrations from the Alexander Turnbull Library

REED

Front cover (clockwise from top left): F-66497-1/2, page 309; F-F-20196-1/2, page 400; PAColl-0783, F-1201-1-4, page 352; PAColl-0614, F-22740-1/4, page 417; PAColl-0+25, F1149-35mm-28, page 407; PAColl-0614, F-69-35mm-B, page 437; G17071-1/2, page 258; F-139885-1/2, page 305; AAQT6401, A36966, page 401; PUBL-0015-09, page 39; PAColl-3082, G-1792-10x8, page 312
Spine: 47253-1/2, page 337
Back cover (left to right): PAColl-0975, G-10246-1/1s, page 184; F-18732-1/1, page 297; PAColl-0089-26, C-16005-1/2, page 347; Matthew Wright, page 452; C-026-002, page 69; DA-02096, F-2096-1/4-DA, page 360; PAColl-3042, G-313-1/1, page 122; PAColl-6303-08, C9624-1/2, page 382; F-49007-1/2, page 343; PAColl-0614, F-1392-35mm-11A, page 430

The publisher acknowledges the assistance of the History Group of
the Ministry for Culture and Heritage in the publication of this book.

Reed Publishing (NZ) Ltd
Te Karuhi tā tāpui o Reed (Aotearoa)

Established in 1907, Reed is New Zealand's largest
book publisher, with over 300 titles in print.

For details on all these books visit our website:
www.reed.co.nz

Published by Reed Books, a division of Reed Publishing (NZ) Ltd,
39 Rawene Rd, Birkenhead, Auckland 10.
Associated companies, branches and representatives throughout the world.

ISBN 0 7900 0955 2
First published 2004

A catalogue record for this book is available from the National Library of New Zealand.

Editors: Carolyn Lagahetau, Brian O'Flaherty, Susan Brierley, Eva Chan
Cover designed by Sally Fullam

Printed in China

Contents

Introduction

New Zealand's past is a rich tapestry woven of hope, ambition, wars, utopian dreamers, rogues and occasional heroes. All running — as has been observed more than once — at speed. There are people alive in twenty-first century New Zealand who were the movers-and-shakers of the twentieth; and it takes but a few who-knew-who links to go directly back to the nineteenth. Few countries offer such combinations of immediacy and depth.

Our past also lives around us. Century-old ferries ply the Waitemata from Devonport to Queen's Wharf. Commuters in Wellington ride daily on the electric suburban rail system introduced by the first Labour Government. Buried in the deep south, down the main street of Riverton, is the original cottage of John Howell, an early whaler who dreamed of a utopian future. Just a few minutes' drive out of New Plymouth it is possible to climb through the earthworks at Te Arei, where the first Taranaki war ended in 1861.

This book offers a broad-brush interpretation and narrative of New Zealand's life and times since about 1800. There are many lines of enquiry we might follow, a point highlighted by the general histories of Keith Sinclair and W.H. Oliver published within a year of each other at the end of the 1950s.[1] Other general historians have highlighted race relations,[2] politics and nationalism,[3] or cast a new framework altogether.[4] All reveal our general past from different perspectives, and the interplay is itself of value. New Zealand's past contains layers of meaning, and — to paraphrase Karl Popper — deeper truths can often be teased out through discussion. This does not mean that historians should dredge through the work of their peers looking for unintended ambiguities or trivial discrepancies between sources on which to condemn. Debate requires a generous and co-operative approach if it is to produce conclusions of worth.

History also demands abstraction. From a twenty-first century perspective, nineteenth-century settlers were racist, sexist, over-rational and determinist. So too were the 'jingoes' of the early twentieth century. However, they did not think

so themselves, and we have merely to look at what settler bureaucrats filed as 'miscellaneous' to gain an instant picture of the conceptual gulf between past and present. We share language, heritage and relations with the past, but to assume we share meanings is misleading. The key challenge is to understand that past in its own terms. A related challenge is expressing it — finding a balance between the language needed to breathe life into text, and the understated vocabulary demanded of a subject where the implications of even common words may change over time.

Yet some ideas have remained surprisingly constant, though framed in different ways as the decades have gone on. These include the ideal of home ownership, our egalitarian thinking and the cultural cringe. Many questions flow from this line of thought. Were we ever truly equal? Why do New Zealanders uphold the ideal of the quarter acre, sometimes to the point of establishing lifetime debt for it? Where did the 'cultural cringe' come from, and how did it affect us? Why were our early-to-mid twentieth-century sentiments focused almost wholly on Britain? What part did New Zealand's early race relations play in setting up the country?

I have sought answers to some of these queries through the narrative — answers that, I hope, will help place the wider truths of New Zealand's past into context, allowing us to better understand where New Zealand is today. Of course, in a book of specified length it is impossible to answer all questions, or to describe every event. Nor would such a monstrous tome be convenient to read. Content must be relevant to purpose, and neither omission nor new thought equate to error. Some of my conclusions vary from those of some colleagues in the field, and I have outlined my reasoning and evidence where appropriate. Apart from the use of debate as a means of teasing out the deeper meanings of the past, history demands ongoing and careful reconsideration as our changing understanding of the world allows us to ask new questions.

The text is drawn from a range of documents, diaries, manuscripts, private papers, official reports and statistical records culled from diverse sources, including

the Alexander Turnbull Library, the Auckland War Memorial Museum, the Christchurch Public Library, the Hawke's Bay Museum, the Hastings District Council, the National Library, the Queen Elizabeth II Army Museum, the RNZAF Museum, and Archives New Zealand among others. Some material has been used indirectly, via earlier research done for my previous books, and I am grateful to the many archivists and librarians who have assisted me over the years. Like all general histories, this book also uses other publications both as sources of occasional detail, and in the more important sense of knowing how others have seen the past. I thank those who have generously given their time to comment on aspects of the text and have given me permission to quote from their work and to use images they have supplied, including Barry Gustafson, Richard Jackson, Olwen Morgan, Nigel Prickett, Sir John White and Colin Wynn.

I remain indebted to the editorial and production teams at Reed, particularly Peter Janssen, who asked me to write this book, Peter Dowling, Carolyn Lagahetau, Eva Chan and Brian O'Flaherty. This book is almost wholly illustrated from the collection of the Alexander Turnbull Library and I am grateful to the staff of the photographic section, especially Heather Mathie who took on the challenge of processing my order for 600-odd images. All reasonable efforts have been made to locate copyright holders, if applicable, for any copyrighted material not otherwise authorised or covered by reasonable 'fair dealing' provisions.

Finally, this book reflects two decades of ongoing research in New Zealand history, including post-graduate work, along with my enduring interest in sociology, ethnography and the sciences, and my interests in writing as a skill of its own. A number of people have materially helped me along the way, and I remain especially grateful to my wife, Judith, for tolerating my anti-social writing habits.

Matthew Wright
March 2004

CHAPTER 1

The first settlers

New Zealand was born and shaped by gigantic forces, a rugged landscape squeezed from colliding crustal plates and carried on an aeons-long journey across oceans, an odyssey that continues today. The first and largest New Zealand, Rangitata — the 'Tasmantis' of the south — disappeared under erosion as it moved. New lands rose. Five million years ago, 'Cook Strait' was in the Manawatu. Later the world entered an era of ice ages. Great glaciers rumbled down from the Southern Alps into Otago and Canterbury. This was also an age of fire. The North Island was dominated by the Oruanui volcanic field near Lake Taupo, where an immense eruption perhaps 30,000 years ago obliterated much life in the central plateau.

So much of the world's water was locked up in ice during these years that the seas dropped. At the most recent glacial maximum some 20,000 years ago, New Zealand was half as large again as it is now. Cook Strait was a deep bay battered by ferocious 'Wellington' winds. Much of the land was scrubby, though forests grew on sheltered slopes and in Northland.[1] The world entered a further inter-glacial period around 14 millennia ago, bringing a sharp rise in sea level, separating the North Island and the South Island and inundating what had been coastal plains. Forests came and went, but by around 2000 years ago both islands were heavily forested, with mainly podocarp forest in the north and beech in the south.[2] Another Taupo eruption in the second century AD changed the pattern, covering 20,000 square kilometres of the North Island in ignimbrite and a further 30,000 with tephra.[3]

No human eyes saw this disaster, and as late as 1960 historians could argue that readers had the 'luxury of choice' when deciding precisely how and when New Zealand was first settled.[4] Stories of fairy folk, moa hunters and Moriori added a layer of myth to popular understanding, but perhaps the biggest problem was the persistence of settler-era beliefs, some of which were still being promoted in fringe literature of the late twentieth century.[5] The underlying misconception was the nineteenth-century diffusionist notion that 'primitive' cultures were incapable of innovation; new developments could only come from successive waves of migration by more 'sophisticated' peoples.

The associated idea of a fleet depositing Maori into New Zealand around 1350 was largely devised by late nineteenth-century ethnographer S. Percy Smith.[6] It was popularised in the *School Journal*,[7] and was still being taught in primary schools in the 1960s, becoming an immutable popular 'truth' in the process. Yet the actual evidence was flimsy. Settler-era renaissance man William Colenso dismissed the whole concept of canoe migration as a 'mythic rhapsody' as early as 1865,[8] and one historian has suggested that the idea was integral to settler ideas of nation-founding, creating a past that befitted New Zealand's aspirations as a better Britain. Maori bought into the idea for similar reasons.[9] This certainly seems true; Te Rangi Hiroa (Sir Peter Buck) was a leading advocate.[10] In fact, the fleet theory became popular at precisely the time when the children of the settlers were styling New Zealand as the greatest of Britain's children, 'chief junior' in the wider Empire. Smith provided vicarious origins that were at least as heroic as those of the mother country. The fleet myth grew with the new ethos and was not seriously questioned until that whole ethos was falling into disrepair in the 1970s. Then, David Simmons demonstrated that Smith had reorganised Maori tradition to create a coherent but misleading tale.[11] Only Ngati Kahungunu spoke of a 'fleet',[12] and this may have referred to coastal voyages.[13]

What actually happened emerged slowly as systematic archaeological analysis got under way in the wake of the Second World War, bolstered by technical developments which transformed the ability of archaeologists to reconstruct time-lines. But it was a slow process even so, and argument raged for decades as the evidence trickled in. Smith's dates of a 925 discovery and 1350 settlement were initially replaced with a range extending from the first centuries AD to AD 800. Later there was a suggestion, based on rat remains dated to AD 50–150, that humans visited New Zealand at that time.[14] Carbon dating later suggested that the Pacific rat pre-dated known Polynesian settlement by at least 1000 years;[15] though the jury remained out because the pattern did not match the origins of the rat in the Pacific.[16] Other evidence suggested human settlement on other dates; seabed sediments off the Hawke's Bay coast suggested that forests had been burned off there as early as AD 600, prompting one proposal that Polynesians arrived about that time.[17] However, the discovery could not prove the cause of the blazes,[18] and this evidence was isolated, whereas any significant human presence would have left interrelated traces ranging from old campfires to artefacts, village sites, patterns of agriculture, storage pits and midden heaps.

Discovering where New Zealand's first settlers came from was another contentious process, closely entwined with timing. Hawaiki, the traditional home, was clearly an abstraction, but nineteenth-century explanations were tied up in thinking about race, the concept of 'progress' from savagery to civilisation — and the idea that 'primitive' peoples were trapped in an earlier stage. This blinded successive archaeologists to the patterns shown by the available evidence.[19] Theories were put forward in an environment where personal status was often as much at stake as the ideas being discussed. This was punctuated by such dramatic exercises as Thor Heyerdahl's *Kon Tiki* expedition of 1947, which showed that with a little help from a tug, modern medicines, radio and food stocks, a 'traditional' Inca raft could drift across the Pacific.[20]

One outcome of all this was a public perception that the origins of Polynesians in general, and Maori in particular, were unknowable, or that any theory, however odd, was as credible as any other. This certainly fuelled the 'fringe' thinking of the late twentieth century, some of which was based on uncritical and out-of-context acceptance of old writings and ideas, this time filtered through 'New Age' theology.[21] In fact the question did have an answer. By the 1980s a wide range of consistent and interlocking evidence from multiple sources − linguistic, archaeological, cultural and even mathematical[22]− showed that people first came to New Zealand from central-east Polynesia, including the Cook, Society and Austral islands, as the last stage in the spread of modern humans across the Pacific from the Bismarck Archipelago.[23]

Polynesia itself was settled by explorers from the western Pacific, who originated in Taiwan − and, by inference, China − around 5000 BC. By about 1500 BC this wave of expanding peoples had reached the Solomons, and continued to move east in double-hull canoes, picking islands up over the horizon by observing cloud patterns and the fishing habits of seabirds. Sophisticated navigational techniques that combined star sightings with wind and sea observations made return and repeat voyaging possible. These explorers − arguably the greatest mariners in the history of the world − employed a system of upwind exploration from each island, making the return journey from an unsuccessful foray much safer. This focused the thrust into the central latitudes where winds favoured that technique,[24] and there is evidence that some Polynesian explorers reached Peru, which explains how the Southeast Asian coconut got to central America − and how the South American kumara reached the Pacific islands.[25] However, this method did not work outside the central Pacific, where the wind patterns were different. New Zealand took longer to find.[26]

By the late 1980s, New Zealand's settlement date had been pinned to around AD 1000, plus or minus several hundred years,[27] on the basis of a wide range of evidence, including climatic analysis that identified 'warm periods' with favourable voyaging conditions.[28] This was refined during the 1990s to the latter end of the range,[29] as archaeological work in the Pacific islands revealed that the places Maori came from in East Polynesia were settled between AD 800 and 1000.[30] There was also no evidence of human occupation in northern New Zealand below an ash layer deposited by an eruption of Tarawera, initially dated to 1260,[31] and later to 1314.[32]

Other methods, including pollen analysis, revealed a national picture consistent with that finding.[33] There was deforestation in central Otago during the same period,[34] and a near-identical picture in the Takitimu mountains of western South-land, where charcoal deposits again dated to 600 years ago were thought to be evidence of deliberate fires.[35] The broad picture shows sustained deforestation in Northland around 1450–1500; Bay of Plenty around 1350–1400; Taranaki around 1550; north Canterbury around 1400; and Otago around 1300–1550.[36] There are some dates outside these ranges, and natural fires complicate the story; pollen analysis draws no distinction between deliberate and accidental burning. However, the broad consensus of the late 1990s was that Polynesians settled in New Zealand in the early-to-mid fourteenth century, a date coincidentally similar to the one Smith suggested. This made New Zealand the last large habitable land-mass in the world to be settled by humans. There was at least one return journey. New Zealand obsidian has been found on Raoul Island,[37] and there is some evidence that the Kermadecs were used as a staging-post.

Migration may have begun with an initial exploration, followed by multiple arrivals from several East Polynesian islands.[38] This 'starting population' could have been as high as 500, though genetic analysis suggests that Maori could be descended from a smaller group.[39] The fact that Polynesian pigs and chicken are absent from the archaeological record suggests that settlers arrived in a few small groups over a short period and that return or repeat voyaging was minimal;[40] though some have argued that tropical pigs and chickens did not survive the voyage, or perished in the New Zealand environment.[41] In any case, Polynesian ocean voyaging ended about the same time New Zealand was settled — indeed, island cultures began diverging from each other much earlier, implying growing isolation and putting the settlement of New Zealand at the end of the great voyaging epoch.[42]

Exactly where the Polynesians landed is unclear. Some archaeologists argue that multiple voyagers swiftly settled all the coastal sites, a pattern that broadly matches the oral tradition of individual canoe arrivals.[43] Other theories suggest the base was Northland or the bar of the Wairau River in the northern South Island.[44] But, in any event, Polynesians quickly spread through New Zealand.

Maori, moa and fire

New Zealand's first explorers found a temperate world very different from the tropical one they had left. The early era is sometimes named after Tamatea, the legendary figure associated with exploration, extensive fires,[45] and the longest place-name in New Zealand.[46] These first settlers were free of most disease, apparently because their population was too low to support the viruses common in more densely settled countries.[47] The first population grew rapidly, fuelled by a rich diet of birds, seals and other wildlife. Some analysts postulate growth of around 1 percent per annum, but the bounteous early food supply probably fuelled a higher rate, and other estimates put growth at up to 3.7 percent.[48] Modern comparison with the way Pitcairn Island was populated suggests that such rates could have been possible.[49]

More permanent settlements soon emerged, including gardens,[50] and these may have come first as the Polynesians tried to re-create the lifestyle of their island homes. However, bird and animal life soon became a primary food source. Seals, fish and shellfish were important at various places and times, and some estimates suggest that up to half the total food supply was provided by moa.[51] The effects on the environment were significant. A number of species were hunted to extinction,[52] and a significant proportion of the forest cover was burned off in the process, partly as a means of flushing game, partly by accident when cooking fires or blazes

set to clear land got away. Ease of capture was probably not the only reason why New Zealand's fauna was hunted. The Polynesian settlers arrived at the end of the Waiherere warm period,[53] an 80-year climatic optimum shared by the rest of the world. While the 'Cool Sporer Minimum' that followed from about 1350 had only minimal effect on air temperature, the shorter growing season and drier weather made gardens that much harder to keep. The South Island, where much of the moa hunting took place, was particularly ill-suited to tropical plants by this time.

Moa are one of the best-known extinct birds in the world. Species ranged from the 250-kg *Dinornis giganteus* to the 20-kg *Euryapteryx curtus*,[54] but it took years to sort out how they disappeared because nobody could believe that New Zealand's earliest settlers had devoured them. Walter Mantell found evidence of fires, human habitation and moa bones in Taranaki during a 'dig' in 1847, but did not think moa were on the menu, and it was the early 1850s before he found enough remains to demonstrate the point.[55] Even then, nobody could agree that Maori had done the hunting, and William Colenso argued in 1864 that Maori had not been around long enough.[56] Julius Haast put the pot on in 1869 when he announced, on the basis of his excavations around the Rakaia river mouth, that ancient inhabitants had eaten moa in vast quantity, taking just the choice cuts and leaving the rest to rot.[57] This caused a sensation. But Haast did not think Maori had done it, hypothesising 'moa hunting' people who he believed preceded them.

In fact, a growing body of evidence — including the discovery of 'industrial' cooking and processing complexes — painted a picture of a bird with low reproductive

Above left

Moa captured the imagination of Victorian-age settlers, though reconstructions such as this *Illustrated Sydney News* effort of 1865 owe more to fantasy than reality.

Artist unknown, Alexander Turnbull Library, B-158-026

Above right

Otago University registrar Augustus Hamilton reconstructed this moa around 1899, put it into the Dunedin Botanical Gardens, and persuaded Te Rangi Hiroa (left), medical student Tutere Wi Repa and missionary Koroneho Hemi Papakakura to attack it.

Photographer unknown, Alexander Turnbull Library, PAColl-1308, F-2887-1/2

rate falling prey to a burgeoning Polynesian population.[58] It was a common pattern: neolithic humans had reduced many species through overhunting, and the idea that it might have happened in New Zealand was explored in the 1950s, when Roger Duff argued that Maori prehistory was divided into 'moa-hunting' and 'classical' eras. However, it was the 1960s before the Polynesian migrants were widely accepted as a significant agent in the disappearance of moa.[59] There is evidence that related causes included habitat destruction,[60] albeit partly from human intervention.[61] Moa were also prey to the giant Haast's eagle, but the latter apparently died out because its prey vanished – not the other way around.[62]

Extreme estimates have suggested that moa vanished within a generation. Other studies propose up to 200 years.[63] Carbon dating has been only a partial help, as there are wide uncertainties and the oldest dates can be discounted because they do not accord with the wider pattern of evidence.[64] Hunting certainly assumed industrial proportions. Hunters would venture into the high country during the incubation season, snacking on moa eggs while searching for prey with the help of snares and dogs. Some moa were butchered on the spot and the joints carried to great oven complexes, where the meat was cooked in its own fat.[65] Other birds would be portaged intact for dressing at the cook-site, leaving the wasted parts – particularly heads and necks – to rot. This diet was leavened in some areas with Polynesian plants, notably taro, yams and kumara.[66]

Unfortunately, this Tamatea-age paradise did not last. While moa hunting probably did not lead directly to extinction,[67] human intervention was also associated with the elimination of the forests in which moa lived.[68] The dogs and rats brought from Polynesia also had had an effect, and moa hunting appears to have been at an end by the beginning of the seventeenth century.[69] Early European settlers were excited by suggestions that they still lived,[70] but these claims were soon dispelled, and alleged sightings since are not credible.[71] Other birds on the menu included shag, kaka, penguin, weka, pukeko, shearwaters, tui, kiwi, wattle-birds, parakeets, albatross, hawk, falcon, quail, owls, geese, swans and oyster-catchers among others, all of which have been found in midden heaps.[72] Around 35 species, including all moa, became extinct during the period; by comparison, 11 species are known to have become extinct since 1840.

Similar arguments apply to loss of bush during the Tamatea period.[73] This has been confirmed by archaeological studies and historical documentation,[74] and debate has been polarised between loss by natural causes,[75] and loss by human intervention.[76] In fact both are true. Volcanic activity, climatic variations, storms and droughts had devastating effect.[77] These factors were overlaid by fire-lighting, evidenced by the increase in forest destruction that became apparent around 600 years ago.[78] This was a new factor, and estimates indicate that up to half the total forest cover in New Zealand was burned off after the Polynesians arrived.[79] Destruction varied from rapid and widespread annihilation to a more piecemeal approach, as in Palliser Bay where bush was nibbled back as the new settlers made room for gardens.[80]

Tangata whenua

Early Maori society underwent broad change around the late fifteenth century, a point underlined by new styles of artwork and gardening patterns,[81] though to arbitrarily identify a switch is misleading. There was continuity alongside innovation, and we may more accurately say that this period saw a broad cultural shift in New Zealand. This occurred for many reasons, not least being that by the late 1400s New Zealand's natural bounty was drying up. Moa were becoming scarce, and gardening could not make good the difference. The fifteenth century was also apparently a rather chilly and tumultuous one for New Zealand, with volcanic activity, earthquakes and even tsunamis around the country. Wave height at Kapiti Island was estimated at 11–15 metres,[82] which could have dislocated local coastal settlements.[83] As in Europe, climate was not the sole or decisive arbiter of change, but it was one of many factors contributing to the pattern.[84] Some analysts suggest that Smith's 'great migration' took place during this period as a series of coastal voyages around New Zealand.[85]

Classic Maori life was based around semi-permanent settlements usually associated with resource sites, and was less mobile than in the earlier period.[86] Even at the best of times, producing food occupied most of the available labour for extended periods, and archaeological investigation of middens has revealed that the range and quantity was less than during the bounteous archaic period.[87] Available horticultural land was maximised by excavation.[88] Pa were a particular feature of this world. They were sometimes fortified villages, more often forts, and sometimes constructed to protect food stores — an indication of the importance placed on resources in a resource-poor land. They predominated in the North Island.[89] Archaeological work has shown that most appeared after 1500, probably related to the fact that a combination of resource competition and scattered population created demand for the tactical defence of particular areas.[90]

Maori occupied and drew identity from the whole country, but there was no 'Maori nation'; the people did not have a formal name for either themselves or the land. The North Island was sometimes called Te Ika a Maui. Some tribes referred to

Below left

Maori fishing on the Whanganui River around 1844, a scene little changed from pre-settler days.

John Alexander Gilfillian, Alexander Turnbull Library, E-273-q-018

Below centre

A 'New Zealand warrior' in 1778.

William Webb Ellis, pencil and ink, Alexander Turnbull Library, A-264-002

Below right

Maori fascinated the British public after Cook's first voyage in 1769.

Sydney Parkinson/R.B. Godfrey, Alexander Turnbull Library, A-111-105

it as Aotea or Aotearoa — though this was not common and the name was also applied to Great Barrier Island. Sometimes the South Island was Te Waka a Aoraki or Te Wai Pounamu.[91] These were functions of isolation; there were no other peoples or places to distinguish. For Maori, the distinctions lay within their own society, and they took great care in defining those structures both from location and ancestry, itself sometimes traced back to a founding canoe.[92]

Classic Maori society revolved around a dynamic and changing set of social structures, based principally on the hapu, which might comprise a number of whanau, extended families.[93] Sometimes groupings of hapu refocused as a wider organisation usually known as iwi. They occupied rohe (territories), but there was significant flexibility between all these groups. Hapu and iwi formed and broke up over time. This fragmentation was a function of resource limitation; as some have argued, the main social group — the hapu — had to be large enough to collect the food and raw materials it needed, without overstraining what was available. Seasonal resources such as shellfish or rookeries also implied mobility, which was not conducive to large-scale political structures.[94]

Maori society was divided — like Polynesian and, for that matter, European — into elite and commoners. Upper strata included ariki and rangatira, both standing above tutua. Experts — tohunga — had a status of their own, as did elders, or kaumatua, in some situations purely because they survived where others had not. Average life expectancy at birth was about 24, though those who survived to their teens might live into their early thirties. This was not radically different from contemporary Europe. Sites excavated on the Wairau bar

reveal that many women there died aged around 23–25,[95] suggesting childbirth was a killer. Status was also intimately related to mana, a personal attribute that could be won or lost through behaviour, achievements, defeat, victory or even turns of fortune, and which was generally more important to ariki and rangatira than to tutua. Mana helped define rights to resources, and in this way the resource dynamic continued to intensify, underpin, create and refine custom.

Resource maintenance had to be balanced against economic, social and political pressures. Warfare was part of the mix, though the settler-era idea that Maori were innately savage was an overstatement. Maori society did not have professional full-time soldiers. Toa (warriors) were also farmers, fishermen, hunters, builders and labourers. They were trained in fighting arts as one of the tasks they were expected to do; and to this extent the warrior tradition formed part of the social order.[96] Fighting was important at social and political level, as was individual fortune in battle; mana could be won or lost depending on the outcome. But fighting was also subject to a range of controls generally derived from the fact that conflict was an expensive luxury.[97] Negotiation and the customs of utu and muru — formalised systems of exchange — were more important. This engagement between society and war differed from that of eighteenth- and nineteenth-century Europe, where warfare was glorified but where combatants were usually also specialists; and this partly explains why early European explorers classified Maori as having a warlike society.

By the same token, however, we should not understate warfare as arbiter. Hawke's Bay's leading pre-European historian, J.D.H. Buchanan, suggested that many classic-era battles were 'trials of strength' akin to football matches.[98] In fact warfare was genuinely violent, seriously fought, and often lethal. The key point is that it was closely integrated with Maori society at many levels and controlled by social systems.

Waimate Pa, Taranaki, during 1839.

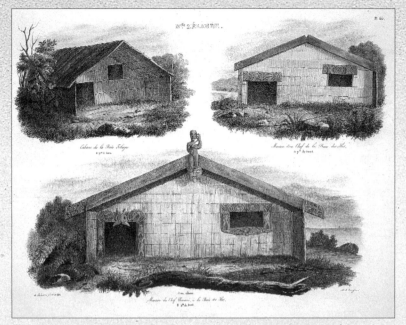

Maori did not have the surplus resources to build massive structures, and although Joseph Banks found a carved meeting house at Tolaga Bay, elaborate buildings of this kind were more generally a nineteenth-century development. Prior to that time decoration was more restrained, and some houses were temporary structures only, designed to provide shelter for short periods while the people gathered food. These buildings were sketched by Dumont D'Urville's artist Louis Auguste de Sainson in 1827.

Inset: Louis Auguste de Sainson, Alexander Turnbull Library, C-010-024
Below: Louis Auguste de Sainson, Alexander Turnbull Library, B-052-008

Another of de Sainson's drawings, a 'cabin' in Torrent Bay on the northwest coast of the South Island.

Louis Auguste de Sainson, hand-coloured engraving, Alexander Turnbull Library, PUBL-0038-1-18r

Life was hard during the 'classic' era. Archaeological evidence reveals that Maori were strong, robust, relatively tall and highly active, but short-lived because their lifestyle took its toll on their bodies. Some skeletons reveal damage to the spine and collarbone caused by carrying heavy loads.[99] Others show signs of neck arthritis, suggesting extended arm use, as from paddling.[100] Agriculture was based around intensively tilled gardens, which produced kumara, yams and gourds. The introduction of kumara has been reconstructed and an 'experimental' period has been identified, varying from region to region, followed by consolidation, in which sophisticated storage methods were utilised. Fern root was eaten but not cultivated, though there is evidence that natural bracken regrowth occurred in older gardens, forcing Maori to find new horticultural land but providing a good resource for the root.[101]

Hunting continued through the 'classic' period, and birds on the menu included wood pigeon, tui, weka and native parrots. Coastal communities made extensive use of seafood, and rats and dogs were also eaten. The range and variation of diet depended on season and location, and Maori sometimes travelled considerable distances to exploit seasonal food supplies. A great deal of effort went into preserving food for later consumption: kumara were stored in pits, seafood was often dried, while animal and birdlife was cooked, then packed and sealed with its own fat into containers.

Maori made tools and utensils from available resources, including stone, wood, flax, bone, shell and vegetable fibres.[102] Clay was available, but the art of pottery had been lost during the earlier migration to East Polynesia and was not rediscovered in New Zealand. Population estimates suggest there were less than 3000 Maori in the South Island by the late eighteenth century, although the total population was at least 100,000. This was largely a function of climate; kumara and some other plants were viable only in the North Island after the Little Ice Age began to bite.[103]

Canoes on the Whanganui River.

The extent to which this society changed over time is unclear. Oral tradition was about identifying contemporary place and recorded details appropriate to that purpose, not the information sought by Western historical tradition. Abel Tasman made few observations during his brief 1642 visit, not enough to compare with the 'snapshot' Cook and du Fresne captured in 1769–73. What does seem certain is that these eighteenth-century visitors themselves triggered change; and that change became dramatic as other Europeans arrived.

The great southern land

Towards noon we saw a large high-lying land, bearing south-east of us at about 15 miles distance; we turned our course to the south-east, making straight for this land... . We resolved to touch at the said land as quickly as at all possible...
– Abel Tasman's Journal, 13 December 1642.[104]

The early seventeenth century was an age of crisis in Europe.[105] New religious beliefs, patterns of thought and fresh political ideals were given impetus by a subsistence crisis brought on in part by the onset of the Little Ice Age.[106] Long-standing political, economic, social and religious structures bent or broke before this multi-founded process of change, and the 'effects of war', as Theodore K. Rabb put it, compounded the crisis.[107] Politics, philosophy and religious thought were reshaped, setting the scene for the 'age of reason' and, with it, the philosophies that Europe's first explorers and settlers brought to New Zealand.

Much of this crisis bypassed the Netherlands, seven provinces which drew strength from their 1588 unification and a sustained effort to make Amsterdam the financial heart of Europe. The Vereenigde Oostinsche Compagnie (VOC) – the Dutch East India Company – was established to work the East Indies spice trade in 1602. Based at Batavia, modern Jakarta, it fought its own wars and made its own treaties to secure Dutch trade against British and Portuguese interests.

By the fourth decade of the seventeenth century much of Asia was known, Japan was contacted, and the VOC began looking further afield into areas that mapmakers had yet to fill, huge blanks on the charts that artists sometimes filled with dragons and sea-monsters. Legend hinted at a lucrative trade with the wealthy inhabitants of a huge continent thought to exist as a counter-weight to Europe, though nobody knew who these might be. Fanciful popular imagination portrayed everything from men with faces in their stomachs to people who walked on their heads. They were, after all, on the bottom of the world, but wiser heads prevailed in the VOC, where Jan Carstenz charted part of western Australia in 1623, and Francoijs Thyssen mapped a portion of the southern coast four years later.[108] This was believed to be part of the great southern land, but how far it extended was unknown. Spanish and Portuguese explorers had crossed the Pacific on five occasions, and Ferdinand de Quiros penetrated to 26 degrees south, finding Espiritu Santo but no continent.[109] In 1615, Willem Schouten and Jacob le Maire rounded

New Guinea and cast out across the Pacific at a latitude of 30 degrees south —
again without locating land.[110] Around 1641, Abel Tasman (1603–1659) and fellow
officers Isaac Gilsemans (c1606–c1647) and Francoijs Visscher (c1600–1645)
decided to explore the waters south and east of Australia, and in January 1642
Visscher prepared a 'Memoir Concerning the Discovery of the Southland'.[111]

The Batavia Council authorised the voyage in August. Tasman was given the
fluyt *Zeehaen* ('Seacock') and larger *Heemskerck*, 'victualled at all points' for a year,
and carrying 'a quantity of precious and other metals for bartering purposes'. The
plan called for a journey to the VOC base at Mauritius, then south to 52 degrees,
'or at most 54 degrees', before sailing east to the longitude of the Solomons 'or
somewhat father [sic] east'.[112] Trade was uppermost in the minds of Governor-
General Maria van Diemen and his council. Separate instructions urged Tasman not
to tip locals off to the value Europeans placed on gold, and to 'prudently prevent
all manner of insolence' from the sailors.[113]

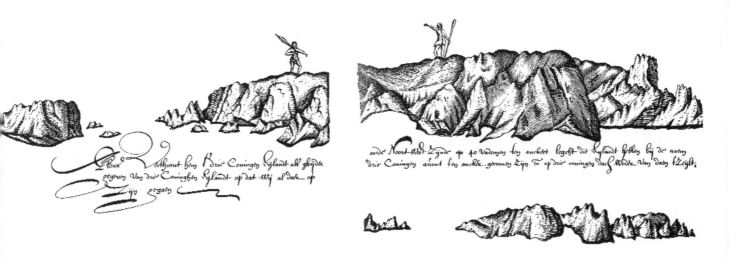

Tasman set out from Batavia in mid-August 1642 and reached Mauritius in late September.[114] Bad weather forced them to abort the run south at 49 degrees, and they sailed east, sighting the south coast of Tasmania on 24 November. They struck east again on 5 December and eight days later the lookouts sighted Punakaiki on the South Island's west coast. Needing to replenish water, firewood and fresh food, Tasman turned north, closing with Cape Foulwind but giving the rugged shoreline an offing. By 16 December they were off Farewell Spit, and spent the next day running 'along a low-lying shore with dunes'.[115] Late on 18 December the fleet dropped anchor in Taitapu (Golden Bay), east of the Takaka river mouth. Soon after dark, two waka — 'prows', to Tasman — approached the Dutch vessels, and the occupants 'began to call out to us in a rough, hollow voice'. Although equipped with a 'vocabulary' that VOC administrators thought might be useful, Tasman's men 'could not understand a word'.[116]

These people were Ngati Tumatakokiri, whose seventeenth-century population has been estimated at 400–500. Although one historian has suggested the blasts they blew on pukaea may have been intended to frighten away ghosts,[117] they were more probably challenging the unknown strangers.[118] Under this circumstance, Tasman's reply — to order 'one of our sailors (who had some knowledge of trumpet-blowing) to play them some tunes' — seemed an acceptance of the challenge.[119] Ngati Tumatakokiri repeated their blasts, answered from the *Zeehaen* as well. Tasman had no idea that the trumpeting might have a specific social meaning to Maori, but ordered 'double watches ... and to keep in readiness all necessaries of war'.[120] His priority remained fresh water, and he ordered a meeting on board the *Heemskerck* next morning to discuss ways of getting it. The *Zeehaen*'s senior officers crossed in a cock-boat, and were still on board the flagship when Ngati Tumatakokiri approached, ready for the fight that had, by their understanding, been arranged the night before. Tasman's journal recorded people of 'ordinary height' with 'rough voices and strong bones', whose hair was tufted and 'tied fast in the manner of the Japanese ... surmounted by a large thick white feather...'.[121]

Nine waka were soon paddling around, carrying more than 100 toa. Tasman's

Three Kings Islands and its giants. 'A view of Drie Coningen Island, when it is northwest of you at 4 miles distance', the text reads, and 'A view of Drie Coningen Island, when you are at anchor on the northwest side of it in 40 fathoms; to this island we give the name of Drie Coningen Island, because we came to anchor there on Twelfth Night eve, and sailed once again on Twelfth Day'.

men 'held up and showed to them, as before, white linens', but Gerrit Janszoon, skipper of the *Zeehaen*, was becoming uneasy. Maori outnumbered the soldiers on the vessels, and he decided to send the cock-boat back to the *Zeehaen* with a warning not to let 'too many of them on board'. The cock-boat crossed safely, but as its crew began the return journey to the *Heemskerck*:

> ...those in the prow before us, between the two ships, began to paddle furiously towards us ... struck the *Zeehaen*'s cock-boat so violently ... with the stem of their prow that it got a violent lurch, upon which the foremost man in the prow of villains, with a long blunt pike, thrust the quartermaster Cornelis Joppen, in the neck several times with so much force that the poor man fell overboard...[122]

The toa 'fell upon' the crew of the boat and 'overcame them by main force', killing three and fatally wounding a fourth. Three survivors, including Joppen, swam to the *Heemskerck*, where they were picked up by the pinnace. The Dutch 'diligently fired our muskets and guns' as the Maori paddled away, while the pinnace 'well-manned and armed', collected the cock-boat.[123] Tasman ordered his small fleet to sea, and as they hoisted their sails, they counted 22 waka, half of which, 'swarming with people, were making for our ships'.[124] More shots were fired. Tasman, angered by the 'outrageous and detestable crime',[125] dubbed the area 'Murderer's Bay'. It was New Zealand's first example of cultural miscommunication.

Tasman still needed water, but they were beset for five days by a storm in the Taranaki bight. This probably prevented them finding Cook Strait,[126] though Tasman suspected there was 'a passage through' on the basis of the tide.[127] Christmas was celebrated with fresh pork and wine, and as the weather settled the Dutch sailed north. They anchored off the Three Kings on 5 January and found a bay with a freshwater stream, but surf and the sudden appearance of 'men of tall stature' on the hills above deterred a landing.[128] An attempt next day to get water also failed and Tasman decided to quit 'Staaten land' altogether, shaping course for Tonga.

A British endeavour

Tasman's reception at Golden Bay quashed further Dutch effort to explore the southern continent. The partial coast of 'Nieu Zeeland' — a name possibly coined by map-maker Johan Blaeu — hung like a question mark on European charts.[129] It took Europe more than 130 years to find the answers. By the eighteenth century the British and French were at odds with each other in Europe, India and around the world; after the Seven Years War, the French translated this rivalry into a fresh effort to explore the globe. With commercial and colonial opportunities at stake, Britain had to follow. However, rival expeditions to the Pacific in the 1760s invariably took advantage of equatorial winds to sail from the Horn through Polynesia — missing the South Pacific.[130]

James Cook (1728–79) captained the *Endeavour* for his first voyage to the South Pacific.

John Webber, Alexander Turnbull Library, A-218-009

Sir Joseph Banks (1743–1820), naturalist on board the *Endeavour*.

Thomas Phillips, Alexander Turnbull Library, A-038-017

A journey into those southern waters was not nevertheless long in coming. The eighteenth century was the 'age of reason', an unprecedented flourishing of philosophy, arts and the sciences. Geographers wanted maps of the world, botanists and biologists hoped to find and classify new species, and the Royal Society wanted to measure the distance between Earth and the sun. This could be done by making observations of a transit of Venus. An effort to take advantage of a 1761 transit failed, and calculations revealed that another would be visible in 1769. In late 1767, Society officials – wanting widely spaced observations – proposed that hydrographer Alexander Dalrymple should lead a naval expedition to observe it from the Pacific. The Admiralty concurred, but proposed Lieutenant James Cook to lead it instead. The scientific contingent was led by Joseph Banks, a wealthy Fellow of the Royal Society,[131] who assembled a group that included astronomer Charles Green, artists Sydney Parkinson and John Buchan, and naturalists Dr Solander and Herman Sporing.

View of the North Side of the Entrance into Poverty Bay, & Morai Island, in New-Zealand.   1. Young Nicks Head   2. Morai Island.

J. Parkinson del.   R. B. Godfrey Sc.

View of another Side of the Entrance into the said Bay.

Left above

The *Endeavour* leaving Whitby for the Thames, where she was fitted out for the long voyage to the South Pacific.

Lionel T. Crawshaw, Alexander Turnbull Library, A-110-019

Left below

Two views of the entrance to Poverty Bay as seen by Cook's artist Sydney Parkinson (1745–71).

Sydney Parkinson/R.B. Godfrey, Alexander Turnbull Library, PUBL-0037-14

25

Cook raised his pendant in the *Endeavour*, ex-*Earl of Pembroke*, at the end of May 1768 and began preparing for sea.[132] Anti-scorbutics were in vogue, and in addition to the usual salted meats, flour, pulses, biscuits and livestock, Cook was ordered to take pickled cabbage, thinned orange juice, carrot marmalade and malt, and to report the effects to the Admiralty.[133] These stocks joined the usual private stores, scientific equipment, water and other gear needed for a long ocean voyage, all shoe-horned with 94 men — including the scientists and a dozen marines — into a vessel 106 feet (32 metres) long.

'Secret' instructions — published shortly after he left Britain in July 1768 — required Cook to look for the missing continent by running south to 35 degrees, then west 'until you discover it, or fall in with the Eastern side of the Land discover'd by Tasman...'.[134] *Endeavour* reached Tahiti in April 1769, where Cook observed the transit. They sailed south with Tahitian chief Tupaia on board, found nothing at the specified latitude, and turned east. Early in October the *Endeavour* reached Turanga-nui — Poverty Bay. Here, by a riverbank, Cook had his first meeting with Maori, the Rongowhakata. As at Golden Bay, the *Endeavour* was outside Maori experience; they first thought it was a floating island or bird, the Englishmen initially regarded as gods.[135]

Cook had no reciprocal illusions. He had been given 'hints', which were no more useful than Tasman's 'vocabulary', but had the advantage of three months in Tahiti. Tupaia was also to hand, and it was 'an agreeable surprise' to find that Maori 'perfectly understood him'.[136] In fact both Maori and Tahitian were derived from the same language, proto-Tahitic.[137] Comprehension was not perfect, but Maori responded to initial calls in Tahitian by 'florishing [sic] their weapons over their heads and danceing [sic] ... upon this we retired until the marines had landed.'[138] One of the Englishmen recognised the challenge as a 'Dancing War Song' that was

Cook found the strait that bears his name and used Queen Charlotte Sound as his main base in the South Pacific. This map was drawn by John Ryland (1753–1825) from Cook's original.

John Ryland, Alexander Turnbull Library, MapColl833aj/1773/Acc.422

'Calculated in my opinion to Chear [sic] Each Other and Intimidate their Enemies...'.[139] This rapport did not prevent bloodshed. By the end of the day two Maori – Te Maro and Te Rakau – were dead.[140] Next day there was more shooting. Unable to get water, Cook eventually found what he wanted a little way up the coast. So began six months in New Zealand. Cook charted the coastlines. Banks and Solander collected specimens, met Maori, and developed a 'snapshot' of classic pre-contact Maori society.

He was just one step ahead of the French; Jean de Surville reached the South Island three weeks after Cook touched Poverty Bay. Cook had already claimed New Zealand *in toto* for Britain – a paper claim, but in any event, had de Surville beaten him to the punch, the spectre of 'southern men' sipping wine and devouring canapes in France's southernmost *département* seems a less likely outcome than an eighteenth-century political accommodation with Britain. Cook himself reached the South Island in January 1770, discovering a refuge in Queen Charlotte Sound which he used as a base during his two later voyages into the Pacific.

Cook has always received the proverbial good deal from New Zealand historians, in part because of the exaltation of all things British during the mid-twentieth

HMS *Endeavour* approaches Young Nick's Head in this twenty-first-century oil by Colin C. Wynn.

RNZN/Colin C. Wynn

century. In a wider context this is less justified. Cook was an innovative and skilled commander, yet arguably many of his brother officers had similar traits — skills deriving from the need for any naval captain to act independently, responsibly and successfully during long months out of contact with the Admiralty. Although more sensitive than many of his peers towards indigenous people, Cook mishandled some contacts, ultimately with fatal consequences. His greatest strength was his skill as a navigator — he was not perhaps in the league of his near-contemporary William Bligh, but was competent and sure-footed nonetheless. His first voyage was achieved without the aid of the Harrison chronometer, a device too experimental for Cook to take in 1768, though he had them for his second and third voyages. He mapped most of the New Zealand coastline and a significant proportion of the Australian, and some of the charts remained in use more than a century later; the errors over Stewart Island and Banks Peninsula were spectacular but minor given that he did not have opportunity to examine these areas in detail.

CHAPTER 2

Agents of change

European explorers nosed into New Zealand's coasts and inlets during the last decades of the eighteenth century. Marion du Fresne, George Vancouver, Alejandro Malaspina and Antoine-Raymond-Joseph de Bruni d'Entrecasteaux led expeditions to New Zealand in the last two decades of the eighteenth century. Settlement was another matter. John Thomson tried to interest England's Secretary of State Henry Dundas in a New Zealand colony in 1792. He thought 'fifty sober men', a hundred sepoys (Indian soldiers), and the same number of convicts could get in by setting 'one tribe against another' and allowing the British to force the loser to terms. Maori would be forced to co-operate via hostages, but Thomson did not envisage this in a negative sense. On the contrary, 'by being taught and well treated' the hostages would 'introduce civilisation and render the country ... an asylum for distressed mariners'.[1]

The idea found little favour. The British Empire of the eighteenth century was a trading empire, and in any case territory claimed was not always territory conquered. New Zealand had no apparent wealth to offer, and Britain had other priorities as the French Revolution and rise of Napoleon threw Europe into chaos. Contact, when it came, was driven by trade. Britain's huge merchant marine and

French explorer Jules Sebastien Cesar Dumont D'Urville made several voyages into the South Pacific during the late 1820s. Here his 'schooner', as the original caption put it, is surrounded with 'New Zealand canoes'.

Louis Auguste de Sainson, Alexander Turnbull Library, PUBL-0034-2-350 navy devoured masts, sails and rigging. Proposals to obtain flax rope from Norfolk Island for Indian merchant shipping were floated in 1785 by Sir George Young and Sir John Call.[2] Young waxed lyrically about the qualities of New Zealand flax, which 'may be obtained at a much cheaper rate' than Russian cordage.[3] Lord Sydney, finalising the 'heads of plan' for a South Pacific penal colony the following year, proposed obtaining flax and masting timber from New Zealand.[4]

Plans floated in March 1787 called for visits to New Zealand 'for the flax-plant' — though Maori escaped the fate of the Tongans, where colonial authorities hoped to procure women.[5] New Zealand was not a serious contender as a prison venue, and proposals to establish a special facility in New Zealand for Botany Bay inmates convicted of sodomy fell on deaf ears. A satellite prison was, however, established on Norfolk Island where Lieutenant-Governor Philip King planned to use convicts as a labour force to process local flax. When the plant proved troublesome to handle he decided to obtain Maori advice, though it was 1793 before two arrived, captured near the Cavalli Islands by the crew of the *Daedalus*. Neither were flax-workers.[6]

Larger-scale exploitation was spurred by renewed war, which interrupted supplies of mast and spar timber from the Baltic. Late in 1794, Captain William Bampton sent the *Fancy*, under Edgar Dell, into Doubtless Bay to get timber for refitting a ship in India. After landing, Dell sailed on to the Hauraki Gulf and the Thames (Waihou) river mouth, where Cook had reported stands of trees. In three months, Dell's men felled 213 of them, mostly kahikatea.[7] Other ships followed; the *Hunter*, *El Plumier* and *Betsey* among them. Ultimately, however, New Zealand timber did not prove durable and the trade was virtually at an end by the early 1800s. Flax also proved less useful than initially thought; tests at the Chatham Rope Yard in 1818 revealed that 'New Zealand hemp bore little more than two thirds the weight' of equivalent rope from Riga and Chile.[8]

Hunters had better luck. Cook reported whale pods and seal colonies, and by 1800 both were in demand for oil, skins, fur and occasionally meat. Seals were to be had for the plucking, and Captain William Raven took the *Britannia* into Dusky Sound late in 1792 for the purpose. The seal skins he brought back to Australia opened the flood gates; the following year Bampton took his *Endeavour* across the Tasman — not Cook's ship, but a creaky old East Indiaman — and others followed.

Below left

Dumont D'Urville discovered French Pass the hard way in 1827, nearly losing the *Astrolabe* to a combination of tidal rip and shallow water.

Louis Auguste de Sainson, Alexander Turnbull Library, B-052-004

Below right

Tolaga Bay Maori 'dancing' on board the *Astrolabe* in 1827.

Louis Auguste de Sainson, Alexander Turnbull Library, B-052-021-1/2

Many sealers arrived after the Australian rookeries were hunted out, a rough bunch who generally worked away from the main centres of Maori population, usually Fiordland and Stewart Island or further offshore. They were later joined by whalers, a polyglot band of Americans, British, Spanish and Russian ne'er-do-wells. There were whaling stations in Dusky Sound by the 1790s, but their heyday came in the 1830s when many stations opened around the southern South Island and eastern North Island, including Whale Island (1835), Awarua (1836), Turanga (1837), Waikokopu (1837), and Waikawa.

Traders gravitated to the Bay of Islands, an area of dense Maori settlement that initially had a bad reputation in the wake of du Fresne's death after a clash with Maori. However, Samuel Chace brought the *Harriet* into the area in 1802 without problem. Robert Rhodes took the *Alexander* there the following year, and in 1805 the Lieutenant-Governor of New South Wales, Philip King, remarked that the 'frequent intercourse' had been 'very advantageous'. European goods and food were highly prized, particularly potatoes. The vegetable had been introduced to the Bay of Islands in 1794, and King reported that Maori were using it 'not only for their own advantage' but also to supply the whaling ships 'very liberally'.[9]

Joseph Toms, Thom or Thoms, also known as Geordie Bolts (1798–1852), established a whaling station next to the Ngati Te Ra pa at Paremata, early in the nineteenth century. By the time artist Samuel Charles Brees (1810–65) sketched these images in the early 1840s, Toms was also running an inn and cross-harbour ferry.

S.C. Brees, Alexander Turnbull Library, A-343-005

S.C. Brees, Alexander Turnbull Library, PUBL-0030-05-3

This painting of Te Kopi whaling station in Palliser Bay probably dates to 1844.

Samuel Charles Brees, watercolour and gum arabic, Alexander Turnbull Library, B-031-025

Trade and prejudice

Timber merchants, sealers and whalers brought Europe to New Zealand whether Maori liked it or not. The process was driven by opportunism, greed and private deals, untrammelled by regulation or much conscience on the part of some Europeans. Small wonder that Maori occasionally objected, but it was not one-sided exploitation. Maori also sought contact and trade deals, a point not obvious to British thinking channelled by 'fatal impact'.[10]

The relationship that developed was unprecedented. Two peoples — each energetic, confident and capable — viewed each other through the tinted glass of their own cultural concepts, lenses so ubiquitous as to be invisible. Efforts to identify and solve the misunderstandings that followed were coloured by the same cultural lenses. The problem was complicated by the fact that each had only recently learned the other's language. In the early period, 'Church Missionary Society Maori' — used in the Treaty of Waitangi — differed from 'Catholic Maori' and from 'trader Maori'. 'Whaler Maori' was different again, a pidgin which diverged from both languages. A standard lexicon was not established until later in the nineteenth century, though the main issue was less British phonetic trans-literation than the fact that nuances were often missed, further masking differences in assumptions. All these issues made even straightforward deals complex. As one historian has argued, each party in the sex-for-guns trade in the Bay of Islands believed they were getting the better part of the arrangement.[11]

However, the equation was not even. Maori had no contact experience and no frame of reference other than their own with which to understand what was happening. The British did have that experience — but filtered it through a mechanistic, empirical and positivist world view. This had emerged from the eighteenth-century 'age of reason', and treated societies as if they developed in linear fashion from 'low' to 'high', 'savage' to 'civilised'.

These limitations framed British thinking in ways so widespread they were

unaware of the distortion. The mechanisms were subtle, the results calamitous, and the issue was tied up in changing attitudes to race. It was the late eighteenth century before European biologists decided that 'savages' were the same species as themselves, and even then, all were classified as lower than civilised 'gentlemen'. It was a linear structure; humanity 'progressed' directionally from black to white, from small to large, and each supposed step was associated with particular behaviours. However, Maori displayed many characteristics that the British had reserved for 'civilised' people — and from this emerged the notion of the 'noble savage', the first fumbling effort to classify Maori. It was a bad fit. To different observers Maori were variously child-like, cunning, spendthrifts, rapacious, energetic or lazy. Such precepts channelled thinking away from real exploration of Maori cultural concepts in their own terms. Even William Colenso, one of the most capable intellectuals in settler New Zealand, was imprisoned by the concepts of his day.

The main result of British conceptual bias was a range of ideas, linked to concepts of market competition, which suggested that Maori would become helpless victims of a 'superior' culture, with lethal results — a fear expressed by the Church Missionary Society (CMS) in particular. By this logic, Maori could be best helped by introducing them to British society, and the argument was over whether to do this by isolation and education, as the Anglican church wanted, or by integration into a colonial world.

In hindsight the flaws of such thinking seem clear. Yet to some extent Maori *were* victims of Europe. Disease was an indiscriminate and uncontrollable killer. Epidemics in the late 1790s had devastating effect, and early missionaries recorded waves of whooping cough, influenza, tuberculosis, measles, the common cold and venereal disease.[12] Maori helplessness in the face of killers that even European science did not fully understand, coupled with exaggerated accounts of depopulation, helped fuel 'fatal impact' thinking, though disease was not thought likely to be decisive. 'Many other causes combined at the same time to work the destruction of the natives', self-confessed 'Pakeha Maori' Frederick Maning wrote;

European goods soon became a currency of rivalry for Maori, and did not take long to spread through the country, often in advance of the Europeans. Edward Ashworth (1814–96) made this pen-and-ink sketch of Waingaroa Maori in the early 1840s.

Edward Ashworth, Alexander Turnbull Library, A-208-022

...continual excitement, over-work, and insufficient food, exposure and unhealthy places of residence, together with a general breaking up of old habits of life, thinned their numbers. European diseases also assisted, but not to any very serious degree...[13]

Such sentiment blinded the British to the fact that Maori took an active hand in the early contact process. Some sought passage to Australia. Others went to Paris and London. Most did so with the help of patrons such as Thomas Kendall, but eager trade deals, which King took to mean that Maori were 'very tractable',[14] were actually a reflection of Maori proactivity. The earliest prominent agent of contact was Te Pahi – 'Tippahee' to contemporary Europeans – a rangatira. Another was Ruatara – 'Duaterra' or 'Dewaterra' in contemporary British spelling – who sailed to Port Jackson on board the *Ferret* in 1805. He returned with a variety of animals and European products.

Maori gained a good deal of knowledge about the British in the process, but translating that into understanding was an issue; cultural frames of reference simply did not connect. The gulf was evident in the response to Christianity. Evangelisation of the gospel to Maori was invariably followed by claims of conversion, but even in the late 1830s, a generation after the Church Missionary Society arrived in New Zealand, A.N. Brown was told by Maori that the Bible did not 'come down from Heaven', it was written by missionaries and 'sent to Paihia to be printed'.[15] Conversion was nominal well into the nineteenth century. 'What was all that nonsense about?' a dying Te Rauparaha told a minister who had just given him the last rites. 'It won't make any difference to my health.'[16] Christianity took its place alongside other European customs, selectively adopted by Maori to overlay and shape – but not supplant – traditional beliefs. The identification of sectarian difference with inter-hapu rivalry underlines the point.

Partly for these reasons, Maori response to Christian teachings did not develop

The 'flogging parson', Samuel Marsden (1765–1838), in 1833.

Richard Read, pencil and wash, Alexander Turnbull Library, A-039-038

Marsden's vicarage at Parramatta, west of Sydney, around 1810. By May 1818 a dozen Maori were at the associated school, 'occupied in the acquisition of useful arts', including 'rope-making and twine-spinning'.

Edmund Thomas, Alexander Turnbull Library, G-19192-1/2

as the missionaries expected, but this was not through lack of trying. Samuel Marsden, Chaplain of the New South Wales prison colony, led a drive to establish the society in New Zealand after meeting Maori who had travelled to Sydney in the first decade of the nineteenth century. King initially refused to let Marsden go, fearing a repeat of the 1809 *Boyd* massacre, but Marsden had good relations with Ruatara, who studied at the Parramatta missionary school in 1809–10; and in 1814 King lost his ability to hold the 'flogging parson' back when Marsden purchased a ship. Carpenter William Hall, rope-maker John King, and school teacher Thomas Kendall pioneered the way, setting up a station at Rangihoua under Ruatara's protection, and the missionaries themselves followed soon afterwards. Marsden and his ministers, meanwhile, pressured the New South Wales administration of Lachlan Macquarie to bring wayward Bay of Islands visitors into line. Macquarie concurred, and although New Zealand was outside British authority, made Kendall a Justice of the Peace, while Ruatara ('Dewaterra'), Hongi ('Shungee') and Kawakawa ('Korra Korra') were given 'power and authority' to carry Macquarie's orders out.[17]

Left above

Mission station at Kerikeri — 'Kiddeekiddee' in contemporary parlance — established in 1819, and seen here around 1830.

Artist unknown, Alexander Turnbull Library, PUBL-0031-30

Left below

Waimate North mission station, near the Bay of Islands, based on a drawing by Cyprian Bridge around 1845.

Cyprian Bridge/J. Whymper, Alexander Turnbull Library, PUBL-0144-1-330

New Testaments donated by the British and Foreign Bible Society are distributed to Taranaki Maori, 1842. Translating the Bible into Maori and distributing it was a key priority for the CMS missionaries. However, it was the early 1840s before even the New Testament was available in quantity.

Working Men's Educational Union, Alexander Turnbull Library, F-029

Kendall's school opened in 1816 with 33 pupils, a figure that rose to 50 before the children were diverted to food-gathering. More than 60 attended during 1817,[18] and Maori also attended Marsden's school across the Tasman at Parramatta, a double benefit from Marsden's viewpoint, as he thought that exposure to 'civilized life' in Australia would be useful, apart from any skills they might pick up at the school.[19] How successful the 'conversions' were is debatable; to some extent the Maori converted the missionaries sent to New Zealand, rather than the other way around. Both Kendall and William Yate found sexual partners among Maori, and Kendall was apparently tempted by Maori beliefs almost to the point of abandoning Christianity.[20]

Mission staff took credit for Maori prosperity, but the fact that results 'far exceeded' expectations should have been a clue to the processes.[21] Maori were actively using European contact to improve their lot. This was only vaguely perceived by the missionaries, though they recognised Maori as 'men of strong intellects' who 'in general possess a spirit of enterprise and enquiry'.[22] Chiefs vied to have a station under their own jurisdiction, and when Hongi took control of the second station at Kerikeri in 1819, war almost followed. Other missions were slower to arrive, in part because of fractious inter-hapu politics; one opened at Te Puna in 1822 and another at Paihia the following year. The Methodist Missionary Society set up a Wesleyan station at Kaeo in 1823, but it was sacked in 1827 and shifted to Mangungu on the Hokianga, under the patronage of Nene. Catholicism arrived later in the 1830s. The key shift in Northland was probably the death of Hongi Hika in 1828; as William Yate noted at the time, Hongi had rejected Christianity as fit only for slaves.[23]

However, the fact that Maori were active agents did not mean they could always control the outcome. European cultural practices and trade goods influenced Maori in many ways, including a transformation of everyday life as tribes swung into

Left above
European trade goods
transformed Maori economics,
switching the focus to producing
potatoes and flax for trade.

Louis Auguste de Sainson, Alexander Turnbull
Library, PUBL-0034-2-387

Left below
Cyprian Bridge sketched this
'ordinary New Zealand pah
with potato plantations around
it' in 1845.

Cyprian Bridge, Alexander Turnbull Library,
A-079-031

producing flax and potatoes for trade. Te Pahi and Ruatara were the early architects of this agricultural revolution, which was restricted initially to Northland. To
some extent higher-yield European vegetables facilitated the transfer of available
labour to producing trade goods, but short cuts were nonetheless adopted to
minimise effort in other areas, notably techniques for letting some food, such as
corn, fester as a way of shortening food preparation times.[24]

Rising demand for consumables such as tobacco, clothing, liquor, seeds and
munitions locked Maori into an economic relationship with Europeans, and European goods — including blankets, mirrors, needles, pipes, pots and clothing — soon
became part of a new currency of mana. Europeans could not explain it. 'The great
madness,' Maning wrote in 1863, 'was for muskets and gunpowder. A furious
competition was kept up ... After the demand for arms was supplied, came a perfect

furore for iron tools, instruments for husbandry, and all kinds of Pakeha manu-factures ... A few years ago the madness ran upon horses and cattle; and now young New Zealand believes in nothing but money'.[25] Such thinking missed the cultural context in which European products were placed by Maori.

Goods were usually paid for with potatoes, pigs and flax, and Maori also offered access to women, often via temporary marriages – though this was not

Maori bartering pigs and potatoes with a merchant, thought to be Joel Polack, probably at Kororareka.

John Williams, Alexander Turnbull Library, A-079-017

what Governor Philip King had in mind in 1805 when he referred to 'frequent intercourse' in the Bay of Islands.[26] Whether the women were willing is another matter. There were reports of crews 'forcing the women to prostitute themselves',[27] and there is also evidence that Maori men forced some women into associations for trade purposes. While some women were perhaps willing, the process almost certainly led to a diminution of the status of women in Maori society.[28] Progeny seldom survived; women were reported to 'generally procure abortion', though a few children were 'preserved' – apparently on the promise that the father would return.[29]

Control of this trade was almost wholly with Maori at first; as Kendall protested, 'They dictate to us!'[30] Prices seem to have fallen as supply rose. 'It used to be 25 hogs for a single musket', Ensign McCrae of the 84th Regiment reported in 1821, but it was 'now generally 15, or 200 baskets of potatoes'.[31] These were still steep. Much depended on negotiating skill; another trader at the same time exchanged a musket and 'some powder' for 18 pigs.[32]

Taua and muskets

War swept New Zealand for half a century from the 1790s. War parties, many of them eventually armed with muskets, roamed over unprecedented distances, and in the face of them entire peoples undertook heke (migrations) on a scale that had not been seen in 200 years or more. People from Kawhia moved south. Waikato moved to Kawhia and Taranaki, and Hawke's Bay was virtually deserted by its traditional occupants, some of whom did not return until well into the settler period.[33] Up to 40,000 Maori were dislocated, either through enslavement or migration.[34] To this can be added casualties of perhaps 20,000 – albeit spread over the period – but still about 19 or 20 percent of the estimated late-eighteenth century population.

Collectively the 500-odd battles of the period have been dubbed 'musket wars' and often viewed as a poor second in the historical mind to the wars of the 1860s. This seriously understates both their size and extent, and the pivotal role they played in establishing the Maori world found during the settlement period. This has partly been an outcome of the heavy focus on 1840 as a divider; in part a function of source limitations. Documentary material is largely restricted to land court records, oral evidence given two generations later in a quite different context and for a different purpose.[35] Even these were not examined in detail until the 1990s.

Perhaps for these reasons the wars never attracted the close attention of either general historians or military specialists, and the first detailed narrative did not appear until 2000.[36] The same historical doldrums also meant that it was the late 1970s before historians began to really question the settler-era notion that the wars had been a reaction to European contact, principally fought with European weapons.[37]

In fact, while settlers and guns all had effect by the mid-to-late 1830s, this particular cycle of warfare started in the eighteenth century, before the main contact period;[38] as a number of analysts have shown, the fighting, alliances, negotiations and resolutions were framed around traditional Maori structures.[39] They were also principally fought with traditional Maori weapons. To call these struggles 'musket wars', and to place Europe as the central trigger, is to mislead.

Left
William Strutt (1825–1915) made this pencil-and-wash drawing of 'the Maori war dance' probably in the late 1850s. The imagery was not dissimilar from that of the 'musket wars', two generations earlier.

William Strutt, pencil and wash, Alexander Turnbull Library, E-453-f-001

Below
A 'war speech, previous to a naval expedition'. Te Rauparaha, in particular, launched campaigns over water during the 'musket wars' era.

Augustus Earle, Alexander Turnbull Library, PUBL-0015-09

'Meeting of the artist and Hongi at the Bay of Islands, November 1827', one of the most famous images of the 'musket wars' era.

Augustus Earle, Alexander Turnbull Library, G-707

However, the wars were still different from earlier conflicts, a point that requires explanation. It has been shown that some of the wars that began the cycle in the eighteenth century were fought over a range of socio-cultural issues,[40] but no wholly convincing explanation for the scale of the fighting that followed has been raised — and particularly of the way that local disputes were translated into long-range affairs. This point demands deeper investigation than is perhaps practical at general level, but the broad finger of suspicion points to general social change consequent on rising population, compounded by the physical limits of resources. The late eighteenth century was not an easy period for Maori. Population continued to grow, and depending on estimate was anywhere from 100,000 to 150,000 by about 1770.[41] The lower figure is generally thought more likely, but either way it was climbing within the framework of economic and social systems that had emerged around a lower population, of which resources were among several underlying factors.[42]

Prevailing climatic conditions may have contributed, though they were probably not decisive. The Maunder Minimum ended around 1710, and the weather became a little warmer, promoting longer-term crop growth and perhaps fuelling a rise in population. However, this was followed by a general downturn in the last third of the eighteenth century.[43] Tree-ring analysis has shown that New Zealand's ten-year average summer temperatures of 1780–89 were half a degree less than for an equivalent period in 1720–29. Glaciers reflected these shifts, though not in synchronicity; the Franz Josef was on the advance as early as the 1770s.[44] Around 1800 the temperature in New Zealand dropped again.[45] Although fluctuations of a degree or less were trivial at a personal level, they were combined with chaotic weather patterns, including unprecedented wet periods, droughts and periodic but erratic heatwaves.[46]

A 'New Zealand war speech', originally engraved in sepia by J. Stewart after another Earle original. The imagery captures the korero that usually preceded each action in the 'musket wars'.

Augustus Earle, Alexander Turnbull Library, PUBL-0022-160

Maori, of course, did not stand idly by while this happened, and there is evidence of a drive to expand gardens during the early nineteenth century, notably by means of fires to clear land or push game towards hunters. Dumont D'Urville recorded 'huge fires' inland of Cape Palliser in 1827.[47] Herbert Guthrie-Smith found evidence in the 1880s that his property at Tutira had recently been under bush, though it was clear when Europeans arrived.[48] This suggests an active reaction to shortages, matching responses to similar weather patterns and rising populations in Britain, but late eighteenth-century Maori were at a disadvantage by comparison with British farmers, because they did not have high-yield European crops such as wheat and potato.[49] The key point is that it was apparently a shared issue across New Zealand.

The wars that began in the Waikato around 1790 — which provided reciprocal justification for some of the battles of the 1820s — were explicitly triggered by resource disputes.[50] Similar pressures appear to have been felt in Northland, where wars began flaring during the first decade of the nineteenth century and raids began pushing south in 1810. This was before the factors of potato and differential access to European goods took decisive hold, though these are usually cited as reasons for the long-range raids. Maori, in short, were pushing against the limits of their food supply; and — as in Europe — traditional social systems were coming under strain. Of course, resource limitations were not the sole factor, but they contributed.

Resources also provided one mechanism by which traditional short-range systems of warfare and diplomacy gained a long-range aspect, as hapu looked ever-further afield to obtain what they needed or to get away from local pressure. Waikato, for instance, hoped to obtain resources held by Ngati Raukawa near

An idealised image of Te Rauparaha's attack on Kaiapoi.

Te Rauparaha, perhaps the most successful chief of the 'musket wars' era, established a loose Ngati Toa empire in central New Zealand.

Cambridge. Pressure from Waikato and their allies produced at least one utu debt there, and prompted Ngati Raukawa chief Te Whatanui to get his people clear. In 1819 he led them to Hawke's Bay and the rich Roto-a-tara resource centre, about which he had been told by Nga Puhi.[51] That drew in Ngati Kahungunu and their allies, triggering a further cycle on the basis of traditional dispute mechanisms in the Hawke's Bay region, but this time with links into distant Ngati Raukawa areas. Meanwhile, Waikato looked to the Kawhia and Taranaki resource bases, citing utu against Ngati Toa, under Te Rauparaha. The latter's migration to Kapiti and the South Island was one outcome, again drawing in relatively distant but richly resourced areas and adding a further long-range aspect. All of this was essentially traditional systems writ large, but eventually a new phenomenon followed — the loose 'empire' that followed Te Rauparaha's conquests, which was a different socio-political structure from traditional iwi, and closer to some contemporary African kingdoms.

All these developments suggested a society in flux, where old systems were under stress and new were emerging. Europe arrived as the cycle accelerated, although the effect was not so simplistic as suggested in the 1890s, when Dom Vaggioli condemned the 'thoughtless, nay stupid introduction of arms' to New Zealand, an act comparable to 'putting razors in babies' hands'.[52] Such sentiments were wrong on two counts. Despite impressions, the wars were not initially fought with muskets. Most taua in the northern wars of 1817–21 had two or three — numbers with propaganda value only — and on at least one occasion, Hongi Hika refused to use the muskets he had.[53] Nor were the weapons forced on Maori. Muskets became a currency of rivalry well before they were available in sufficient number to have tactical value, and Maori actively sought to procure the weapons

Henry Williams trying to reach
Matamata in 1836. The original
caption identifies the Europeans,
left to right, as Henry Williams,
Alfred Nesbit Brown, Dr Fairburn
and Mr Morgan.

Henry Williams, Alexander Turnbull Library,
PUBL-0031-1836-1

both from the British — in the face of missionary protests — and from American sailors, who were 'free from restraint'.[54] The quality of these weapons was questionable, but this was less crucial to Maori than possession.

Deliveries in tactically useful quantities began in 1821, when Hongi obtained the first major batch after a trip to London. He was showered with gifts and sold the presents in Sydney on the way back, using the cash to buy several hundred muskets — and, in that single stroke, becoming the most powerful military leader in the South Pacific outside the Royal Navy. He used the guns to extract utu from Ngati Whatua,[55] though apparently not to force wider changes on society.[56] Other hapu and iwi followed suit through the 1820s, and the arms race accelerated towards the end of the decade; more than 6000 muskets were imported in 1830 alone. By this time most toa had one, and the epithet 'musket' could reasonably be applied to the wars of the 1830s.

Clearly the wars would have had a large-scale dimension whether Europe had found New Zealand or not. But we should not understate the effects of Europe in the latter part of the period. Fighting during this period was eventually underpinned by European food, weaponry and, on at least one occasion, transport.[57] Europe also had disproportionate influence at the contact points, such as in the Bay of Islands, where old mechanisms of rivalry were played out with new currencies, notably competition for missionaries and trade goods. These helped push tensions within Nga Puhi during 1818–21.[58] But this did not apply outside the European zone, where triggers continued to reflect traditional issues. Waikato and Ngati Whatua, for instance, organised a joint taua in 1821 in part because Waikato wanted to obtain utu from Ngati Toa after the 1790 battle of Hangakaka.[59]

Right above
Maori queue to receive the
word in this idealised image
of missionary work.

Artist unknown, Alexander Turnbull Library,
PUBL-0151-2-014

Right below
This 'night scene in New Zealand'
was published in 1837, again
capturing the imagery of
missionary work as they liked
to see it at the time.

William Wade, Alexander Turnbull Library,
PUBL-0031-37

Perhaps the most decisive of Europe's products was the potato, which grew more easily than kumara and offered more energy for weight. Again, the potato did not arrive until the cycle of warfare was well established, but it facilitated the long-range aspect and certainly made Te Amiowhenua – 'the encircling of the land' – possible. Nga Puhi embarked on the first of these mighty raids, a trek that encompassed Northland, Hawke's Bay, Wellington, Taranaki and Auckland. Other campaigns covered hundreds of kilometres, as in 1822–24, when Ngati Tuwharetoa and Ngati Raukawa trekked from Taupo to Hawke's Bay, then up the coast to Mahia. Perhaps the longest was the 1836 raid by Te Puoho from Golden Bay to Tuturau, near Bluff.[60] It is difficult to see these being accomplished without the potato; and potatoes also enabled those back home to survive without part of the labour force. During the pre-European period, toa could not abandon their gardens and fisheries for long. By 1820, Nga Puhi could, and others followed. Slaves captured during the campaigns helped bolster the labour force, further tipping the resource calculation.

Muskets increased the lethality of battles, particularly during the 1830s when the new weapons became widespread. Although death rates during this period were not as high as has sometimes been claimed, they were still high and even apparently survivable wounds sometimes proved fatal, perhaps months afterwards as Hongi himself discovered the hard way in 1828. In a society where relationships were based on reciprocity, the higher death rate served as an additional device for extending and perpetuating grievance, and under these circumstances the question is not why the wars occurred, but how they ended. Fighting intensified during the 1830s, gaining lethality as taua gained muskets, and even the 1839 battle of Te Kuitianga on the Kapiti coast can be considered part of the cycle.[61] However, although there were a few tussles over the next few years, as in 1842 when Ngati Tamatera and Te Arawa attacked Ngaiterangi,[62] fighting was over for practical purposes by the early 1840s.

Missionaries credited themselves. The CMS spread down to Kawhia during the period — and there were even two isolated missions on the Kapiti coast[63] — and ministers were invariably regarded as peacemakers. They also brought opportunities for trade, though the flow was not a significant factor behind war's end because the primary dynamic was not access to European products. One historian has suggested that land sales helped defuse tensions by removing disputed territories,[64] but this is less convincing. Although these factors affected Wellington and the Bay of Islands as early as 1840, it was the 1850s — well after the wars ended — before European land purchases became widespread enough to be decisive. Furthermore, the act of defining boundaries in order to transact them was itself sometimes trigger for conflict. The more crucial settler influence was the fact that the British actively intervened to prevent or end fighting, as for example at Pakiaka during 1857.[65]

We therefore have to seek other reasons for the 'musket wars' petering out, and the main factors seem to have been a combination of exhaustion and the rising tide of European settlement. Huge casualties, coupled with migration and the massive drain warfare placed on resources — even bolstered by the humble spud — meant that Maori had fought themselves to a standstill by the late 1830s, just as the British began appearing in numbers.

This prompted a new focus on a relationship with British government and settlers, a relationship which itself was affected by the legacy of the wars. Fatalism, coming in the wake of the psychological exhaustion that followed the huge casualties and dislocation of the period, seems to have been a factor behind the wave of conversions to Christianity in the late 1830s. Migrations turned traditional occupation on its head, and occasionally — as Richard Barrett and William Wakefield discovered in Wellington — the occupier was not the only claimant.[66] Traditional loss of rights associated with defeat in battle produced a skein of precedents that complicated government land purchases. War-weariness also affected attitudes to colonisation. Ngati Whatua unease at possible further attack from the north prompted them to invite William Hobson to establish his capital on the Waitemata shores in 1840. In some places, settlers were seen as a new tangata whenua (local people), as in Hawke's Bay, where Ngati Whatuiapiti chief Te Hapuku asked 'to have Europeans to replace my tribes now nearly extinct'.[67]

The wars also gave Maori relatively up-to-date weapons and introduced them to European-style warfare. Musket pa emerged, geared against guns, and the step from those to cannon-proof defences in the mid-1840s was straightforward. This was one cause of the exceptional Maori performance during the New Zealand wars a generation later. One historian has also proposed that the musket wars were unifying, prompting new iwi identities that were then 'frozen' as a result of the settlement process.[68] However, while the pre-contact process of change in socio-political structures and land associations was to some extent brought to a halt by the arrival of the settlers, the cultural energies that had pushed that dynamic along were instead transformed. They emerged later in different form such as the King movement, syncretic religions such as Pai Marire, and other responses to the arrival of Europe.

The hell-hole of the Pacific

Europe settled in New Zealand while the 'musket wars' flared. Most permanent arrivals settled around the Bay of Islands, where around 60 were living in the CMS stations at Rangihoua, Kerikeri and Paihia by 1827. The number jumped when Waimate opened four years later. Others settled at Kororareka (Russell), a trading community on the east side of the bay. The Hansen family tried to make a living there from 1819, joined in the mid-1820s by deserters and convicts. Traders were soon joined by sawyers, carpenters and blacksmiths. Several hundred other Europeans lived in the district, including the missionaries, their staff and families.

This painting by Dumont D'Urville's expedition artist Louis Auguste de Sainson reveals the Kororareka beach in 1827 before European settlement reached its riotous peak.

Louis Auguste de Sainson, Alexander Turnbull Library, B-052-006

Above

An engraving based on Joel Polack's 1838 picture of Kororareka township. According to Polack, it was the best anchorage in the Bay of Islands, 'possessing the best holding ground', and 'sea room for beating in and out of the bay and out of a strong tideway' lay opposite the town. This may explain its growth.

Joel Samuel Polack, Alexander Turnbull Library, PUBL-0115-1-front

Centre

Shipping in Kororareka Bay, 1840.

Artist unknown, Alexander Turnbull Library, PUBL-0064-2-TP

Below

S.C. Brees' painting of the 'town of Kororareka', 1840s.

Samuel Charles Brees, Alexander Turnbull Library, B-031-017

Most were attracted by trade with Maori. During the 14 months from January 1830, 60 vessels carried exports worth £37,980 and imported goods valued at £23,350.[69] These figures translate to early twenty-first-century values of around $7.5 million and $4.6 million, and most of the profit ended up in the pockets of Australian merchants. Figures for January to September 1830, for instance, reveal that £18,426 worth of New Zealand goods were imported into Sydney, including just over 500 tons of flax, 35,200 linear feet (9990 metres) of timber, 36 tons of maize and 500 gallons of whale oil.[70]

Kororareka became New Zealand's first town, with a population of around 100 by 1830. Its floating population was higher. Anything up to 30 ships could bring two or three hundred sailors ashore at once. Most wanted grog, food and women, usually in that order; lack of any of these — or an excess of drink — led to trouble. The problem was that Kororareka was outside the jurisdiction of New South Wales, and settlers thumbed their noses at precedent that suggested that the law applied to them outside Australia. Maori had little influence; in theory the town came under Nga Puhi's jurisdiction — the southern alliance before 1830, the northern after a brief war that year. However, not all townsfolk respected Maori authority, and missionaries were effectively powerless over the traders, rouseabouts, criminals and ne'er-do-wells.

When trading opportunities were saturated, a few merchants tried to gain a competitive edge by theft, sabotage and assault. Debts were often uncollectable — on one occasion a Sydney-based debt-collector was set upon, tarred and raupo-feathered. Another loser was Jewish merchant Joel Polack, who was run out of town after losing a gunfight on the beach. This went on against a riotous background of drunken high jinks, street brawls, prostitution, gambling, occasional theft and corruption on the part of visiting transients. Justice was erratically enforced by what one observer later called an arbitrary 'club-law system'.[71] Kororareka gained the epithet 'hell-hole of the Pacific', and the real question is how it functioned so well under the circumstances. Part of the answer is percentages; drunken sailors were not a majority, and sorting out what to do with them early in the morning was not too difficult. In those respects the seedy side of Kororareka was no worse than in many port towns. Respectable citizens did what they could to curb the excesses, as when a temperance society was formed in 1836.[72]

Early European traders settled with Maori, among them Barnet Burns, who landed on the Mahia coast in the 1820s and gained a moko.

Artist unknown, wood engraving, Alexander Turnbull Library, PUBL-0074-front

The real problem was that lack of legal government allowed the more boisterous to thumb their noses at authority, gaining sometimes disproportionate notoriety in the process. As early as 1819, John Bigge led an enquiry into allegations that sailors were mistreating Maori in the Bay of Islands.[73] Statutes were passed in 1817, 1823 and 1828 with the intent of improving behaviour in New Zealand, but none had any effect. The final straw was the *Elizabeth* affair of 1830, when Te

Rauparaha paid Captain John Stewart 'about 16 or 18 tons of flax' to carry a taua to Banks Peninsula.[74] Stewart was considered an accomplice in the kidnapping and murder of Ngai Tahu that followed, but the 'atrocious crimes' occurred outside British territory, spurring a lengthy legal debate in Britain.[75] Stewart was never indicted despite efforts by New South Wales authorities to catch him.[76]

In the wake of the incident the Governor of New South Wales, Ralph Darling, suggested appointing a Resident. However, New Zealand was not legally British territory, nor was the Colonial Office enthusiastic. James Busby reached the Bay of Islands in May 1833 with a letter of authority from King William, but had no legislative power and no practical means of asserting British law or protecting Maori. A Colonial Office bill intended to give him legal standing failed to pass the New South Wales legislature; and Darling's successor, Richard Bourke, refused to provide either troops or special constables.[77]

Busby's lack of teeth soon prompted a crisis. The *Harriet* was wrecked on the New Plymouth coast in mid-1834, local Maori held the crew hostage, and Bourke responded by despatching HMS *Alligator* to rescue them. In the fracas that followed three pa were attacked, canoes burnt and several Maori killed. Busby bore the brunt of the fallout for not reacting first – though he had not been told of the *Harriet*'s misfortune and had nothing to respond with in any case. This did not prevent talk of his ineffectual character and possible sacking. Bourke finally decided not to replace him, but Busby continued to suffer from lack of real power. He could have been made a magistrate, as Allan Gardiner was in Natal during the same period, but nothing was done.[78]

Europe came to the rest of New Zealand while Busby sat at Waitangi. Whaling spread dramatically during the mid-to-late 1830s. Traders – including the itinerant Polack – sought opportunities inland. A few Europeans settled with Maori, among them Barnet Burns, who was left standing nervously on Mahia Peninsula with his trade goods.[79] He allowed himself to be tattooed. Burns was not the only European to do this, but tales of Europeans becoming 'chief' of various tribes reflected

HMS *Alligator*'s boats off the Taranaki coast, late September 1834, trying to 'get Mrs Guard and her children from the New Zealand savages'.

Thomas Woore, Alexander Turnbull Library, A-048-008

European thinking rather than actuality. The spread of Europe to New Zealand was assisted by missionary evangelism, a shift from the commercial ideals of the 1810s largely driven by the arrival of Henry Williams as head of the CMS in New Zealand. He initiated, among other things, an effort to translate the Bible. Fragments of the Old Testament were prepared in the late 1820s, but the focus switched to the New Testament in the early 1830s. Henry's brother William Williams took on the task of translation, and 23-year-old William Colenso arrived at Paihia in late 1834 to print the texts. Some 5000 copies of the New Testament were handed out after Williams finished the job in late 1837.[80] Colenso translated elements of the Old Testament, but Robert Maunsell's full translation was not available until 1858.[81]

Detail from the journal of Edward Markham (1801–56), showing the flag Busby organised for Nga Puhi in 1835.

Edward Markham, Alexander Turnbull Library, MS-1550-120

Sovereignty and governorship

The Treaty of Waitangi emerged from an uneasy fusion of British pragmatism, administrative weakness, penury and humanitarianism. The problem was balancing the hands-off approach espoused by the CMS with pressure to formally control the growing European settlement. This initially seemed to be in the 'too-hard' basket. Britain had many world priorities in the 1830s, and New Zealand initially seemed more liability than asset. Money was unavailable to underwrite a colony,[82] and Busby was left to handle the growing problem of European rampancy alone.

He turned to Maori for support, trying to draw them in via the issue of New Zealand-built ships lacking registration papers and flags. Flagged vessels, registered via Busby's office, were less likely to be impounded when they got to Sydney, and in March 1834 just over two dozen local chiefs assembled on the lawn outside Busby's Residency at Waitangi to select the flag.[83] Busby hoped this would lay the groundwork for unity, but although Maori were finally prodded into picking an emblem, most did not subscribe to the British view of flags.[84] Busby nonetheless persisted, envisaging a 'tribunal' of chiefs, which would allow New Zealand to evolve into a British protectorate.[85] This did not go down well in the Colonial Office, where Lord Glenelg — formerly CMS vice-president — felt Europe had a responsibility to 'civilise' non-Europeans for their own protection. An 'Aborigine Protection Society' had already been formed in response to reports of Maori mistreatment, and in this environment Glenelg could not endorse settlement.

Chance provided Busby with his next opportunity. New Zealand was part of the British sphere, but without a formal declaration of British government the country was legally open to any claim, and there was a scare in 1831 when the French warship *La Favourite* was reported to be on her way to annex New Zealand for France.[86] That crisis passed, but then in 1835 the self-styled Baron Charles Phillipe Hippolyte de Thierry loomed into view. He had purchased land near the Hokianga, apparently intending to establish an independent French enclave, perhaps with help from Tahiti. Busby responded with a 'Declaration of Independence' that was signed by 30-odd chiefs in October, and which he continued to peddle until the late 1830s. The declaration was accepted by the Colonial Office to the extent that its signatories were sought for the Treaty of Waitangi, which superseded it.[87]

How serious the French threat was remained unclear; de Thierry reached New Zealand in late 1837 with colonists he had picked up in Sydney to find that his land had been sold. This prompted a bizarre tirade in the *Sydney Gazette*. 'I am an Englishman at heart,' he wrote, 'but the study of my life will be to support the independence of New Zealand under some civilised ruler ... and to save this fine people from the degradation and destruction which would inevitably follow its subjection to the British crown.'[88] There was talk of him being appointed French Consul in 1838, prompting brief effort in London to remind the French that New Zealand was a British sphere.[89] Parisian officials concurred. In the end, de Thierry proved a chimera; Busby suspected he was mad.

Reconciling the humanitarian concerns of the CMS and the Colonial Office with the need to establish colonial government in New Zealand remained a problem, intensified by Busby's weakness. 'He has no power, no authority,' the Aborigines Committee of 1836 concluded.[90] Colonial Office officials thought Busby was incompetent, and although the Secretary, James Stephen, ruled out action as late as November 1837,[91] renewed inter-hapu warfare in the Bay of Islands prompted Busby to request a warship. Bourke despatched HMS *Rattlesnake* from Sydney with Lieutenant William Hobson on board. The crisis had blown over by the time Hobson arrived, but the European population in New Zealand was rising towards 2000 and Hobson suggested a 'trading factory' system similar to that used earlier in India, though he knew the idea was probably going to be unworkable.[92]

William Hobson (1792–1842), first Governor of New Zealand.

James Ingram McDonald, Alexander Turnbull Library, G-826-1

Pressure to do something rose yet again in the late 1830s. Long drought and regulations fixing Australian land at 12 shillings an acre — around $100 in early twenty-first-century money — helped prompt many would-be pastoralists to seek new opportunities in New Zealand's grasslands. Some deals were conducted remotely in Sydney, as when W.C. Wentworth and his partners purchased 20 million acres from visiting South Island chiefs.[93] There was also interest further afield as New Zealand drew attention from social dreamer Edward Gibbon Wakefield and his New Zealand Company.

The prospect of cowboy land sales and an independent, private government was unacceptable — for slightly different reasons — to the CMS, Busby and the Colonial Office. Hobson's 'factory' proposal joined a missionary petition and a report from Busby on Glenelg's desk,[94] and in late 1838 Glenelg proposed a consul who would report directly to the Colonial Office.[95] But nothing had been done by the following

February, when Glenelg relinquished office to the Marquis of Normanby. The leisurely pace was partly a consequence of three-month communications between New Zealand and London, and partly due to staff shortages, as the office had only some 25 clerks to deal with 50 colonies.[96]

In light of hints that Normanby intended to act, the New Zealand Company sent the *Tory* scurrying around the world — though her hasty departure was not, as legend has it, to forestall a Colonial Office effort to stop them. The Colonial Office found out in advance, but the only response was a fresh flurry of bureaucracy.[97] Permanent Undersecretary Sir James Stephen thought colonisation 'inevitable'.[98] Events took a new pace in May when Stephen canvassed legal opinion, telling the Attorney-General that the Colonial Office intended to get a 'cession of sovereignty' from 'the chiefs of New Zealand' and wondering whether the colony could be temporarily attached to New South Wales.[99] In mid-June Stephen went to the Treasury for authority to fund the cession, specifically budgeted at £4005 — around $800,000 in early twenty-first-century New Zealand dollars — of which a quarter was for 'presents for [the] natives'.[100] He got the cash, with one rider. Nothing could be done without the 'indispensable preliminary' of the 'amicable negotiation with and free concurrence of the native chiefs'.[101] Treasury Pro-Secretary G.J. Pennington was less concerned with humanitarianism than finances. Forced annexation had led to war before, and wars were expensive.[102]

This laid the groundwork for instructions to Hobson, drafted by Stephen and signed by Normanby. Hobson would get the 'free and intelligent consent' of Maori to accept British sovereignty, negotiating with 'principles of justice, sincerity and good faith'.[103] Unruly Europeans would be rescued from 'the evils of a lawless state of society'.[104] Stephen also intended to halt the 'dangers' posed by 'mere land jobbers'.[105] This drove the policy of pre-emption, copied from earlier precedent on the American frontier where the Crown had acquired sole right to buy land. It had a double benefit as far as the Colonial Office was concerned. By giving the colonial administration a land monopoly and an injunction to buy cheap and sell high, Normanby also hoped to make land acquisitions self-funding from a relatively small investment, and the Colonial Office justified this with the argument that most of the land was 'of no actual use' and 'possesses scarcely any exchangeable value'.[106]

Much of the approach was underpinned by prevailing humanitarian concerns, evidenced in Colonial Office insistence that Hobson organise schools and crush the 'savage practices of human sacrifice and cannibalism'.[107] Hobson was in London and quick to query the instructions. Did the orders apply to both North and South islands? If he could not persuade Maori to stop cannibalism, was he authorised to 'repress these diabolical acts by force'?[108] Normanby admitted that too little was known about the South Island to make a decision, but if it was 'uninhabited except by a very small number of persons' who were of 'savage state, incapable from their ignorance of entering intelligently into any treaties' then British occupation might become a 'matter of ... duty to the natives'.[109]

Hobson left London in late August 1839 intending to secure sovereignty over New Zealand by treaty, and reached Sydney four months later to discover a new and awkward situation. Rumour that the Colonial Office was intending to pre-empt land purchase in New Zealand had been circulating for months, spurring local merchants to rush across the Tasman and secure land themselves. One of the most prolific was William Barnard Rhodes, who sailed from Sydney on his barque *Eleanor* in October 1839 and toured New Zealand, making extensive purchases in North and South islands. The deals were hasty, shoddy and vague, typified by Rhodes' Hawke's Bay experience. He 'bought' territory from the Mahia Peninsula to Cape Turnagain, but failed to negotiate with the appropriate people, and the exact details of what changed hands seemed unclear even to Rhodes. To some extent boundaries had to be unclear; as Edward Jerningham Wakefield found out, Maori were 'unused to dealing in land according to our notions'.[110]

However, the variations in Rhodes' claims also suggest sloppiness and certainly haste on his part. He told his partners he had bought 1,401,600 acres in a 30-mile (48-km) deep block between Cape Turnagain and Mahia. When he registered his

purchase with the government of New South Wales, however, the deeds specified 1,228,000 acres and a depth of 20-odd miles (35 km). Nor was he clear about the price. He told his partners that he had spent 'about £150', but revealed to the Land Claims Court that he had handed over £50 in cash and goods to the value of £323 — roughly $73,000 in early twenty-first-century money, paltry even by nineteenth-century standards.[111]

The New Zealand Company also 'purchased' central New Zealand during late 1839. From the British perspective this was likely to undermine the effort to gain sovereignty by agreement. The merchants, however, viewed Colonial Office policy as interference, protesting to Hobson in early January.[112] Governor George Gipps responded by proclaiming jurisdiction over New Zealand and reserving all land purchases to the Crown, a declaration that reached New Zealand with Hobson late that month. The pressure was now on to get the treaty organised. Hobson and his secretary J.S. Freeman had prepared notes, broadly echoing Normanby's instructions, which Busby reworked into something slightly different. He submitted the new version to Hobson on 3 February.[113] In this draft, Hobson's idea to have New Zealand ceded in stages was transformed into a plan by which Maori would accept British sovereignty from North Cape to the Manukau estuary and the Thames. In exchange they would be treated as British and guaranteed possession of their 'forests, fisheries and other properties', until they wanted to sell them to the Crown. This explicitly meant only the areas on which Maori actually lived or which they used; other lands were defined as 'waste' and, as far as the British were concerned, were up for grabs.[114]

William Colenso (1811–99) — missionary, printer, botanist, linguist and pugilist. Colenso was one of the few to write down what he saw at Waitangi in February 1840.

Photographer unknown, Alexander Turnbull Library, F-5028-1/4

Henry Williams, translator of
the Treaty of Waitangi.

Charles Baugniet, Alexander Turnbull
Library, C-020-006

Opposite
A 1949 reconstruction of the
signing of the Treaty of Waitangi.
Although idealised in many
respects, and inaccurate in
specific details, Leonard Mitchell's
artwork captures the essential
theme of a British ceremony
conducted with due pomp and
circumstance.

Leonard Mitchell, Alexander Turnbull
Library, A-242-002

The details were further amended in the final version of 4 February. Restricted sovereignty disappeared, as did the claim on 'waste lands' and with it the implicit restriction on what was — and was not — Maori property. Busby and others on the ground in New Zealand were under no illusion that Maori identified with all of it, in spite of what the Colonial Office wanted. Conceptually, this was less a problem than the distinction between sovereignty and land ownership, which was perhaps the more crucial intellectual issue at the time. None of the drafters were sure that Maori understood the difference, and efforts to come up with wording to clarify it were flawed by haste and the lens of nineteenth-century rationalism.

The three clauses of the final treaty were further muddied by translation. Hobson managed to get the CMS on side as instructed, and late on 4 February asked Henry Williams to translate the treaty ready for a meeting with Maori next morning. Williams did the job with the help of his son Edward, apparently fluent in everyday Maori but not a trained translator, and they sat down to preserve the 'spirit and tenor' of Busby's wording in just a few hours. Inexperience was not the only pitfall; there is some evidence that the draft Williams had been given did not include the words 'forests and fisheries'.[115]

Irrespective of this blunder, the final result was coloured by Williams' motives and inexperience. He used 'ratou taonga katoa' to refer to property — a term which meant a good deal more to Maori than Williams apparently thought it did. The result, as one historian has pointed out, was that Maori later argued for rights to resources that the British drafters did not intend, and which were not in the English version.[116] The other main problem was Williams' use of 'kawanatanga' — 'governorship' — to mean sovereignty. In the Declaration of Independence, the translation had been 'mana', a word with obvious implications to Maori. This mistranslation was compounded when Williams came to the clause guaranteeing Maori possession of their lands until they sold them. For 'possession', he selected 'rangatiratanga', which was actually a better match for 'sovereignty'.[117] Hobson used it in that sense two months later,[118] and it was also translated that way by missionaries in other Maori documents, such as a letter by Tamati Waka Nene that has survived in Colenso's papers.[119]

In short, Williams' translation was problematic even by the standards of his day, a point so well recognised that there were accusations of deceit. In the 1890s, Catholic monk Dom Vaggioli even classified Williams as the 'treaty's arch-manipulator', though sectarian difference doubtless played a part in Vaggioli's thinking.[120] Williams' motives were extensively debated during the late twentieth century re-analysis of the treaty,[121] and there has been suggestion that he may have felt the treaty would not be accepted if chiefs thought they were going to lose their authority.[122] There seems some truth in this, but it is also clear that the situation was further complicated by the cultural gulf. John Flatt, for instance, told a Lords Committee in 1838 that Maori: '...do not think anything of sovereignty... . Their simple view is, that their land may be cultivated, and that they may be benefited by that.'[123] This logic led the British to fear confusion between

NEW ZEALAND
JOURNAL OF
Agriculture
JANUARY · 1949

sovereignty and land ownership, not realising that the real confusion might be between sovereignty and chieftainship.

Charitably, Williams was doing his best to resolve these issues in wording that Maori would be likely to accept, but irrespective of any intent to dissemble, it seems clear from his choice of vocabulary that he did not have the wit or information to truly translate the treaty. His apparent effort to 'spin' the whole in order to sell it to Maori simply compounded the problem. Colenso — the more capable intellectual — might have done better. But Colenso also suffered from cultural centrism, and in any case was never asked.

As it happened, Williams' translation did not survive unadulterated. On the morning of the fifth Busby wanted amendments. By this stage Maori were assembling on the Residency lawn, and Busby ended up in the house with Hobson and Williams, making changes. They finally emerged on to the 'delightfully situated lawn' in front of the house, where a 'spacious tent ... tastefully adorned with flags' had been set up.[124] Even the weather co-operated. 'Nature,' Colenso wrote, had 'consented to doff her mantle of New Zealand grey.' Colourful policemen, sailors and officials wandered about on the emerald lawn, contrasting with Maori who turned out in the more muted tones of their own formal dress, leavened with 'woollen cloaks of foreign manufacture'.[125] Inside the tent, Hobson and his officers arranged everything to impress:

> In the centre of the narrow raised platform were the Governor and captain of the man o' war in full uniform, on the Governor's left were Mr Busby, and the Roman Catholic bishop in canonicals, his massy gold chain and crucifix glistening on his dark-purple-coloured habit, on the right of his Excellency were the members of the Church of England Mission, in plain black dresses...[126]

The rangatira spent the day considering the treaty as read aloud to them by Williams, with supplementary explanations by Hobson, but all did not go as smoothly as it could have. At least one European fluent in Maori complained to Hobson that the 'native speeches were not half interpreted by Mr. Williams, neither were His Excellency's remarks fully interpreted to the natives'.[127] He apparently portrayed the treaty as an 'act of love' by Queen Victoria towards Maori.[128] This did not wash well with Maori, who initially disliked the arrangement, though to some extent this was also a function of hui, where all points of view were expressed before being considered. During the morning Te Kemara pointed out 'in his energetic, peculiar manner' that Busby and the missionaries had already bought land[129] — an embarrassing point. Other points of view followed, including those of Tamati Waka Nene of Ngati Hao, who believed there would be commercial opportunities. His arguments ended the meeting that evening, and Hobson announced that they would reconvene on the seventh.

Tamati Waka Nene.

Joseph Merritt, Alexander Turnbull Library, A-255-019

Next morning, however, 'not less than 300' Maori were back at the Residency, 'talking about the treaty, but evidently not clearly understanding it'. There had been confusion over times. Hobson arrived from the ship 'in plain clothes', and decided to 'take the signatures' of those who wanted to sign. However, as it was not a 'regular public meeting' he refused to accept further debate.[130] Pompallier then 'pushed forward' and asked: 'That the natives might be informed that all who should join the Catholic religion should have the protection of the British government.' Hobson, 'with much blandness', concurred, adding that he was sorry Pompallier had not asked earlier, as 'your desire should have been embodied in the Treaty'.[131]

Williams objected on the basis that this protection applied to all denominations by default, but Hobson insisted and Williams 'accordingly commenced' to write a 'grave announcement ... for the benefit of all', declaring that Maori who joined the Anglican, Wesleyan or Catholic churches — or, and this was Colenso's point — retained what Williams called their 'heathen beliefs' ('ritenga Maori'), would all receive the same protections under the Treaty. There was no reaction when he read it out, 'the Maories [sic] being at a perfect loss, [as to] what it could all mean'.[132] As one historian has noted, some early twenty-first-century commentators suggested that this was a 'fourth' clause of the Treaty.[133] In fact the clarification was simply for Pompallier's benefit and he left as soon as it was read out.[134] Williams'

An 1880s reconstruction of the signing of the Treaty of Waitangi — but probably not intended to represent the main ceremony. The Treaty was signed in many places around the North Island under circumstances like this.

Artist unknown, Alexander Turnbull Library, A-114-038

objections were also correct. Although Anglicanism played an important role in the life and times of the day, Britain was legally a secular state in 1840. In any case, the remarks were neither on the treaty that was signed that morning, nor had been raised when the treaty was considered by Maori.

Once Pompallier's objection was out of the way, Hobson had Williams re-read the treaty. At first no one wanted to sign, so Hobson decided to call out names, starting with Hone Heke Pokai — 'known to be most favourable' towards the Treaty.[135] As Heke was about to place his mark, Colenso interrupted and asked whether Maori actually understood it. 'I have spoken to some Chiefs,' he continued, 'who had no idea what ever as to the purport of the Treaty.' Hobson remarked that he had done all he could to make sure they did, 'and I really don't know how I shall be enabled to get them to do so. They've heard the Treaty read by Mr W.'[136] After some discussion with the others he threw the onus for explaining it back to the CMS. Heke then signed, the first of more than 40 who placed their marks, while two others made 'long speeches against the signing' in the background.[137] Twenty-six had signed the 1835 Declaration of Independence — and their acceptance of the new treaty was a significant legal step. Hobson waited out the seventh, and the following day proclaimed the new colony with a 21-gun salute and flourish of flags from the *Herald*.

Hobson then circulated the treaty around New Zealand, with results that reflected the way European authority had penetrated the hinterland. Northland, the Waitemata and the Waikato were well covered by government officials, but other regions relied on ad-hoc measures. William Williams, now at Turanga (Gisborne),

HMS *Herald* — literally the herald of the Treaty of Waitangi for many Maori around New Zealand — in Sylvan Cove, Stewart Island.

Edward Marsh Williams, Alexander Turnbull Library, A-083-005

was told to get signatures from the East Coast and collected about 40 in Poverty Bay during April, but abandoned plans to visit Ahuriri (Napier) for the rest.[138] Coverage elsewhere was thin. Hobson was laid low with a stroke, and Willoughby Shortland sent Bunbury to get signatures in the *Herald*. He annexed the South Island by cession on 17 June, but otherwise the main targets were the remaining signatories of the 1835 declaration. This brought Bunbury to Hawke's Bay in June, looking for Te Hapuku, who had signed as late as 1839. The chiefs Waikato and Mahokai happened to be visiting and also signed,[139] but Bunbury did not seek out others in the area and most Ngati Kahungunu did not sign.[140] National patchiness was compounded by the fact that not every chief was prepared to sign, but over 500 signatures were nonetheless collected on multiple sheets, including several to an English-language version.

Maori had various reasons for signing. Tamati Waka Nene saw the treaty as a means of extending the trading relationship with Britain.[141] For Hone Heke, signing was apparently an assertion of mana.[142] Others saw it as a means of getting the blankets and tobacco offered during the ceremonies, though this sometimes prompted dispute. 'Next morning,' one signatory recalled, 'the things came with which the Governor intended to pay us for writing our names' — a disappointment, because 'there was not much tobacco, and only a few blankets'.[143] This prompted a 'fierce squabble',[144] an argument repeated around the country, causing some nineteenth-century critics to classify it as a 'blankets treaty'.[145] A few changed their minds, motivated in at least one case by the paucity of blankets,[146] returning the gifts in an effort to nullify their decision.[147] In the Waitemata, the prospect of British military protection was arguably a motive — a legacy of the musket wars,[148] though it is possible Ngati Whatua misunderstood Hobson. His

William Williams, East Coast missionary and brother of Henry Williams.

Charles Baugniet, Alexander Turnbull Library, PUBL-0031-37

Rawiri, a 'fully tattooed chief' of Taranaki, drawn here in 1856 by William Strutt (1825–1915).

William Strutt, Alexander Turnbull Library, E-452-f-006-3

point that the treaty guaranteed land ownership left some 'very much alarmed ... for they thought that perhaps a great war expedition was coming...'[149]

Understanding varied, and as at Waitangi, the problem was not lack of effort to explain by the British, but cross-cultural misunderstanding. Waitemata Maori, listening to the explanation of the treaty, felt the 'meaning ... was so closely concealed we never have found it out'. As Frederick Maning noted, this was a 'polite Maori way of saying that ... [the speaker] was talking nonsense'. One message was 'understood well', however:

A Maori woman from Taranaki, mid-1850s.

William Strutt, Alexander Turnbull Library, E-452-f-009-2

...he told us plainly that if we wrote on the Governor's paper, one of the consequences would be that great numbers of pakeha would come to this country to trade with us, that we should have an abundance of valuable goods, and that before long there would be great towns, as large as Kororareka, in every harbour in this whole island. We were very glad to hear this, for we never could ... get half muskets or gunpowder enough, or blankets...[150]

A few chiefs did perceive the structure the British had in mind, though still expressing it within the framework of Maori understanding. When Bunbury explained the treaty to Te Hapuku, the chief suggested that Maori would be made slaves, and demonstrated what he meant by drawing a 'sort of diagram' on a board, 'placing the Queen by herself over the chiefs as these were over the tribes'. Bunbury assured him that 'it was literally as he described it, but not for an evil purpose ... but to enable her to enforce her execution of justice and good government equally amongst her subjects'.[151]

CHAPTER 3

Shadows of Empire

If anyone could be called settler New Zealand's founding father, it would probably be amateur hypnotist and would-be social climber Edward Gibbon Wakefield. Half a dozen towns from New Plymouth to Christchurch were directly or indirectly established as a result of his efforts, and he brought nearly 9000 settlers to New Zealand in the process. Propaganda issued by the New Zealand Company guided the public perception of Wakefield well into the twentieth century, building the myth of a nation-founder at a time when New Zealand was trying to perceive itself as a nation. The truth is less applauding. His vision was bold in scope and execution, but the facts about both Wakefield and his enterprises have a tawdry banality well removed from the image of glorious settlement. Greed, incompetence and wild misconception created a witches' brew of deed and misdeed that shaped New Zealand: physically, by locating half the main centres, and morally by contributing to race-relations issues that reverberated into the twenty-first century.

For all that, we must not wholly demonise Wakefield. As his biographer argues, the truths of his life are both better and worse than we might imagine.[1] He was a complex character, well known for his lack of scruples — arguably an outcome of his dysfunctional family upbringing, producing an adult whose belief in a basic immorality of humanity was probably heightened by his exposure to post-Napoleonic politics from 1815. Ill-health crippled him after 1840, and on the basis of his volatile behaviour and wild mood swings, it has been argued that he may have suffered from bi-polar disorder. He was unquestionably complex, defying efforts by biographers to reduce his character to a few clear traits.[2]

Wakefield developed his colonial ideas during the late 1820s while serving a term in Newgate prison, detailing a neo-feudal utopia designed to escape the woes afflicting Britain's unplanned and chaotic world, while at the same time retaining the 'better attributes' of the 'old society'.[3] The key to it was 'waste lands' that could be purchased cheaply by settlement company owners and on-sold at a price sufficient to entrench a wealthy land-owning class. Company profits would fund the import of cheap labour, which Wakefield envisaged would come from the 'thousands and tens of thousands of half-starved semi-maritime' people in the 'north and west of Scotland'.[4] These workers would allow the wealthy to live a leisured lifestyle, while the 'thrifty' among them could — 'after working some time

Edward Gibbon Wakefield (1796–1862) wrote *A Letter From Sydney* to expound his colonial theories. He was elected to the Wellington Provincial Council, but contracted rheumatic fever in 1855 and never really recovered. Depressed, he withdrew from the public world.

Abraham Wivell/B. Holl, engraving, Alexander Turnbull Library, A-042-023

Edward Jerningham Wakefield
(1820–79) was the only son of
Edward Gibbon Wakefield. Best
known for his propaganda work
Adventure in New Zealand, he
emigrated to New Zealand in the
early 1850s, entered politics, and
after a brief term spent the next
quarter-century intermittently
standing for re-election.

Artist unknown, engraving, Alexander
Turnbull Library, PUBL-0128-001

Joseph Somes, New Zealand
Company secretary.

John Wood, Alexander Turnbull Library,
C-043-007

for wages' — become landowners themselves, replaced by other workers brought in by the company on the profits of its role as land wholesaler.[5]

Such thinking was broadly founded in the Calvinism of the day, which stereotypically portrayed labourers as lazy and often drunken wastrels, authors of their own misfortune — but a group who might redeem themselves given incentive to save. Perhaps because his otherwise radical ideas were so closely founded in popular ethos, Wakefield's ideas quickly gained ground. He was wooed by the National Colonisation Society when he was released from prison in 1830, launching into his new occupation with a good deal of enthusiasm. However, an effort to establish an Australian colony foundered in 1835 after a dispute over land prices, and in the opposition from James Stephen.[6] New Zealand seemed a good alternative. A 'New Zealand Company' had been established as early as 1825, sending two ships under James Herd to the South Pacific. But the government refused to issue a charter and the proprietors gave up after making a dead loss of £20,000.[7] Wakefield decided to try, forming the New Zealand Association, but the jump from that to colonising company required parliamentary approval and was opposed by the Colonial Office, where Stephen thought the colony would 'infallibly' exterminate Maori, and in any case considered the idea too vague.[8] Wakefield then published specific plans, alarming both the Colonial Office and the CMS with his fantasies of Maori desperate to be colonised and a conveniently hospitable New Zealand aching to be purchased.[9]

The idea remained in abeyance until early 1839, when news came of the Colonial Office proposal to obtain pre-emptive purchase rights.[10] Wakefield hastily formed the New Zealand Land Company on a capital of £100,000,[11] hired most of his extended family for senior positions, and got to work. He intended the venture to be largely self-funding, and some 1100 sections in the first town were put up for sale in London at £1 per acre. Colonists were promised a 75 percent rebate on travel costs, but the real targets were speculators, lured by promise of spiralling value once the colony was established.

The ploy worked. British investors swallowed Wakefield's promise of a profitable Arcadia, and 1000 sections were bought by people who had no intention of moving. They did so in the belief that 'extensive tracts' of the 'most fertile' land had been 'already purchased and secured'.[12]

In fact Wakefield had the name of the first town — Wellington — but nothing to actually sell. The company ship *Tory* was still on its way to New Zealand; she had set sail in May with Wakefield's younger brother, Colonel William Wakefield, on board. Lack of news did not prevent the company offering more land in August, this time in the 'Hokianga, Kaipara, Manukau' and 'the islands of Waiheke and Paroa' among other places.[13] Meanwhile, the company sent the *Cuba* racing off to New Zealand with a surveying team. The colony ships *Oriental*, *Aurora* and *Adelaide* followed in mid-September — filled with 'labourers especially of the agricultural class'.[14] The *Glenbervie* left in October, loaded with the 'Machinery, mills, steam-engines, agricultural implements ... and goods of various other descriptions'.[15]

All this was based on the assumption that the *Tory* had reached New Zealand and that Colonel Wakefield had bought land suited to his brother's schemes. There was no backup plan,[16] and the whole edifice would have come crashing down like a pack of cards if there had been a hiccup. As it happened, the *Tory* reached New Zealand on 16 August after a record 96-day passage. They watered at Ship's Cove, clashed with local Maori, then sailed for Port Nicholson.[17] This area was occupied by several hapu of Te Ati Awa, who had migrated from Taranaki during the wars a few years earlier and felt far from secure. Te Rauparaha's loose Ngati Toa empire stood to the west. He was not a safe ally, and two hapu, Ngati Mutunga and Ngati Tama, had left for the Chathams in 1835.[18]

Colonel Wakefield offered another form of escape. Through sale, leading chiefs Te Wharepouri and Honiana Te Puni-Kokopu could not only reinforce their mana over territory disputed with Ngati Toa but also gain powerful allies.[19] Wakefield was delighted with their 'lively satisfaction' when he offered to buy land in the area.[20] His instructions, penned by Gibbon Wakefield, exhorted him to:

> ...constantly bear in mind that the profits of the Company must, in a great measure, depend on the judgement which you may exercise in selecting places of future location ... it should be your especial business to acquire spots which enjoy some peculiar natural advantage ... Wilderness land ... is worth nothing to its

Above left

Te Ati Awa leader Honiana Te Puni-Kokopu was born in Taranaki and, with other Te Ati Awa chiefs, led his people to the Wellington region in 1832 as a result of the 'musket wars'. Their tenure was not secure, which is why Te Puni and Te Wharepouri welcomed the Wakefield settlement, and Te Puni sided with the colonists during the 1846–47 war. Pallbearers at his funeral in 1870 included Native Minister Donald McLean.

Charles Heaphy, Alexander Turnbull Library, PUBL-0011-02-2

Above right

Te Wharepouri, also known to New Zealand Company agents as 'Dark Horse'.

Charles Heaphy, Alexander Turnbull Library, PUBL-0011-02-1

native owners ... We are not, therefore, to make much account of the utter inadequacy of the purchase money according to English notions of the value of land...[21]

For all that, the company needed Maori on side and Gibbon Wakefield hoped goodwill would come from reserving a tenth of any purchase 'in trust ... for the future benefit of the chief families of the tribe'. This was not quite the benevolence it seemed; the aim was to make chiefs landowners within Wakefield's iron-clad society. For this reason, he told his brother not to 'make reserves ... in large blocks' as this would cause Maori to 'continue savage'.[22]

Long-time New Zealand resident Richard 'Dicky' Barrett interpreted, though his 'whaler Maori' was arguably more hindrance than help.[23] Certainly Te Wharepouri's real reasons for sale did not surface. By late September they had settled on a price of about £400 worth of goods for the district.[24] Te Wharepouri divided them into six, though there were seven hapu in the area,[25] and this was not the only problem. Colonel Wakefield had been exhorted to 'most clearly set forth' the boundaries, 'not merely in words, but in a plan attached to the written contract'.[26] However, when it came to the crunch, they discovered that it was 'almost impossible ... to buy a large and distinct tract of land, with fixed boundaries'.[27] Maori did not define land in such terms. The combination of uncertain border, uncertain tenure and mis-division of the goods was a time bomb for which the fuse was lit even as the first settler ships left Britain.

The New Zealand Company ship *Cuba* at anchor in a northwesterly breeze off Port Nicholson heads, 1840. Barrett's Reef is visible to the right in this watercolour by New Zealand Company draughtsman Charles Heaphy (1820–81).

Charles Heaphy, Alexander Turnbull Library, A-144-003

Wakefield moved on in October, arriving off Kapiti just after a battle between Ngati Toa on one side and Te Ati Awa and Ngati Raukawa on the other, spurred by the sale of land in Port Nicholson. The ship's doctor, Ernest Deiffenbach, tended the wounded. Wakefield had heard of Te Rauparaha in England, and as Wakefield's biographer Philip Temple argues, probably left the old chief until last so as to be preceded by rumour of the *Tory*'s power.[28]

From Te Rauparaha's perspective the ship was a threat; the chief held his loose empire partly by controlling the supply of muskets, and his problem was how to stop the new arrivals distributing weapons to anyone but himself.[29] What followed was bizarre. By Wakefield's account, he secured much of the Ngati Toa empire. Te Rauparaha thought he had sold only a couple of pieces of land. Wakefield sailed on, and by November was in the South Island, where he 'purchased' more land. A few days later he took three Wanganui chiefs on board the *Tory* and 'purchased' land from them. The deal was completed later by Arthur Wakefield, who thought he had secured 40,000 acres for £700. Other deals in Taranaki were left for Barrett to conclude in his whaler Maori. Before year's end the company had laid claim to virtually the whole of central New Zealand, 20 million acres from the north of Taranaki to Pito-one (Petone) and into the northern South Island.

They were just in time. The company ship *Cuba* arrived off Petone in early January 1840, bringing surveyor William Mein Smith, but the settler ships were just days behind and Smith had no time to complete his work. Hopeful migrants poured onto Pito-one beach with their cases, trunks, goods and furniture — including 25,000 bricks and at least one piano — to discover they would have to camp. The cargo, including goods that various would-be traders had brought with them, was dumped below high-tide mark and ended up 'washing about in the sand'.[30] There were surprises all round. Te Wharepouri had been promised settlers as part of the deal,[31] but assumed this meant 'nine or ten' Europeans — one in each pa, who could 'barter with the people'. When he saw 200 or more pouring from every ship he almost decamped.[32] The pantomime was somehow emblematic of the whole enterprise, and to cap it off the settlers learned the hard way that the valley was a flood-plain.[33]

Smith had been instructed to 'adhere to the conditions on which the land orders have been sold', though the form of the town was 'left to your own judgement and taste'.[34] Faced with swamp in the Hutt Valley, Colonel Wakefield thought the colony might fare better on the south side of the harbour near Pipitea pa, which he called Thorndon. There was precious little land there either, but there was no going back, and more than 1300 settlers were deposited in the Hutt Valley and Wellington that year alone, complete with their furniture, ploughs, ironmongery by Cottam and Hallen, and an array of 'Manning's Portable Cottages' — prefabricated homes that came complete with 'joists, floors, doors and glazed windows'.[35]

Although New Zealand Company propaganda displayed the Hutt Valley as flat, open and fertile with a navigable super-Thames running through it, the region was actually a swampy alluvial valley dominated by a wandering river.

Samuel Charles Brees, Alexander Turnbull Library, PUBL-0033-1847-168

Henry Petre's residence at Petone.

Samuel Charles Brees, Alexander Turnbull
Library, PUBL-0020-14-1

Right

With Petone and the Hutt Valley
unsuited to large-scale settlement,
company officials turned to flat
land in the south of the harbour.
Wiremu Tako Ngatata had led his
people to the Thorndon flat after
Ngati Mutunga departed, and by
1840 about 80 Maori lived in the
Pipitea pa, seen here. There were
other settlements in the vicinity,
some of which had not agreed to
the land 'sales' by Te Puni and Te
Wharepouri. But that did not
stop the settlers.

William Mein Smith, Alexander Turnbull
Library, C-011-005

Right below

Charles Heaphy titled this 1841
watercolour 'Thorndon flat and
part of the city of Wellington' —
an overstatement, but the town
nonetheless had a solid air of
establishment barely a year after
it was founded, helped along by
prefabricated buildings.

Charles Heaphy, Alexander Turnbull
Library, C-025-010

Above

Te Aro flats provided early Wellington with most of its flat land, seen to advantage in this 1841 Heaphy watercolour. Mount Victoria rises to the left of the frame, the Aro Valley to the right.

Charles Heaphy, Alexander Turnbull Library, C-026-002

Left

William Wakefield's house, on the hill behind Barrett's Hotel, Wellington.

Samuel Charles Brees, hand-coloured engraving, Alexander Turnbull Library, A-109-032

Left below

Much of the Wellington area was clad in forest but was sold as farm sections and the trees cut down. Some of the timber disappeared into the maws of sawmills such as this one at Kaiwharawhara.

Samuel Charles Brees, Alexander Turnbull Library, A-109-033

Company officials came to Wellington armed with an ideal grid-plan, though this seems to have been more for inspiration than a serious proposal. Practical reality tempered social perfection, though the actual town plan still optimistically draped straight roads and oblong sections over rugged terrain and Maori settlement alike.

MapColl832.4799gbbd/1840/Acc.316

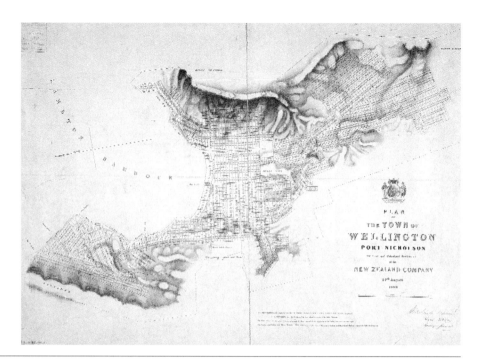

The second Wakefield colony was set up in Nelson during 1841. Allotments were more generous than Wellington, though most again went to speculators. By mid-1842 there were 2000-odd settlers on site, but only 526 of the 1000 allotments had been sold, and 364 of these belonged to absentee landlords. The result was inevitable: the colony lacked capital, the poor squatted, and Arthur Wakefield — nominally in charge — had to legitimise their holdings by lease. This torpedoed the economic basis on which the colony was meant to operate. These difficulties did not prevent the Wakefield towns in the Hutt Valley, Thorndon, Nelson and later New Plymouth and Wanganui growing over the next few months. Prefabricated buildings created a swift air of permanence, the building boom provided initial employment, and early trade with Maori was lucrative. Settlers also arrived at regular intervals, some doubtless drawn by the propaganda of Company secretary John Ward, whose outrageous portrayal of a flourishing Eden might be considered New Zealand's first work of fiction:

> The extensive forests offer an inexhaustible supply for the wants of many generations... . Flax ... appears to be indigenous and inexhaustible ... an almost incalculable source of riches ... Peaches are plentiful in the season at Hokianga; figs, grapes, oranges, melons and the Cape gooseberry, thrive uncommonly well ... Strawberries and raspberries grow in abundance ... the latitude and climate are suitable to the olive...[36]

Nearly 9000 would-be migrants swallowed these words and were disappointed.[37] Nor did apparent early successes resolve deeper problems ranging from the failure of Wakefield's social dream to the incompetence of company officials. Ultimately, failure reflected the divergence between a simplistic and absolute theoretical construct,

The Governor and Court of Directors of the New Zealand Company request the honor of

Mr: Duppa's

Company at a Breakfast at the West India Dock Tavern, on Friday the 17th September at two o'Clock, to celebrate the departure of their Second Colony for the Settlement of Nelson in New Zealand.

New Zealand House,

7th September 1841.

The favor of an answer is requested on or before Monday next the 13th instant, on receipt of which, Cards of Admission will be forwarded.

Artist unknown, Making New Zealand Collection, Alexander Turnbull Library, 119NMZ-1/4

and the fuzzy truths of a complex real society. The emigrants were considerably more capable than Wakefield imagined, and came to better themselves – not re-enter a world of hungry semi-slavery at the hands of industrialists and landowners. Many left as they could afford to do so, replaced by others from Britain and Australia who were less constrained by Wakefield's efforts to slot them into a social position. Within a few years many were looking beyond company lands, finally derailing the economic constraints with which Wakefield had hoped to lock in his class-based society.

This was not the only problem. Wakefield envisaged a local land-owning elite, but company vessels usually brought labourers, not landowners; and the wealthy who did arrive ended up competing with speculators back in London.[38] It was an unequal struggle that by 1843 was prompting a good deal of protest, and the issue was compounded by geography. Wellington had little land for the 'country sections' Wakefield had promised. A lucky 30 settlers got what was available, by lottery; and in late 1840 William Wakefield had to offer the rest of them land in Wanganui. Dubious title there laid the foundation for a long dispute.

Capital remained short. The Britannia Hotel and Store opened in mid-1840, and owner J. Pierce deigned to list prices, declaring that the 'competitive system of puffing, much practised in the old world' had no place in New Zealand, and he therefore 'refrains from introducing prices', instead inviting 'a trial'.[39] He was joined by others; T. Roskell's store 'at the west end of the beach' offered 'spirits (wholesale and retail), tea, coffee, sugar, tobacco and cigars, prime rose Cork butter, cheese, hams and pork' among other stores.[40] J. Telford's shop, at the other end of the beach, offered a similar range. R.W. Elsdon opened a 'commercial inn and tavern' offering 'wines, spirits, ale and porter' along with 'cold joints'.[41] But until the hinterland was settled there were few customers. Competition was tight, and

'Potie' of 'Port Nicholson' was apparently the mistress of Nelson hotelier William Wright. Maori-settler liaisons of this kind were not uncommon.

Isaac Coates, Alexander Turnbull Library, A-286-017

penniless labourers and families continued to pour in. Most ended up without work. Some were hired by the company, billowing the wages bill to over £1000 a month in Nelson alone by 1843. This was not sustainable, but a plan by company official Frederick Tuckett to offer the men individual contracts, paying them in allotments of land, did not go down well. Nor were allotments part of the Wakefield system, which was intended to keep the poor off the land.

Later company settlements were no better handled. New Plymouth was initially settled by the Plymouth Company, which merged with its parent in 1840. There was no harbour adjacent to the intended colony, nor could Maori provide the settlers

Right

Nelson in 1845; an air of prosperity belies the faltering scheme.

Francis Dillon Bell, Alexander Turnbull Library, A-252-019

Below and below opposite

An 1842 panorama of Nelson harbour and town. One feature of Wakefield's colonisation scheme was 'instant towns', rising up almost overnight with the help of prefabricated buildings from England. Others were quickly built by settlers eager to move out of temporary accommodation.

John Waring Saxton, Alexander Turnbull Library, PUBL-0011-06-2 and PUBL-0011-06-3

with enough food, as they had elsewhere. The shoddy land deal remained a bone of contention; there was a good harbour at Waitara, but both Crown and Maori refused to allow the company to have it.

Slabs of the 1839 Wellington purchase were disputed by Ngati Toa, who also opposed a drive to purchase more South Island land during 1843. These protests were mistaken for 'bounce', defiance of British authority. The situation was complicated by snail's-pace Crown efforts to resolve pre-Treaty land issues; and one outcome was the 'Wairau incident' of June 1843, a brief and bloody battle in which Arthur Wakefield and 25 others died.

Left

Settlers arriving at New Plymouth were initially housed in these barracks, built with Maori labour. An upstanding version of Mount Egmont/Taranaki rises behind.

Charles Heaphy, Alexander Turnbull Library, PUBL-0048-01

Hobson's choices

William Hobson faced a multitude of problems as he recovered from a stroke during early 1840. His infant administration was penniless, commanded 90 soldiers, and had yet to secure wide agreement to the Treaty of Waitangi. Pre-Treaty land claims had yet to be tackled, and New Zealand Company officials were uneasy about the potential loss of their 1839 'purchases'.[42] There was talk of a private French colony at Akaroa, under the aegis of the Nanto-Bordelaise Company. Captain Langlois of the whaler *Cachalot* had 'purchased' 30,000 acres on the peninsula in 1838, and eventually persuaded the French government to support a private venture to exploit fishing opportunities. The colonists were on their way by early 1840. To cap it off, the New Zealand Company declared self-government in May.

Hobson dealt with it all systematically. He sent two magistrates and several constables to welcome the French and remind them that New Zealand was British.

The New Zealand Company prompted more decisive steps. Hobson learned of their declaration of self-government late on 21 May, considered it treason,[43] and before the day was out issued a proclamation seizing the North Island by cession. Shortland was despatched on the *Integrity* to raise the Union Jack over Wellington. Thomas Bunbury formally annexed the South Island three weeks later off Cloudy Bay. These were immediately driven by Hobson's political problems, but were implicit in the British understanding of the Treaty of Waitangi. The Colonial Office began promoting the treaty around Europe to forestall other efforts. Meanwhile the British government issued a post-fact charter for the New Zealand Company, legitimising the operation within the gamut of colonial sovereignty.

These difficult beginnings set the theme for successive colonial governments in the early 1840s. The bold assertion that British power had been declared over New Zealand — and the assumption by the Colonial Office that this was true — was at odds with local reality. In practice, Hobson and his successors Willoughby Shortland and Robert FitzRoy had to balance Colonial Office requests, the increasingly strident demands of the New Zealand Company, and difficult race-relations matters against a penurious reality. Lack of funds, military weakness and lack of settler numbers highlighted the fact that Crown control was only nominal in the face of superior Maori numbers and power.

Perhaps the biggest issue for the successive regimes of governors Hobson, Shortland and FitzRoy was the 'waste land' argument. It stemmed in part from a Colonial Office interpretation of the Treaty of Waitangi. To the new Secretary of State, Lord John Russell, indigenous property rights extended only to the lands that Maori actually occupied and cultivated, and he asked Hobson to 'define on the maps of the colony the lands of the aborigines.'[44] This was not Hobson's

Auckland was founded as colonial capital more by chance than design. William Hobson intended to site the capital at Okiato, near Russell, but it was tied up with the 'old' land purchases made illegal by the Treaty of Waitangi. A power vacuum in the Waitemata, legacy of the 'musket wars', made settlement easier there. Felton Mathew surveyed a site in late 1840 and the new capital was set up early the following year. New Zealand Company officials in Wellington were bitterly disappointed. The fact that the colonial administration could be housed in this relatively modest structure is indicative of the relatively ad-hoc nature of government at that time. The building was destroyed by fire in 1842.

Edward Ashworth, Alexander Turnbull Library, E-216-f-005

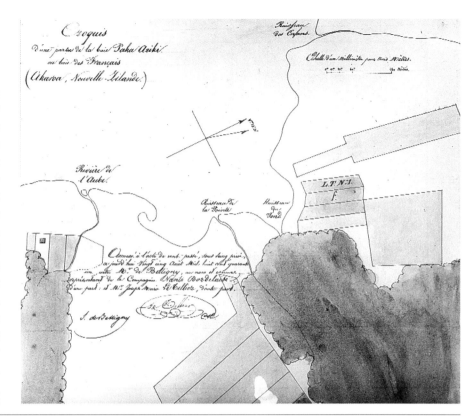

Akaroa was tipped as the site of a Nanto-Bordelaise Company colony. Captain C.F. Lavaud of the frigate *L'Aube* reached Auckland in July 1840 to tell Hobson what was happening, refusing to recognise Hobson's government until formal notification of the British claim arrived from Paris. Hobson sent special magistrates to hold courts and remind the would-be French claimants that New Zealand was British. Subsequent Foreign Office representations secured the British claim to New Zealand over that of its European rivals.

Artist unknown, Nanto-Bordelaise Collection, Alexander Turnbull Library, qMS-1407-080

understanding of what Maori had agreed to, but the Colonial Office attitude played into New Zealand Company hands. Agitated by the potential loss of their purchases, Company officials claimed that the law did not recognise anything other than ownership by occupation, and the Treaty was nothing more than 'a praiseworthy device for amusing and pacifying savages for the moment'.[45]

Hobson's lack of effective clout goes far towards explaining his apparent spinelessness, his premature death in 1842, and the consistent bad press delivered by historians to both his regime and those of his successors Shortland and FitzRoy. All three have been portrayed as preludes to a heroic George Grey (1812–98), the crusading, brilliant, eccentric idealist whose administration shaped the country from the late 1840s. In fact the main reason for the difference between Hobson and Grey was administrative. Auckland-based government could not keep tabs on Wellington, still less anything further south. The Wairau massacre prompted calls in Wellington for local government, which FitzRoy — by contrast with Hobson or Shortland — viewed favourably. But his concept of municipal powers fell short of what the Company had in mind, and they were further alienated in 1844 when he abandoned the pre-emption provisions of the Treaty of Waitangi, playing into the hands of Auckland landowners.[46]

Grey's New Zealand Government Act of 1846 split New Zealand into two provinces. The southern, New Munster, was based on Wellington, and came under a Lieutenant-Governor — explorer and adventurer Edward Eyre. Both provinces had their own two-house legislative assembly who reported to a General Assembly in Auckland; and most of the Wellington administrators, with the exception of

Life at home in the new colony. Sonia Bambridge and son William (1842–?), at Purewa in the mid-1840s.

William Bambridge, sepia ink, Alexander Turnbull Library, qMS-0122-074

Colonial Secretary Alfred Domett, a career civil servant, were Company men. This compromise provided an on-the-spot administration, reinforcing the authority of the Crown and providing better control of the European settlers. Grey's system, however, would not have been so effective had there not also been a shift in the ground relative to Maori — a consequence of the war that broke out with Nga Puhi in 1844.

Flagstaffs and regiments

Although invariably lumped with the conflicts of the 1860s and 1870s, the northern war of 1844–46 was very different from its successors. The struggle set Hone Heke Pokai and Te Ruki Kawiti against Tamati Waka Nene and the British. In some respects it reflected traditional Nga Puhi relationships, in which the British played a third party. However, historians have struggled to explain why fighting erupted, or what it meant. To T.L. Buick, writing in the 1920s, it was a 'rebellion',[47] though this is not how Heke saw it. Subsequent analysis has been more realistic,[48] though still problematic — one historian attributed the war in part to the death of Heke's first wife, who had otherwise restrained her hot-headed husband.[49] Ultimately, however, causes transcended personalities; had Heke not sparked the war, trouble would probably have brewed one way or another.

The cause was the conceptual gulf between concepts of sovereignty and chieftainship — though it is simplistic to blame the confusion solely on Henry Williams' use of 'rangatiratanga' in the Treaty. In fact the misunderstanding reflected practical experiences across a broad range of activities, and it was here that the key grievances generated. As far as the British were concerned, chiefs were free to run

Robert FitzRoy (1805–65) was appointed Governor of New Zealand in 1843. During the northern war of 1845 he issued debentures to fund government — exceeding his authority — and was sacked by a Colonial Office that did not comprehend the realities of the penurious colony.

Artist unknown, H.J. Schmidt Collection, Alexander Turnbull Library, PAColl-3059, G-1318-1/1

their tribes within the framework of British laws. Maori, however, interpreted British duties and ordinances as interference with their own power. In the Bay of Islands the issue was compounded by the fact that Nga Puhi felt abandoned after Hobson moved the capital to the Waitemata. Many had signed the treaty expecting to receive settlers and trade. However, 'in our part of the country ... the pakeha did not increase in numbers, but on the contrary, began to go away to the town at Waitemata ... Tobacco began to be scarce and dear; the ships began to leave off coming.'[50] When they discovered that the cause of the price-rises were customs and harbour duties, Maori 'at first did not believe' because 'you all said you were not slaves ... but all free men'.[51]

Heke Pokai (c1807–50), adopted the first names Hone Wiremu (John William) when he and his wife were baptised in 1835. He was the first to sign the Treaty of Waitangi — and among the first to become disillusioned with it. Here he stands with his second wife Hariata, daughter of Hongi Hika, and Te Ruki Kawiti.

Joseph Jenner Merrett, Alexander Turnbull Library, C-012-019

By 1844 Heke was determined to do something about it, though — despite his anti-colonial rhetoric — he did not want to destroy his economic relationship with the British.[52] His dispute was with what he considered to be government interference in Maori authority, a point underlined by his target — the symbol of British sovereignty, fluttering from the flagstaff above Kororareka, which Heke himself had given to the British. On the night of 8 July, he sent his men to fell it. There is some evidence that Heke interpreted the flag as a rahui pole, used to warn of a ban or restriction, and Maori certainly 'expected there would be fighting.'[53] However, FitzRoy had no force to hand, and in any case preferred diplomacy. He sent Archbishop Selwyn to meet Maori, then came to the Bay of Islands himself, removing customs duties in September.

At first all seemed well, but FitzRoy's concession did not relieve the wider underlying tensions, and Heke knocked the flagstaff down a second time in early January 1845. FitzRoy responded by putting a price on Heke's head and asking Nene to guard the pole. The latter agreed, but although Nene's men boasted of capturing Heke and 'smoking him' — spending the reward on tobacco — they made no effort to stop Heke when he brushed past them on the night of 19 January. He

Kororareka 'on the morning before the assault', March 1845.

G.T. Clayton, Alexander Turnbull Library, C-010-022

hacked the staff down a third time and sauntered back to his canoe with the words 'Heoi ano.' ('That's enough.')[54] The British considered the act a 'brazen declaration of war'.[55] FitzRoy called for more troops and sent 30 men of the 96th Regiment to guard the flagstaff — now re-erected with reinforcing. Meanwhile Williams circulated 300 copies of the Treaty of Waitangi around the Bay of Islands. The arrival of the regulars also had an effect. Maori had not seen British troops before:

> Now, these soldiers had red garments; they did not work, or buy and sell, like other pakeha people; they practised every day with their weapons, and some of them were constantly watching as if they expected to be attacked every moment. They were a very suspicious people, and they had stiff, hard things round their necks to keep their heads up, lest they should forget, and look too much downwards, and not keep their eyes continually rolling about in search of an enemy.[56]

The soldiers were joined by around 250 marines and 'special constables', but Heke was undeterred. 'I will cut down the flagstaff... . The soldiers are not gods; lead will kill them.'[57] Kawiti joined him, and they launched an attack on the night of 9 March. British forces included 45 sailors from HMS *Hazard*, which was anchored offshore. Heke's men took the blockhouse and felled the flagstaff, but the battle devolved to a pot-shot struggle in the town and Maori did not advance even after Joel Polack's powder store was accidentally blown up.[58] This gave the British time to evacuate to ships anchored in the bay, and the *Hazard* opened fire as Maori and settlers surged forwards to pillage.[59]

Heke disassociated himself, proclaiming that the looters were neither his nor Kawiti's.[60] FitzRoy waited for elements of the 58th Regiment to arrive from Sydney and in late April launched an expedition under Lieutenant-Colonel William Hulme. This landed in the Bay of Islands in early May, attacked Pomare's pa, then marched inland through rain to Lake Omapere, where they were joined by Nene's men outside Heke's incomplete Puketutu pa. Heke had 200-odd men to hand, and Kawiti provided a force variously cited as 140 or 300,[61] which camped outside the pa. Hulme opened fire with rockets, then sent the bulk of his men to take the incomplete rear,

Te Ruki Kawiti (c1770s–1854) of Ngati Hine was known to the settlers as 'The Duke', and had a formidable reputation as both fighting chief and peacemaker. He was heavily involved in the 'musket wars' and refused at first to sign the Treaty of Waitangi. He changed his mind, but then sided with Heke in 1845.

(Artist unknown, Alexander Turnbull Library, F-37353-1/2)

96th and 58th Regiments in action at Puketutu, 8 May 1845. Lieutenant Egerton's rocket battery is visible to the right in this painting by Major Cyprian Bridge of the 58th Regiment.

Cyprian Bridge, Alexander Turnbull Library, A-079-008

where they were engaged by Kawiti's force. The British got the better of it, but by arrangement Heke sortied into British forces in front of the pa. The storming party rushed to help, Kawiti attacked them in the rear and Hulme decided to withdraw. Maori had scored a tactical victory, but at the same time it was clear that they ran second to the regiments in open battle. Neither Heke nor Kawiti missed the lesson.

A tussle between Heke and Nene's forces followed at Te Ahuahu while the British regrouped, now under Colonel Henry Despard. By June they were ready to attack Heke's pa at Ohaeawai, south of Waimate, and some 600-odd soldiers and 250 of Nene's men set out from Kerikeri. Just getting there was a struggle; Despard remarked that 'Scarcely a rivulet was passed that some of the guns did not upset...'.[62] They battled their way to Ohaeawai, but a five-day siege did not crack the defences, and Despard's decision to storm the pa produced only disaster. With 70 wounded and ammunition running short, the beleaguered Colonel had to abandon the attempt. Heke's forces slipped away, and Despard got the blame for what Major Cyprian Bridge called defeat at the hands of a 'mob of savages'.[63] In fact the British repulse was not solely due to Despard's ineptitude. Heke and Kawiti had learned from their experience, refused to engage in open battle and set up a modified musket pa that offered protection against cannon fire — they had out-thought and leapfrogged the British.

FitzRoy decided to negotiate, but his failures were the final straw for the Colonial Office, and he was sacked in September. His replacement was Captain George Grey, the capable, ruthless, autocratic and idealistic administrator of South Australia, who reached Auckland in November 1845. Negotiations had reached a point where FitzRoy believed peace could be organised, but Grey thought the chiefs' letters were merely a device to gain time, and demanded a fresh expedition to attack Kawiti's new pa. The force that left Auckland on 7 December included 800 regulars and a naval brigade, backed by three 32-pounders, an 18-pounder, two 12-pounders and other artillery. This arsenal was pitted against Kawiti's new fortress of Ruapekapeka — 'The Bat's Lair' — another modified musket pa built on a hillside south of Kororareka. Grey asked Nene's ally Makoare te Taonui to detain Heke at Hikurangi, while Despard advanced across 18 miles (30 km) of rugged

terrain. It took days, in part because Despard insisted on building staging posts, but they were in position by Christmas and began a massive bombardment. Maori were 'almost deaf with the noise ... the air was full of cannon-balls', and the palisades 'began to disappear like a bank of fog before the morning breeze'.[64]

Heke arrived with 60-odd men on 10 January, but Despard did not move until next day, when he discovered that the defenders had withdrawn — only Kawiti and a dozen men remained behind, exchanged brief shots with the British, then withdrew. Stories circulated that the Maori had left the pa because it was Sunday and they intended to pray.[65] There were also suggestions that Kawiti and Heke planned to draw the British into the bush behind the pa, then ambush them 'as if they were wood-pigeons'.[66] There was a skirmish in the bush, but the loss of 12 dead and 30 wounded did not dent British strength and this 'ambush' theory has been dismissed by some historians.[67]

In fact the whole battle was another tip-and-run exercise; neither Heke nor Kawiti sought to tackle the British head on, instead dancing away, boxer-like, before the blow could fall. In theory this strategy could have allowed the two chiefs to extend the war, exhausting the British, but in practice it was Heke who ran short. He and Kawiti arrived at Pomare's pa a week after the battle and agreed to cease hostilities. Their people 'could not live on fern-root and fight the soldiers at the same time'. Nor was dispersing among Nga Puhi an option. 'After talking over this plan for some time,' an observer recalled, 'it was found it would not do, for already some chiefs ... had said they would give up anyone who came to them ... rather than bring war against themselves.'[68] The only other option was peace. In this respect the northern war was closer to the old inter-tribal conflicts: a limited struggle where lack of resources forced a negotiated end. Grey offered a pardon,[69] Heke and Kawiti kept their looted property, and the flagstaff remained down.

Some historians have taken Grey's magnanimity to mean that the northern war was a Maori victory.[70] However, the issue is less clear-cut. Although Ruapekapeka had been designed to force the British into peripheral actions, the British were able to continue the war, whereas Heke and Kawaiti were forced to a halt. Grey's subsequent actions reflected FitzRoy's aim of fighting with 'justice and clemency'.[71]

Above left
Colonel Henry Despard (c1784–1859) led British forces and kupapa against Ohaeawai in mid-July 1845.
Cyprian Bridge, Alexander Turnbull Library, A-079-005

Above right
Battle for Ohaeawai, ink and wash sketch by Sergeant John Williams of the 58th Regiment.
John Williams, Alexander Turnbull Library, E-320-f-002

Charles Heaphy's sketch of the
Ruapekapeka defences, noting the
flagpole knocked over by a lucky
shot early in the siege. What this
does not show is the slope that
gave the defenders a significant
advantage.

Charles Heaphy, Alexander Turnbull
Library, B-043-015-3

War was costly for the indebted colony, and other flashpoints demanded attention.
When opportunity came to make an expedient peace, Grey did so. The fact that he
continued to investigate ways of keeping Heke and Kawiti under control through
1846 is an indication that he recognised the potential threat they still posed, but
not that it reflected sudden military impotence.

In a military sense the failure of Heke's war to spread among Nga Puhi suggests
that the British had checked northern Maori. The visibility of the regiments was
probably a factor, and so was their performance. In open combat fought on their
own terms, the professional soldiers were extremely capable, and British artillery
counted for much even in battles fought on Maori terms. Non-combatant Maori
had been eager to see the 'full strength of the soldiers put forth, that we might see
what the utmost of their power was',[72] and they got it at Ruapekapeka in a storm
of noise and fire. Restraint also carried a practical benefit; war damaged the
economic relationship with the settlers, and few chiefs were prepared to sacrifice
what they had gained.

Grey withdrew half the force to Auckland, but they had not been there long
before they were sent to a new war in Wellington. This southern tussle broke out
largely as a result of the shoddy land purchases of the late 1830s. By early 1846
Ngati Toa were directly threatening settlers in the Hutt Valley. Raids in March
prompted Grey to declare martial law, which he enforced with the help of 400 men
of the 58th, 96th and 99th Regiments under Hulme. Their presence did not prevent
the Battle of Boulcott's Farm in May, when Upper Whanganui chief Te Mamaku led
a force of around 200 against 45 regulars of the 58th under Lieutenant G.H. Page,
pinning the British in a stockaded barn. After about an hour Page led his men to
engage the foe directly and, with the help of a small party of militia that happened
to arrive soon afterwards, drove Te Mamaku's much larger force back over the Hutt
River.[73]

Left above
Boulcott stockade after the Battle of Boulcott's Farm, graves of the regimental soldiers in the foreground.

George Hyde Page, Alexander Turnbull Library, B-081-002

Left below
Fort Richmond in the central Hutt Valley was designed by Captain Compton on US blockhouse practice, and first occupied in April 1846 by part of the 58th Regiment. The bridge is an 1844 structure built for the New Zealand Company.

S.C. Brees/Henry Melville, Alexander Turnbull Library, A-109-030

What followed demonstrated Grey's ability to find lateral answers. He had Te Rauparaha seized on pretext of treason, a *coup de main* that effectively decapitated the Ngati Toa empire and prompted Te Rauparaha's nephew Te Rangihaeata to withdraw to Horokiwi. Here he was attacked by elements of the 65th Regiment and local militia, with 150 Ngati Awa, but after a mortar bombardment Te Rangihaeata abandoned the position. In this way Grey effectively replaced Te Rauparaha's loose polity with one of his own. It was a cheap victory, and when combined with the results of the northern war the effects were significant. British presence was still a shadow of Empire, but the balance was shifting. By the end of the 1840s, the settler state was in a position to assert itself with caution.

Some 400 men of the 58th, 96th and 99th Regiments arrived in the Hutt Valley during March 1846 to enforce martial law after raids by Ngati Toa.

Shades of Grey

Mr Colenso told me they [Ngati Kahungunu] seemed doubtful about selling the whole of Moturuahou [sic] Island that they wanted several reserves on the island, and Mr Colenso advised them to have a clause inserted in the deed giving them free rights to their vessels entering and leaving the harbour besides such other rights as would no doubt be to their advantage, although *it does not appear to me essential that the natives require such advice when they are in treaty with the British Govt.*

– Donald McLean, 11 November 1851[74]

Government attitudes to Maori and the Treaty of Waitangi steadily hardened during the 1850s. This reflected a general Empire-wide transition from more humanitarian ideals towards the tougher imperialist sentiment of the later nineteenth century, itself a function of changing British thought. In New Zealand, the shift was made possible by Grey's victories of 1846 and the ongoing influx of settlers, which tipped the balance just enough to give Grey leverage that Hobson had not enjoyed. What followed was a combined outcome of pre-existing issues, misfired plans, misunderstandings and the workings of fate, along with cynical efforts to drive land purchase deals.

Grey had his own ideas about how to handle the land purchase process, but he inherited problems that required drastic action, not least of which was the mess left by Wakefield. An added complication was the Colonial Office interpretation of the Treaty of Waitangi, reflecting the 1844 opinion of a House of Commons Committee. Under pressure from the New Zealand Company, this committee concluded that the Treaty of Waitangi represented 'injudicious proceedings'. The problem was 'waste lands' — territory not physically occupied by Maori. The Colonial Office began pressuring Grey to acquire them, as originally intended in their instructions to Hobson. As Colonial Secretary Lord Stanley told Grey, 'all lands not actually occupied in the sense in which alone occupation can give a right

A 'terrible and fatal man', George Grey (1812–98) was just 28 when he was appointed Governor of South Australia. He became Governor of New Zealand in 1845 after FitzRoy's dismissal and made an early splash with his military campaign to end the northern wars. He followed this with his controversial 'flour and sugar' policies and introduced representative government to New Zealand. He was appointed Governor of South Africa in 1854, a post he held until 1861 when he returned to New Zealand, finding that the representative government hampered his latitude. By this time he was well offside with the Colonial Office, and was dismissed in 1868 amid remarks that he was unlikely to be re-employed. After a brief effort to be elected to the British Parliament, he entered New Zealand politics in 1874 and became Premier in 1877.

Photographer unknown, Alexander Turnbull Library, PA2-2509, F-92895-1/2

of possession, ought to have been considered as the property of the Crown'.[75] These attitudes drew protest in New Zealand from Sir William Martin, who argued that 'the whole surface of these islands ... has been appropriated by the Natives ... Nowhere was any piece of land discovered or heard of which has not been owned by some person or set of persons'.[76]

Grey did not dissent; as he remarked to the new Colonial Secretary Earl Grey, 'even in the most densely inhabited portions ... are very large tracts of land claimed by contending tribes to which neither of them have a strictly valid right'.[77] In practice, however, he could not seize the 'waste' lands, and instead set up mechanisms for Crown purchase, abolishing the Protectorate Department and putting the protection of Maori rights into the hands of officials such as Donald McLean. He also intended to maximise returns to government, pushing land sales 'so far in advance of the wants of the European settlers as to be able to purchase the lands required by the Government for a trifling consideration...'.[78] Agents such as McLean, Henry Kemp and Walter Mantell came under pressure to conclude sales at the lowest price. Grey envisaged the main payment would be through ongoing trade and his 'flour and sugar' policies — a deliberate effort to educate Maori and provide them industry; in short, to 'assimilate' them into the British economy.

To some extent it was an attempt to force Maori to become 'British'. However, as far as Grey was concerned the plan was also a way of helping Maori help themselves. As early as April 1851, Donald McLean noted in his diary that 'it would be an excellent thing if the natives would join with the Europeans in purchasing sheep, or shares. It would be a yearly revenue to them, which would always be increasing, and ... lead to their eventual wealth and improvement.'[79] Such sentiment defined the way the British saw Maori; official reports for decades afterwards invariably began with descriptions of 'industrial pursuits'.[80] What Grey, McLean and their successors variously missed or hoped to change was the point that Maori economics were geared around traditional social structures.

Grey facilitated flour mills and other factories, and set up 'industrial schools' to teach Maori how to use them. Establishment costs were significant: the Whanganui Industrial School of 1853 absorbed more than £1500 in government money and a further £200 from the CMS for the land. Most were effectively small farms. By 1856, Te Aute had more than six acres in wheat, four in potatoes and 13 in grass. Principal Samuel Williams believed he could 'confer a benefit' on Maori by 'teaching them to cultivate their land in a proper manner, also to look after their stock, milking &c'.[81] But Te Aute staggered and then folded — 15 pupils in 1856 had fallen to just four by 1859, when Williams closed it. He put the failure down to poor accommodation, hard work demanded of the pupils, temptations of high wages in adjacent stations — and the 'excited state of the native mind on the Land question'.[82]

The reality of the 1850s was that Maori could not be 'assimilated' by having British values rammed down their throats. This did not prevent the British trying long after the assimilation horse had clearly bolted. As late as 1862, William Baker

Yorkshire-born Edward John Eyre (1815–1901) reached Sydney in 1833 with £400 and settled on the Hunter River. His restless spirit drove him to explore the interior, including a pioneering 13-month continental crossing from Adelaide to Albany in 1840–41. He returned briefly to England before being appointed Lieutenant-Governor of New Zealand under George Grey. The latter was less impressed, and the two fought a near-continuous turf war until 1853, when Grey displaced Eyre.

Artist unknown, Alexander Turnbull Library, F-11991-1/2

decried the indiscipline he saw at the Turanga church school as symptomatic of Maori social systems, condemning the lack of 'prompt and cheerful obedience' as 'one of the greatest evils', making it 'more imperative that it should be strictly enforced at their public schools'.[83]

The irrelevance of British culture to Maori hampered Grey's efforts to kick-start Maori industry on the British model, but this was not the only problem. Maori were also hobbled by debts and the fact that the majority of their income went on consumables — some of which were purchased because European goods had become part of a currency of rivalry, a development the British misinterpreted as 'frivolous' spending. Industry, in any case, was not cheap. A mill set up at Warea in 1846–47 cost £150, paid in pigs to the builder, William Henwood. He was also the operator, and Maori soon found that the cost of construction and operation outstripped returns; the mill was abandoned in the early 1850s. Nor were mills always set up for economic reasons; in the late 1840s mills themselves became a brief focus of rivalry, as a result of which uneconomic numbers were set up in some areas, none in others. Hapu in Taranaki even came to blows over siting one.[84] Government assistance helped improve the economics, but the wheat market crashed in 1856. Prices fell from 12 to 3 shillings per bushel and Maori agriculture effectively collapsed.[85]

Some British were puzzled by the failure of Grey's system, but the only explanation officials could come up with was that Maori had 'got into dissipated habits and squandered the money in debauchery at Auckland and Wellington, and in the purchase of useless and extravagant articles'.[86] Efforts to rectify the problem reflected this attitude, as at the Kohimarama conference of 1860 where McLean told chiefs that:

> The education of your children, greater attention to the cultivation of the soil, the
> erection of better houses to live in, and the acquisition of European property will,
> I sincerely trust, claim your chief attention, when you return to your people.[87]

One of the problems was that the playing field was not quite as level as Grey and his government imagined. It was difficult for Maori to get credit; nor could their products command the prices fetched by the same products grown by settlers. Another and more serious issue was Grey's personal influence; he insisted on taking a lead role in the distribution of funds. The results were erratic, and ultimately Grey's 'flour and sugar' initiatives did little to improve Maori economic status.

Land sales provided the bulk of Maori income during the 1850s, but such arrangements had a built-in end point and the cultural gulf guaranteed problems. Government land-buyers envisaged sale in the British sense, but Maori did not share that vision. It has been argued that Maori had three means of transferring rights: take tupuna — ancestral rights; take raupatu — by conquest; and tuku whenua — by gift.[88] British requests to buy territory did not fit this framework, and many Maori concluded that the British only wanted the 'shadow of the land'.[89] After a sale, Maori continued to use the land as they always had, which caused ructions. When Ngati Kahungunu hunted on government land in Hawke's Bay during 1855, Resident Magistrate Alfred Domett admonished them:

> It is not your land. The white people do not go upon your land without your leave.
> In like manner, you would not go on the Queen's land … without leave of the white

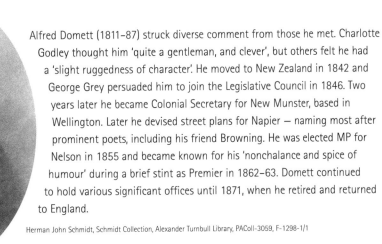

Alfred Domett (1811–87) struck diverse comment from those he met. Charlotte Godley thought him 'quite a gentleman, and clever', but others felt he had a 'slight ruggedness of character'. He moved to New Zealand in 1842 and George Grey persuaded him to join the Legislative Council in 1846. Two years later he became Colonial Secretary for New Munster, based in Wellington. Later he devised street plans for Napier — naming most after prominent poets, including his friend Browning. He was elected MP for Nelson in 1855 and became known for his 'nonchalance and spice of humour' during a brief stint as Premier in 1862–63. Domett continued to hold various significant offices until 1871, when he retired and returned to England.

Herman John Schmidt, Schmidt Collection, Alexander Turnbull Library, PAColl-3059, F-1298-1/1

men who are living upon it & paying for it to government... . This conduct of yours is very bad ... If you had no land of your own there might perhaps be some excuse for you. But you have plenty of land at Te Apiti, Kairakau, Waimarama and elsewhere you can hunt.[90]

Donald McLean (1820–77), the archetypal 'canny Scot' and chief land buyer in Hawke's Bay and the Wairarapa. Controversial even at the time, he became known to Maori as the 'Great Taniwha' and his activities eventually produced grievances from Wanganui to Napier. Yet he exhibited sensitivity towards Maori in other respects and gained a reputation as a race-relations fire-fighter, the national 'Maori doctor'. Much of this was doubtless due to his knowledge of the language – a fluency that would have been flavoured with a strong Hebridean accent.

Photographer unknown, Alexander Turnbull Library, PA2-2603

Maori knew something was different, but the issue was understanding the difference. The British similarly framed strategies through their own lens. In 1851, for instance, Colenso warned government land-buyer Donald McLean that 'land originally given as a gift from one chief to another does not empower the recipient to sell but to hold for himself and successors'.[91] But he did not question the concept of transfer. It took half a century for European authorities to recognise some of the cultural realities,[92] and the problem was not explored in detail until the 1980s.[93] In the 1850s, particularly when combined with the attitude of agents such as McLean, this array of hidden misunderstandings was a recipe for trouble.

The hardening of land policy was driven in part by necessity,[94] in part by conscious decision. The national effort initially focused on the Wairarapa and Hawke's Bay as a direct result of unauthorised pastoral expansion out of the Wellington region, combined with New Zealand Company ambitions in the same areas. These first purchases into densely populated Maori areas allowed government officials to develop and refine policies later applied at national level, and the initiative came from the New Zealand Company. By the mid-1840s it was clear to Edward Gibbon Wakefield that his dream had misfired, but he was far from defeated and concocted the idea of a Church of England colony. This was brought to fruition by John Robert Godley, whose Canterbury Association was formed in 1847 on promise of land in New Zealand. Wakefield meant the Wairarapa, some 20,000 acres of grassland that Robert Stokes had reached as early as 1841.[95] But although Shortland's suspension of pre-emption gave the company a free hand, William Wakefield would not commit to purchase.[96]

Some settlers, led by C.R. Bidwill, Frederick Weld and his business partner C. Clifford, decided to make their own deals with Ngati Kahungunu. None knew anything about sheep, but Weld leased an area for £12 per annum and depastured merinos on it in May 1844. By 1846 there were nearly 20 privately leased pastoral stations in the Wairarapa. Early difficulties managing the flocks were resolved by hiring shepherds, and within two years Weld made a personal profit of around £4000,[97] around $800,000 in early twenty-first-century money. This was simply stunning at a time when many Wakefield settlers were struggling to make ends meet. Grey's re-imposition of pre-emption rendered this illegal but this did not stop the pastoralists, and Grey had to tread a fine line between enforcing the law and stifling settlement.

Above

A party explores the shores of Lake Wairarapa in the early 1840s.

William Mein Smith, watercolour, Alexander Turnbull Library, B-062-021

Left and below

Big sky, big country. The 'great Wairarapa district' contrasted sharply with the narrow valleys of Wellington. Hunters soon gave way to pastoralists eager to strike leasing deals with Maori — thumbing their noses at government in the process.

S.C. Brees/Henry Melville, hand-coloured engraving, Alexander Turnbull Library, E-070-009

S.C. Brees/Henry Melville, hand-coloured engraving, Alexander Turnbull Library, E-070-008

Wakefield asked Grey to grant the New Zealand Company land in the Wairarapa that year, an area that briefly became the new national focus of settler expansion. Francis Dillon Bell and interpreter George Clarke approached Ngati Kahungunu in February 1847 and discovered that none was prepared to sell while it was possible to get a return by leasing. All Grey could do was issue a circular letter threatening to force the Europeans off if Maori did not sell. This stalled at the first recipient,[98] and in October government warned settlers that further leasing could result in prosecutions.[99] However, Grey did not push the effort and instead turned to the South Island, where the huge Wairau block was purchased during 1847 and the Canterbury-Otago block a year later.[100] The Company remained eager to secure land in the Wairarapa, and a second government effort got under way in mid-1848,[101] despite staunch opposition from Colenso, who was running the Ahuriri mission. Domett thought the minister might 'feel a peculiar interest in the formation of this [Church] settlement',[102] but Colenso turned down a request to butter up chiefs, penned a dire warning to the CMS, then wrote to Eyre and Domett that he:

> ...cannot conscientiously aid or assist or ... use any influence which I may possess over the native chiefs to prevail upon them to alienate the whole of their Lands to the Crown, or to accept ... scattered or detached parcels or blocks among the whites.[103]

Eyre – diplomatically – put this down to a misunderstanding,[104] but in the end it was academic. Ngati Kahungunu wanted £16,000, four times Kemp's budget, and Grey turned his attention to the more sparsely populated Akaroa and Canterbury, a decision that simply spurred the Wairarapa squatters on. Some had already spilled north into Hawke's Bay and it looked like more would follow.[105] Ngati Kahungunu wondered about sale, and in mid-1849 Eyre received several letters offering land.[106] Armed with this proposal, the Lieutenant-Governor hit on the idea of surrounding the Wairarapa with lands that could be leased to settlers at lower prices than Wairarapa chiefs were prepared to accept. He nominated Walter Mantell to negotiate, but Grey viewed Hawke's Bay as a sideline, preferring direct ways of undercutting leasing in the Wairarapa. The job went to Donald McLean, who had made a name for himself tidying up the Wakefield mess in Wanganui. By late 1849 McLean was halfway through negotiating with Ngati te Upokoiri for part of the Manawatu.[107]

McLean's influence has been invariably underestimated. His plans for the Wairarapa revived encirclement on the basis that Ngati te Upokoiri ties gave him an opening into Hawke's Bay. This was out of line with Grey's policy, but McLean was determined – possibly for personal reasons[108] – and when Eyre told him to investigate purchases in the Manawatu and Wairarapa, McLean replied that he would go to Ahuriri 'where some of the Principal Chiefs concerned in the sale of the Districts ... are residing'.[109] Grey rejected the proposal,[110] but Eyre passed the

Left above

An 1858 view of Waipukurau Pa, central Hawke's Bay. The scene eight years earlier when Donald McLean arrived to buy land would have been similar.

Joseph Rhodes, watercolour, Alexander Turnbull Library, A-159-027

Left below

Ahuriri Lagoon, another Joseph Rhodes watercolour. Settlement had spread this far north from the Wairarapa by 1850, well in advance of effective government control.

Joseph Rhodes, watercolour, Alexander Turnbull Library, A-159-033

message to McLean with an out-clause; he was to 'report what steps you consider it desirable to take' to buy land in the Manawatu and Wairarapa.[111] As far as McLean was concerned, this meant pushing Ahuriri, and it appears McLean finally sold the strategy to the Governor.[112] By early January 1851 he had been offered 'Haretaonga [sic] and Ahuriri from end to end'.[113]

When bargaining began for the Waipukurau block in April 1851, McLean discovered that Ngati Kahungunu knew about Grey's intentions, and Te Hapuku talked McLean up to £4800 for the Waipukurau block,[114] around $980,000 in early twenty-first-century dollars and more than McLean wanted to spend. The result was that he had to push both the Ahuriri and Mohaka deals to the edge of failure.[115] Grey's 'flour and sugar' assistance and an economic relationship with settlers were considered part of the payment.[116] Academic analysis has concluded that McLean offered concessions to keep the door open for future sales,[117] and the point has also been made that some problems can be attributed to mismatch of culture rather than a deliberate attempt to defraud.[118]

McLean turned his attention to the Wairarapa in 1852, using his connections with Te Hapuku as a lever. Virtually the whole Wairarapa changed hands over the next few years, and although other land was sold around New Zealand, the Wairarapa and Hawke's Bay remained the main focus of the government purchase strategy for years. Grey made a lightning trip through the area in early 1853, and the result was a general arrangement to sell further blocks. Negotiations were apparently complete by the end of 1853, when Ngati Hawea chief Kurupo te Moananui wrote to McLean to explain that he was organising the lands for sale and intended to come to Wellington for payment. Four sales followed while Kurupo te Moananui and Te Hapuku were in Wellington over Christmas 1853, without consultation with their people.

Te Hapuku (c1797–1878), Ngati Whatuiapiti chief and prominent land-seller in Hawke's Bay.

Samuel Carnell, S. Carnell Collection, wet collodion glass negative, Alexander Turnbull Library, PAColl-3979, G-22221-1/4

This began a national policy of pressure on chiefs to sell directly. Speed was of the essence as settlers poured in. To give McLean fair context, the process reflected the settler assumption that Maori should adopt British principles, but the approach as McLean adopted it was still out of line, and he was heavily criticised by contemporaries. However, his promotion to head the Land Purchase Department put him in an unassailable political position, and the policy was embedded when Governor Thomas Gore-Browne decided Maori relations were Imperial, putting them under his own authority. But he left McLean alone to proceed.[119] The sales that followed were unprecedented: in the 21 months from mid-1856 to March 1858, some 771,673 acres in the Bay of Islands, Whangarei, Auckland, Thames, Kaipara and Wellington districts changed hands for a grand total of £24,870.[120]

There were two interrelated outcomes for Maori. Land sales became part of a currency of rivalry, but McLean's system led to the promotion of one chief over another as agent, causing old oppositions to flare. The process diminished chiefly authority, because many parted with land without properly discussing it with their people. This was evident early on when various Waikato hapu protested the activity of Te Wherowhero, among other chiefs, who had sold the Waitemata and Manukau blocks without adequate consultation.[121] Trouble flared particularly in Hawke's Bay, which provided four-sevenths of the total sold by Maori in the 1855–56 period. Selling land had evidently become part of a 'race for mana' between Ngati Kahungunu, led by Kurupo te Moananui, and Ngati Whatuiapiti, led by Te Hapuku.[122] War broke out between them in late 1857. McLean hastened to distance himself, but it was a direct outcome of his purchase system, and Samuel Williams rammed the point home at the time.

CHAPTER 4

The road to Erewhon

Settlers poured into New Zealand during the mid-nineteenth century, a relentless movement punctuated by two great booms in the early 1860s and 1870s, and by dips during the depths of depression in the late 1860s and 1890s. The rate of this movement — boosted by the industrial-strength migration policies of private enterprise and government — was explosive. The 1858 census revealed 59,413 Europeans and 56,049 Maori,[1] though distribution was not even and areas such as the Waikato and the East Cape of the North Island were almost wholly populated by Maori. Settler society had nevertheless arrived.

Their world view was shaped by a potent mix of industrial ideology, new philosophies of reason, new Calvinist evangelism and new economic theory.[2] This combination goes a long way towards explaining both why settlers came to New Zealand and the society they built — with its nod to egalitarianism, the do-it-yourself ethos, dreams of private home ownership, the 'quarter-acre paradise', gridwork street patterns, and emphasis on job security. It was also another reason why the New Zealand Company failed. Settlers came to New Zealand with a mood for change, but not the society Wakefield handed them.

Oakes colliery explodes.

Artist unknown/Author collection

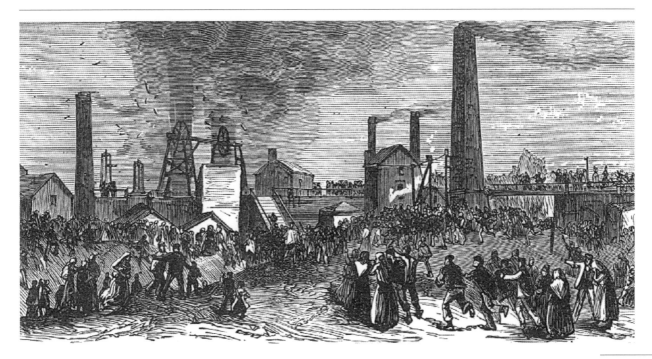

New worlds

The ideals of New Zealand's mid-nineteenth-century settlers can be traced to industrialising Britain. The 'industrial revolution' was one of the discontinuities of Western history, driven by a range of social, economic and scientific developments that emerged through the eighteenth century. The key forces were an agrarian revolution — which demanded land, obtained in many rural areas by turfing off tenants and 'enclosing' the common fields — and a technical shift in production methods. A combination of new engineering techniques and labour shortages triggered the invention of machines to meet cloth markets, machines that required a retinue of unskilled supplicants to tend them.[3] Much of the labour force came from the dispossessed rural poor, who drifted into the industrial towns. The mews and narrow streets of these urbs — the only open spaces amid a 'forest of chimneys'[4] — filled a dual role as community gathering places and sewers.[5] Towns grew with frightening and uncontrolled pace, pushed by the influx from the fields, pulled by demand for labour. Efforts by Ned Ludd and his supporters to change the pattern by smashing the steam looms did not halt the tide.

These shifts turned 'early modern' society into a structurally modern one, where people relied on employment to survive. Some town workers' homes did not even have kitchens; meals were pies and hot potatoes purchased from street vendors.[6] Factory owners made vast profits by paying 'Johnnie' just a 'penny a day', masking the fact that the British economy expanded little between 1760 and 1820.[7] At a time when the rural pie was shrinking the industrialists, traders, administrators and

Right and opposite
'Here and there; or, emigration a remedy'. This *Punch* parody of July 1848 — one of Britain's crisis years — actually contained a fair dollop of truth about the realities of both nineteenth-century Britain and the colonies.

Artist unknown, wood engraving, Alexander Turnbull Library, PUBL-0043-1848-15

Alexander Turnbull Library, PUBL-0043-1850-01

HERE   AND   THERE;

OR, EMIGRATION A REMEDY.

bankers managed to transfer most of the wealth to themselves. Food shortages triggered by inclement weather compounded the problem. Poaching and theft became the only way some country-folk could keep their families fed, but government response addressed only the symptoms.[8] Songs, nursery rhymes and stories mourned a lost rural idyll, and many people found succour in religion. John Wesley evangelised the gospels to northern, Midlands and South Wales working classes. When the Anglicans rejected 'Wesleyanism', he founded the Methodist church. The Evangelicals infused new life into Anglicanism. The upheavals of industrialism, the ethos that went with it, and food shortages caused by oscillating weather patterns[9] helped prompt new emphasis on the more abstemious teachings of Protestantism, ultimately expressed as renewed Calvinism — a philosophy of material self-sacrifice for later moral reward. The link was explicit. As R. Vaughan declared in 1843, the 'strength of Protestantism' was a 'strength on the side of industry, of human improvement...'.[10]

One of the first to rationalise these upheavals was Adam Smith (1723–90), who is credited with inventing the idea of the 'invisible hand' in markets — though he only mentioned the concept once in context of foreign trade.[11] However, his ideas were further developed by David Hume (1711–76), who drew on the economic doctrine of Jean Bodin — a sixteenth-century advocate of burning witches — to lay the groundwork for a philosophy based on the assumption that all interactions should be based on self-interest and open competition.[12] During the early nineteenth century these ideas were extended by clergyman Thomas Malthus

The Needlewoman at Home and Abroad.

AT HOME. ABROAD.

(1766–1834) and financier David Ricardo (1772–1823) into dogma, and as Eric Hobsbawm has pointed out, it is impossible to argue that their motives were anything but partisan.[13] Malthus even disclaimed the 'right of the poor to support', arguing that starvation would eliminate the unemployed. At the time, William Cobbett decried Malthus as a 'monster' whose theories 'furnished unfeeling oligarchs' with ammunition.[14] This was also true of Ricardo's 'iron law of wages', which suggested that employer benevolence would distort the labour market, a point seized upon by industrialists seeking to maximise profits.

Such theories derived from and fitted the puritanical mood of the day, and did not take long to implement. In 1820 the London Merchants offered a petition to Parliament urging 'freedom from restraint'.[15] They found an ally in the people, who funded taxes on corn through higher bread prices. Successive bad seasons following on from the calamitous 'year without a summer' in 1816 had helped put food at a premium,[16] and by linking abolition of the 'Corn Laws' to the free market, Britain's industrial elites were able to push their philosophy to society at large.[17] The edifice was given validity in the 1850s when Charles Darwin — inspired by Malthus — built market competition into his theory of natural selection. Herbert Spencer then championed the notion as proof that pure competition was a natural state.[18] Such thinking keyed from and re-expressed the Calvinist ideals of the period, which had already blamed the misfortunes of the poor on their own failings. The notion that they should be punished for it flowed with these ideas. 'The workhouse,' the Reverend H.H. Milman wrote in 1832 to Edwin Chadwick, 'should be a place of hardship, coarse fare, of degradation and humility; it should be ... as repulsive as consistent with humanity.'[19]

The problem was that the theorists had reached their conclusions by observing a world in disarray, and their conclusions rested on simplistic assumptions. In reality it was naive to expect that simple market exchange and contract could wholly explain or supplant the complex social interactions of their society;[20] and the German philosopher Karl Marx — whose theories were founded in the same chaos — produced ideas that were ultimately just as impractical. Nor did the people stand idly by. The British government almost collapsed in the face of social change in 1816 and again in 1830. Popular opposition by the 1830s was oriented around the Chartists, a cause that emerged from Robert Owen's failed union movement and as a reaction to the moderate parliamentary Reform Bill of 1832.

Crop failures between 1838 and 1843 prompted the epithet 'hungry forties', a situation not helped by the fact that purist liberal capitalism proved anarchic. The rational economies of the period swung wildly between violent booms and catastrophic busts. The 'railway mania' of the 1840s gave Britain multiple competing railways between a few centres, but failed to provide a national transport network, and then the railway stock bubble burst. This contributed to the general economic crisis of 1847, which fed into political crisis in 1848.[21] Britain avoided calamity by a whisker in the face of Chartist agitation. European governments — which shared these problems — fell over, and these experiences prompted some thinkers to temper early theories. John Stuart Mill suggested that minimal education, state protection of start-up industry, and regulated working hours would be needed to make the economy operate properly.[22]

Even with Mill's input, however, Britain's poor faced an insecure future, and while the formation of 'class' in the Marxist sense was a complex process, obscure enough in some British city settings to prompt historical debate later,[23] the wealthy of the day feared a popular revolution. However, there were alternatives. Jerusalem may not have appeared among England's dark satanic mills, but optimists hoped it might be built in the green and pleasant lands of the colonies. The philosophy of the day favoured migration as the answer to social issues,[24] and Robert Horton organised systems for the mass-export of paupers as early as the 1820s. The poor pushed, flocking to the migrant ships. The wealthy also felt impelled to seek greener fields; some with a little capital felt they could make better use of it in virgin territory. Whether they were consciously seeking to build a new and perfect world is arguable. Theorists such as Wakefield held high hopes, but his dream failed, and although one historian has argued that New Zealand's settlers were Arcadian,[25] the reality for most migrants was practical. The conservative wealthy saw emigration as an escape from chaos. The poor hoped to better themselves. Chartists and radicals also left, hoping to escape persecution, and there is good evidence that the radical agenda was dropped once they had emigrated.[26]

The voyage to New Zealand

The rate at which New Zealand was settled during the mid-nineteenth century was simply extraordinary. The first government census in 1851 revealed a European population of 26,707. Most had arrived in the previous 15 years, many by subsidised passage with the New Zealand Company. By the next head-count in 1858 their numbers had doubled, and by 1864 there were just over 171,000.[27] Only a small proportion was natural growth; in the 1861–65 period, for instance, about 15,000 settlers were born in New Zealand but another 90,000-odd arrived by sea.[28]

These increases understate the true scale of movement. Tens of thousands poured into New Zealand during the gold rush days – and tens of thousands poured out again, part of a gigantic floating population that surged around the Pacific in pursuit of the precious metal. Most were Australian. In the year to 31 March 1862, some 29,454 men arrived in New Zealand, of whom 24,243 came from Australia. Only 794 were from Britain,[29] though these were more likely to be permanent; the tyranny of distance translated into a return cost that few could meet. In other respects, New Zealand – however bad – was an improvement on 'home'. This was particularly so in the 1870s, when many migrants were labourers.[30]

'The emigrant's daughter' – although families usually emigrated together, this 1861 sketch captures the pain of parting for ever from friends, family and home. Only the very wealthy could afford a return journey from halfway round the world.

Thomas Graham, Making New Zealand Collection, Alexander Turnbull Library, F-84-1/4-MNZ

The Canterbury
Association

John Robert Godley (1814–61),
mover-and-shaker behind the
Canterbury Association, was
inspired by Ireland's plight during
the potato famine. Plans to settle
1,000,000 Irish in Canada were
soon dropped, but a meeting with
Wakefield triggered a new plan
for an Anglican Church
settlement in New Zealand.

Photographer unknown, Alexander Turnbull Library,
F-1079-1/2

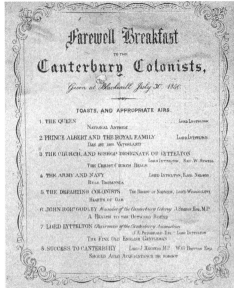

Above right
Creator unknown, Alexander Turnbull
Library, F-1213-1/2-MNZ

Centre
Farewelling the Canterbury
colonists, Gravesend, September
1850. The first four settler ships
reached Lyttelton at the end of
the year.

Alexander Turnbull Library, PUBL-0033-1850-199

Below
The *Lady Nugent* at sea, sketched
by G.R. Hilliard en route to New
Zealand late in 1841. 'Our ship at
times appearing to fly up into the
clouds and again as if to descend
from a watery Mountain into the
very bottom of the sea', he scribbled
in his journal. 'Felt very qualmish.'

George Richard Hilliard, Alexander Turnbull
Library, A-113-016

The Canterbury Association

Above

A romanticised view of life on board the *Randolph* Canterbury settler ship en route to New Zealand in late 1850.

Artist unknown, Alexander Turnbull Library, F94-1/4-MNZ

Centre

Passengers from the *Cressy* at Lyttelton, 1851. An engraving from an original sketch by William Fox. Those who could not afford transport had to hike across the Port Hills to Christchurch.

William Fox/Thomas Allom, Alexander Turnbull Library, PUBL-0001-2

Below

The 'great plain' of Canterbury as seen by William Fox in 1851. The Canterbury Papers described the scene as a 'complete wilderness, with the exception of the farm of Messrs Deans...' adding that wide grasslands would require 'no labour' to maintain livestock.

William Fox, Alexander Turnbull Library, A-195-014

The reasons people were leaving Britain are clear, but why they chose New Zealand is not. The 90-day journey under sail compared unfavourably in time and cost with the ten it took to cross the Atlantic by steamer.[31] Land was more expensive, and even with assisted passage, New Zealand offered fewer prospects than Canada, the United States or even Australia.

For these reasons, New Zealand intercepted less than one percent of the total emigrating from Britain during the period.[32] Still, the fraction who made the journey had reason. Some historians argue that the main factor was evangelising by officials and colonial boosters such as Charles Hursthouse, Richard Taylor and Thomas Cholmondeley. Frederick Campbell, working for a company that acted as broker for the New Zealand Company and the Canterbury Association, recalled years later that:

> ...it was necessary to know as much as possible about the colony, from books, from the tales by people who had been there, and from 'other sources'. These other sources, I found to be from the fertility of their own imagination, and I am afraid I soon became an apt scholar ... I knew more about New Zealand in those days, than I do now after 44 years residency here. Yarns like how easy it was to: 'Go into the bush, catch a pig, and kill it for dinner'. 'Throw a line with a hook into the river and pull out a fish for breakfast'. 'Make a few holes in the ground, cut up a bucketful of potatoes, plant them, then dig up enough to last you for a year'. 'Live outdoors, as houses were superfluous, and all you needed was a blanket to lie down and sleep out anywhere — all year round'. 'Grow roses which were always in

'The emigrant's farewell', a scene repeated time and again as settlers departed for destinations afar.

James Fagan, Alexander Turnbull Library, C-015-001

bloom'.... We used to say what jolly fellows the natives were, so the Wairau Massacre came as quite a shock, but we did make light of it to clients...[33]

The extent to which settlers were taken in is unclear, though raw percentages suggest not many were. Fantasy New Zealand did not compare with the well-reported realities of New York, Sydney or Cape Town as a place of opportunity — or as a road to the frontier for the die-hards who wanted to hack a living from virgin soil. Those who found New Zealand appealing may have had a healthy cynicism; propaganda raised expectations but did not convert. 'I left England because I was sick of it,' William Hay wrote in 1865, 'and believing that I should better my condition by so doing....'[34]

The fact that dips in migration to New Zealand correlate with depression and war in the colony suggests there was reality behind the decision. At an individual level there were many reasons for making the journey, including 'betterment'. Campbell himself took the decision 'at some evil hour in November 1850', making the voyage on the *Bronte*.[35]

The voyage to New Zealand — three months from Gravesend or Plymouth to Auckland, Wellington, Lyttelton or Port Chalmers — remained a remarkably constant experience. The difference between the cabin passages of the 1840s and 1850s and those of the 1870s and 1880s was not great. Steam sped the Atlantic crossing, but sail remained prime mover for the journey to New Zealand until the end of the settler period in the late 1880s; and the usual route took them to the Cape of Good Hope and east through the Roaring Forties.

Dinner time 'on board the first emigrant ship for New Zealand'. Real ships, even in 'cuddy' class, were considerably more cramped.

Artist unknown, Alexander Turnbull Library, A-109-054

DINNER ON BOARD THE FIRST EMIGRANT SHIP FOR NEW ZEALAND.

Although steamships regularly crossed the Atlantic by the mid-nineteenth century, the journey to New Zealand was made by sail for decades.

Artist unknown, Alexander Turnbull Library, G-17245-1/2

A few came out in style. Thomas Tanner chartered a ship to carry his servants, gold plate, pedigree animals, furniture, books and family to New Zealand.[36] But he was a rare breed, and for the majority with enough cash, cabin passage offered a comfortable, entertaining, genteel and relaxing journey of gastronomic excess.[37] During one crossing at the end of 1861, F.W. Hamilton reported living 'in the very best style having fresh meat of all kinds every day, fresh fish, sweet cream, and all kinds of fruit preserved in bottles'.[38] A succession of feasts was part of the sales-pitch, and actually appears to have materialised for the wealthier passengers. Breakfast, lunch, dinner and supper were seldom less than banquets. Various hot boiled or roast meats — often joints and choice cuts provided fresh from on-board livestock — were invariably accompanied with cold or jellied meats, roast fowl, hams, cheeses, boiled vegetables, pies, broths, bread, biscuits, jams, conserves, puddings and nuts, all laid on the groaning board for cabin passengers whose appetites had been whetted by deck games and sea air.

Some of this gluttonous cornucopia came from private supplies, renewed where opportunity permitted. Deal boatmen 'bought oranges off from shore' at '20 a shilling' when the *Palala* anchored offshore in early 1880, bound for New Zealand. Later, as migrant schoolmaster William Rainbow recorded, boatmen delivered 'macaroni, haricot beans, lentils, & a suit of oilskins and boots for me'.[39] Occasionally cabin supplies ran out, forcing passengers to subsist on steerage rations, but while some captains preferred non-stop passage, others were prepared to stop for food along the way if fortune permitted. 'The captain had promised to heave to off Tristan d'Acunha [sic],' Charlotte Godley wrote from the South Atlantic in March 1850, 'and send off a boat for potatoes and pigs ... unluckily ... the wind changed when we came pretty near it...'.[40]

Left above

Settlers bound for New Zealand celebrate New Year's Eve 1864.

Artist unknown, Alexander Turnbull Library, B-064-022

Left below

Divine service on board the *Pegasus*, New Zealand bound in 1865.

Artist unknown, Alexander Turnbull Library, A-277-020

Cabin passage still had its hazards. 'Woke in the night and found rat sitting on my face,' Rainbow wrote a few days out from Deal in early 1880.[41] Seasickness was another problem, and most thought the storms 'wretched',[42] though the results could not be confided in genteel society; as Godley wrote to her mother, the 'wretchedness' of the first days at sea were 'not a thing to be spoken of'.[43] Things improved further south. 'Everything soft & mild & ship heeling over like a rocking chair,' Rainbow penned a week or two out of Deal.[44] Quoits, reading, chatting and lessons helped fill the hours, but 'ship life became monotonous after a time'.[45] Night offered entertainment. 'Tonight I have been sitting on the poop for a time watching the phosphorescence of the sea,' Rainbow wrote in February, 'I have seen the Southern Cross ... not so striking as it is reputed. Orion is glorious ... and the Milky Way & Magellan Cloud [sic] — a cluster of stars dim thro' great distance. There are others — glorious, but I don't know them.'[46]

At times the ships sailed in company. 'Twenty-six ships all in sight together from the mast,' Charlotte Godley wrote early in 1850 after being becalmed on board the *Lady Nugent*.[47] Cyrus Davie took the opportunity to swap ships, jumping from the *Sir George Seymour* to the *Randolph*.[48] Off the Cape of Good Hope it was a different story. They had been promised 'dusty weather' and got it, 'tremendous waves, as they seemed to me, and we sprang our fore-top mast and lost some ropes, and a sail or two much torn'.[49]

For those without the means, the voyage was another matter. A steerage passage was an ordeal amid cramped, damp and airless spaces below decks. Food was supplied as part of the ticket, but some captains failed to stock promised supplies, either through incompetence, or deliberately to reduce costs. A steerage diet was usually boiled salt beef or pork, potatoes or rice and sometimes peas or lentils, prepared in giant cauldrons and doled out. On some ships hours might pass before everybody was fed, and if the food ran out steerage went hungry. Nutrition was marginal at the best of times, and there was at least one reported case of death by starvation.[50] Dysentery was common. Pneumonia sometimes followed otherwise minor colds. Scarlet fever, mumps, measles and chickenpox were clear dangers. Children were particularly vulnerable and for many families the voyage was one of unrelieved tragedy, as their offspring died one after another.

Settler ship at sea. 'Frigate' construction was in vogue by the mid-nineteenth century, complete with fake gunports.

Artist unknown, Alexander Turnbull Library, G-2543-1/1

The voyage often threw together folk from disparate walks of life. William Rainbow's fellows in 1880 included a 'German couple' and three children; a 'tall slip of a Scotch boy' on his way to visit his uncle; and a doctor. The cabin next door was 'highly mixed' and included a 'gas engineer ... with a crank about him that we are the lost tribes of Israel'.[51] Charlotte Godley's fellow passengers on the *Lady Nugent* of 1850 included wealthy aristocratic scion Algernon Tollemache, on his way to see £15,000 worth of land he had bought in New Zealand. He brought with him his dog, 'three maids', and a 'family whom he is helping to emigrate ... with five very naughty, dirty children.'[52] Others included:

> ...one lady, Miss Borton, quite young and rather pretty, though neither aristocratic nor very bright... . Mr. Bulkeley, cousin to Sir Richard, going out to New Zealand to join his regiment, the 65th; Mr. Nicholson, who has just left Oxford — his father is some rich man near Leeds ... Mr Robinson ... has been a merchant at Calcutta ... and a smart young Mr Lee, one of many brothers, going out as a settler, Mr Wakefield ... and a Mr. Elliott, who knows all about everything but is careless about his h's and is taking out a steam engine.[53]

Aristocrat, merchant, engineer, officer and one of the prestigious Wakefields seemingly had little in common, but even Elliott's Cockney origins and his interest in engineering did not prevent him joining other 'cuddy' passengers at dinner, or in the six a.m. wash on deck. Wealth — not breeding — defined status, and folk of very different lives mixed and mingled. Despite efforts by cabin passengers to keep the poop deck to themselves, steerage inevitably met cabin settlers. Some of the latter deliberately sought the company of 'emigrants'.[54]

In some respects this reflected British society of the day, which was being redefined around wealth and behaviour, but shipboard life refined and focused the phenomenon, putting disparate people into contact in a way that could not have happened in London, Leeds or Liverpool. For this reason, although fleeting, the voyage to New Zealand cannot be discounted as one of several elements behind new social structures in the antipodes. Certainly there is evidence that the voyage was a symbolic *rite de passage*, a literal means of highlighting the shift from a comfortable society to the new world of the colonies. The ships were more than a means of transport; they were devices for making that social transformation — a factor that partly explains the importance the ships gained in many genealogies. At this level, the journey was a voyage of permission.

Artist unknown, Alexander Turnbull Library, F-48401-1/2

An egalitarian society?

The colonial world into which Britain's migrants poured was very different from the one they had left. Charlotte Godley's discovery that New Zealand's aspirant genteel included wealthy butchers[55] — a contradiction in terms back 'home' despite the widening of class — highlighted a familiarity that New Zealand shared with other colonies of the period, but not mother England. This was the origin of New Zealand's egalitarian ethos, but, as always, received truths must be treated with care. There is a difference between what 'egalitarian' meant, and what it was assumed to mean.

The ideal seems to have emerged from a combination of deliberate aspiration, mixed with event and environment. Many settlers hailed from a narrow slice of middling Britain, many of the wealthier were urban, and most emigrated with a mood for change. This group widened further in the New Zealand environment, rising — often through hard personal work — to fill the middle and upper ranks of society. Although called 'middle class' because of their origins and lifestyle, the wealthiest were actually New Zealand's elite, a nobility in all but birth. Many aspired to genteel life, yet most also exalted a hard day's work — a practical expression of the Calvinist ideal. This widened definition of gentility allowed station owners, businessmen, merchants, brokers and colonial administrators to engage in hands-on work, yet also ape the leisured rich of Britain.

By British standards this created a society of contradictions. It was socially acceptable for station owners to spend the day drenching sheep — or direct staff on the job — then retire to the homestead and dine on bone china plates, perhaps washing the meal down with a few glasses of claret. A doctor, whose hands-on profession had ranked with that of barber a century earlier, could become a respected part of society. This difference between the imported British concept of the leisured wealthy, and the actual settler incarnation of a hands-on, hard-working elite, was often reconciled with various symbols and rituals. This could be as simple as a change of clothes after work, itself practical yet symbolically

Short on stature, big on status: Isaac Earl Featherston (1813–76) emigrated to New Zealand in 1840 as surgeon-superintendent on the *Olympus*, settling in Wellington where he ran a medical practice alongside his political interests. Eventually politics won the day. When war with Maori broke out in 1860, Featherston lobbied Maori and later led a kupapa unit on the march around Mount Egmont. He returned to Britain in 1871 as Agent-General for New Zealand, where he organised the Vogel settlement drive — sending more than 70,000 emigrants to the colony.

Photographer unknown, Alexander Turnbull Library, F-5051-1/2

underlining the shift of role. A settler housewife, for instance, could remove her house-soiled apron and replace it with a decorative one at the end of a day.[56] Timing also played a part. Hands-on activity in working hours could be replaced by genteel behaviour in the evenings or on Sundays. The notion survived its society and re-emerged during the twentieth century in, for instance, the ability of a Prime Minister such as Keith Holyoake to renovate his bach, clear the section or indulge in a spot of weekend house-painting, without being frowned upon.[57]

This ethos was accompanied by a relaxed familiarity, itself partly an outcome of the mind-set created by migration — the desire to drop the old world, road-tested during a three-month voyage in which all were effectively thrown together. The hardships of the first settlements acted as a further leveller, as did early back-country work when would-be wealthy and poor sometimes worked shoulder to shoulder. To be on first-name terms became a mark of respect, and anything that smacked of the old ways was protested. When Napier shopkeepers and mechanics were barred from a ball run by Donald McLean in March 1868, 'A Napier Tradesman', writing to the *Hawke's Bay Herald*, complained that 'snobbishness' was 'now rampant'. Shop owners and tradesmen were being sneered at by 'sheepocrats' and 'devotees' of the Hawke's Bay Club.[58] Vertical familiarity was unthinkable in Britain and underlines the general point that New Zealand settler social structures were not the tight European 'brotherhood' of Karl Marx, but a more nebulous and flexible arrangement defined by behaviour and economic standing.

The upper ranks of this society were a kind of supercharged middle class, not a nobility of the British kind, but this did not prevent some elite eventually considering themselves lords. George Bell of Wantwood held himself aloof, as did G.H. Moore of Glenmark, who typically received his estate manager in the library and, if he absolutely had to get into his 77,000-acre run, took his carriage.[59] Waipukurau pastoralist Henry Russell was so imperious that he gained the nickname 'Lord H'. Others adopted trappings of patronage, as in 1892 when staff of John Harding's station 'assembled in full force' at his house on Boxing Day to 'partake of that gentleman's hospitality and receive the Christmas gifts he so liberally provides for them...'.[60]

A cut-off point of around ten staff has been suggested for this behaviour,[61] but styles were personal, sometimes reflecting the aspirant 'would-be' rather than the more confident 'have'. The majority of New Zealand's gentry derived no shame from soiling their hands or consorting with workers. George Carlyon — a veteran of Crimea and the archetypal officer and gentleman — insisted on directing his staff on his sprawling Gwavas property despite knowing nothing about sheep.[62]

The desire to escape British life meant that most poorer migrants rejected servility as a career. Few had come to New Zealand to be servants, and figures from 1851 indicate that domestics made up just 2.85 percent of the workforce in

'Miss Absolon', a pencil sketch usually attributed to Charles Heaphy.

Charles Heaphy, pencil and watercolour, Alexander Turnbull Library, qMS-0613-096

Auckland and a miserable 2.02 percent in Nelson.[63] Typical servants' wages hovered around £25 per annum in Wellington in 1847–48, rose to a maximum of £40 in 1850, and by 1852 some domestics were earning £50. In Nelson, the rate doubled between 1847 and 1852.[64] This suggests both a seller's market and a sustained effort to attract and retain staff. Yet there was no shortage of one-time servants arriving in New Zealand. For women in particular, employment in Britain often meant being servants, and nearly 70 percent of a sample of 4028 single women who emigrated during the 1857–71 period had been employed in some form of domestic service in Britain.[65] The number who found the same work in New Zealand is unclear. Although 1858 figures reveal 1927 'domestics', out of a European population of 59,238, this included those working in lodging-houses. For the 17 years after 1874, the 'domestic' classification included wives, widows, sons and daughters at home, and the 8795 women and 3582 men who listed themselves as 'domestics' out of a total population of 299,514 in 1874 were not all servants.[66]

A more useful picture emerges from the chorus of complaints by the elite. To some extent this fuelled the do-it-yourself ethos. Genteel Taranaki settler Jane Atkinson thought she could manage without a servant 'provided I have not more than three people besides myself to do for'.[67] She eventually hired the highly efficient Ann Foreman — who became pregnant and left.[68] Jane Moorhouse hired nine different servants over a three-year period between 1867 and 1870.[69] Mary Hobhouse, wife of the Bishop of Nelson, first hired a 'very nice creature of 14', then a 'young lady as housemaid' — but the latter 'soon captivated the soft-hearted Mr Philpotts' and Hobhouse had to replace her with 'a little girl of 15'.[70]

Isaac Featherston lays the foundation stone of the Houses of Assembly, Wellington, 1857. The former Wakefield colony won the hard-fought battle to become national capital in the mid-1850s, a decision pushed in part by the difficulty of governing New Zealand from its northern end at a time when communications were poor.

William Fox, Alexander Turnbull Library, A-018-021

The picture seems clear. Poorer migrants found work as domestics, but only until they could 'get on', often by marriage. This was to the frustration of the elite, yet unsurprising. Most migrants came to New Zealand to better themselves. Nor was the situation unusual. Although New Zealand's domestic percentages were down by comparison with those at 'home' or in other colonies, servant numbers had been dropping around the British Empire since the eighteenth century. New Zealand was extreme, but not out of line, and ultimately the local elites had to grin and do their own laundry. Many did so without complaint. After all, hard work was a mark of Calvinist-inspired colonial gentility.

Did this mean that New Zealand lacked class structure? Settler society has been sliced and diced many times by historians.[71] It has been pointed out that the 'undiluted' application of Marx is fraught with difficulty because his theories emerged from old industrial society, not colonial.[72] Certainly it seems clear that New Zealand did not have a class society in the popular Marxist sense, though perhaps the Weberian cultural-economic definition might be made to apply.[73] Much of the debate depends on what is defined as 'class'. Deference, impassable social barriers and birth had been traditional definitions in Britain, and their apparent lack in New Zealand – combined with powerful evidence of social mobility – has often been mistaken for lack of a sign of real equality.

Ultimately, however, New Zealand society defined much of its own reality. There were classes of a sort, but money, land, office and behaviour counted for more in settler New Zealand than Britain, where birth and traditional barriers added to the mix. In settler-era New Zealand their lack reduced the 'horizontal' links, preventing an early arrival of the Marxist 'brotherhood of workers', and reinforcing the 'vertical' element by comparison with England or Europe. However, the opportunity for the penniless to 'get on' disguised the fact that barriers still existed along the way. David Balfour fell from gold prospecting to swagging in the 1860s, worked his way back to become a respectable and respected station manager and family man by the mid-1870s, but could advance no further.[74] Others had the same experience. There was only so much room at the top, and once the middle-class gentry and elite oligarchs had established themselves, poorer settlers had little opportunity for improvement beyond a certain point. Jocularities and a good deal of apparent success at 'getting on' hid the point that New Zealand settler society was stratified.

Jane Maria Atkinson, nee Richmond (1824–1914).

Photographer unknown, Alexander Turnbull Library, F-79203-1/2

Life at the top

During the settler period New Zealand's main currency of social rivalry was wealth, often translated into land,[75] and the earliest pastoralists quickly accumulated most of it for themselves, exploiting early growth to entrench themselves at the top of the heap. This uppermost rank was a closed shop, an oligarchy that was financially and politically so far ahead of the pack as to beggar comparison even with their nominal peers. They dominated provincial and national life for decades. The

The home of William Bishop,
Matai Valley, around 1844.

Charles Heaphy, Alexander Turnbull
Library, A-144-011

so-called 'long ministry' of the 1860s and 1870s was one outcome — a party-less and shifting alliance of politicians drawn from the leading pastoralists and businessmen. One historian has argued that they were stunned by their own success,[76] and while others suggest that the power of these groups should not be overestimated,[77] there is no doubt that the oligarchs held sway where it counted. Even government bent before their activities. It was not without reason that William Rolleston once asked whether Minister of Defence and Auckland businessman Thomas Russell represented the government — or whether the government was there to represent Russell.[78]

This image is made all the more extraordinary by the fact that the main oligarchs were, numerically, in the minority — a few dozen families, nationally, through the settler period. The next step down were still elite, a group we might call 'gentry', who held most of the rest of New Zealand's key wealth and power. Gentry families numbered in the hundreds. So-called 'lower middle-class' or 'respectable' folk beneath them were vastly more numerous, a significant proportion of urban dwellers, small-to-medium landholders, usually agriculturalists and mixed-crop farmers. Those at the upper end blurred into the gentry; those at the lower into the 'working classes'. During the depression of the 1880s all these — with the exception of the top oligarchs — blurred further as part of a general down-shift.

The power of the gentry came from the sheep's back, and it came early. Wakefield's effort to control property access came to nothing when there was territory to lease beyond company lands. The first such snake in his Eden was the Wairarapa, where Ngati Kahungunu concluded deals with would-be pastoralists spreading north from Wellington during the mid-1840s. This group were a mixed bunch, initially ignorant of their trade, but all with money and ambition. Nearly

Grasmere Station, probably during the 1860s.

Daniel Louis Mundy, Alexander Turnbull Library, F-50828-1/2

half were Scots, and there were three doctors, a lawyer, six surveyors and two self-proclaimed gentlemen among them.[79] The fleece soon turned to gold; wool reached 11 and three-quarter pence per pound in Wellington auctions during 1845, and by 1850 typical prices had topped a shilling.[80] Estimates suggested that £540 starting capital – around $110,000 in early twenty-first-century money – could return net profits of £1200 after five years. Some did better. Early Wairarapa settler Frederick Weld obtained £4000 profit from a turnover of £6000 in 1850.[81]

Once the pastoral floodgates had opened in the Wairarapa the way was clear for others to surge into Hawke's Bay, Otago, Canterbury and Marlborough. Sometimes, as in the Tiffen enterprise in Hawke's Bay and the Weld effort in Marlborough, the pioneers were Wairarapa settlers moving further afield. As time went on and these pastoral provinces became better established they attracted interest from British pastoralists and investors, all hoping to multiply their cash faster in the colony than they could at home. Hector Smith reached Hawke's Bay in 1858 with £8000, which he spent on 12,000 acres near the Ruahine Range. Just four years later Algernon Tollemache offered to acquire the property on a lease-to-buy arrangement of £1400 per annum for 11 years, followed by a cash settlement of £14,000, around $1.22 million in early twenty-first-century money. Smith 'very nearly took' the 'good offer'. Instead he 'did a wise thing' and bought an adjoining run for £12,000.[82]

Others boot-strapped themselves from nothing, including Hebridean shepherds Allan and John McLean, who held half a million acres of Canterbury by 1858.[83] William Rolleston (1831–1903) reached Lyttelton in 1858, decided to 'turn shepherd at once',[84] and within three years had his own run, Mount Algidus. Once Laurence Kennaway (1834–1904) had got his coastal land into 'comparatively habitable order' he hastened inland in search of 'available sheep-country', finding 40,000 acres near the Rakaia River.[85] It was a case of the quick or the dead; as Kennaway wrote, latecomers lost out or ended up in 'furious dispute' with neighbours over the boundaries.[86]

By 1861 wool exports were valued at some £524,000, second only to gold and streets ahead of the next highest, timber, which stood at a miserable £19,000.[87] The means of producing this bounty was owned by a very tiny proportion of the colony's total population. Less than a fifth of all settlers worked in the agricultural and pastoral sector at this time, and numbers on the stations — including the labourers, shearers and farmhands — were smaller still.[88]

Differential fortunes highlighted the relationship between oligarch run-holder and lesser gentry. In 1878 there were 215 flocks of more than 10,000 sheep in Canterbury and Otago, but only 11 were of 50,000 or more. One, Morven Hills, ran up to 130,000 sheep and had one of the largest woolsheds in the world.[89] Holdings were not always private — New Zealand's largest landowner of the day was the New Zealand and Australian Land Company, which had stations totalling nearly 600,000 acres by the 1870s.[90] Australians also bought land privately, as in March 1876 when the Joshua Brothers of Melbourne bought part of the Kereru and Otamauri estates, some 33,000 acres and 26,000 sheep, for £35,000, aound $34.1 million in early twenty-first-century money.[91] At least part of the success of these sheep-lords came from a dynamic adaptation of diverse cultures; as one historian has noted, farm management and pastoral business practices were American.[92] Social values, of course, remained strictly genteel.

Once pastoralism got going there was nearly as much to be made from supplying the stations, trading their wool, and acting as agent for the shipping companies, though the window did not stay open for long. By the late 1850s the

Pastoral wealth was built on the sheep's back. This is shearing, 1864 style, complete with manually pressed wool. The station owner looks on.

Illustrated Sydney News, Alexander Turnbull Library, PUBL-0169-1864-001

oligarchs — among them several McLeans, Ormond, Molesworth, Riddiford, multiple Williamses, various Campbells, miscellaneous Rhodes and several unrelated Russells — had gained an unshakeable position from which they also derived political status. They were characterised not only by their wealth but also, initially, by their youth. Many were no more than 30 when they accumulated their fortunes, and few bettered John Ormond. This 'resolute' man of 'great mental power' was 17 when Eyre appointed him Clerk of the New Munster Executive Council. He had his first pastoral run by age 20; and by 27 was on the Hawke's Bay Provincial Council, a body he had been instrumental in creating.[93]

Below this strata — but still of the aspirant genteel — were lesser pastoralists, agents, industrialists and merchants. They were a wide group, occasionally divided by historians into multiple sub-classes,[94] all part of wider 'middle-class-derived' settler society. We might call them New Zealand's gentry, of which the oligarchs were an elite sub-group. They were often back-country pastoralists, or operated lowland mixed-farms, and included businessmen, agents or merchants in the towns. Most aspired to gentility, and regarded themselves socially — though not financially — in the league of the oligarchs. They frequented the same clubs, aspired to the same ideals, and hobnobbed whenever possible.

At first this did not mean luxury living. Mary Hobhouse remarked that there were 'some rich sheep owners' around in 1860, but 'most of the gentry here' lived in conditions no better than that of 'a comfortable farmer or tradesman at home...'.[95] Gentility implied behaviour as much as money, and as always embodied paradox. Calvinist personal restraint sat poorly with the opulent display of wealth demanded by status, and while some gentry displayed the fruits of fortune in houses, buggies, clothing and a lavish lifestyle, others drew pride from being seen to be frugal, though this did not mean doing without.

Mary Elizabeth Hobhouse, nee Brodrick (1819–64).

Photographer unknown, Alexander Turnbull Library, F-46810-1/2

There is some evidence that these opinions were geographic; that God-fearing northern English and Scots settlers angled towards a lifestyle of personal self-denial and guilt assuaged by philanthropic gift in a way that earthier southern English did not.[96] But ultimately the decision was personal, and there were wide variations, most obvious in the homes many built for themselves.

Low, sprawling, single-storey dwellings sprang up across Hawke's Bay, Otago, Marlborough and Canterbury in particular during the 1850s and 1860s. With verandahs and floor-to-ceiling French windows opening into rooms of opulent luxury, these 'colonial mission' homes were a perfect match for the social demands of the time. Drawing rooms, servants quarters — even ballrooms in some of the later incarnations — along with wide grounds, occasionally a tennis court, croquet ground or other sports facility, helped set station homes apart from the dwellings of the staff. Early homesteads were often supplanted by mansions imitating the

country homes of England. Most were fashionably in wood, but a few were cob, concrete or — as in the case of John McLean's huge North Otago home, brick. Most were architect-designed, many in Queen Anne style, others neo-Gothic, still others classical. Almost all the elite had one, the difference between 'frugal' and 'extravagant' often emerging as a predilection to extend an existing home instead of building a new one.

Many were surrounded with pleasant gardens and English-style woodlands. Canterbury's Telford family preferred an 89-acre block of native bush, but they were in the minority. Most who could afford it planted English trees by the thousand, and the Rhodes family imported English birds to sing in theirs.[97] Sports facilities were *de rigueur*; William Pember Reeves had lawn tennis courts installed at Risingholme, his mansion near Christchurch. In Hawke's Bay, R.P. Williams had a 'very elegant and chaste' house at Mangateretere, surrounded by ornamental gardens and a croquet lawn.[98] John Ormond owned two: one on his Porangahau property and another near Hastings, while his neighbour Thomas Tanner spent tens of thousands on a mansion on his Riverslea property, and when Sir William Jervois came to stay in 1883, Tanner spent a fortune redecorating.[99] All were outstripped by Dunedin-based W.J. Larnach, who poured £125,000 into a Gothic mansion on the outskirts of town — a home that, in name at least, became his castle.[100]

Towns featured as much as country in the lifestyles of New Zealand's settler gentry. Much of the inspiration for pastoral lifestyle — with its middle-class aping of the elite — actually came from British cities, themselves creations of the middle class,[101] and town houses were popular, a focus for urban social life and rivalry. Dunedin's genteel homes congregated on Maori Hill; in Christchurch they clustered around Fendalton.[102] Some houses were rented for a few hundred pounds per annum, or built for under a thousand, but some people went further. Former

Dundee businessman James Watt had a £7000 mansion built on Napier Hill during the 1870s, a figure equating to nearly $700,000 in early twenty-first-century money.[103] Watson Shennan's 'Threave' soared to three storeys above Dunedin's High Street in 1904. Not all town houses were in the urbs. John Bathgate's was 10 miles (16 km) from Dunedin and set in 240 acres of park-like gardens; while Thomas Tancred grew wheat in the rural grounds of his 'town home' near Christchurch.[104] Elsewhere, town houses were built amid wide grounds between urban streets, sprinkled with fountains and ornamental shrubs, and sometimes the town house became the main family dwelling.

The pastoralists were joined in the towns by an urban gentry of bankers, brokers, speculators, moneylenders, agents and industrialists. Many gained their wealth on the back of pastoral fortune; Thomas Cawthron made an estimated £240,000 from his 30-year stranglehold on Nelson's shipping agencies.[105] The urban elite often gained government offices ranging from Provincial Superintendent — in the case of Wellington's Dr Isaac Featherston — to Agent General. James Fitzgerald was immigration agent, police sub-inspector and then editor of the *Lyttelton Times* before becoming Christchurch Provincial Superintendent in 1853.[106]

One of the pivots on which genteel life turned was 'the club'. Middle-class gentlemen's clubs usually included dining rooms, private bars, ballrooms, libraries, reading rooms, office facilities, billiards rooms and places for large-scale social functions. Socially they reinforced the gap between the have and the have not, providing a framework within which rivalry for status could be played out among the elite. Important business deals were often conducted at 'the club', and disgrace was tantamount to social suicide. Stiff entrance fees and subscriptions denominated in guineas, the currency of the genteel, acted as gatekeeper. But this was not something military men had to worry about; membership was usually free to officers.

William Hort Levin (1845–93), right, championed Wellington — including the Te Aro reclamation, for which he is being pilloried here — and was one of the principal shareholders in the Wellington and Manawatu Railway Company.

William Hutchison, Alexander Turnbull Library, A-095-022

No. 26.—THE TE ARO RECLAMATION.—"Too many cooks spoil the broth."

Marriage was an essential ticket to status in the higher social circles. Many self-styled elite were married when they emigrated. Others married in New Zealand, and although it was a 'buyer's market' from the woman's perspective, genteel men could also go 'home' to find a spouse. Colonial pastoralists were accorded immense status in England, where there was a surplus of women. Colonel George Whitmore, a widower, went to England to meet and marry his second wife in 1865. Wakarara pastoralist Hector Smith married while on a visit to Scotland the following year.

Left

Napier was one of New Zealand's larger urban centres for many years. This is 'The Grange', alone on Napier's hill, mid-1870s.

Photographer unknown, Alexander Turnbull Library, F-110489-1/2

Below

Wealthy Hawke's Bay pastoralists eagerly sought places on Napier's hill for their town houses, including Donald McLean and John Ormond, but they had to compete with the town jail — lower left — and Hukarere, centre. This picture was taken in the late nineteenth century.

Photographer unknown, Alexander Turnbull Library, F-29565-1/2

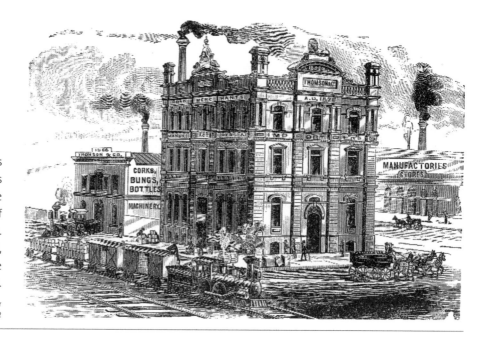

Many urban elite made fortunes on the backs of import businesses and industries, often rivalling the pastoralists. This is a group of Dunedin businesses in the 1870s. The locomotives are fanciful, though underlining the importance of railway at the time.

Working Men's Educational Union, Alexander Turnbull Library, D-010-012

Algernon Gray Tollemache (1805–92) was one of the few English nobles among New Zealand's self-made elite and became one of New Zealand's wealthiest men during the settler period. He was one of the early investors in the New Zealand Company.

Photographer unknown, Alexander Turnbull Library, F-5090-1/2

Pastimes were often designed to assert status — visitations were usually announced with a calling card, received by a servant who could acceptably tell the would-be visitor that the owner was 'not at home', even if everyone knew that they were. Elegant parties were another means of showing status and spending spare cash. Adela Stewart recorded one soiree for 60 at her Katikati home that began with two hours of dancing. Dinner was served at 10 p.m., followed by dances — 28 in all — before soup was offered at 2 a.m. There was more dancing before tired party-goers dispersed into the dawn, except for the ones found 'coiled up in floor corners all over the rooms' late next morning.[107] Such overnight roistering was not a rare occurrence. In 1892 the McHardy family, living at remote Blackhead station, brought 100 guests by coach from Waipawa to a woolshed ball that lasted until the following morning.[108]

Exotic destinations beckoned for those with enough cash. Hawke's Bay pastoralist Henry Tiffen went to Japan during the 1870s, just a few years after it was opened up to the West. Other wealthy settlers toured the United States, Africa or Europe. Often these were interim stops on a journey 'home', where New Zealand elite slotted into the top of middle-class British society. Sometimes they stayed for years in the Imperial capital, coalescing in a kind of New Zealand enclave in Kensington. Many also drifted back 'home' to retire. Some historians argue that a return to Britain was often the rationale of the drive to make a colonial fortune, and the exodus of aged sheep-lords from New Zealand certainly suggests so.[109]

Among the oligarchs who made the return journey was a fabulously wealthy Algernon Tollemache, whose assets were estimated at more than £1,267,000 when he died in 1892 — around $188.5 million in early twenty-first-century money,

Above

This mail coach negotiates the Waimakariri river bed.

Photographer unknown, Alexander Turnbull Library, PAColl-5155, F-19613-1/4

Centre

Coaches crossing the Maungatoetoe Stream, between Waiouru and Tokaanu, Central Plateau.

Photographer unknown, Alexander Turnbull Library, PAColl-5155, F-19571-1/4

Below

Bullocks were the heavy-haulers of the settler period, not fully supplanted until the early twentieth century. These teams worked in the Stratford district.

James McAllister, James McAllister Collection, Alexander Turnbull Library, PAColl-3054, F-12361-1/1

though direct comparison is slightly misleading.[110] Less well-heeled gentry who retired to the 'old country' included Herbert Meyer, worth £41,000 by 1869, and Christchurch's J.C. Aitken. A few, such as Henry Russell, were poorer; he had spent a fortune in the vain hope of demolishing his political enemies in New Zealand, was hammered by the downturn of the 1880s, and returned to Scotland poorer, though perhaps wiser.[111] Those who retired in New Zealand displayed a similar range of fortunes. Sir David Monro (1813–77) was worth more than £50,000 when he died,[112] a typical fortune of the self-made gentry and a respectable sum for the day. Their numbers were leavened by the handful of oligarchs who took wealth to a higher plane. John Ormond was estimated to be worth £400,000 when he died, and G.H. Moore's Glenmark estate was valued at £350,000 in 1882.[113] These figures were simply staggering.

Pastoral techniques

A classic settler-era shearing shed, Rangitikei district.

New Zealand's early wool fortunes were fuelled by a brisk export market. Britain demanded fine wools, and world markets were driven further during the early 1860s by the American Civil War. Most pastoralists dabbled in meat, but early experiments with salt, oats and other preservers were dismal. Carcases were often boiled down for their fat; Hawke's Bay pastoralist R.P. Williams, for instance, processed around 30,000 carcases in the 1875 season, rendering them into 300 tons of tallow which was exported the following year at £48 per ton.[114]

Pastoralism was the 'scientific' farming of the age, harking to American rather than British practice and demanding huge areas of back-country. The main bottleneck was the cost of renewing pasture. Hand distribution of fertiliser and grass seed was expensive, and pastoralists would instead set light to huge areas of scrub. The remains were trampled into the soil by roving flocks. Grass seed — typically Yorkshire fog, cocksfoot, couch or danthonia — could then be spread. This was cheap and got around the shortage of farm equipment, but had a built-in end-point because burning and grazing exhausted poor back-country topsoils. D.P. Balfour wrote that the sheep were 'in the last stages of starvation' when he arrived at Gwavas in 1873. The difficulty was that as 'crushing' was a spring activity, farmers kept every animal they could through the winter. This was a sin, according

Pastoral techniques

to Herbert Guthrie-Smith, transgressing 'the first and greatest of pastoral commandments'.[115] Yet most had no choice but to overstock if they were to crush the fern and get the grass growth.

Within a few decades some back-country areas were suffering shingle slides. By 1910 large parts of Guthrie-Smith's Tutira, crushed and burned for 30 years or more, were inundated with manuka. Hector Smith had a problem with thistles on his Wakarara property and ordered his staff to weed them while he went fern crushing. But John Chambers told C.W. Richmond that thistles had been worth £10,000 to him in improvements, because they prevented fern regrowth.[116]

One of the biggest problems was roaming stock. Tutira station owners C.H. Stuart and T.C. Kiernan suffered 30 percent losses in 1877,[117] but at up to £50 a mile, fencing was frequently unaffordable. Shepherds were often employed at station borders, doubling as hunters. Once or twice a year musters were taken to get the wool. At Mangawhare, David Balfour's musters typically took a fortnight, and stragglers missed in earlier years could often add to a flock — in February 1874, Balfour found he had 100. Another year there were more than 1000.

Most runs were under-manned. Te Haroto, midway between Napier and Taupo, reached 160,000 acres by 1890 — yet ran only 24,000 sheep with four permanent

Dipping at Clayton Station, Canterbury, January 1892. Few nineteenth-century treatments were effective. Arsenic worked against fly-strike but damaged the wool and was dangerous to sheep and farmer. The main enemy was scab, not conquered nationwide until the 1890s.

Photographer unknown, Alexander Turnbull Library, PAColl-4624, F-2358-1/2

Pastoral techniques

staff to manage them. Gallomy Station, in Otago, ran 75,000 sheep on its 129,000 acres in the 1870s; and after rabbits tore through the area stock levels dropped to less than 30,000.[118] Rabbits were certainly a major problem. Phosphor-radium poison evidently had an impact in Otago,[119] but in general efforts to control the problem with rabbit-proof fences, hunting and poisoning were not highly effective.

Disease often defied control. Scab — a burrowing parasite — appeared in Nelson in 1845. By 1846 it was in the Wairarapa, and cases were recorded in Riccarton in 1848.[120] Imported sheep also had it; F.W. Hamilton discovered an outbreak in a flock he was bringing out from Britain in late 1861.[121] Legislation to limit movement around New Zealand was introduced to control the problem, but what was really needed was better medication. Footrot, a fungal infection, was attacked by running sheep through blue-stone or lime-filled yards — though to little effect. Guthrie-Smith was one of many who endured 'endless labour in paring the hoofs of the limping brutes'.[122] Up to a quarter of his ewes were lame during the early 1880s. Lungworm was another problem. Guthrie-Smith lost three-quarters of his weaners to the parasite when the problem was at its height. 'Everywhere sheep-farmers were dosing their young sheep with turpentine and oil, or attempting the smoke cure with sulphur.'[123] John Chambers recommended intra-tracheal injections.

Bringing sheep into New Zealand was itself fraught with problems, as Hamilton found the hard way. The flock he brought in from Britain survived scab during the journey only to be poisoned on landing:

> Last Saturday we landed the sheep ... all over the Country here is a onerous shrub called Tute which affects all sheep newly landed. Sunday nearly all of ours were tuted, they were taken with spasms and lockjaw and seem to be in awful pain. We bled nearly all of them and gave them ammonia, but in spite of all we could do we lost thirty of them which amounts to something at £65 a head.[124]

Efforts to find a breed that could cope with New Zealand conditions ran through most of the available types. Romneys were introduced to Wellington in 1852, but most pastoralists settled on the merino. Gilbert merinos were described as 'one of the finest results of rational breeding of the present time' in a November 1861 advertisement, while Henry Tiffen, G.G. Carlyon, G. Hunter and W. Lyon bought Negretti merinos in Wellington a month later at an average price of £43.10.0 — about $3800 in early twenty-first-century money. The breed fell out of favour during the following decade, replaced in the North Island largely by Lincolns; and in 1877 one newspaper reported that there had been a 'complete usurpation' of long-wool breeds in Hawke's Bay.[125] The same was not true in Canterbury, where merinos reigned supreme until the advent of the frozen meat trade.

Opposite above
Moving sheep in the late 1880s.

Edward Roper Stapleton Sandys, Alexander Turnbull Library, C-075-008

Opposite below
Shearing was a family affair when the camera appeared.

Photographer unknown, Greig Collection, Alexander Turnbull Library, PAColl-5713, F-58360-1/2

Pastoral techniques

Respectable folk and working life

Decent settlers filled the middle ranks of New Zealand's society, respectable folk of modest income who shared ideals and familiarity with the upper strata. Respectable income and lifestyles fanned across a wide spectrum, shading at the top into the genteel and at the bottom into the skilled tradesmen. Some historians subdivide this group into 'respectable', 'decent', and classes between.[126] Others prefer to put the lower end of the respectables into the 'working class'. However, to overclassify can be misleading. Reality was blurred by social mobility and the ethos of familiarity. There was also a difference between perception and reality; inherited British thinking prompted popular definitions that did not always correlate with the realities of New Zealand.

The respectable ideal put professionals at the top — including academics, teachers, doctors, lawyers and bank managers — along with small businessmen and small-to-medium landholders, agriculturalists and mixed-farmers. Publicans, farm managers, store-owners, and self-employed tradesmen or artisans such as tailors, carpenters, farriers and saddlers were usually assigned to the lower end. In practice, income and behaviour counted as much as occupation, and while New Zealand's respectables were internally stratified, they were also more of a continuity than division into fixed 'classes' implies. Ambition fuelled movement, as for Robert Cole, the Ross publican who saved enough to buy pastoral property in Timaru; or Meeanee publican R.D. Maney, whose rags-to-riches-to-rags career on the back of

Below left

Edward Dobson (1816–1908) became Canterbury Provincial Engineer at a time when such professions were emerging as respectable occupations.

Photographer unknown, Alexander Turnbull Library, PA2-2445, F-32835-1/2

Below right

Arthur Dobson (1841–1934), one of Edward's sons, discovered Arthur's Pass while exploring west of Otira in 1864, though he did not name it himself. Later he was involved in a project to build an east–west rail link through the pass.

Photographer unknown, Alexander Turnbull Library, F-5041-1/2

Maori debt spurred national controversy.[127] Savvy tradesmen such as Henry Shacklock or Josiah Firth could become big businessmen, joining the elite without being thought 'above' their station. Others were not able to move so far. John Hislop, educationalist extraordinaire, took an active role in Dunedin's civic affairs after retiring — but public office in the town was a lateral shift from his former career as first Secretary of Education.[128]

Many respectables came from the Wakefield settlements, and a high percentage were urban dwellers. Respectables dominated town boards and councils; and their lifestyle, aspirations and ideals provided one foundation of the 'pavlova' society of the twentieth century. Those of modest means could rise into positions of local authority without great difficulty. The lifestyle was aspirant gentility with more work stirred in. Most were eager to get on, among them Mary Taylor (1817–93), one of the few self-employed women. She and a friend had an 'objection to sedentary employment', and were helped by 'gifts and loans' to buy land in Wellington, where she set up a shop in 1850. 'How we work!' she wrote to a friend.[129]

Respectable folk also lived in the country, often as agriculturalists or in small mixed-pastoral lowland areas. Most were helped by policy as government sold small blocks of land in the hope of creating an agricultural economy to rectify the lack of such basics as vegetable supply. During the 1870s, Canterbury's lowland mixed-farms multiplied from 300 to around 1000 holdings.[130] This does not mean that small-holders were a 'sturdy yeomanry' predestined to become the farmers of

This family pose outside their cob house, Canterbury, in the 1860s.

Photographer unknown, Making New Zealand Collection, Alexander Turnbull Library, F-172-1/4-MNZ

the twentieth century — close settlement was patchy for decades. However, like the urban respectables, most small-holders were ambitious, and the more successful were able to elevate themselves. Some did so by founding towns, a vehicle for social advance even for the elite — as, for instance, in the 'father' of Matamata, Josiah Firth.[131]

Other respectables worked for pastoralists. Managers were at the top of the scale, effectively lower-middle class, often considered semi-genteel themselves. When Donald McLean's manager Thomas Condie left the Maraekakaho estate in 1876, he was given a silver tea service by the station employees and feted at a dinner in Hastings' Clarendon Hotel.[132] Reputation was everything; a skilled manager such as Balfour could demand £200 per annum or more, perhaps $19,500 in early twenty-first-century money, though direct comparison is difficult. Managers and senior staff could be 'poached' by other station owners, and Balfour turned down offers while he was at Gwavas. Although even £100 was an adequate annual wage for much of the latter nineteenth century, only overseers and perhaps head shepherds approached this figure. Ordinary shepherds, bullock drivers, ploughmen and other skilled hands could receive anything between £40 and £80, though some were paid less.

Charles Weitzel's 'European Hotel' at Charleston on the South Island's west coast, late 1860s. It was built the year before to cater for the gold rush trade. Hotels were invariably lucrative, a ticket to respectability and social ascent.

Photographer unknown, Alexander Turnbull Library, F-11550-1/2

VOTE FOR <u>SAM</u> BROWN!

"WE'LL RUN HIM IN."

Settler towns were bustling venues for the respectable. This is 1860s Dunedin, a dense-packed and vigorous provincial capital.

Alexander Turnbull Library, D-010-012

Respectable women did not hold an exalted position and often achieved prosperity indirectly, frequently through marriage — though at first, married women had no rights and were effectively propertyless. Some got around this by signing contracts with their husbands. Limited rights were provided by the New Zealand Married Women's Property Protection Act of 1860. These were broadened by a further act in 1870, though New Zealand still lagged behind Britain in regard to married women's property. Although Victorian women were denigrated as 'the weaker sex', prone to 'vapours' and 'ennui', they usually stopped fainting once out of corsets.

Working classes

The bottom of New Zealand's settler social heap included semi-skilled or unskilled labourers, bottom-of-the-range farmers, and servants. As with the respectables, the group encompassed a range of incomes and skills, shading from lower-respectables down to itinerant swaggers. Some, with semi-permanent jobs in town, were able to set up households, rent 'workers cottages' — even own their own if they did well enough. Their numbers included the assisted settlers of the 1870s, who hacked a living out of virgin bush in central Hawke's Bay and the Manawatu. Others were unskilled or semi-skilled workers, men who eked out a living on piecework and temporary jobs. Evidence points to seasonal movements between town and country.[133] Many of these people worked at anything from hay-carting to general labour, tree-felling, road-making, and later rail-laying and tunnel-digging.

Working-class thinking was not that of the middle class, but most still aspired to the quarter-acre section and job security; and photographs reveal that many also aspired to the dress of the respectable. Language was often coarser — respectables preferred not to say some words, while the working classes used them with abandon. The offensive words were not all those of the twentieth century. One of the worst expletives in the evangelical settler age was 'damn', politely censored with a dash — and later transmuted to the word 'dash' by other echelons of society.

Income reinforced many differences. Working-class drinks included cheaper spirits such as gin or bulk-brewed beer; and workers were meant to be drunk more often than the genteel. Sometimes they did drown their sorrows in liquor, though it might be more accurate to say that they were seen doing so, while the genteel got drunk in private. Food certainly differed. Making-do was the name of the game; stews and scrag-ends took the place of joints, dripping substituted for roast

William Bambridge (1819–78) in his bed, October 1846. Many emigrants started off in one-room cottages, which remained the mainstay of the working-class settler.

William Bambridge, sepia ink, Alexander Turnbull Library, qMS-0122-043 beef as a sandwich filling. Household furniture and equipment was repaired rather than replaced. All this was essential to survival at the bottom. Typical workers' wages in Auckland, for instance, hovered around seven shillings a day in the late 1840s — this when a pound of tea was two shillings and sixpence, and bread two shillings a loaf.[134]

Working-class women had a particularly hard life. Many had not only to keep house at a time when every domestic task was done by hand but also to put in a day's work on their farm, in the family store, or on the piecework that gave them 'pin money'. A few found other paid work. Sarah Self, who emigrated to Auckland with her husband in the early 1860s, got a job as a seamstress in an Onehunga dress shop at six shillings a week with promise of more once she had learned the trade.[135] Self used the cash to make her own life more comfortable. 'I do not earn much at present as I do not know much about the trade,' she wrote later, 'but I earn more than my washing comes to.'[136] Sometimes women were the only breadwinners. Like men, women in every walk of life had to adapt to the new environment, and in so doing found new strengths.

A settler puts out a chimney fire, mid-1850s.

William Strutt, Alexander Turnbull Library, E-453-f-003

Being working class was not quite the trap it had been in Britain. Some, such as D.P. Balfour, rose into the ranks of the respectable. Others remained labourers, but that did not reduce familiarity with their employers. The group was initially not a majority — lack of labourers, indeed, was one of several body-blows that took down the Wakefield enterprise. The figures did not change much. In 1851 Auckland, some 491 men put themselves down as labourers out of a workforce of 8840. In Russell there were six out of a workforce of 402.[137] While such figures

Huts on Mesopotamia during the late 1860s. Washing lines give an air of establishment.

William Packe, Alexander Turnbull Library, A-196-015

must be taken with a grain of salt — pride, self-promotion, misclassification and falling through the statistical net undoubtedly contributed to an understatement — they are indicative. It was a consequence, in part, of early ambition to 'get on' and the fact that Britain's working poor could not afford to migrate. The shortages were keenly felt; a sustained effort to import labour during the 1870s bore fruit, however, and one historian has suggested that the rural labour pool stood at around 60,000 by the early 1890s. This included labourers who worked elsewhere in the off-season, including railway and road-builders, coal miners and fowlers.[138]

Left

Charles and Elizabeth Kerr pose outside their tiny cob cottage with Elizabeth Ritchie and a Mr Hill, around 1870.

Photographer unknown, Murray Collection, Alexander Turnbull Library, F-55441-1/2

Below

Living in a raupo whare did not reduce the need for a washing line. This soldier's family were photographed around 1863, probably in the Waikato.

Lieutenant-Colonel William Temple, Alexander Turnbull Library, F-4135-1/2

Country poor included the very smallest landholders, settlers brought in often by assisted passage and set up, by policy during the 1870s, in North Island bush-land. Some were paid for work on railway by grants of land — which they then had to clear with back-breaking effort. Many set up dairy farms, though it was the 1880s before this really became a viable activity. There is evidence that many poor rural families made ends meet collectively, adding the income from the land to 'pin money' earned by the wife — often through piecework or short domestic jobs — and anything the children could earn. Rural and small-town schools were often short of pupils as a result of child labour; in 1886, the Havelock (North) school even had to delay opening because most of the pupils were working on the Riverslea hop garden.[139]

Unskilled workers often found employment on the stations. Station working life, for the most part, was arduous and unrewarding. Wages were low, the hours long, accommodation often dubious,[140] and without much time off or the means to go anywhere station hands frequently spent their evenings drinking together. Some stations hired up to 50 men on a permanent basis. Other staff were itinerant, moving from station to station in gangs as the work came and went. Ploughmen, shearers and wool classers often booked themselves ahead with station owners and worked at a variety of locations. Many developed a regular clientele, and the better among them had good connections across wide areas of New Zealand. Seasonal or short-term threshers, harvesters and shearers could earn around 30 shillings a week.[141]

The bottom end of the working scale included swaggers and ne'er-do-wells who sought work wherever they could find it. They were a minority, but could be found in many parts of the back-country, sometimes alone, often in pairs or groups. Numbers swelled in the early 1860s as miners fell out of the gold rush; shrank in the 1870s; and grew again in the mid-1880s as the economy crashed and permanent work fell by the wayside.

Urban boosters

All the threads of settler society came together in the towns, urban landscapes that inherited much about their life and times from the middle-class urban creations of contemporary Britain,[142] and much about their look from the rugged frontier of contemporary America. Town boards and councils were a preserve of the respect-able, and the urban environment also generated and hosted one of the key icons of the New Zealand cultural scene — the quarter-acre section. Despite the persistent myth of the rugged bush pioneer, New Zealand settler society at all levels was urban in attitude, ideals and outlook. Location was less important, though New Zealand was surprisingly urbanised from the outset; more than 40 percent of all settlers lived in towns as early as 1881, nearly a fifth in towns of 25,000 or more.[143] By 1911 half the population lived in towns,[144] but these statistics understate the importance of the urban centres, which were key gathering places for folk from the

hinterland. Country gentry, itinerants, labourers and seasonal workers swarmed into town for social contact, to buy clothes, food, tobacco, alcohol and the necessities of life, to get entertained, pleasured and drunk. Labourers often oscillated between town and country, following the work as the seasons changed.[145] All lived a lifestyle and had attitudes to town that, in Britain, would have stamped them irredeemably urban.

There is no question that the towns were the real focus of the settler world. In town the settlers could find the markets, banks, industries, shops, and hotels essential to any lifestyle, and the towns offered opportunities for skilled workers: plumbers, farriers, smiths, carpenters. Early Wellington traders included three

cabinetmakers, one turner, two fishmongers, three coffee-house keepers, one lithographic printer, four bakers, four butchers — and nine publicans.[146] The flurry of centres such as Christchurch, Auckland or Dunedin with their bustling shopping streets, theatres, hotels, parks, gardens, museums, libraries and up-to-date newspapers contrasted sharply with the rural idyll. Dunedin's Vauxhall Gardens offered diversions ranging from a 'pavilion of pleasure' to ballrooms and flower gardens.[147]

There was much of the wild West in the towns; the visual differences between Hastings, Minnesota and Hastings, Hawke's Bay — or for that matter Palmerston North, Christchurch, Invercargill or Hamilton — were academic. All shared a gridwork street pattern, their town centres bristling with grandly fronted shops, clapboard hotels featuring wide verandahs, sash windows, and hitching posts. Moleskin or canvas trousers were in vogue on both sides of the Pacific, including the 'jean' cut developed by Levi Strauss. Even spelling reflected a common theme. 'Honor' was preferred to 'honour' in settler New Zealand, 'clamor' instead of 'clamour', 'druggist' to describe a pharmacist.[148]

Gentry with political ambition looked to provincial capitals such as Christchurch, Dunedin, Napier, Auckland, New Plymouth and Wellington as venues to vie with one another. Even after the provincial system was abolished in 1876, these towns reflected the entrenched political, economic and social interests of the gentry. A few viewed their own priorities as synonymous with their town — business rivalry was sometimes commuted into town rivalry, which found expression in competition for major town monuments and buildings. For any aspirant landowner, founding towns was a way of asserting status, and towns also offered profit from sale of sections. Wellington businessman William Levin drew

New Plymouth, probably during the late 1850s.

Photographer unknown, Making New Zealand Collection, Alexander Turnbull Library, F-1098-1/4-MNZ

status from the Manawatu town named after himself. Once a town had been established the chance of a newcomer successfully setting up another nearby was slim, though many tried — evidenced by such close-aligned centres as Levin and Shannon.

Towns, like the colony as a whole, were promoted by residents as desirable, go-ahead places even when they were not. Boosters typically included the local newspaper editor, arguably because by so doing they could improve the circulation of their papers. Storekeepers had vested interest in pushing their towns. Politicians too were often town boosters, at least up to the turn of the twentieth century when the rise of a new farming class pushed rural interests ahead of urban.[149]

The heady mix of boosterism and middle-class idealism also provided settler towns with their physical shape. This was particularly evident in the housing sections, which became the essence of New Zealand's urban landscape and reflected various ideals, including the middle-class notion of insular privacy, concepts of 'progress', a desire to reject the congested mews of Britain's industrial cities, and theories about street layout and social structure. While town planners such as Auckland designer Felton Mathew drew on British cities for inspiration — in his case, Bath[150] — the majority applied gridwork designs. These were an expression of the utopian dreams of the day, a conscious effort to eliminate the perceived causes of England's urban problems and provide what James Buckingham called 'social balance'.[151] Paradise was defined by symmetrical streets with clearly delineated parks, spaces for public buildings, and room for quarter-acre sections. All these were essential elements of the colonial town, and not just in New Zealand. It was an explicit rejection of the conditions found in London, Manchester, Leeds, Sheffield and other long-established English cities, where the poor congregated in filthy dead-end cul-de-sacs.

The government landing terrace, Timaru, during the 1860s.

Photographer unknown, Alexander Turnbull Library, PAColl-7469, F-5329-1/2

Town planners, suffused with the notion that physical dirt was associated with moral corruption, argued that wide streets offered social, moral and physical advantages, including the fact that it was hard for poor communities to use them as living spaces, and the practical point that they did not act as dirt-traps.[152] In New Zealand this concept was embodied in law: the Municipal Corporations Act 1876 required roads to be 66 feet wide.[153] Although this included footpath and berm, it was far in excess of the needs of foot and horse traffic. Wider streets were occasionally reserved to separate industrial zones from residential, rich from poor. F.W. Engels referred to such districts as 'separate territories, assigned to poverty'.[154] It was an apt observation; Frederick Utting's 1866 plan for Tauranga, or the Canterbury Association plan for Christchurch, included manicured green belts and parks as a way of splitting zones.[155]

The grid was not always practical. The New Zealand Company crossed the world with plans for Wellington that, naturally, did not fit the terrain,[156] though there is evidence that this was an ideal rather than an effort to create a real town layout. Landscape forced designers to compromise, as in Frederick Tuckett's plan for Nelson or Alfred Domett's Napier, though others were more obstinate. Frederick

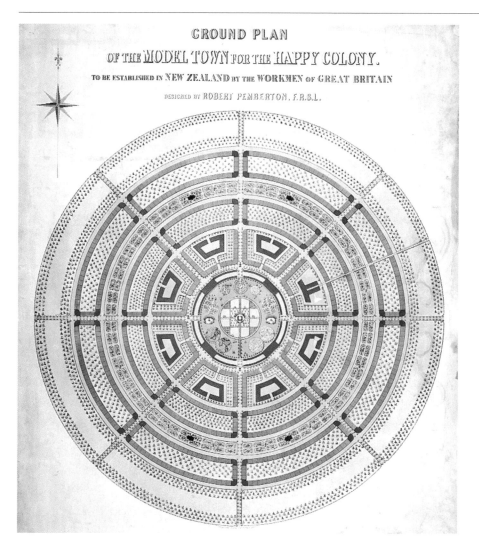

Robert Pemberton's 'Ground Plan of the model town for the happy colony to be established in New Zealand by the workmen of Great Britain'. This 1854 design, intended to map the spheres of existence — terrestrial and celestial — reveals that idealism had not died. The centre was designed to hold a miniature farm. Beyond lay the first circle, containing four colleges, conservatories, workshops, swimming baths and riding schools. There were also circles for factories and workshops, with orchards separating housing areas. The fourth circle carried an arboretum and horticultural gardens, while the whole was surrounded by a three-mile-circumference park.

Robert Pemberton, Alexander Turnbull Library, Plans-80-077

'Plan of the City of Wellington'
was drawn up for the New
Zealand Company in 1839 to the
latest social concepts; a gridwork
street layout with functionally
separate regions and an overall
physical order that contrasted
sharply with the chaotic mews of
London. However, the evidence
suggests it was more talking point
than serious effort. New Zealand
Company surveyor William Mein
Smith was instructed to use his
own judgement on site, making
'ample reserves for all public
purposes; such as a cemetery, a
market place, wharfage and
probable public buildings...' in
such a way that the 'beautiful
appearance of the future city'
would be 'secured' — even at the
expense of profit to the company.

Samuel Cobham, Alexander Turnbull Library,
MapColl 832.4796a/1839/Acc.1269, F-51659-1/2

The 'real' plan of Wellington laid
gridwork streets over swamp and
hill. Some aspects never
materialised, including canal
access to the Basin Reserve, then
projected as a harbour.

Francis Molesworth, Alexander Turnbull Library,
MapColl-832.4799gbbd/1841/Acc.16266,
F-124686-1/2

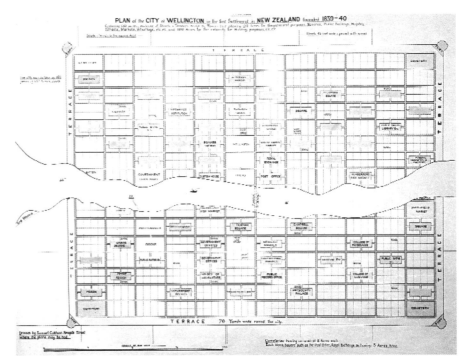

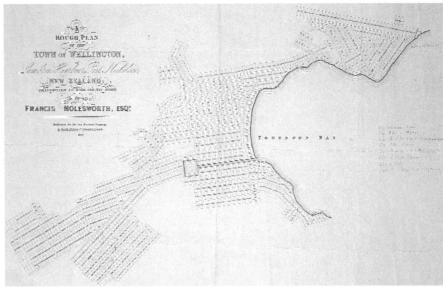

Carrington's 1842 plan for New Plymouth rammed the grid across hill, dale and stream.[157] Sometimes, as in Henry Tiffen's Havelock North or in Martinborough, the grid was tempered with a Union Jack motif.[158] Plains offered better opportunity for urban gridwork perfection. Large-scale examples included Hastings, Christchurch, Hamilton, Invercargill and Palmerston North, and many smaller centres were also laid out the same way, Carterton, Levin and Timaru among them.

The town grid encapsulated the sections thought ideal for middle-class urban life, where settlers could bring their families up in the privacy demanded by the middle-class ethos. The suburban section was also a device by which working classes could elevate themselves. If they could afford one, they could adopt some of the lifestyles of the genteel. Another driving force behind the urban section, as

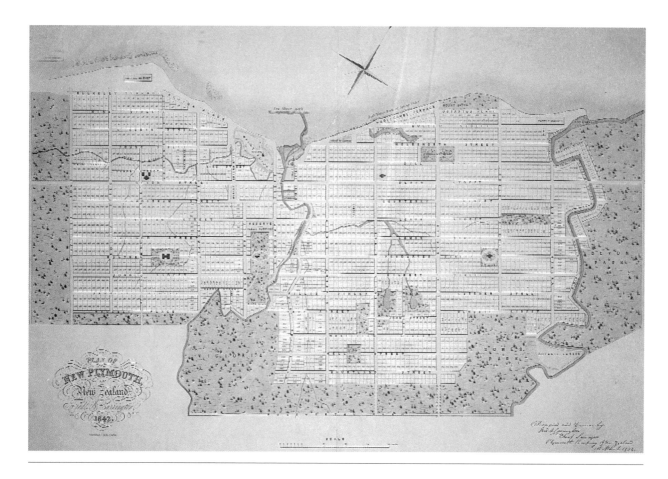

one historian has argued, may have been survival. The quarter-acre provided enough land for a subsistence garden, hens and perhaps a goat or a sheep; working-class families who relied on piecework or seasonal employment were less likely to starve.[159] Indeed, domestic poultry and the vegetable patch remained a feature of suburban gardens into the 1970s. It was an old pre-industrial tradition transplanted to the antipodes, given particular impetus by the fact that industrial working-class Britishers suffered for lack of it. This argument must be tempered with the fact that many urban sections were an eighth of an acre, and some workers could not afford to buy or rent even this much land. But that is not to diminish the importance of the ideal in the settler mind.

This was the origin of New Zealand's 'quarter-acre' ideal — driven from below, pushed from above — a utopian dream for middle class and workers alike. The fact that many settlers had emigrated in search of security also provides insight into the other New Zealand phenomenon — owning the house and quarter-acre. Suburban house ownership in New Zealand was traditionally higher than elsewhere in the world, remaining so to the end of the twentieth century. So important was getting property in one's own name that generations of New Zealanders were prepared to get heavily into debt for it. This phenomenon was unprecedented, its origins unprosaic. The poor of industrial Britain had been reliant on indifferent employers for livelihood and housing, never knowing when they might end up on the street. Settlers came to New Zealand to escape this fate.

Frederick Carrington's design for New Plymouth slammed the grid across the available landscape, making concessions only for waterways.

Frederick Alonzo Carrington, Alexander Turnbull Library, MapColl-832.295a/1842/Acc.1928

Above and right

Insular middle-class Christchurch around 1860. These views from the Provincial Buildings highlight gridwork streets with fenced, insular residential sections — still rough-hewn at this stage, but clearly discernible and harbingers of a quarter-acre future.

Photographer unknown, Alexander Turnbull Library, F-346367-1/2
Photographer unknown, Alexander Turnbull Library, F-75383-1/2

Left

Christchurch, looking towards Armagh Street and Cathedral Square, around 1854.

Photographer unknown, Alexander Turnbull Library, 75389-1/2

Below

House and garden on Napier's hill, probably early 1870s; ideal living for middle-class urbanites. Picket fences, limed streets and organised gardens give a solid air of establishment less than 20 years after the town was founded.

Photographer unknown, Williams Family Collection, Alexander Turnbull Library, F-29576-1/2

Suburban Auckland, 1858-style; this is Grafton Road.

Settler society and its anomalies

Historians have offered various theories about how settler society fitted together. One suggestion has been that, in an absence of easy transport, settler New Zealand consisted of clusters of local communities. The evidence certainly seems to point that way, particularly as some areas developed special community spirit — notably Havelock North, 'our village' to its people for decades.[160]

In the 1980s, one historian made the radical proposal that, by numbers, settler society was made up of single and kinless men wandering alone from place to place, binge-drinking, fighting and suing each other.[161] This idea prompted a good deal of debate, but ultimately was too reductive — cutting society down to a few simplistic numbers — to be credible. The idea did not adequately explain, for instance, why men went to the time, expense and effort of suing each other if they had no more than passing social contact. One of the well-known responses to real loneliness — suicide — was also at its historic low during the period.[162] As another historian asked, why was frustration-driven violence limited to fisticuffs in a country that bristled with small-arms, known to have been carried by men on the spree?[163] Some suggested that 'atomisation' simply revealed truths about one of several male lifestyles in New Zealand, and studies of women's culture revealed a society that was the very antithesis of atomisation.[164]

In fact, settler society was filled with community interactions at all levels. The letters, newspaper reports, diaries, memoirs and photographs from the period reveal a dynamic social world. The desirable building block was the nuclear family. In spite of a huge demographic imbalance, the marriage rate was at an all-time high during the 1855–74 period, some 8.97 per thousand, peaking in 1864–66 at over 10 per thousand three years running. This contrasted with the average 6.78 per thousand of the 1875–94 period when New Zealand was in depression.[165] By comparison, apart from a brief peak during the Second World War, twentieth-century rates were typically around 7 to 8 per thousand. In 1858, more than 49 percent of European males over 15 were either married or widowed, though the figure varied regionally. In underpopulated and pastoral Hawke's Bay, the figure was 27 percent.[166] Around 30 percent of the population in the 1871–91 period were married,[167] which was a reflection of the high percentage below marriageable age. In 1881, of 185,941 unmarried males, some 104,876 were under 15.[168] This suggests a social pattern in which those who could get married usually did, although the figure remained skewed because there were far more men than women.

The importance of family and marriage is underlined by the fact that the very moment when women were at their rarest was also the period when the highest percentage of men and women met and married each other. This demands some explanation, given the ratio of men to women. Part of the reason was that the demographic imbalance was not as severe as raw numbers suggest. In the 1840s and 1850s the ratio of men to women was around three to one, not helped when thousands of gold-hungry men poured into the country during the 1860s.[169] Unfortunately, knowing that 29,884 women joined 63,285 men during the 1861–65 period is not very useful, because a good number of the miners moved back to Australia.[170] A better indication is in the ratio of the 9369 women and 11,167 men who arrived during the 1867–70 period.[171] The demographic imbalance was also not even, either across age-brackets or from region to region. Pastoral provinces generally had a lower than average percentage of women.[172]

So there was better balance in the larger towns and agricultural communities than we might think.

However, there was still a major imbalance at national level; some back-country areas were almost wholly male, and settler authorities did something about it, importing single women in their thousands. They were viewed as potential wives and domestic servants. A study has shown that nearly 70 percent of a sample of 3737 single women who arrived between 1858 and 1871 were aged between 15 and 24, and 95 percent were under 30.[173] Many sought marriage as a means of bettering themselves, and were often very young; Ellen Hewitt, for instance, married 'only three weeks' after her fifteenth birthday and was a mother at 16.[174] Back-country shepherds and labourers actively sought to meet these women, as evidenced by such pleas as that of 'A Bachelor', who wrote to the *Otago Witness* in 1870 with a call to 'inaugurate a marriage office in connection with the Labour Exchange' as a way of getting 'respectable single men' to meet potential wives.[175]

Unmarried men had a society of their own. When not looking for wives, they actively sought the company of their peers, evidenced by the proliferation of boarding houses, which were decried by the *New Zealand Times* as 'crowded dwellings' whose denizens were 'glad to escape to the public house'[176] – where drinking with good mates and punching well-known rivals were popular social activities. One historian, taking kauri bushmen of the Auckland province as a case-study, demonstrated that this culture was family-oriented to a point, hard-drinking, and looked after each other in the towns – particularly when fights broke out.[177] This suggested a single men's society of close-knit groups, and the point was picked up generally by another historian, who argued that data suggesting mobility, hitting and drinking reflected the behaviour of the lumberjacks, road-builders, navvies, shearers and milling gangs who migrated together around New Zealand in search of employment.[178] Much of New Zealand's tradition of 'blokes together' originated in this period.

Being an itinerant did not mean isolation. Ernest Weston (1866–1926) and his brother Harold (1865–1958) took to the road as swaggers, but did not lose contact with each other, or their families, or become drunk and litigious.[179] Settlers such as David Balfour – who ended up alone on runs out of circumstance – built social ties with their neighbours. Balfour's memoirs and diary reveal much about this kind of far-flung community.[180] Occasional loneliness on his back-country leasehold did not drive him to drink – if anything, his experience hardened his thinking the other way. 'Beware drink, it is a treacherous thing,' he later warned his children, adding: 'To avoid running into debt you must be sober.'[181]

The conclusion is clear. Although some settlers gathered into sociable groups or work gangs, and spent their free time getting drunk together and hitting each other, while a few wandered alone thinking about family, these were but part of New Zealand's rich settler culture. Wider society was built around and relied on a broad range of social connections, particularly marriage and family ties, 'work gangs', friendship, club, sports and business associations. The result was a complex, socially active and vibrant settler world.

CHAPTER 5

Desperate times

The two great threads that shaped New Zealand – race relations and settler society – came together during the 1860s and 1870s. These decades were a crunch period for the young colony and left a direct stamp in the form of towns, railways and roads which continued to shape New Zealand into the twenty-first century. It was a curious age. Settler society was heavily distorted. A small group held much of the wealth and wielded effective political power; the population was imbalanced towards males; and private enterprise had not built an effective infrastructure.

These issues were compounded by physical problems. Settler New Zealand consisted of settlements expanding from isolated centres. Communication was poor and funding to build roads and rail to link them unavailable. Initial administrative arrangements had to reflect this reality, and the provincial system established by the Constitution Act of 1852 was Grey's effort to resolve the problem. The two provinces of Grey's first years were replaced by several, including Auckland, Wellington, Marlborough, Nelson, Canterbury and Otago, each under an elected Superintendent – an all-powerful administrator answerable to the local Provincial Council and inevitably elected from the ranks of the gentry or oligarchs. Provincial Councils controlled their own immigration, education and public works policies, along with their debts. They were not fixed; Hawke's Bay split from Wellington in late 1858 after an argument over the Wellington provincial debt – none of which had been spent in Hawke's Bay. Southland split for similar reasons from Otago, then re-amalgamated as a way of restoring its tremulous fiscal position.

Candidacy for Superintendent was usually cause for character assassination, as in Hawke's Bay where Alexander Alexander told Donald McLean that while Alfred Domett had 'no wish to become superintendent of Hawke's Bay', he would 'act if called'. Domett was opposed by a significant faction, but Alexander's opinion of them was not high. Henry Tiffen had 'considerable official influence', Henry Russell was 'disliked by everybody', Joseph Rhodes was a 'donkey', and T.H. Fitzgerald a 'scheming Jesuit'.[1] A few years earlier Fitzgerald had been dismissed by Domett as a 'desperate sneak',[2] but he got the job despite such sentiments. There was no love lost between them – Fitzgerald soon decried Domett as 'indolent'.[3]

In theory the provinces were subsidiary to central government, which was elected on a property-based franchise that included about 20 percent of all settler males. In practice the General Assembly – based in Wellington after 1865 – was

Government House, Auckland, soon after opening in 1856. The transfer of central government to Wellington less than ten years later was something of a coup for the former Wakefield colonists, who had been agitating since 1840 to have government moved there.

Photographer unknown, Alexander Turnbull Library, F-2657-1/1

less effective, particularly as parliamentarians were drawn from the same elites who ran the provinces. There were no parties as such, and the response to the first elections for central government in 1853 was apathetic to the point where there were problems even finding candidates in Otago. Politics were splintered, and even efforts to reinforce central government, championed by E.W. Stafford and C.W. Richmond among others, were arguably de facto methods of improving the lot of particular provinces.[4]

This was not the only weakness of the provincial system. Public works were poorly co-ordinated, erratic and usually geared to support the interests of the gentry. Rail was an election-winning issue in Christchurch, where William Moorehouse was made Superintendent on a transport platform. Driving a tunnel from Lyttelton to Christchurch demanded world-beating engineering,[5] but many other public works languished despite soaring provincial debts. Canterbury was not alone. In Hawke's Bay, the Provincial Council elected in 1859 voted money for roading and £125 for the prison, but £250 voted towards a hospital was barely sufficient. Patients were charged to stay, and it took an outbreak of typhoid in 1876 before a bigger institution was authorised.[6]

New Zealand wars: Waitara to Waikato

Race relations reached crisis point in the 1860s. Although local affairs were devolved to provincial government, land purchase and 'native affairs' were handled by the Governor – Gore-Browne considered Maori an Imperial matter; and after an 1856 compact gave provinces the net revenue from land sales, the pressure was on to

Thomas Gore-Browne (1807–87)
and family around 1859. Left to
right: Mabyl, Thomas, private
secretary Captain F.G. Steward,
Harriet, Harold.

Photographer unknown, Urquhart Album,
Alexander Turnbull Library, F-2658-1/1

buy. The system was essentially developed by Donald McLean, with the tacit but
hands-off approval of Gore-Browne; it has been argued that while this provoked
war within Taranaki and Hawke's Bay Maori, it fuelled unification elsewhere.[7] This
was social as much as political, and Te Heuheu called meetings near Taupo in 1856
to discuss what British agents described as a 'Maori Parliament'. The aim was to
halt the steady process of disempowerment, highlighted by land sales. Te Heuheu
also hoped to implement changes to British law, by treaty, putting arrangements
'on a footing more satisfactory to the Native race'.[8]

The gathering attracted rangatira from much of the North Island, laying the
groundwork for what became known as the King movement. In early 1858, at the
urging of Wiremu Tamihana, Te Wherowhero was elected as Potatau I – a name
that highlighted the integral part British goods played in Maori society. Core
support was quintessentially Waikato, and adherents were required to place their
territory under protection of Te Wherowhero's mana. It was considered co-rule
with the settlers.[9] However, at least one historian has noted that although the
symbols of power were easy to set up, maintaining an institution new to Maori was
more difficult.[10] Not all responded – the traditional enemies of Waikato were
notably absent – and some hapu joined or left as expedient.[11]

One of the key priorities was halting land sales, which the King movement,
Kingitanga, recognised as a mechanism of disempowerment. The difficulty was that
Maori relied on sales to fund consumables, and efforts to restrict expenditure
included bans on drinking. Some settlers thought Maori were 'ingenuous' for
thinking that 'simply making a King would be enough to heal their wounds'.[12] Yet
Te Wherowhero provided a focus, and was succeeded in 1860 by his son Tawhiao,

underlining the persistence of the movement. A land buyer's report of early 1860 offered one reaction, while the movement 'effectually put a stop to sales of land to the Government...', it also would also stop 'further bloodshed, by preventing lands from being sold by claimants with doubtful titles; or ... by rightful and acknowledged claimants, against the wishes of the majority of those interested'.[13] These sentiments, however, were lost amid the government notion that Kingitanga was separate sovereignty – illegal under the Treaty of Waitangi.

All these developments might have led to fighting, but the war that actually broke out in Taranaki in 1860 was only indirectly related, and certainly cannot be put down to Maori aggression, as the settlers tried to argue.[14] It was mainly about land, a sore point in Taranaki as a result of the New Zealand Company's efforts. Land Commissioner William Spain reached a 'verdict in favour of the Company's having effected a valid purchase' in 1844.[15] However, the settlers wanted more, and dispute between Maori over selling in the Bell Block area led to a 'fatal affray' in August 1854,[16] followed by a larger-scale battle in December. Native Secretary C.L. Nugent thought there was no danger to the settlers and suggested that government interference might be 'fatal to the prosperity' of the district.[17] However, Gore-Browne

Fighting during the 1860s spread across the central North Island.

Artist unknown, Alexander Turnbull Library, MapColl-832.16hkm/1868-1869/Acc.5862

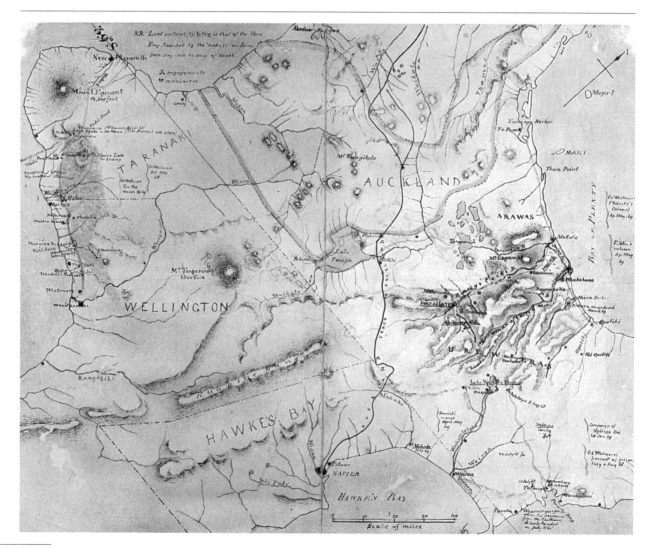

issued a proclamation declaring that any Maori fighting in the district would be 'treated as persons in arms against the Queen's authority'.[18] Meanwhile there were calls to confiscate the land of Kingite supporter and Te Atiawa chief Te Rangitake, also known as Wiremu Kingi.[19]

The *casus belli* was the 600-acre Waitara block, which contained the harbour New Plymouth lacked. Te Teira was prepared to sell; Te Rangitake was determined not to. In early 1859 Gore-Browne went to New Plymouth to see if he could settle their differences. There is some evidence that both McLean and local land buyer Robert Parris failed to brief Gore-Browne adequately. After addressing Te Teira, Gore-Browne received an offer of sale, which he accepted — out of ignorance, according to one historian. McLean did not correct him.[20] Te Rangitake remained opposed to the sale, and when surveyors arrived in February 1860 to start marking out the block, his people intervened. Gore-Browne responded vigorously, sending HMS *Niger* to stand offshore while part of the 65th Regiment under Colonel C.E. Gold took punitive action. Tensions spiralled. Settlers poured into New Plymouth, and the town was soon bursting with refugees, including Te Teira's people.

The war that followed was the first of a series that engulfed the central North Island over the next 12 years.[21] They fall into two broad phases: the early 1860s, when the economy was booming and Imperial regiments bore the weight of the fighting; and the late 1860s, when New Zealand was in depression and local militia took up the sword, with the help of allied Maori.

Interpretations range from heroic nineteenth-century views founded in fatal-impact notions to post-colonial suggestions that the settlers only just won in the face of Maori resistance.[22] However, although 'revisionist' thinking effectively discredited the old view of the wars, it did not replace it with an adequate military evaluation.[23] Revisionists made little effort to consider the tactical skills of different British field commanders or consider how the British took measure of Maori defences. In fact, after the Ruapekapeka experience, the Engineer Depot in Chatham identified specific ways of breaking such defences.[24] Sapping techniques were successfully used in the first Taranaki war, and the failure to use these in the Waikato can be put down to the campaign commander. The unprecedented artillery deployed at Gate Pa was yet another method for getting in, but here Maori introduced a different system of deeper trenches, and in wake of that the British introduced a new strategy. Each side, in short, was actively adaptive, changing to meet new threats as the other came up with them — a deadly game of tactical leapfrog.

The first Taranaki war surged on through 1860. Most of the fighting took place in and around the Waitara block, and as in the northern war 16 years earlier, Te Atiawa made use of tactical mobility, sometimes holding pa only long enough to force engagements before withdrawing. Skirmishes at Te Kohia and Kaipopo highlighted the strategy. There was a heavier battle in June, when 350 British under Major Thomas Nelson came up against 400-odd Te Atiawa under Hapurona, defending two 'rifle pa' at Puketakauere. The British were rebuffed, throwing the advantage to Te Atiawa who surged into Waitara.[25]

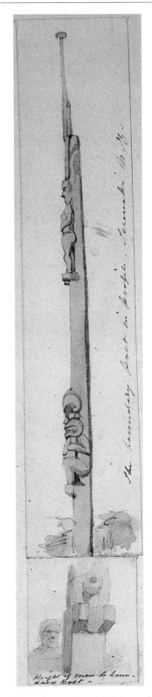

A boundary post erected to mark Maori land near Bell Block and the Waiwakaho River, nicknamed 'FitzRoy's pole' by the settlers.

William Strutt, Alexander Turnbull Library, E-452-F-015-1/2

Taranaki militia and the Royal
Marines, supported by sailors
from HMS *Niger*, attack Waireka
pa on 28 March 1860.

Artist unknown, Alexander Turnbull Library,
PUBL-0098-02-24-06-lower

Fighting peaked with an assault against three pa in the hills upland from the
Waitara block. Rifle pits, light palisades acting as barbed wire, and entrenchments
made clear to Major-General Thomas Pratt — the overall commander of Australasian
forces who had swept in to take control — that these defensive positions could not
be taken easily. Maori held the first only long enough to force the British into
wasted effort, but resistance was more prolonged at the second, Huirangi. Pratt
declined to expend his men in fruitless frontal attacks and instead threw a sap
forwards under cover of which his men could approach the defences with impunity.
By early January 1861 the British had dug themselves to within 50 yards of
Huirangi, and Te Rangitake withdrew to the third and last pa, Te Arei. This was a
tougher nut to crack, perched on a hillside with cliffs protecting its flank to the
north. However, in early February the 65th Regiment secured a rise nearby, which
allowed them to build a redoubt and start a sap. Although Pratt was heavily
criticised by a public that associated military competence with heroic assaults, his
tactics worked. By mid-March the siege was over,[26] and Te Rangitake sought peace.

By this time the focus had switched to the King Country. Settlers were putting
pressure on available land. George Grey had been reappointed in 1861 and tried to
negotiate with Tawhiao in January 1863. Mid-year in Taranaki, in which Waikato
were implicated, gave Grey a pretext to act. Maori north of the Waikato refused an
ultimatum, and on 12 July part of the 14th Regiment crossed the Mangatawhiri
River. So began the Waikato war, which ultimately drew in a significant proportion
of British regimental forces outside India, mostly at British cost.[27] Maori initially
held the Hunua Ranges, flanking British positions and bringing pressure to bear on

Maori fire into British positions at Pukerangiora in this drawing by Lieutenant H.S. Bates of the 65th Regiment.

Henry Stratton Bates, Alexander Turnbull Library, NON-ATL-0121

Manukau settlers, and the first thrust in September brought 200 Ngati Maniapoto and Ngati Pou to Pukekohe. British forces were supported by irregulars, including a force under mercenary commander Gustavus Ferdinand von Tempsky. Skirmishing continued while British commander Lieutenant-General Duncan Cameron waited for the 12th Regiment to arrive from Australia and for new shallow-draught gunboats to be completed.[28]

In late October the British advanced up the Waikato. The gunboats helped Cameron reduce the defences at Meremere, and the decisive battle took place in late November at Rangiriri, a bottleneck between the Waikato River and Lake Waikare. Around 500 Maori held the fortifications, against which Cameron could bring 1500 soldiers. However, he made the mistake of launching a frontal assault and took heavy losses. What followed was surprising: Cameron belatedly ordered a sap, but next day a white flag rose over the defences. Cameron took it as a sign of surrender and sent the troops in. Maori, however, simply wanted to negotiate – they had run short of ammunition. Cameron insisted on surrender, and over 180 Maori were taken prisoner.[29]

This opened the way into the Waikato, and by mid-December the regiments were in Ngaruawahia. Tawhiao withdrew to the Waipa valley, unwilling to accept the British demand for total surrender of his land. However, the British did not immediately follow. Cameron had 7000 men, but many were occupied keeping his logistics line open, and he could not advance far or fast until the supply situation improved. This gave Tawhiao time to prepare defences in the crucial Rangiaowhia agricultural district. Cameron declined to engage and sent just over 1200 men on a flank attack into Te Awamutu, which they reached on 21 February. This forced Tawhiao to pull out of Paterangi, but he declined to engage in open battle and threw up fresh defences at Rangiaowhia, just east of Te Awamutu. They did not hold when the British approached, and the vital agricultural area fell to Cameron.[30]

The British now controlled the economic heart of the Waikato, and the war ended at Orakau – 'Rewi's Last Stand', as the Rudall Hayward movie called it. Rewi

Maniapoto was opposed to fighting there, but factions in Ngati Raukawa and Tuhoe prevailed. Maniapoto then joined them and work began on fortifications. At the end of March, von Tempsky's Forest Rangers and part of the 18th Regiment, the Royal Irish, launched an assault on Orakau pa, which had about 300 defenders including some Ngati Kahungunu and other East Coast tribes. It was a bitter struggle tinged with moments of chivalry, its end driven by lack of water in the pa. Although Maori declined a call to surrender on 2 April, the only other option by this stage was a break-out, and while the garrison successfully punched through the British lines, they were pursued and run down by cavalry, suffering heavy casualties.[31] As always, fighting on British terms was risky, but on this occasion Maori had little choice.

Tawhiao threw up more fortifications in the southern King Country and there was talk of further military action, but Grey sought a settlement. It has been argued that the key factor was Cameron's reservations about attacking rifle pa,[32] but the post-fact opinions of the field commander and at least one newspaper editor should not be overplayed.[33] Cameron, whose heroically unsubtle assaults contrasted sharply with Pratt's skilful use of saps, did not express his glum opinions directly to Grey until 1865,[34] and they were but one part of a wider mix that included Imperial reluctance to keep supporting the war.

The fact was that by April 1864 the regiments had staged a successful invasion of the Waikato, in spite of Maori use of rifle pa. However, Cameron's insistence on frontal assaults when other tactics were known to be more effective was well recognised at the time, and he was castigated in the *Herald* for failing to use what the editorial called 'superior science'.[35] The result was high cost in lives and money – none of which the British could readily afford. New Zealand provided just £3031 of the £400,000 spent on local military activity during 1861, roughly $265,000 out of $35 million in early twenty-first-century money.[36] To this extent, Maori strategy worked, though not for the tactical reasons implied by the revisionist view.

Rewi Manga Maniapoto (1815–94).

Photographer unknown, Alexander Turnbull Library, F-52801-1/2

The British advance into the Waikato was a full-scale invasion, on par with any other Imperial war of the period. This is a camp en-route.

Photographer unknown, Alexander Turnbull Library, F-48082-1/2

Britain's problem was that the Waikato campaign absorbed many of the available regiments outside India; and in 1863–65 the British were fighting in Umbeyla, the Peshawar valley, Bhutan, Jamaica and Arabia.[37] Trouble was also brewing in Abyssinia.[38] To have a significant portion of the regiments tied up in a small corner soaking up Imperial funds was increasingly impractical, and this was the main factor behind their withdrawal.

In any case, Cameron had actually met Grey's declared objectives of July 1863 by the time he attacked Orakau. After Ngaruawahia was occupied, Maori put peace feelers out. Tamihana told Cameron that 'I don't say that peace is made' – but he would not continue the fight unless Grey brought it to him by attacking Waipa.[39] Grey was thus in a position to enforce terms, confiscating land north of the Puniu River. In a wider sense this was consistent with Imperial strategy, which often resolved the problem of the 'thin red line' by switching to diplomacy at first opportunity.[40] This was certainly the case in New Zealand, particularly given

Right above

King Matutaera's whare, Ngaruawahia, 1864.

Daniel Manders Beere, D.M. Beere Collection, wet plate glass negative, Alexander Turnbull Library, G-96095-1/2

Right below

Cavalry of the Defence Force charges at Orakei, after a painting by Frank Malone. Out of food and water, Maori had no choice but to take the regiments on in open battle.

Frank P. Malone, Alexander Turnbull Library, PUBL-0197-3-569

prevailing fatal-impact theory and Grey's amalgamation policies. There was a vague idea that the wars might reduce Maori, and newspaper headlines such as 'How to save the Maori from extermination', appeared in May 1864.[41] Maori wanted peace for their own reasons; Tamihana wrote to Pompallier in August to say that the war was over, adding that it 'would have ceased had it ended at Rangiriri'.[42]

Attention turned to Tauranga, where the harbour had been occupied by the British in January 1864 in order to cut off one route of supply to Waikato Maori. Some tribes in the district, notably Te Arawa, were supporters of the Crown, but Ngai te Rangi were not, and there was talk of illegal munitions sale. British forces at the Monmouth Redoubt were under instruction not to provoke Maori, but there was skirmishing in early April.[43] Local chief Rawiri Puhitake decided to build a pa and invited them to attack it – even offering to construct a road. Colonel H.H. Greer did not rise to the bait, so Puhitake built a pa just outside Tauranga, Pukehinahina – Gate Pa. By late April Cameron had assembled 1700-odd men at Tauranga to attack it, backed by the Royal Navy and artillery that included howitzers, 8-inch mortars and a monster Armstrong gun hurling 110-pound shot.[44]

This fearsome arsenal was brought to bear against the 235 defenders at the end of April. It failed. The pa, as the *Herald* correspondent later put it, had been 'scientifically constructed' by Maori and withstood even the enormous Armstrong gun.[45] The toa, deep inside solid earth bunkers, were shocked, stunned and concussed but alive – and recovered fast enough to repel an attack by the 43rd

Below left
A fanciful reconstruction of Maori answering William Mair's offer to let the women and children go free from Orakau. The act was usually attributed to Maniapoto.

Wilson and Horton, Alexander Turnbull Library, C-033-004

Below right
Frederick Aloysus Weld (far left) and his wife Filumena Mary Anne Lisle Phillipps Weld (second from left) with Sir Charles Clifford (right, back), Jessie Cruickshank Crawford and Francis Louise Tollemache. As Premier briefly between 1864 and 1865 Weld inherited the politics of the New Zealand wars.

Photographer unknown, Alexander Turnbull Library, F-34967-1/2

Regiment and the Naval Brigade. The British lost 35 dead and 75 wounded, versus total Maori casualties of perhaps 25.[46] However, Maori slipped away that night under cover of bad weather, leaving several British wounded who had been captured during the fighting and had been well looked after.[47] Cameron went back to Auckland, leaving Greer with orders to attack at once if Ngai te Rangi started to build a new fort. This led to a battle at Te Ranga in June, where Maori tried to defend a half-completed structure and lost nearly 120 toa, including Puhitake. British casualties were nine dead and 39 wounded. It was decisive, and a settlement was reached in July.

Booster engines

The tumultuous events of the 1850s and early 1860s took place in an environment of vigorous economic expansion. This growth was a paradox; the settler economy had minimal infrastructure, widely separated main centres, virtually no national communication other than coastal shipping, and relied heavily on non-renewable resources such as gold. Yet it expanded with near-explosive haste. In part this was a function of accounting; a shift from one timber mill to two represented 100 percent growth in that sector. After the economy was established, a shift from 99 to 100 mills represented only a one percent increase.

However, growth was spectacular even stripped of its statistical illusions. The main reason was that the population was expanding, and the new arrivals wanted land, housing, shops, business opportunities, farms, entertainment, clothing and goods. These demands created lucrative investment opportunities, and the capital that poured in boosted the economy still further. Once New Zealand had a reputation as a good investment the process became self-fulfilling, and as long as dynamic expansion continued, massive returns became possible from very little capital. Strategies for maximising growth included 'talking up' prospects, further fuelling the rate — which attracted yet more investors keen to exploit the opportunities. Growth, in other words, produced growth, and investors effectively surfed the wave as the economy unfolded.

There were two problems with this bounty, which was fairly standard for frontier societies worldwide. The first was that it was artificial — eventually the wave would break, potentially even before the flood of settlers subsided. The enhanced rate of growth also disguised the fact that the underlying economy, as it emerged, was not in good shape. The balance of payments was appalling. Annual deficits soared from £1,123,000 in 1861 to £3,599,000 in 1864, and there was a deficit most years from 1861 to 1876.[48] The distortions created by debt, bad balance of payments and no sustained income were compounded by the fact that the mechanisms that had allowed a handful of ambitious middle-class settlers to super-boost their fortunes also affected the way everything else developed.

In theory, the provinces were part-funded by profit from state land purchase, but this was never enough and the difference had to be borrowed via such legislation as the Loan Act 1856, which obtained £500,000 by way of debentures offered at 4 percent on the London market.[49] In 1863 the New Zealand government tried to borrow £3 million at 5 percent, but when the British government refused to underwrite the loan, the only way of getting the money was to issue £1 million worth of short-term debentures at 8 percent as bridging finance. Provincial governments also raised debts, as in 1860 when Canterbury borrowed £300,000 to pay for an ambitious railway system. Auckland borrowed £500,000 three years later. Political tensions rose with the debts: as we have seen earlier, Hawke's Bay separated from Wellington and Southland from Otago in response to the fiscal position of the parent province. Independent borrowing spurred wider worries about

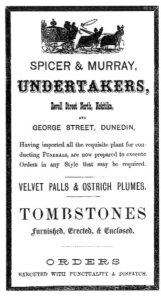

Artist unknown, Alexander Turnbull Library, F-31932-1/2

Opposite above

H.G. Robley (1840–1930) sketched Gate Pa early on 30 April 1864, detailing defences that had been thoroughly calculated by Rawiri Puhitake and his toa. Palisades were intended as delaying obstacles, while the defenders remained safe behind earthworks and in deep trenches, some linked by tunnels.

Horatio Gordon Robley, pen and wash, Alexander Turnbull Library, A-033-007

Opposite below

British artillery at Gate Pa just after sunrise, 29 April 1864. General Sir Duncan Alexander Cameron, bearded and holding a shooting-stick, leans on the gun carriage wheel. Soldier to his right straddles a Cohorn ('Coehorn') mortar.

Photographer unknown, Alexander Turnbull Library, F-29252-1/2

New Zealand's credit rating, and in 1867 central government moved to consolidate the debt – borrowing another £7 million for the purpose.[50]

Private capital flowed in through trading banks, family connections, or companies established for the purpose. These included the New Zealand Loan and Mercantile Agency and the Northern Investment Company, the latter formed by leading pastoralists with the aim of borrowing money from Scottish investors.[51] Other money came from former Australian pastoralists, among them 'Ready Money' Robinson of Cheviot, whose 93,000 New Zealand acres were worth a quarter-million pounds in 1882.[52] Several Australian-backed companies also operated New Zealand runs, including Robert Campbell & Co. of Otago.[53]

Right above

Gabriel's Gully, mid-1860s. It did not take long for Gabriel Read's discovery to become the hot news of the South Pacific. This 'tent city' was one result.

Photographer unknown, Alexander Turnbull Library, F-31007-1/2

Right below

Gabriel's Gully, transformed into a lunar landscape of pit and heap.

Photographer unknown, Alexander Turnbull Library, F-2662-1/4

Opposite above

Chinese miners came to New Zealand, following the gold. Some eventually returned to China. Here Ah Sam and Joe Quin prepare for market.

Photographer unknown, Alexander Turnbull Library, C6165

Opposite below

A glimpse of New Zealand's 'wildest west': Ahaura goldmining settlement at Napoleon Hill, Grey County, looking down Prince's Street East. Shantytowns like this, often complete with casinos, burst into life near many diggings.

Photographer unknown, Alexander Turnbull Library, PA-0-530-25

The provincial system, which split New Zealand into competing and semi-autonomous regions, added further strain. Provincial development was lumpy. Auckland became the prime industrial-agricultural region, with 60,201 acres under cultivation in 1858.[54] This was about half the national total and produced, among other things, 28 percent of the national potato crop in 1869.[55] Auckland also housed 102 of the 406 factories in national operation by 1867, including 30 sawmills — a third of the national total — 11 grain mills, seven breweries, seven brickworks, four fellmongeries and ten flaxworks among others.[56] The value of this plant was double that of the next highest province, Otago.[57] Pastoral and agrarian products such as wool, oats, hay and wheat were focused in Canterbury, Otago, Marlborough and to some extent Hawke's Bay. In 1869, nearly half the national oat crop — the 'fuel' for New Zealand's horses and beasts of burden — came from Otago and most of the rest from Canterbury. Almost two-thirds of the wheat was grown in Canterbury, and more than half the barley.[58] Getting this from place to place was reliant on coastal traders. Efforts by provincial governments to rectify these issues were limited, in part because general philosophy dictated hands-off development, in part because these governments were dominated by oligarchs whose focus was inevitably on their own interests and local regions.

Left

Early gold mining: a slightly romanticised image from the late 1850s.

Working Men's Educational Union, Alexander Turnbull Library, D-010-010

Opposite

Industrial-scale mining with floating dredges dominated the long-term gold industry, notably on the West Coast and near Alexandra. This example — known as the Manuherikia Dredge — operates on the Manuherikia River just outside Alexandra.

Photographer unknown, Alexander Turnbull Library, F-62537-1/2

Below

Gold-rush days in Thames. The North Island attracted its share of hopeful prospectors, and when the yellow metal was found at the south end of the Coromandel there was a rush there. These structures stand at Moanatairi Creek around 1868, with the chimney of the Moanatairi Battery just visible up the valley in the centre frame. The Prince Alfred Hotel stands to the right, on the corner of Coromandel Street.

Photographer unknown, Alexander Turnbull Library, F-65407-1/2

Banks quickly followed the gold miners. This is a BNZ branch on the diggings in 1864.

The economy was initially trans-Tasman. In 1861 some 61 percent of all exports by value went to Australia and 37 percent to Britain. However, the British share rose at the end of the decade and on into the 1870s, hitting 80 percent by 1876.[59] This emphasis pre-dated the frozen meat boom by nearly a decade,[60] and the early focus on Britain is given greater weight by the fact that much of the exported material by value in the 1860s was gold, initially sold via the Melbourne market.[61] Eliminating gold from the equation skews the earlier export figures more heavily in favour of the mother country. Imports painted a different picture: just over half came from Australia during 1861, and trade was still significant in 1876.[62] In 1870, imports to New Zealand from all sources included £114,188 of apparel; £215,164 of boots and shoes; £636,936 worth of drapery; and £61,789 worth of hats. This compared with £175,210 worth of ironmongery and £95,6870 worth of spirits, not including £9125 of gin, £25,114 of whisky, and rum to the value of £16,104.[63]

The other main problem of the period was that New Zealand's settler economy was extractive. Even pastoral operations had only limited life without fertiliser. Timber, kauri gum and gold could be harvested only once. Yet gold, in particular, was the foundation of New Zealand's fortunes in the early 1860s. Most of the precious metal came from Otago. Dunedin was established by the Lay Association of the Free Church of Scotland in 1848, on a modified Wakefield system where lack of capital and minimal farming activity restricted settlement to the town and environs. The pastoralists who spread into the hinterland during the 1850s were migrants from Australia and Canterbury, let in particularly by new grazing regulations in 1856. Infrastructure was minimal – roads were 'canals of liquid mud' – and European exploration of the interior was patchy.[64]

Maori knew of gold in Otago, but the metal had little value in pre-European times. Settlers were told of nuggets the size of 'a small potato' being tossed back into the Molyneux River. Such stories tantalised hopeful prospectors, and 'at least one party of settlers attempted to discover the El Dorado...' in 1852.[65] Another, led by Thomas Archibald, spent three weeks scouring Otago rivers in the hope of finding the metal. Other parties were more successful, but their small finds were 'suppressed, as likely to cause mischievous results' or 'neglected, as of trivial import'.[66] There was a political issue; Otago authorities faced an uphill battle to preserve the ideals of their neo-Scottish settlement and did not want it disrupted by rowdy miners.

By the end of the decade, however, the idea that gold might rescue a flagging economy was gaining ground and official rewards were offered. In early 1861 roadmen found gold in the upper Lindis gorge. There was a 'small rush', but the 'general yield was not encouraging'.[67] Then in late May the prospector Gabriel Read, armed with a butcher's knife, tin dish, spade, and 'about a week's supply of provisions', checked a 'large area of country' in the Tuapeka district, discovering 'prospects which would hold out a certainty that men with the proper tools would be munificently remunerated'.[68] There was a brief rush with 'highly satisfactory' results; and when the first shipment of 5056 ounces came down to Dunedin the floodgates opened. As an official report remarked, 'thousands were bitten by the gold fever, and abandoned their ordinary pursuits to "try their luck" at the diggings'.[69]

By Christmas there were 14,000 gold-seekers in the district, though numbers fluctuated radically. Discoveries near Cromwell prompted a surge there; other prospectors moved up the Mataura Valley. More prospectors checked the Clutha headwaters, and William Fox found gold in the Arrow River. Over the next few years, tens of thousands of men arrived, prospectors whose working lives spanned the Pacific from California to Victoria and Otago. By far the majority came from Australia – 24,243 in the year to July 1862.[70] Almost as many hurried back the other way; 16,386 to Australian destinations in the year to 31 July 1862. Some re-crossed the Tasman when more gold was found soon afterwards in Otago, a movement decried officially as 'senseless panic'.[71] But the two-way trade continued: 7303 moved back to Australia in the following 12 months, crossing paths with 31,762 coming in over 12 moths to 31 July 1863. By then the boom was largely over, and miners poured out across the Tasman in 1864, while incoming hopefuls dropped to less than 2000.[72] The population of Otago oscillated violently and estimates suggest the population on the fields peaked at around 24,000.[73]

The statistics make several things clear. Although some fortune-hunters came from America, Britain and from within New Zealand, around 80 percent came from Australia; and many went back there when the New Zealand lodes were worked out. A few stayed, moving on to prospects in Nelson, the West Coast and Thames. Still others – like David Balfour, or Australian businessman Alexander Burt – entered the New Zealand workforce. How much the miners made is debatable. There is an oft-quoted shibboleth that only shopkeepers and publicans made money on the gold frontier, but the 500,000-odd ounces extracted in 1862–63 implied an average annual yield of around 21 ounces per miner. Most seem to have been able to make ends meet.

The discoveries revolutionised New Zealand. One historian has argued that anti-Chinese prejudice was introduced with the gold miners; that the influx of labour accentuated egalitarianism – and that it introduced new 'fondness for gambling'.[74] Gold became a significant export; the £753,000 worth exported in 1861 was New Zealand's single biggest income-earner that year, outstripping wool at £524,000 and timber at £19,000.[75] The bonanza had its effect on Otago. A report at the time claimed that Dunedin 'assumed the dimensions of a city', 'agricultural villages' became 'important inland towns', and the 'large and important town of Queenstown' was established. Much of this was puff; Dunedin still lacked a proper sewerage system and was prone to epidemics.[76]

However, Otago's population rose, inland areas were populated, towns were established, and provincial revenue soared on the back of export duty and miners' licences, reaching some £78,587 in 1862. Against this had to be netted the costs of running the fields, £35,270 in 1862 for Gold Field Department staff salaries, escort services, buildings, hospitals – and the £1000 reward to Gabriel Read 'for discovery of Tuapeka', approximately $87,000 in early twenty-first-century money.[77] Most of the gold went to Melbourne; in 1863 the amount shipped to Australia amounted to four-fifths of the total. This was credited with obscuring the importance of the Otago field in Britain, an 'error ... not confined to the illiterate'.[78]

The Otago rush marked the beginning of New Zealand's golden years. Other gold was found elsewhere in the South Island and in Thames, and for a few years the metal became New Zealand's most valuable export. Some 674,499 ounces went overseas in the year to 31 March 1866.[79] But the auriferous nirvana did not last long. By 1867 the Otago 'rush' was over. Gold still came from the West Coast, around Havelock, and the Thames fields, but further practical extraction demanded

Gold mining at
Addison's Flat, Buller.

Photographer unknown, Alexander Turnbull Library,
F-14986-1/4

large-scale industrial processes. This did not stop an ongoing national search for easier lodes. In 1867 the Hawke's Bay Provincial Government offered £1000 to whoever discovered gold there, and George Whitmore secretly sent parties to look. Gold eventually was found in the province, but in no great quantity.

The end of the Otago gold boom coincided with a crunch in the wool market, as prices were forced down by a glut of cheap products from the expanding American frontier, which was shaking down after the end of the Civil War.[80] Some historians have suggested that the downturn was the start of a 'Long Depression', 30 years of economic stagnation alleviated only by an artificial upturn in the 1870s. An editorial in the *Hawke's Bay Herald* in early 1868 attributed the depression to over-government, bankruptcy of the provincial governments and a falling market for surplus sheep. The solution proposed by the paper was fresh industries and direct taxation of absentee landowners.[81] George Maunder, who emigrated to New Zealand in the late 1860s, lost his job as a wool presser at Ahuriri in 1870. 'I do not know what I shall do next,' he wrote to his sister. He had already decided not to go to Auckland 'as things are very dull there'. Optimistically, he thought flax, sheep and cattle offered hope.[82]

Pai Marire and Te Kooti

The economic crisis came just as the New Zealand wars entered a new phase. Fighting flared in North Taranaki during late 1863. However, the military details of the 1864–66 period — notably war in South Taranaki and the 'Lame Seagull' march by Cameron — are less crucial than a context that included the withdrawal of the regiments after a spat over cost, and arguments over local militia driven by personal rifts within the governing oligarchy.

Maori feeling was refocused by a new religious movement that emerged in Taranaki during 1862, called Pai Marire by founder Te Ua Haumene. He portrayed Maori as a lost tribe of Israel and spoke of revelations from the angel Gabriel. In a

Hori Kingi te Anaua, John White and Te Ua Haumene, around 1860. As founder of Pai Marire, Te Ua was demonised by the settlers, but his original aims were peaceful. Born around 1825, he became a lay reader in the Wesleyan mission, where he discovered the Old Testament. This formed the basis of his subsequent teachings, and he was inspired to found Pai Marire after a vision in September 1862. Pai Marire gained a range of followers, and the radical faction gained power after the battle of Te Ahuahu. John White (1821–91) was Resident Magistrate in the Wanganui district, former interpreter and a key figure in the government effort to resolve Maori issues peacefully. He wrote extensively on Maori life and times, and edited the repudiation movement newspaper *Te Wananga*.

Photographer unknown, Alexander Turnbull Library, PA2-2856, F-103545-1/2

wider sense this was a standard response to Old Testament teachings, reflected many times around the world, and more than once in New Zealand. One analyst has identified coincidental similarities between traditional Maori and Hebrew cultures, providing a likely mechanism by which the connection was made.[83] Militarist adherents gained power over the movement after the battle of Te Ahuahu in April 1864, in wake of which they began seeking wider support. Strategies included taking the dried head of Captain Thomas Lloyd around local tribes. When combined with such practices as speaking in tongues and dancing around a mast-like niu pole, this confirmed the image of Pai Marire as savage killers in the settler mind, a concept not challenged until the twentieth century.[84] Lloyd's head was eventually retrieved by regimental interpreter Charles Broughton, who rode into Waitotara and asked for it.[85]

In battle, Pai Marire warriors used the cry 'Hau Hau', a name the settlers applied to the movement, though the teaching that an upraised hand deflected bullets did little good at Sentry Hill in April 1864. Nearly 300 Pai Marire attacked the British redoubt, over 30 were killed and as many more wounded. The movement assumed a new dimension in early 1865 when Kereopa te Rau arrived in the Bay of Plenty, intending to win over Hirini te Kani, the principal Heretaunga chief. They still had a British head, which one witness saw 'with a cap of the 70th on. They pretend to make it speak.'[86] While in the district these people killed the Reverend Carl S. Volkner in his Opotiki church, mutilating the body and drinking his blood from the church chalice — an act that sent shock waves through the colony. Much of the often hysterical settler response to Pai Marire can be traced to these events, and Kereopa was later hanged for the murder.

Pai Marire spread down the East Coast during the next few months, but their invitation into Hawke's Bay by Te Hapuku was a function of earlier disputes over land sales. Full attention did not swing to Hawke's Bay until mid-1866, as the war in Taranaki drifted to a halt in a succession of skirmishes.[87] The movement was adopted by Ngati Hineuru of Te Haroto, part-way between Napier and Taupo. By mid-1866 they were effectively at war with Ngati Kahungunu, a conflict driven by long-standing disputes over distribution of the original Ahuriri purchase money.[88] Tough talk seemed likely to give way to violence several times during the year, but though Ngati Kahungunu tried to draw the settlers in amid rumour of a planned attack on Napier, Donald McLean sought to negotiate. This strategy prevented any actual fighting until October, when two battles were fought on the same day at Omarunui and Petane between settler and Ngati Kahungunu kupapa — 'collaborators' — on one side; and Ngati Hineuru and Pai Marire on the other.

The settler victory at both locations was so decisive that there was talk of a massacre even at the time. Some post-colonial analysis has suggested that Pai Marire at Omarunui, particularly, were innocent victims.[89] However, the documentation makes clear that they rejected multiple offers of surrender.[90] The battle was also fought in context of the emotion whipped up by Volkner's murder and general fear of the Pai Marire. As far as settler authorities were concerned, although the

group at Omarunui included women and children, they meant mischief. McLean was apparently tipped off about '...a plan ... under which a general movement of the disaffected Natives was to take place ... and that this place [Napier], if feasible, was to be the point of attack, but if not, then an attempt was to be made to attack Wairoa and Poverty Bay'.[91] Given the reputation of Pai Marire, McLean took such reports in deadly earnest. As he told Stafford, he intended to collect a force:

> ...to be able to deal conclusively with the intruding Hau Haus, which I trust may be done without bloodshed, for able as I shall then be to surround them with an infinitely superior force, I trust to obtain their submission, and by that means to absolutely crush out the danger which at present menaces the district.[92]

Politically, McLean also needed a moral victory over hapu wavering towards Pai Marire, and he got it. The true crisis on the East Coast did not come for several years. Meantime, fighting flared again in South Taranaki, this time at the hands of Nga Ruanui leader Titokowaru.

One of the finest strategists of the period, Titokowaru ran second fiddle to Te Kooti in the public eye, but gave colonial forces under Lieutenant-Colonel Thomas McDonnell and Colonel George Whitmore a run for their money. However, suggestions that Titokowaru brought Maori to the 'brink of victory' by threatening government control of the coast from New Plymouth to Wellington are overstated.[93] This was not militarily feasible. As a skilled tactician, Titokowaru certainly made life problematic in South Taranaki, but Wanganui was held by 600 men of Whitmore's militia, a superior force. The only tactical danger came at the end of 1868 when the militia were switched to the East Coast to deal with Te Kooti. Titokowaru and his 400-odd toa did not take advantage of it, and by mid-January 1869 Whitmore was back. His force besieged Titokowaru's pa of Tauranga-ika at the beginning of February, and were about to assault it when Titokowaru's force suddenly evaporated. He had apparently fallen for another man's wife, lost mana, and with it the support of his men – fleeing with a £1000 bounty on his head, around $90,000 in early twenty-first-century cash.[94]

The last phase of the wars revolved around Te Kooti Arikirangi te Turuki (c1830–93), who founded another syncretic religion, Ringatu, and was one of the most complex and multidimensional characters of settler-era New Zealand. He was a charismatic leader, deeply intellectual, faultlessly loyal to his friends, and – despite efforts in the late twentieth century to downplay the point – also vindictive and directly or indirectly responsible for a good deal of death and suffering.[95] He had worked for the settler authorities, fallen out with his employers in 1866, and was tried as a spy in Napier. McLean exiled him to the Chathams. Te Kooti believed

Major-General Sir George Stoddart Whitmore (1830–1903) came to New Zealand as military secretary to General Sir Duncan Cameron and was involved in the Taranaki War during 1862–63. He sold his commission and bought property in Hawke's Bay, but was subsequently prominent as a commander in the colonial militia, leading multiple campaigns against Te Kooti and Titokowaru in the late 1860s. These were as much characterised by settler politics as by fighting, not helped by Whitmore's combative temperament.

William Henry Whitmore Davis, E. Ellis Collection, Alexander Turnbull Library, PA2-0604, F-5306-1/2

he had been wrongly imprisoned, but his calls for a trial fell on deaf ears. In mid-1868 he and his followers seized the schooner *Rifleman* and landed near Gisborne. He was pursued as an escaped prisoner, attracting support from disaffected Maori.[96]

At a military level, Te Kooti did not seriously contest the government, and his two largest engagements – Ngatapa and Te Porere – were poorly handled. However, he ran an effective guerrilla campaign, alarming settlers on back-country stations. David Balfour, on his leasehold mid-way between Napier and Wairoa, recalled that 'for about four years I very rarely lay down at night without a loaded rifle for my bed mate ... my pen entirely fails me now to paint the fears, troubles and anxieties that I (and all others in the district) had during these next four years, principally through undefined dangers ... in my case, as I was often alone, imagination would often conjure up something to be afraid of and render me truly miserable'.[97] However, government response was torpedoed by an absurd feud between Stafford and McLean, and further undermined by arguments between McLean and Whitmore. This led to both McLean and Ormond joining the opposition party of William Fox in late 1868, action decried by the *Advertiser* as the 'most unconscionable instance of ratting ever known in the Colony'.[98]

When Te Kooti struck Poverty Bay at the end of the year McLean tried to get a relief expedition sent from Wairoa, but argued with the local commander, and meanwhile Te Kooti established a stronghold at Ngatapa. Whitmore was authorised to lead a force against it, although the *Hawke's Bay Herald* – the mouthpiece of the Ormond-McLean faction – suggested that he possessed 'neither the confidence nor the goodwill of either Maori or European'.[99] McLean feared the Colonel might

Allegations that the battle of Omarunui had been a 'massacre' circulated within days of the fight in October 1866. It was certainly a decisive settler victory, as intended by organiser Donald McLean. Colonial troops and kupapa crossed the Tutaekuri River, foreground, to attack the village.

Photographer unknown, Alexander Turnbull Library, F-111457-1/2

alienate the kupapa and asked government to rescind their decision, but Native Minister J.C. Richmond told him it was too late. The tone of McLean's letter to Ngati Porou summed up his feelings. 'It is not of my doing that Colonel Whitmore is going thither to do the work which has been so nearly finished by you. But now he has got there, you must unite in attacking the Hau-Haus ... Mr Richmond will be there to give directions in case of any troubles arising out of Colonel Whitmore's management.'[100]

Whitmore superseded Poverty Bay militia commander Captain Westrupp — an old McLean supporter — whereupon McLean withdrew his support from the Poverty Bay campaign, and with it the Hawke's Bay militia and around 700 Ngati Kahungunu. He also organised a separate campaign into the Urewera, defying a government ban on independent provincial action. Whitmore 'had relied on the Napier natives to complete the investing force' at Ngatapa,[101] complicating a difficult siege which ended with Te Kooti's escape. Some of the defenders were summarily executed by kupapa, to the horror of the militia. As one recalled: '...8 had that morning been shot in camp ... we saw the bodies ... lying out in a row, amongst whom I recognised Renata Tupara, Wi Kipa etc; altogether some 150 are supposed to be killed'.[102] Nor did the Wairoa campaign achieve anything, because Te Kooti did not retreat from his stronghold when Whitmore approached, and the Wairoa group could not intercept him inland as intended.[103]

As a result Te Kooti was able to raid Rauporoa, near Whakatane, in March 1869. Immediately afterwards he led about 100 followers to Mohaka in northern Hawke's Bay, massacring 57 Maori and seven settlers, including John Lavin and his family. David Balfour and several others reached Mohaka with a relief column and joined a group looking for Lavin. They found them dead, and Balfour reconstructed what happened from the positions of the bodies. The three children, aged about four, six and eight, had been playing by the river when Te Kooti's men appeared. The children fled, but had not gone far before they were tomahawked from behind. Lavin apparently realised something was wrong and hid with his wife in manuka scrub on a flat behind the house, but they were quickly located. Lavin returned fire with a revolver, but a:

...half-caste Hauhau [sic], who knew Lavin well ... called out 'Lavin, come and take your children with you.' They (the Lavins) thinking it was some friend ... showed themselves and were instantly shot dead and died in each other's arms.[104]

Balfour found the empty revolver still in Lavin's hand and later dug their graves. Post-colonial analysis suggests complex motives,[105] but the children had been murdered in cold blood by any standards, and government response was decisive. Whitmore and 600 armed constabulary were transferred to the East Coast

and, against McLean's objections, launched a systematic invasion of the Urewera with the support of kupapa. That ended Te Kooti's threat to the East Coast, but a change of government later in the year introduced more political complications. McLean became defence minister under Fox. Whitmore was sacked, and responsibility for a campaign to crush Te Kooti fell on Ormond, who organised it from Napier in his capacity as Hawke's Bay Provincial Superintendent. The embittered Whitmore later claimed that Ormond was so obsessed with cost cutting that the appointed commander, Thomas McDonnell, 'rarely had a complete day's ration at all, never knew when to expect a convoy, and was always absolutely without reserve'.[106] Ormond, for his part, told McLean that he was 'positively getting ill with work and worry'.[107]

By this time Te Kooti was operating from Te Porere, south of Taupo. McDonnell rendezvoused with the Hawke's Bay kupapa at Moawhango and advanced across the Rangipo Desert in heavy rain while Ngauruhoe belched ash and smoke. It was an apocalyptic start, but Te Kooti was no strategist and settler forces had little real difficulty taking the pa. Te Kooti fled to the King Country. Never missing a beat, the *Hawke's Bay Herald* took the opportunity to blame his being 'let loose in our midst' on the 'criminal neglect of the late Ministry'[108] – an attack on Stafford. McLean tried to negotiate with Tawhiao but, thanks to what Whitmore called 'our imbecile management of affairs',[109] was unable to persuade the King to hand the rebel leader over. McDonnell was made scapegoat because, according to the bitter Whitmore, 'Mr Ormond was too influential a member of the party, and Mr McLean too necessary to it, to be called to account.'[110]

Te Kooti left the King Country and was pursued by Ngati Kahungunu, Te Arawa and Ngati Porou. After a final engagement in mid-February 1872 the religious leader fled again into the King Country, where he remained a fugitive until his pardon in 1883.

Colonel Thomas McDonnell (1832–99).

William James Harding, Alexander Turnbull Library, PA2-2599, G-4882-1/4

Te Kooti was besieged by colonial militia and kupapa at Ngatapa at the end of 1868, but Te Kooti's strength had always been guerrilla warfare, and the Ngatapa fortification lacked water. He eventually fled with a handful of followers.

James Crowe Richmond, Alexander Turnbull Library, A-048-011

Priming the fires

New Zealand was in dire straits by the late 1860s. The economy was faltering and the combination of King Country, Te Kooti and Titokowaru showed that the state had yet to penetrate the North Island. It was a complex plight which Julius Vogel – Colonial Treasurer from 1868 – hoped to resolve with a grand strategy to build an infrastructure, bring settlers in, and settle the North Island hinterland. Some historians have suggested his policy was a precursor of twentieth-century state intervention.[111] This is debatable. Vogel occasionally espoused his own brand of social idealism, but his main initiatives were a response to the 1860s, and he was probably trying to rekindle the boom years of the gold-rush days in the belief it would set the fires of economy burning.[112] Nor were his proposals far out of line with prevailing thought. Nineteenth-century politicians were not mindless ideologues demanding state minimisation at all cost. In New Zealand's expanding frontier world, private enterprise could only succeed when working co-operatively with the state; the debate was over the balance point, and Vogel was shifting the fulcrum but not the fundamental structure.

Rail had been a particular theme of public debate for years, as much tied to prestige as to practical economics. Lines were started in Auckland, Otago and Canterbury, and there were calls for others in Taranaki and Hawke's Bay. The Wellington Provincial Council surveyed an inland link from Foxton to central Rangitikei. Central government convened a Select Committee in 1867 to avert a 'war of the gauges'. However, although they opposed standardising the gauge to 3 feet 6 inches (1067 mm), they recommended continuing the fragmented provincial rail system.[113] Vogel swung to a more centralised approach, though he did not envisage a state rail monolith, wanting some lines run as 'revenue rail' on the American mould and anticipating that private lines could spring from the state initiative. There was also a political motive. Rail led the drive into the central North Island hinterland, and was explicitly used as a political weapon to break the King Country during the 1880s.[114]

Enigmatic social thinker, Colonial Treasurer and sometime Premier Julius Vogel (1835–99) was prime-mover behind the state policies of the 1870s, personally organising funding and contractors for his railway projects. Although driven by his 'absorbing affection' for New Zealand, he was at odds with the provincialists, and the argument came to a head in 1875 over his Forests Bill. Vogel resigned, but not before passing legislation to abolish the provinces.

Photographer unknown, Alexander Turnbull Library, PA2-2831, F-92898-1/2

Vogel managed to find money on the London market, and public works expenditure rose from £284,000 in 1871 to £725,000 in 1872, peaking at £2,332,000 in 1874 — around $228 million in early twenty-first-century money. The railways absorbed a large chunk of this cash.[115] Costs were projected to be £7.5 million over ten years, around $750 million in early twenty-first-century money, and Vogel hoped to offset expenditure by offering Crown land in part-payment to the builders, John Brogden and Sons. His plans were also penurious; the Railways Act of 1870 authorised lines to the cheaper gauge of 3 feet 6 inches, with light rail, narrow tunnels and tight curves — all of which stretched the borrowed money, but which restricted speed and rolling stock for decades afterwards.

None of this was done without debate, and Vogel made enemies of the oligarchs by levelling part of the costs directly on the provinces and trying to secure the loans he needed on the security of six million acres of provincial land. Grey emerged from eccentric retirement on Kawau Island to lead the opposition. Tempers ran high and there was even talk — led from Otago — of separating the South Island from the North. Grey's oligarchs managed to stop part of Vogel's legislation, notably a Forest Conservation Bill, and the only way Vogel could undermine them was by making the state bigger than the provinces were. By 1876, using precedent from the 1858 New Provinces Act, he had abolished the provinces, replacing them with a system of smaller counties, boards and local authorities with far less power. It was overtly driven by local politics, but this was not the only motive. New Zealand was not big enough to compete with itself in the Australasian world. Eight or nine tiny New Zealands could not foot it with six Australias across the Tasman, but one larger New Zealand was on par with any of the Australian colonies.

Rail spread across New Zealand, and by 1874 some £5,575,400 had been allocated for just over 1000 miles (1600 km) of line.[116] About 808 miles (1300 km)

New Zealand's narrow and sinuous track restricted locomotives to small tanks such as the F — until the Fairlie Patent arrived. This is one of the double-ended engines being reassembled near Wellington's Thorndon Station, probably during the early 1880s. The driving wheels were mounted on bogies with flexible steam couplings, which gave excellent adhesion and an ability to surmount the tight curves of New Zealand rail. In service, however, their mechanical complexity counted against them.

Photographer unknown, Alexander Turnbull Library, PAColl-7477, F-4671-1/2

had been completed in the South Island alone by 1879. Gross receipts that year topped £601,000.[117] The North Island was less developed, with some 336 miles (540 km) of rail — including just over two miles of special three-rail incline — pulling in just over £156,000.[118] Usage was heavy. The North Island's 58 locomotives ran more than 712,000 miles (1,146,000 km) and carried 700,000 passengers — many of these repeat journeys, indicative of the value people placed on rail. Perhaps more critical was the bulk cargo. North Island lines carried just over 176,000 tons of freight that year, including wool, timber, minerals, firewood and merchandise. Livestock — tallied separately — included 65,600 sheep and nearly 11,000 horses and other animals.[119] These figures are made all the more spectacular by the fact that the lines were fragmentary.

Settlers from the Wychwood

Vogel's subsidised emigration scheme was broadly intended — like rail — to open up the North Island, and to a large extent it did. The influx transformed the demographic landscape and pushed the settler population from just over 297,654 in 1874 to 412,465 four years later.[120] Natural growth exceeded imported growth in the last four years of the 1870s, and it was not until the depression of the 1880s that the flood fell away.[121]

These new settlers differed from those of earlier decades. The New Zealand government had long coveted labourers, but they were hard to attract until the early 1870s, when they came in droves. Part of the reason was the reduction of rural conditions in Britain, culminating in the 1872 'Revolt of the Fields'.[122] Tenure was unsteady at best, and despite being in the country, the poor did not have the right to enough property to feed themselves. Nor was employment secure, and trouble flared across whole districts. This explains why emigration was often a community phenomenon. Two-thirds of all Oxfordshire migrants, for instance, emigrated to New Zealand in 1874 — a statistical glitch at a time when a disproportionate percentage of migrants came from southwest England.[123]

The experience of Ascott-Under-Wychwood resident Philip Pratley typified the experience. Pratley worked for tenant-farmer Robert Hambidge, and when they struck for more wages in April 1873, Hambidge tried to bring in outside labour. Local women picketed the farm and 16 were arrested, including Pratley's wife, Elizabeth. These 'Ascott Martyrs' were sentenced to short prison sentences with hard labour, souring feeling towards government and employers, and when New Zealand agent Charles Carter touted the benefits of emigration at Milton-On-Wychwood in mid-November, Pratley listened. Within a few weeks he and his wife had left for Ahuriri on board the *Mongol*. Their move paved the way for others in the extended family; and by the end of the decade Pratley's brothers and several other relations had emigrated, some to Timaru, the rest to Hawke's Bay.[124] Chain migration of this kind was common, and often continued for some time — in the case of the Pratleys, one relation finally reached New Zealand with his family as late as 1888.[125]

There was a similar pattern in Lincolnshire, where agent William Burton exploited the popular sense of injustice, promising greater rights of free speech and public assembly in New Zealand. Two thousand left, despite efforts by local authorities to dissuade them.[126] One paradox was Cornwall, which was unaffected by the revolt of the fields, yet, with Oxfordshire, provided by far the highest

Mount Victoria in the early 1870s.

proportion of migrants in the early 1870s. The key factors here were probably the tin and copper industries; the highest migration correlates with the lowest fortunes of these industries.[127]

The journey to New Zealand in the 1870s was different from that of even ten years earlier. Cabin passage was much the same, but Vogel was determined to fix the problems faced in steerage – this was a government effort and the emigrants 'should be made in every way as comfortable as the circumstances of a long sea-voyage will permit ... the consideration of expense is in no way to interfere with arrangements for the security of their health'.[128] Ships' surgeons were asked to haul captains into line and the ships – invariably private charters – were inspected on arrival.

Left

Armstrong and Son's Wanganui smithy, early 1870s.

William James Harding, W.J. Harding Collection, Alexander Turnbull Library, PAColl-3042, G-146-1/1

Below

Settlers arriving in Hawke's Bay disembarked in Napier – then a noisome town hemmed in by swamp. This is a view from Hastings Street looking north to Carlyle Street. The river in the foreground was a flood menace.

William Williams, E.R. Williams Collection, Alexander Turnbull Library, PAColl-0975, G-25613-1/2

J.G. Wilson drives the region's first buggy in this typical southern Hawke's Bay scene of the late 1880s.

This produced some spectacular successes. The *Salisbury* arrived with all on board who had departed Plymouth, a noteworthy achievement.[129] 'Everything that was possible seems to have been done for their comfort on board,' Edward Green reported of the *St Leonards* in September 1873.[130] 'Extreme cleanliness was noticeable in every part of the ship,' another inspector remarked about the *Brerar.*[131] The *Helen Denny* left short on flour, but the captain 'endeavoured, by issuing his cabin stores, to make up the deficiency'.[132]

However, other ships did not meet the standard. Some leaked, and even three months in a leaky boat was intolerable. 'In consequence of the ship *Wild Duck* leaking so much,' ship's surgeon H.L. Diver reported, 'many of the immigrants had to crowd into other berths than their own ... medical comforts were very short of the quantities ordered ... no quicklime ... soup very short, ... soap ditto, very little charcoal ... I consider it a miracle that half my people did not die...'.[133] The *Columbus* received a pasting for failing to provide the 'dietary of young children' and having a broken water condenser.[134] The *Hovding* ran short of supplies altogether, 11 children died, and the Danes on board made a formal complaint when they reached Napier. The commissioners found no great evidence of problem, decided to have local immigration officials charge the captain anyway – and then had to drop it when they discovered that captains could not be charged under the law. Ormond, as Provincial Superintendent, could not 'enter further into the case' once the commissioners had decided not to pursue it – though he was worried about the number of unmarried mothers who had enveigled themselves on board and could not then support themselves in New Zealand.[135]

This was not the only hiccup. The *Star of India* embarked without the 'cheese, carrots and onions' promised in the dietary scale on the migrants' tickets,[136] and Vogel personally castigated the 'gross carelessness' with which the 'despatching and inspecting officers' had handled this ship.[137] Calamity struck the *Woodlark*, which reached Port Nicholson in March 1874 with scarlet fever on board. The disease had killed 18 children during the voyage, and two more died while the ship was in quarantine.[138] The *Surat* wrecked on arrival at Port Chalmers and the settlers lost all their 'clothing, bedding and effects' because the hulk and all its contents were salvaged and 'sold at public auction' despite protests by the survivors. Vogel rectified the problem after the survivors protested to the Governor.[139] A worse fate befell the *Cospatrick*, which caught fire and sank in the South Atlantic.

Many of the settlers were women. They were deliberately sought out to rectify the demographic balance. The Scandinavians were considered highly desirable, and when about 550 Danes were due to arrive in Napier on board the *Hovding* and *Ballarat* in September 1873, one newspaper lasciviously welcomed the 57 single women known to be on board, who with their 'blue eyes and flaxen hair' would 'prove a welcome addition' to the province.[140] How willing these and other Scandinavian women were to emigrate is unclear. Some may have been enticed by subterfuge.

Few found great fortune in the new land. Vogel picked Scandinavians to pioneer the dense bush of the Manawatu, northern Wairarapa and southern Hawke's Bay after noting that a small group did well in Palmerston North in the late 1860s.[141] The popular image of poor settlers hacking lives out of the bush largely emerged from this period, though it was limited both geographically and in time. There were two motives for moving them into the bush. As G.H. Scholefield remarked in 1904, the 'doctrine of progress declared that the bush must be destroyed under the guise of improvements'.[142] However, bush had been a friend to Maori during the guerrilla phase of the wars, and eliminating it was another step towards enforcing settler power.

The first Vogel settlers, mostly from Denmark and Norway, were settled on 40-acre lots in the upper Manawatu during 1871 and given the task of building a

Terrain and life in the cut-over bush of the North Island remained hard for decades. This 1904 picture of the Gate family reveals something of the conditions many faced even 30 years after settlement. Left to right; unknown; Alan or Ernest Gate; Anne Gate (nee Mather) holding Hope; Ernest or Alan Gate; Harriett Gate; unknown on horse; Aaron Gate.

James McAllister, James McAllister Collection, Alexander Turnbull Library, PAColl-0975, G-10246-1/1s

road and tramway to Foxton. Others went into the shadow of the Ruahines, where they helped hack a road through the Manawatu Gorge into southern Hawke's Bay. Early income came from sawmilling, and by the early 1880s enough bush had been cleared to begin dairying. Other Scandinavians were sent to the northern Wairarapa, where they began nibbling into the Seventy Mile Bush from the south.[143]

The majority, however, were settled in southern Hawke's Bay, and most were dismayed to find their farmland clad in thick bush. Access was along a bridle track cleared to serve Oringi and Tahoraiti stations, both of which had been operating in the Oringi clearing since the early 1860s. The settlers were expected not only to fell their own properties, but to pay off their passages and land by clearing bush for the railway. Settlement spread from Norsewood and Dannevirke, and more settlers were brought in during 1874, colonising Makaretu. Altogether around 4000 Scandinavians arrived in the ten years after 1872, and in just 15 the vast tract of bush between Takapau and Eketahuna was reduced to stumps and pasture. Fires completed the destruction in the late 1880s. James Inglis, visiting Hawke's Bay in

Left above

Dairying spread across Taranaki and southern Hawke's Bay during the Vogel period. This is the Rukuhia factory around 1907.

Photographer unknown, Alexander Turnbull Library, G-89356-1/2

Left below

The Maharahara dairy factory in southern Hawke's Bay.

James McAllister, James McAllister Collection, Alexander Turnbull Library, PAColl-3054, F-3560-1/2

Foxton during the 1870s: a typical
settler town in the Vogel era.

1885, condemned the 'wholesale denudation' which, he claimed, would 'exact its retribution in widespread ruin and desolation'. Others had more commercial reservations. J.G. Wilson was later of the opinion that the destruction of bush in his home district of Umutaoroa 'was premature' and 'would have seen a keen market' ten years later.[144]

Poverty remained the biggest problem. State wages of around six shillings a day – less land and passage costs – did not go far, and many settler farms were just staggering to their feet when depression bit. Nor was dairying a panacea. Butter was initially almost worthless and the newcomers had to find other incomes. Manawatu settlers found milling lucrative. In Taranaki and Hawke's Bay 'Jew's Ear' edible fungus proved a winner. It grew naturally, found a keen market overseas, and some £375,000 worth was collected and sold nationally between 1872 and 1904, typically at 3d a pound.[145]

It took time to expand from these small initial holdings. When sections in Woodville were advertised in November 1874, small settlers were swamped by speculators such as H.B. Sealy, who bought 800 acres at 50 shillings an acre and sold them in December 1876 for £800 profit. This was out of the reach of many small-holders. However, by policy, provincial government set aside 20,000 acres which was taken up by the Woodville Small Farms Association, a Methodist group largely formed from work gangs who had built part of the railway line. This typified nationwide initiatives to make land available for small-holders and highlighted a phase of expansion from elsewhere in New Zealand. It also underlined a shift in policy. Complaints that too many 'foreigners' were coming in eventually carried enough weight to deter government from seeking settlers outside Britain – in 1883–84, for instance, there were just 55 Scandinavians among 6267 migrants.[146] Their hardships reinforced the rugged colonial ethos, helping lay the foundations for the twentieth-century ideal of capable, do-anything individualists.

CHAPTER 6

Prelude to a century

New Zealand changed dramatically during the 30-odd years from the mid-1880s. Dashed ambition to build a better or bigger Britain prompted complex responses, including a reassertion of the settler quarter-acre and ideal of job security, both becoming anchors amid economic uncertainty. Britain itself was evangelised, a nostalgic image upheld by the children of the settlers as something which, in an absolute sense, it was not.

Maori continued to decline, settlers penetrated to virtually all useful parts of New Zealand, and the turbulent race relations problems of the early years were resolved by brute force as the North Island Main Trunk Line slammed through the King Country. Maori did not idly sit back and accept their fate; for some decades, however, they lived effectively separate lives and settler society dominated. By the 1890s the main problems of that society were not how two peoples might relate, or how utopian dreams might be brought to fruition, but the difficulties facing a monocultural, male-dominated colony where ambitions to make a bigger and better Britain came crashing down with economic depression.

What followed was unprecedented. New Zealand went into the 1880s without political parties or a real civil service. It emerged from the decade with a party in waiting. The same downturn pushed the deprived together – a movement that soon became militant. These swirled with the other changes of the period, many stemming from the switch to an established society, demanding such institutions

Flax mill at Whakaki, near Wairoa, 1889.

William Williams, Alexander Turnbull Library, E.R. Williams Collection, C-9482-1/2, G-25559-1/1

as a civil service, which had been ad hoc and often personal for much of the settler period. Organised sport also emerged, including the 'rugby' part of New Zealand's twentieth-century ethos. To this was added a change in the position of women and new attitudes to drink.

These changes broadly matched developments around the world, but New Zealand's particular innovations – ranging from the policy of 'estate bursting' to new industrial-relations legislation, the introduction of universal suffrage, and the creation of one of the world's first organised government bureaucracies – led the pack, a point not lost on contemporaries. H.H. Asquith thought the colony was a social laboratory for the world,[1] while Philadelphia academic Frank Parsons went further, declaring in 1904 that New Zealand was the 'birth-place of the twentieth century'.[2]

Swaggers and soup kitchens

The role of the 'long depression' of the 1880s in shaping New Zealand's twentieth century cannot be understated. The crisis emerged in the late 1870s. Vogel had borrowed heavily, and New Zealand's six banks and 16-odd private loan companies[3] had long since followed his lead, offering high rates to attract overseas funds, then lending to local borrowers at even higher rates. Bank advances soared from £3.53 million in 1872 to just over £12.8 million in 1878, mostly borrowed from Britain.[4] Some of the Scottish loans were secured merely on the good name of the borrower – and with most of it going on speculative land ventures, lenders were becoming edgy. The edifice came crashing down in 1878 when the City of Glasgow Bank collapsed, in part a result of its over-exposure in New Zealand.

New Zealand suddenly became a financial hot potato, credit dried up, and New Zealand banks had to restrict local lending. Merchants, traders and landowners who had relied on the cash suddenly found themselves short. Bankruptcies doubled that year,[5] and there was deflation of 16 percent – a historic record – as the land-price bubble burst.[6] Government revenue dropped from a high of £4,167,000 in 1878 to £3,134,000 the following year, and did not rise much afterwards.

George Grey's government responded with cutbacks. Funds for charitable institutions and hospitals – lumped together in the government books – slumped from 2.5 to 1.4 percent of government spending between 1878 and 1879.[7] The administration of John Hall went further in 1880. In the face of annual deficits that ran over £700,000, Colonial Treasurer Harry Atkinson implemented a plan to slash public works expenditure from 37.5 to 28.7 percent of government spending.[8] This killed a just-started Wellington–Manawatu railway and plans to create a North Island Main Trunk Line. Government ran a small surplus during 1881 and 1882, but the retractions took money out of the economy. Labourers found themselves destitute. Shopkeepers and businesses who had relied on their custom found their livelihood threatened, and so it went on. In wake of bank credit restrictions, estate agents began advertising themselves as financial dealers. 'Terms very easy', one

land agent advised potential buyers of a Waikato cheese factory. Charles Osmond, an Auckland 'Land and Monetary Agent', offered mortgages and loans, investment services and estate management alongside his real estate business. So did Edward Wayte, whose 'House, Land and Financial Agency' had both farms and residential properties on sale in early 1884.[9] In a wider sense this was part of a downturn across the British Empire, but thanks to its combination of debt and Calvinist state policies New Zealand felt the pain more acutely.

Politics became chaotic. Government of the day consisted of shifting alliances as the fortunes of one would-be leader or another rose and fell. This kaleidoscope changed with ever-increasing speed in the early 1880s; there were as many administrations between 1880 and 1884 as there had been between 1873 and 1880. The shifts reflected the sense of crisis gripping the country, but neither the Hall nor short-lived Whitaker governments offered much in the way of alternatives, and franchised voters expressed their frustrations at the ballot box. Atkinson's administration lost the next election. However, the bizarre Stout-Vogel alliance that came to power twice in 1884 – interspersed with another brief burst of Atkinson's government – inherited the same economic problems, and was kicked out in 1887 in favour of a further Atkinson-led administration, the so-called 'Scarecrow' ministry which renewed its retractive policies.

Unemployment soared, and even the ranks of land-owning elite and urban entrepreneur were winnowed. Few fell as hard as Thomas Tanner, bankrupted in 1885 by the Northern Investment Company after he defaulted on an £80,000 debt

This family stand in their best for the photographer outside a sawmill house near Invercargill.

Photographer unknown, Wallace Early Settlers Association Collection, Alexander Turnbull Library, F-66205-1/2

– around \$11.2 million in early twenty-first-century money.[10] Soup kitchens opened in Christchurch during 1880–81 as a stopgap, but few of the masses were happy with their lot and there were strident calls for work. This eruption of the poor highlighted a weakness of colonial society. Grey's Destitute Persons Ordinance of 1846 had thrown responsibility for supporting the destitute on their 'near relatives',[11] and the state had no role other than to force relatives to pay. Charitable aid was thrown to provincial authorities in New Zealand with erratic results, and support ultimately relied on philanthropy, itself far less well set up in New Zealand than in Britain.[12]

To some extent this was inevitable. One historian has argued that the settler desire to shed British systems, such as the Poor House, prompted a decision to eschew welfare;[13] in any event the colony had developed in such a distorted way as to make a sustained welfare system unaffordable. But welfare was not entirely rejected by government. Efforts to implement a formal system began in 1877 – well before the crisis erupted – when the first short-lived Atkinson administration toyed with regularising charitable relief. However, fears of creating welfare dependency deterred progress,[14] and the result was that the crisis of the 1880s created social problems that erratic personal generosity could not rectify, even when spurred by Calvinist guilt. Some even cast the crisis as a kind of social Darwinism; the downturn purified the ranks of the employed, allowing the fittest to survive while the undeserving and weak were cast out.[15]

For men like Bill Blackie, a station hand suddenly thrown on the scrapheap, the future seemed bleak. After a stint at pig-shooting he set off from Ongaonga to Wellington, finding 'numerous men' in similar condition, all 'sober, decent workers' who found work 'almost unprocurable'.[16] Blackie eventually reached the South Island and found a few months' work, then returned to the North Island where he oscillated between Hawke's Bay, the Manawatu and Wellington. William Cox spent five years on the road; and even after things began to pick up he was unable to find permanent work.

The plight of the infirm, old and destitute was often desperate during the 1880s, and welfare was patchy at best. This is the Newtown Home for the Aged Needy.

Photographer unknown, C.M. Heine Collection, Alexander Turnbull Library, PAColl-4401-01, G-32552-1/2

The Tarawera eruption

Right

Long thought extinct, Mount Tarawera erupted one dark night in June 1886: a six-hour paroxysm blew half the mountain skywards, triggered earthquakes and sent lava, boulders and ash showering into the area, killing 147 Maori and six Europeans. The sound was audible across much of the central North Island; some people thought it was the guns of a visiting Russian frigate. Three villages were destroyed. Moura slid into Lake Rotomahana, which temporarily became a bubbling mud-pit. Te Ariki was crushed beneath 30 feet (10 metres) of ash, while even Te Wairoa — nine miles (14 km) from the mountain — was swamped with ash and mud. The delicate Pink and White Terraces on Lake Rotomahana, seen here, were obliterated.

Photographer unknown, Alexander Turnbull Library, F-77660-1/2

Right

The remains of Te Wairoa. McRae's Hotel stands half-crushed amid the bleak landscape of ash and mud.

Burton Brothers, Alexander Turnbull Library, F-20459-1/2

Opposite top

Two survivors beside the 'fowl house in which we spent the night'.

Photographer unknown, Alexander Turnbull Library, G-23412-1/2

Opposite below

The Surveyor-General and party on the ashfield at the foot of Tarawera, July 1886. The eruption changed the lie of the land, and the volcano itself was riven apart, its three-peak profile gone.

Photographer unknown, Alexander Turnbull Library, F-80868-1/2

The Tarawera eruption

These itinerant men met and mingled, went about in groups or work gangs and often found lodgings together. Ernest and Harold Weston were among them. The two brothers arrived in New Zealand in 1886, could not find work and took to the road in 1888. Their trek took them from Auckland to Taranaki, Wellington and Hawke's Bay. There were signs of recession everywhere. A 'troll down the main street of Waipawa' revealed that it had been a 'go-ahead town at one time', but things were 'very quiet now'. They went on to Hampden (Tikokino) where they got permission to sleep in a whare with an old Irishman and somebody else from Shropshire. The former was lifting potatoes at 2 shillings a bag. They felt the towns 'on this side of the Gorge' were 'doing more than the other side. Not so many empty houses, wages higher, general hand on a farm gets 25/- a week, ploughman 30/- and so on.'[17]

As able-bodied men, the Westons were among the lucky ones. The disabled and destitute, the elderly, widows and the infirm had little option but to fall on what there was of organised welfare, a system reliant on private gift to leaven the trickle of cash doled out by impoverished and miserly provincial authorities.

Total annual spending by the Nelson Provincial Government on hospitals, aid and a lunatic asylum was around £2700 in the 1860s, but the per-capita rate fell.[18] In Otago, the destitute were helped by the local hospital and erratic grants from government – some £200 had been voted in 1860 for the purpose. Julius Vogel helped establish the Otago Benevolent Society to put this on a firmer footing, but this arrangement was rare, and destitution – including old age – usually meant living in cheaply run and often unpleasant quarters, though these were not numerous. Auckland's total facility amounted to 49 beds in 1880, Nelson's just a dozen. Napier's original building was dismissed in 1875 by the *Daily Telegraph* as 'a miserable refuge in which only the miserable would take refuge'.[19] Women were better catered for in Christchurch, where there was a 25-bed house.[20] Many who could afford it got out altogether: around 125,000 New Zealanders voted with their feet between 1885 and 1892, crossing the Tasman in search of greener fields in Australia.

Rail and race

We stand here, almost in view of what I might call the classic ground of the Maori war … I think we should remember, in doing work of this class, to contrast it with the old days, the days of the past … it is by works of this character – works which are not to set race against race nor people against people, but to unite them together as one people…

– Sir Robert Stout at the sod-turning ceremony of the Main Trunk Line, April 1884[21]

Despite a prevailing air of gloom, some public works were back on track by the mid-1880s. The stalled Wellington–Manawatu railway was picked up by private enterprise; there was also new attention to the North Island Main Trunk Line. This had been long projected as an extension of existing government rail through the Wairarapa and Hawke's Bay, and debate focused on ways of getting across the rugged Napier–Taupo stretch – an issue that became heavily politicised as local business lobbies played their battles out in newspaper columns.[22] Hawke's Bay agitators were joined by voices from Taranaki, but their pressures fell on the stony ground of depression penury. In the end, while the Commission looking into national railway expenditure in 1880 viewed a Wairarapa–Hawke's Bay rail connection as part of a trunk line, cost considerations killed an immediate link.

Race relations provided the spark to restart the process. Maori had neither died off nor been swamped. Efforts to contest disempowerment swung to parliamentary representation and legal action in the 1870s, and the Parihaka occupation of 1881 – though peaceful – made clear that direct action remained an option. The King Country was intact, and although Tawhiao made formal peace that year, the region remained nominally independent. Some locals felt renewed war could not be ruled out – a point recognised by Matamata's Josiah Firth, who built a strong-point next to his house.

Government was eager to eliminate the King Country as a stronghold – and rail offered a way of doing so. At the same time, Rewi Maniapoto and Huatara Wahanui recognised the economic benefit of rail and agreed to allow government surveyors in against Tawhiao's wishes. John Carruthers identified routes to Te

Depression-era capital: Wellington's Te Aro flat in 1884, from Mount Victoria.

Burton Brothers, Alexander Turnbull Library, G-2236-1/2-BB

Awamutu through the King Country, either from the railhead at Waitara, or directly north from Marton. However, Hawke's Bay voices could not be ignored, and when efforts to locate a route began in February 1883, survey parties were sent to investigate lines from both coasts.

Maniapoto's initiatives were not welcomed by all King Country chiefs, as C.W. Hursthouse's survey party discovered. They left Pirongia (Alexandra) on 12 March to identify a route from Te Awamutu to New Plymouth and headed down the Waipa Valley, but were ordered back by local Maori. A second attempt next day met the same result. On the 20th the surveyors made a third attempt, this time with the consent of Maniapoto and Wahanui. They were escorted by Wetere te Rerenga, but when they reached Te Uira they were:

> stopped by a party of Maoris under the leadership of one Te Mahuki, and violently dragged from their horses ... everything was taken from them except the clothes they stood in; they were forcibly led about half a mile, and then thrust into a Maori cook house; their feet were chained, and their hands tied with rope behind their backs; they were then left for forty one hours, during which time they were kept without food. They were finally rescued by the Natives who had been with them when they were captured, assisted by others and by Te Kooti.[23]

Main Trunk Line sod-turning ceremony at Puniu, near Te Awamutu.

Daniel Manders Beere, D.M. Beere Collection, Alexander Turnbull Library, PAColl-3081, G-96175-1/2

Hursthouse's work and that of their counterparts in Hawke's Bay revealed the impracticability of either coastal route. That left only the plateau west of Taupo. The North Island Main Trunk Railway Act of 1884 rubber-stamped the plan, and work began that year with the co-operation and blessing of Wahanui. There was a

small ceremony near Te Awamutu in April, though Hote Tamehana wanted it deferred on the basis that Tawhiao had not given his consent.[24] Stout told a crowd of 1500 that he need not 'point out the good that railways do'. That was not the function of this line; in truth it was a means of linking the diverse halves of the colony:

> He wished the natives to know that the ceremony had nothing to do with the title to the land, nor did it affect their chieftainship ... He wished to impress upon them the importance of attending to their health. If they wished to preserve their race they must preserve their health ... It was important that they should pay attention to their food, and stop taking alcohol.[25]

Tawhiao saw the line as a clear challenge to his independence, and he embarked on various strategies to assert himself, including issuing his own banknotes. It did no good. The Main Trunk inched south from Te Awamutu and north from Marton, hampered more by state penury than politics, bringing the trappings of Europe into the immediate hinterland. Labourers built villages along the way, installed their families, and traded with Maori. To-and-fro traffic bringing timber, steel, iron, supplies and equipment to the railhead reinforced the presence of the state. The railway reached Te Kuiti in 1887, and work began on the Waiteti viaduct south of the town the same year. Progress north from Marton was also good; by the same year, track had been laid 18.5 miles (30 km) north of Hunterville.

In many respects the trunk line was emblematic. Like many changes of the period, it happened whether Maori wanted it or not. Maori continued to decline numerically, settler society continued to expand and consolidate; government officials continued to exhort Maori to 'better' themselves. Yet in many respects the two worlds were separate and, tacitly, settler government preferred it that way. Expensive works such as the Main Trunk Line helped hem in the remaining centres of Maori life, breaking up territories that might otherwise have become strong-holds. However, this did not itself bring Maori into the settler fold. Maori lived mostly in rural settings, and even the ribbons of road and railway did not link all Maori communities with the wider world. When Maori turned up in town, it was often simply to trade. In the Urewera, Europe was barely visible, though sometimes keenly felt.

Maori were by no means quiescent, but responses were hampered partly by the dislocations of the settler period, including the emotional distress of repeated epidemics, and partly by a diffusion of effort. Maori framed responses to settler impact through traditional systems, often re-emphasising existing processes. One of the first was the runanga, known as the komiti (committee) to the missionaries, which established what one land purchase officer called 'petty courts' partly in an effort to limit the direct impact of settler goods and social systems on Maori. The system emerged in Waikato but became pan-tribal, evangelised around the North Island during the late 1850s. It was cautiously welcomed by settler authorities:

As Petty Courts they are really useful; for although the fines and punishments they inflict are generally excessive and, according to our ideas, quite disproportioned to the offences committed, they are always rigidly enforced; and the result has been that drunkenness, which had lately been increasing to a fearful extent among the Natives, has now almost disappeared...[26]

Gore-Browne at one stage toyed with promoting runanga as an opposition to the Kingitanga, but settler governments were generally ambivalent. While legislation such as Fox's Native Lands Bill of 1862 contained a provision authorising runanga to sort out land disputes, the legislation passed by the administration of Alfred Domett actually diminished the power of the runanga as arbiter.

Tensions were inevitable between tribalism and new unitarian movements such as the Kingitanga, the drive to promote Maori through parliamentary representation, or such strategies as the Repudiation Movement of the early 1870s. Other divisions also had effect, as in the Whanganui district where tribes were split between kupapa and Kingitanga. Although efforts by Maori to reassert their position were vigorous enough, total energies were diffused, and some strategies ended up associated with particular iwi. The parliamentary drive had been a largely Ngati Kahungunu response – though, itself, diffused to some extent with the competing Repudiation Movement – and Kingitanga became almost exclusively Tainui. Syncretic religions such as Pai Marire and Ringatu spread the focus yet further.

Other Maori social systems were transformed by cultural contact. As one historian notes, hui gained dimension as forums for discussion – notably to develop strategies for survival and reassertion. Although settler presence prohibited war as the final arbiter, Maori began using the land courts as a venue to air and

William Williams photographed this train at Te Aute, central Hawke's Bay, in 1887. Tender locomotives such as this J-class example were introduced during the 1880s to handle the longer routes being completed by this time. The motley array of carriages is noteworthy.

William Williams, Alexander Turnbull Library, PAColl-0975, G-25481-1/1

resolve grievances.[27] However, this had a down side. Long stays in towns were expensive and, as parliamentarian Robert Bruce declared in 1885, Maori were also exposed there to disease. Discovering that an epidemic had swept a group of Wanganui Maori after they had been in town for a land court hearing, he added what he called the 'demoralizing influences' of the 'lowest class of society' to the effects of European towns. Government could not, he declared, have devised a 'more ingenious method of destroying the whole of the Maori race'.[28]

Legislation associated with the land courts accelerated Maori dispossession. The system was established by act in 1865, ostensibly – as Sir Willam Martin remarked in 1871 – to give Maori 'safe and quiet possession of their lands, free to sell them or deal with them as they might think best, without disturbance or interference from their neighbours.'[29] But the act tried to translate communal holding into individual title by arbitrarily dividing the title between up to ten grantees. In theory they held it in trust for the rest of the tribe. In practice – as Justice C.W. Richmond put it in 1873 – the certificates provided 'each of the grantees with full property in one undivided tenth part of the block – his share becoming liable at once to be taken in execution for his private debts'.[30]

It was a national issue, but the hot-bed of such sales during the late 1860s was Hawke's Bay, where Napier merchant Frederick Sutton was publicly credited with inventing the 'system of grog accounts and mortgages by which the hapless and improvident natives are gradually but surely being divested of their estates'.[31] He was joined by Meeanee settler Richard Maney, among others,[32] and official concern soon followed. In 1867, one official warned J.C. Richmond that Maori had begun to sell land 'in every direction' in the face of unlimited credit with local merchants.[33] T.H. Haultain was more explicit, telling the House that 'unscrupulous

and dishonest persons' had 'encouraged [Maori] extravagance ... to get them into debt, have charged exorbitant prices for the goods they have supplied, and have taken advantage of their ignorance or intemperance to receive mortgage over the lands ... a sure preliminary to transfer on their own terms'.[34]

It became a national scandal and a general focus for Maori feeling across the country. The crisis broke when Thomas Tanner used the system to purchase Heretaunga, grant by grant, in 1868–69. The move was entwined in settler politics, and wild claims flew thick and fast as the scandal erupted. The Reverend Samuel Williams was said to have 'prostituted spiritual influence' to help Thomas Tanner make the deal.[35] John Ormond had supposedly used his political office as Provincial Superintendent and General Government Agent for Hawke's Bay to gain unfair advantage. When the whole affair was investigated by special commission in 1873, Justice C.W. Richmond noted that this latter allegation had 'no foundation whatever',[36] but claims that Tanner had illegally dealt with individual grantees were proven.[37]

The Commission did not, however, give Maori what they wanted; and from this emerged a dual effort by elements of Ngati Kahungunu to improve representation in parliament, and to 'repudiate' land deals. The Repudiation Movement spread from Hawke's Bay to Wanganui,[38] and became tied into settler politics at national level as Henry Russell used it to attack the Ormond-McLean faction. The battle cost him his fortune; and when his funds dried up in the late 1870s the Repudiationists also dwindled.[39] Elsewhere, Maori tried other strategies to retain their property.

New Zealand's only private railway emerged from the ruins of the state effort to build a line out of Wellington to the Manawatu. When the government effort stalled in the face of depression economics, local businessman John Plimmer rallied support and, with William Hort Levin and George Shannon as prominent shareholders, floated the Wellington and Manawatu Railway Company. The line to Longburn was opened in 1886, and the company continued operating until 1908, when it was taken over by the government. This is a W&MR train on the Thorndon gradient in 1892.

Photographer unknown, Alexander Turnbull Library, F-18847-1/2

During the late 1870s Land Court litigants in Wanganui tried — as resident magistrate Richard Woon put it — to '"tapu" several large tracts of country, and to forbid their being surveyed for lease or sale'.[40]

Officials realised Maori were selling land to buy consumables, but put it down to 'improvidence'.[41] In fact Maori were in an indifferent economic position, and this was made worse by the depression of the 1880s. To some extent Maori were insulated from the downturn, in that individuals in traditional society did not rely on paid employment to survive. Yet in other respects hapu and iwi were doubly hit. The steady whittling away of tribal holdings reduced access to traditional food sources. Meanwhile, three generations of European contact had created an economic reliance on European goods, including clothes, tools and industrial products. Rum, cognac and brandy also featured on some shopping lists. Although liquor was not consumed by Maori to anything like the extent imagined by temperance-obsessed settlers,[42] it was certainly used at times as a palliative for the pain felt across whole communities as their way of life crumbled.

At national level fortunes varied. Some did well — Pakowhai, near Napier, was a flourishing community. So was Parihaka, on the Taranaki coast. Some found seasonal work; Maori could be found around the country hiring themselves out as work gangs for the pastoralists, digging ditches or shearing. Elsewhere, however, Maori seemed resigned to their fate. By 1891, Maori comprised just ten percent of the population and held around 17 percent of the land — and that percentage continued to fall.

Sports and games

The 'rugby, racing and beer' tradition of New Zealand's twentieth-century culture was founded in the settler period and matured with the rest of society in the 1880s. Racing was always a genteel activity. Samuel Marsden reputedly brought the first horse into New Zealand as early as 1814. Racing – formal and informal – followed as settlement expanded from the 1830s. However, although local clubs were quickly formed, it was the 1880s before efforts were made to form a national organisation. The New Zealand Racing Conference emerged that decade, largely at the initiative of the Hawke's Bay Jockey Club. Racing was socially divided; many New Zealanders attended race meets, but the mechanisms were elite, notably the bloodstock industry.

Like many developments of the period, the arrival of organised sport at national level in the 1880s was a symptom of a maturing society. In New Zealand's first decades only the gentry and upper echelons of the respectables had time and money for more than casual weekend sporting events; the communications needed

Right above

Racing at Riccarton around 1900.

Photographer unknown, *The Press* Christchurch Collection, Alexander Turnbull Library, PAColl-3031, G-8259-1/1

Right below

Maori took a keen interest in horse racing from the earliest settler period. This 'Maori hack race in full costume' is by well-known settler artist C.D. Barraud.

Charles Decimus Barraud, Alexander Turnbull Library, B-080-031-2-2

Maori Hack Race in full Costume

to run sports at national level were non-existent. All that changed during the 1870s, and by the following decade mechanisms and opportunities to develop organised sport were present.

Rugby swiftly captured interest and imagination. The Nelson Football Club reputedly played New Zealand's first organised football game to rugby rules in 1870, at the behest of Charles John Monro. An inter-town match with Wellington followed. Other clubs began organising matches to the same rules during the next few years, and by the end of the 1880s rugby was a national sport with some 700 clubs and 16 unions. The first international game appears to have been played in 1884, when a New Zealand team crossed the Tasman. This began a tradition which, in the early period, culminated in a 1905 tour of Britain by a team generally known as the 'All Blacks'. We may speculate that the ruggedness of rugby matched that of colonial life in general, striking a chord with people for whom the frontier still loomed close.

Sports and games

Left above

The Reynolds family playing doubles, Christmas 1900.

Frank May Reynolds, Reynolds Album, Alexander Turnbull Library, PA-Coll-2772, F-55994-1/2

Left below

Singles tennis during the 1895 New Zealand Championships, Thorndon.

Photographer unknown, Making New Zealand Collection, Alexander Turnbull Library, F-978-1/2-MNZ

Below

Kathleen M. Nunnely, New Zealand Ladies Tennis Champion, serves in 1889.

Photographer unknown, Alexander Turnbull Library, C-8867-1/2

Sports and games

Sports and games

Above

George Mannering (left) and Marmaduke John Nixon tackle Tasman Glacier around 1895.

Photographer unknown, Alexander Turnbull Library, F-47541-1/2

Left above

H.A.T. Jackson, J. Alexander and A.S. Jackson with their penny farthings around 1889.

Photographer unknown, Alexander Turnbull Library, F-25544-1/2

Left centre

Lawn croquet, probably in the Wanganui region.

Frank J. Denton, Tesla Collection, Alexander Turnbull Library, PAColl-3046, G-17384-1/1

Left below

Swimming was a popular summer activity in New Zealand, again often organised on a club basis. The women in this 1899 picture are members of the Richmond Amateur Swimming Club.

W.E. Sorrell, Alexander Turnbull Library, F-29673-1/2

The road to God's Own

New Zealand's first organised political party emerged in the last decade of the nineteenth century. The Liberals and their policies were a reaction to depression need, and an overdue response to the growing complexity and urbanisation of the period. A new generation was in power, and colonial issues were supplanted by such matters as an ageing populace, urban growth, more developed economy and balanced demography – and with this the need to build roading networks and all the other appurtenances of Western society, including a bureaucracy. Any government would have had to tackle these issues by the 1890s; the Liberals, however, framed their responses around their own thinking. They were helped in part by an economy that prospered on the back of new commodities markets; the annual compound growth in potential GDP during the 1895–1912 period stood at 4.2 percent, up from the 2.6 percent of the depression years.[43]

Local Liberalism had a distinct New Zealand stamp. In Britain, the creed emerged as a political philosophy designed to leaven purist capitalism with a more socially responsible form of government. However, the New Zealand environment with its colonial legacy – including its ideals of security of income and property – was a different beast, and New Zealand Liberals also had to manoeuvre between free-market capitalism on one hand and socialism on the other. They neither totally rejected nor accepted either position, though doing so meant they were criticised both by conservative pastoralists and the radical left. Much was done with the aid of Labour support, a 'Lib-Lab' alliance that finally crumbled just before the First World War. In practice their land reform and cautious attitudes to social welfare were combined with new militarism and a resurgence of Victorian pro-Imperial sentiment. This contrasted with the same movement in Britain, where peace-hungry Liberals fought a guns-versus-butter battle with Conservatives.

John Ballance, self-confessed 'Fabian Socialist' and New Zealand's first Liberal Prime Minister, with his cabinet, 1891. Back row: Richard Seddon (Public Works), Alfred J. Cadman (Mines), John McKenzie (Lands), Joseph Ward (Postmaster-General), William Pember Reeves (Attorney-General). Front row: Sir Patrick Buckley (Attorney-General), John Ballance (Premier).

Photographer unknown, Alexander Turnbull Library, F-52824-1/2

Liberalism took time to reach New Zealand; George Grey set up a Liberal party in the 1870s, but it was the late 1880s before the movement gained the dimensions needed for government, fronted by such diverse figures as the burly West Coast publican Richard Seddon, left-leaning intellectual William Pember Reeves and self-professed 'Fabian Socialist' John Ballance. They were not a party in the twentieth-century sense – there was initially no apparatus, no organisation and little to unify members beyond the platform of reform.[44] Party feeling, it has been argued, did not emerge until after the Liberals were in power.[45] Nor were the Liberals initially very different from the oligarch-based opposition – then called the 'Opposition' – whose own views towards capitalism broadly matched those of the British Liberals. The point was not lost on voters. 'At the ensuing elections,' one *New Zealand Herald* editorial proclaimed in early October 1890, 'the vote will be taken between two sets of politicians, who can hardly be said to have separate political creeds.'[46] Ballance was identified with the Stout-Vogel camp, and Stout was widely expected to be invited to lead the government if the grouping won.[47]

In the event New Zealand went into the 1890s with a government under Ballance. Popular support came in part from disillusion; the old system had failed, governments during the 1880s had made the problems worse, and to this extent, the swing was a protest vote. However, a rising tide of radicalism also played a part. New lobby groups emerged in the 1880s, again a function of the depression, and all with their own methods for solving the crisis. The State Bank league blamed the imprudent lending of banks, calling for government loans at low rates to put the country back on its feet. Radical groups with impressive names such as Knights of Labour or the Trades and Labour Councils blamed labour laws. Others, such as the Anti-Poverty League, thought the oligarch stranglehold on land was the cause of New Zealand's problems. Although no single organisation was particularly large – the Knights apparently peaked at around 5000 members in the early 1890s – they were indicative of a diffuse groundswell of opinion. So it was not hard for the Liberals to find support, a point underlined by the sharp collapse of these radical groups in the 1890s after the Liberals began implementing policies proposed by the Knights in particular. Another factor, at a time when other Liberal policies seemed little different from those of the Atkinson and Stout-Vogel alliances, was the rise of class feeling among the labourers, itself an outcome of the depression, but also in part imported from overseas.

Industrial unrest provided the lever to project the Liberals into power. Strikes rippled through the country in 1890, starting in the Whitcombe and Tombs printing office and spreading to the railways, then the docks – this an import from Australia where there was similar action under way. Stout and Reeves championed the cause, but at a time of high unemployment the labour movement had little clout with employers or government, and the result was a swing to politics by radicalised workers, who threw their support behind the Liberals. This contrasted with the Australian experience where a Labour party emerged, and to this extent the New Zealand experience reflected expediency rather than ideology. Ballance

Right above

A bullock team in Wellington's
Cuba Street during the 1890s.

Photographer unknown, James Smith Ltd
Collection, Alexander Turnbull Library, F-29256-1/2

Right below

Steam meets the Rimutakas. The
best route from the Hutt Valley to
the Wairarapa left a 1-in-15
gradient on the Wairarapa side,
which was tackled with the three-
rail system invented by John Fell.
Half a dozen locomotives
equipped with Fell's powerful
centre-rail grip system hauled
trains up and down the 3.2-mile
(5.1-km) stretch for 60-odd years.
The line closed in 1955.

Burton Brothers, Alexander Turnbull
Library, C-6614-1/2

capitalised on strident calls for labour reform from the industrial sector during his election campaign.

Buoyed by working-class support, and espousing a platform of land reform, the Liberals came to power, and they came with radical ideas. Reeves for one had a Fabian agenda, but inevitably this was tempered by practicality, and the more radical notions could not be achieved overnight or even to their fullest extent — particularly as Atkinson was able to pack the upper house against the Liberals before he left office, frustrating early bills by the new government. The Colonial Office had to intervene to resolve the deadlock, and even then, it was 1892 before Reeves was made Minister of Labour, and 1894 before he could start some of his significant reforms.

Depression legacy produced other problems. There was a run on the Auckland Savings Bank in September 1893, prompting Seddon to issue a public statement designed to restore confidence.[48] It worked, but the government did not get away so cheaply the following year. The Bank of New Zealand had deposits double those of rival banks in 1878, and with this finance issued shares at a premium during the 1880s — adding £200,000 to its profits in the process, around $2.8 million in early twenty-first century money. This gave the bank confidence to make more advances, but their Australian operation suffered heavy losses in 1887 and the BNZ had to transfer £125,000 to cover it. By 1890, when the decision was made to move the bank to England, total losses included £349,000 on the calamitous sale of its international subsidiary Globo Assets, £54,000 on current business, and a further £28,000 on deals in Sydney. Law changes made redemption of notes and coin a first charge on assets, by which time the bank was in a critical situation. The Liberal administration reluctantly stepped in, backing the bank by £2 million — around $300 million in early twenty-first-century money — on a ten-year guarantee.[49]

The most significant development of the first Liberal term was unplanned — indeed, was not even on the agenda of the key Liberal leaders. Individual colonies and local governments had been giving women the vote for some years, but New Zealand was the first country to do so. The suffrage movement in New Zealand also got the vote in less than a decade, a pace that Reeves put down to an expedient alliance with temperance, and it has been argued that Sheppard and the other movers-and-shakers thought women might help tip the vote towards prohibition.[50] However, other historians have identified the suffrage movement itself as being the more decisive step behind women getting the vote.[51]

None of this really explains the shift. In some senses the movement simply reflected a trend towards greater democracy, itself a controversial process. All men were given the vote in 1887, which the *New Zealand Herald* condemned on the basis that it put 'power to pledge or to waste the property of the industrious portion of the community' into the hands of 'the idle and worthless'.[52] But giving all men

Kate Wilson Sheppard (1848–1934), first President of the National Council of Women.

Photographer unknown, Alexander Turnbull Library, C-9028-1/2

Women were heavily involved in cycling during the 1890s, not merely because of the exercise but as a means of social contact.

James McAllister, James McAllister Collection, Alexander Turnbull Library, PAColl-3054, G-12665-1/1

the vote was a difference of intensity, whereas extending it to women was a change in kind. One of the main forces at work was a broad change in the role of women, buoyed in part by the general radicalisation of the era. By the 1880s women in the Western world were moving away from the stereotype of the submissive and ennui-prone housewife, finding work in a variety of roles outside the home, getting involved in organised sport and physical activities – notably cycling – and becoming active as artists, poets and writers. In New Zealand, women found work as teachers, secretaries and clerks; rate-paying women could vote for local authorities and boards.

THE SUMMIT AT LAST.

Artist unknown, Alexander Turnbull
Library, PUBL-0126-1894-01

To this was added moral evangelism. This thinking emerged in the 1880s and eventually became a driving force behind a cycle of general social change that went on into the twentieth century. Where Victorian-era middle classes paid lip service to Calvinist self-denial in matters of vice, the moral evangelists – tiring of the double standard – demanded conformity. Restraint was the order of the day; public displays of affection were policed, farmers even forbidden to allow stock to breed within sight of public roadways. Plunket was founded within this moral framework, as was the Scout movement, imported to New Zealand near-complete from Britain. One of the main pillars of this new ethos was temperance, which refocused existing Calvinist teachings against alcohol. This had always been a theme in settler society. George Maunder, though unemployed, resisted the temptation to join his uncle's business in 1867. 'Of course I could not go into the liquor trade,' he wrote later to his sister.[53] However, the work gangs of the 1880s had other ideas and their excess prompted a backlash, often allied to renewed religious enthusiasms. Women became the main evangelists of alcoholic restraint, and the Women's Christian Temperance Union

Agitation to extend the franchise to women was grist to the mill for many cartoonists. This example was published in the *New Zealand Mail* of September 1893.

Artist unknown, Alexander Turnbull
Library, F-31495-1/2

(WCTU) also provided an organisational framework for the suffrage movement. The campaign was managed by Katherine Wilson Sheppard, who provided much of the national drive, and delegated local affairs to other prominent women such as Helen Nichol, Lily Kirk and Amey Daldy.[54]

The idea found fertile ground on both sides of parliament, in part as an extension of general support for electoral reform, but also because of genuine sentiment for the cause. Vogel in particular sympathised with women, comparing their treatment with that of the Jews, and introduced a Women's Suffrage Bill in 1887. However, there were also powerful voices against, spearheaded by the bullish Seddon, and the bill came crashing to a halt amid his condemnation of 'petticoat government'.[55] Atkinson won the election that year and proposed a new Electoral Bill for 1888, which did not include women's franchise, and the issue was not raised again until the supply debate of 1890, where the majority of the House came down in favour – against Seddon's objections. Again there was no legislative follow-up.[56] By this time there was a ground-swell of popular opinion; as Reeves' wife wrote, women were 'intensely anxious'[57] for the vote.

The problem was getting the shift past Seddon and his supporters. An Electoral Bill of 1891 made no provision for women, but Sir John Hall put up a Female Suffrage Bill, and the whole issue was debated again, still without result. Meanwhile Sheppard organised a petition of more than 30,000 signatures as part of a skilful campaign by the WCTU and Franchise Leagues to raise the stakes. The effort included personal visits, lobbying, public statements and attempts to woo the media. Women's suffrage was included in the Electoral Bill of 1892 but foundered on the machinations of party politics.

Onehunga women voting in the 1893 general election. Leading campaigner Elizabeth Yates was elected Mayor of Onehunga two months later.

Artist unknown, Making New Zealand Collection, Alexander Turnbull Library, F-2834-1/4

Country women lost no opportunity to vote in 1893; this is Dabinet and Young's store, the polling station at Tahakopa, Clutha.

Photographer unknown, Alexander Turnbull Library, McWhannell Collection, C-15837-1/2

Ballance came down against universal suffrage in early 1893; it was election year and he feared that newly enfranchised women would vote against the Liberals. Seddon became Premier that April when Ballance died; and although personally opposed, the portly West Coaster faced a majority opinion in favour. That year's Electoral Bill again included provision for women, which passed the lower house, but the upper was stacked with Seddonites, and this was where the real battle was fought. It was a clever tactic. As one newspaper put it, Seddon's group hoped to 'avoid the appearance of direct treachery ... while at the same time ... insuring that women shall not vote at the next election'.[58] Seddon argued that the 'political and social revolution' had not gone to referendum,[59] and some observers feared a 'great danger of the measure being wounded to death' as a result of his politicking.[60] However, Seddon's attempt to influence three wavering members backfired, and after coming to a knife-edge the bill was passed. It was 'hardly too much to say', one newspaper reported, 'that the enfranchisement of the women has been accomplished by her enemies'.[61] Six weeks remained before the election, barely time to organise registration. 'Female suffrage must be a reality and not a sham,' the *New Zealand Herald* declared, hoping that the vote might introduce a 'higher and better tone' in colonial government.[62]

Women were wooed by both parties, but it is unclear whether the narrow Liberal victory of 1893 can be attributed to their vote. The other main issue of the day was land reform, and there were swings in some areas for other reasons, as in Hastings where the safe seat of Opposition leader Sir William Russell was almost upset by a surprise swing to Thomas Tanner, who apparently put himself forward for revenge, after being bankrupted by the Northern Investment Company, which Russell part-owned.[63]

Greymouth cyclists around 1899.

Photographer unknown, West Coast Historical Society Collection, Alexander Turnbull Library, PAColl-5376, F-96569-1/2

Liberal policies gained momentum during their second term, including a sustained effort to build a new public service. Government offices had existed since 1840, but only the Railways Department grew to any scale, and more extensive general administration was becoming essential by the 1890s as New Zealand society shifted from a relatively small-scale frontier society to an established and urbanised world. The Liberals put their own stamp on the change; their reforms were also part of a general effort to dislodge the personality politics and patronage of the gentry. This had enabled officials such as Donald McLean to effectively impose their personal stamp on policy – and, in other cases, to feather their own nests. As late as 1885, Thomas Kirk had been made Conservator of Forests by Stout as a result of personal contact. Kirk was Stout's neighbour in Tinakori Road and drew his water from Stout's well.

Edward Tregear led the Liberal drive to build the public service, and in line with the 'conservative radicalism' of their approach, policy was based on Royal Commission findings from 1866 and 1880 – with a Liberal spin. To keep the senior public servants in line, Seddon insisted that any salaries of more than £200, around $35,000 in early twenty-first-century money, should come under parliamentary control. Twelve departments were eventually formed, though the old school did not go down without a fight; nor was the new bureaucracy widely welcomed. 'Our first duty is to ourselves,' one cartoonist captioned a picture of new civil servants.[64] Another portrayed the new approach as a spider's web of 'red tape' in which the vulnerable 'Zealandia' had been entwined. The service itself was still not entirely without irregularity; Seddon himself was accused of 'jobbery'. There was an attempt to introduce a Public Service Bill in 1904, reorganising the service, and many of Seddon's personal appointments had to be regularised post-fact in 1907.

These were not the only issues. The old settler system of private enterprise and oligarch-dominated local bodies had left many urban centres without sewerage systems and, in some cases, lacking proper water supplies. Even when local authorities agreed to build waste-disposal systems, the cost was often prohibitive. On top of this there was no organised hospital system. It was a national issue, and as the towns grew during the late nineteenth century the problems of disease grew with them. The situation came to a head in 1900 when bubonic plague appeared in Auckland. Although New Zealand suffered only one case, government responded first with a Bubonic Plague Prevention Act, then a general Health Act that created a new government department and provided officials with authority to deal with sanitary problems and disease, including tuberculosis. Later, in 1909, the department took over the hospitals, a move that paid off four years later when smallpox broke out – and paid dividends again during the influenza outbreak of 1918.

Other reforms reflected a new compact between labour and employers. This was essentially Reeves' initiative, though he had a good deal of difficulty getting his ideas across. His views were on the left, and much of his legislation in 1891 and even 1892 fell victim to the Atkinson-stacked Upper House. It was not until Seddon was in the Premier's chair in 1894 that Reeves made headway; that year, six of his

'Undesirable Bill' – William Pember Reeves (1857–1932), politician, historian and sometime poet. Further left-leaning than his peers – to the point where he called his son Fabian – he introduced compulsory arbitration as part of a raft of industrial reforms in the 1890s. However, the tide of radicalism receded, and he left politics in 1896 to become Agent-General in London. His historical works included *The Long White Cloud* (1898) and *State Experiments in Australia and New Zealand* (1912).

A. Vyvian Hunt, Alexander Turnbull Library, A-122-001

bills were passed through the House, including his key industrial reforms. This Conciliation and Arbitration Act was designed to prod unions into existence, but cut back strikes by forcing compulsory arbitration. No other country had introduced such legislation; although outcomes included the industrial unrest of 1912–13, it essentially established a half-century compact between union and employer.

The following year, fearing that Asian migrants might create a pool of cheap labour and undercut his industrial policies, Reeves tried to have an Undesirable Immigrants Bill passed. The effort failed, and Reeves ended up with the nickname 'Undesirable Bill' as a consequence. Worse, the initiative put him offside with Seddon, who now considered Reeves too radical – and intellectual – to be of use. In early 1896, the Premier packed his Fabian-influenced minister off to become Agent-General in London.

The other Liberal innovation was a rudimentary welfare state. This initially focused around an old-age pension, which Seddon introduced from 1898, meeting a need that was a legacy both of the depression and of an ageing settler society. Many early settlers were approaching retirement age by the 1890s, and while some were able to support themselves, others were not. Destitution was the likely outcome, and in any event Reeves was determined to prevent the 'social evils' of the work-house. In this he was less left-leaning than pro-colonial; it was to escape precisely this fate that many settlers had arrived in the first place. However, there was heavy opposition. Government took four years to implement the pension scheme, and it was finally offered under socially driven criteria designed to restrict it to the so-called 'deserving poor'. Other moves were equally cautious. In 1905 the government initiated the first state housing scheme, limited to Petone. A widow's pension followed in 1908, but here the Liberals, as Michael Joseph Savage later put it, 'left off'.[65]

Bursting the estates?

Perhaps the greatest shift of the Liberal period was their drive to 'burst' the estates. Their crusade against the gentry, which was also waged at government level in the effort to regularise the state services, has usually been seen as the cause of profound social and economic change. The idea came from the 'Fabian socialist' Ballance, and was put into action by John 'Honest Jock' McKenzie, Minister of Lands from 1891. It was one of the few Liberal policy planks to make much progress during their first term. The conclusion has inevitably followed that the Liberals brought down the oligarchs – indeed, one historian even suggested that gentry political rule was 'done' after the Liberal victory in 1890.[66]

This is one of the great shibboleths of New Zealand history. Estate-bursting was promoted as a radical effort to cut the gentry monopoly on pastoral land and open up possibilities for small-holders. But it is untrue to say that the gentry were broken – either financially or in terms of their holdings – during the Liberal period. Politically they were far from a spent force in the 1890s. We also have to

separate declared aims from the policies as implemented. Ballance – a self-professed 'Fabian socialist' inspired by J.S. Mill – envisioned a nation of small landowners. In this he was perhaps the most radical of his peers, but his ideas caught on. Seddon, visiting Walter Shrimpton at Matipiro Station during the 1890s, warned that if Shrimpton did not reduce his holdings, Seddon would do it for him. Aspects of the policy that followed were guided, to some extent, by Reeves' plan to provide perpetual leasehold, allowing small-holders to put all their capital into improvements. These plans were met with horror by the oligarchs; the *Hawke's Bay Herald* – one of several ultra-conservative organs of the gentry – condemned plans for closer settlement and argued that there was no justification for considering landowners 'social pests'.[67]

In practice, however, the Ballance-Reeves-McKenzie triumvirate had to back off from their more radical ideas.[68] Liberal reforms, as implemented, actually extended

William James Mudie Larnach (1833–98), wealthy Dunedin businessman and politician best remembered for his eccentric and fabulously expensive home outside the town, dubbed Larnach's Castle.

many of the policies that governments had been trying to apply since the 1840s, this time adding a financial incentive. All land with unimproved value of more than £500 was taxed at 1 pence in the pound. On top of this Ballance imposed a graduated tax of one-eighth pence in the pound, rising to 2 pence in the pound for land valued at more than £5000. A few estates were actually burst. Cheviot, with 84,000 acres and 110,000 livestock, was exploded into 150 small farms in 1893.[69] Fourteen South Island estates followed by compulsion. In Hawke's Bay – still a pastoral stronghold – 28 were broken by 1912. The main targets were absentee landowners, who were hammered with a further flat 20 percent tax,[70] and those who refused to pay were subject to forced purchase.[71] The national test case came in the mid-1890s. Purvis Russell, a central Hawke's Bay landowner, had moved to Scotland in 1873, and in 1896 the government informed him that his station would be purchased at 'land tax' value. Russell objected, and through prolonged legal battle, postponed the sale until 1900, when he received £21,000 over the tax valuation. Even then he offered £60,000 to retain the land – a tenth of his assets and about $8.5 million in early twenty-first-century money.[72] The station was divided into 57 farms in 1901.

All this created a good deal of high-profile ill feeling, but appearances were deceptive. In 1891 there were 43,777 landholders with more than an acre, of whom a quarter had holdings of between one and ten acres, 584 had more than 5000 acres, and of these, 24 had more than 50,000 acres. Just seven had more than 100,000 acres.[73] This upper end did not fall significantly – there were 112 holdings of more than 50,000 acres in 1896, and in 1911, after 20-odd years of Liberal 'bursting', there were still 90. The average run size at this level dropped by less than a tenth of a percent and still stood at 90,319 acres.[74] The number of holdings of between 5000 and 50,000 acres actually rose from 732 to 926 over the same period.[75]

Members of the Scandinavian community party at the Lowry Bay home of honorary Danish consul Sir Francis Bell, 25 April 1897.

These figures can be boiled down to a single statistic: in 1896, 2 percent of landholders held slightly over 20.7 million of New Zealand's 33.3 million acres of available pastoral land. By 1911 — the last year these statistics were collected — the same 2 percent held just over 19.5 million acres, out of a total national land-holding that had risen to just over 40.2 million acres.[76] Gentry land had dropped from around 62 to 49 percent of the total, absolute holdings had dropped by only 5 percent, and this was hardly sufficient to crumble the land monopolists. Land freed up by 'bursting' amounted to 1.3 million acres.[77] The point is made explicit from the viewpoint of land tax revenue. In a regime that penalised large-holders, the tax take stood at £272,000 in 1896. It rose to £295,000 in 1901, and by 1913 was up to £728,000.[78]

In practice, gentry land was reshuffled rather than diminished. The experience of Tutira station owner Herbert Guthrie-Smith was typical. Alarmed that a Royal Commission had been appointed to investigate tenure of Hawke's Bay properties, he placed his affairs 'unreservedly' in the hands of the Commissioners and resigned the lease on the western half of Tutira station. He was allowed to keep 18,000 acres at quadrupled rent, and the visit ended when the 'Royal Commission, not snatched up to heaven in a chariot of fire as the assembled natives almost seemed to anticipate, proceeded in a cloud of dust on its way to Wairoa'.[79] But in 1905 he was able to lease part of a block north of Te Pohue.[80] Nor were Liberal policies the sole reason for selling. Division of a property between elderly owner and adult children was also a way of getting around death duties, and in some cases landowners wanted to cater for multiple offspring. John Chambers, for example, divided his own estate into sections for his three sons.

The Lowry Bay Yacht Club, picnic, 25 January 1891.

Frederick Halse, Alexander Turnbull Library, PAColl-3041, G-10361-1/2

This process of reshuffling also explains how the number of small-holders effectively doubled. The people who gained were principally small farmers and herd-owners; Liberal policies had less effect on agriculturalists — land under close cultivation went up from 8,893,225 acres in 1891 to 10,698,809 just four years later.[81] The leasehold quick-shuffle was aided by the fact that total settler land-holding expanded, particularly in the North Island. A few runs were broken up amid much publicity and high-profile complaint but, in general, this new land made it possible both for pastoralists to broadly hold their own and for small-holders to expand. The new territories came mainly from a Liberal effort to reduce Maori holdings. Between 1891 and 1911 government purchased 3.1 million acres of Maori land in the North Island, on average at just over six shillings an acre.[82] Small-holding in Taranaki, particularly, was markedly accelerated.[83] Maori tried to resist; James Carroll as Native Minister implemented policies designed to at least slow the sales. However, as we have seen, Maori efforts to maintain their position through these years were disorganised.[84]

Gentry lifestyle during the Liberal years makes clear they were far from a failing breed financially. Rising wool prices after 1895 were coupled with rising yields — more than double per fleece than 30 years earlier.[85] Personal profit rather than inability to pay the land taxes seems to have been the key motive to sell their land. In Hawke's Bay, for instance, J.R.B. A'Deane sold portions of Ashcott, which was valued at £2.16.0 per acre in 1902, for £5 to £15 per acre in 1906. Other pastoralists who leaped on the profit-wagon included E.J. Watt, who sold Tukituki and Longlands stations, and Douglas MacLean, who cut 38,000 acres of Marae-kakaho up for closer settlement.[86]

Lucrative returns helped restore gentry fortunes after a decade of indifference, and most of the elite had cash. C.G. Tripp of Orari Gorge station spent some £4700 on luxuries in 1892 alone.[87] Almost without exception, the gentry took swift advantage of their good fortune. New houses were the order of the day; great mansions rose, some adjacent to the older houses, others in new and wide grounds, such as the 'large and handsome villa residence' built by Blackhead settler Alexander McHardy in 1894.[88] Many spent vast sums on architect-designed structures, including the 35-room mansion Heaton Rhodes gave his wife in 1895.[89] Allan McLean outdid most with a 54-room town house in Christchurch.[90]

New inventions offered another way to spend the lucre in which the gentry were rolling by the 1890s. They vied to buy gramophones, telephones — initially by private line — and anything else that could be run with electricity. The younger John Chambers led the way, installing a private hydro station in 1892.[91] By the turn of the century the wonder-fluid of the age had been widely adopted by those who could afford it, and pastoralists competed to install electric lights, ranges, toasters and refrigerators. Even electric vacuum cleaners were on the shopping list. As the first years of the twentieth century rolled on the gentry replaced their landaus and broughams with motor cars. No expense was spared; Mason Chambers' Meisse steam car, for instance, topped £450 — around $60,000 in early twenty-first-century money.[92] Running costs on these high-maintenance devices were stupendous until garages became widespread. Cars nonetheless became a focus for new rivalry, and the most powerful in the country for some time was a 24-horsepower Wolseley imported by G.P. Donnelly. New technology did not change the behaviour of coaching days:

> Bill Robin was the chauffeur bedecked in uniform and engineer's cap. You can imagine the scene with all aboard. G.P. in the front seat giving Bill Robin instructions (horn! horn!), Princess Irene in one bucket seat at the back and Maud Perry (her daughter) in the other both wrapped in fur coats, the dicky seats seating Iraia Karauria and others.[93]

This British behemoth was apparently capable of 60 mph (100 km/h) — a frightening velocity in an era of rutted shingle roads and pencil-thin tyres. Other pastoralists bought Continental: Edward Mallaby-Goodwin wowed Ashburton residents with a Benz, while Walter MacFarlane of Amuri preferred a De Dion.[94]

When not belting around in fast cars, the gentry partied — often in public. There was fresh media attention to the new social whirl of the 1890s and beyond, as in December 1892 when the *Hawke's Bay Herald* covered a bash held by the McHardys of Blackhead, whose 100 guests were trucked in by the carriage-load to their remote east coast property.[95] In March 1897, Donnelly hired Napier's Gaiety Theatre and invited 250 guests to a ball marking his daughter's birthday. The 'many tasteful dresses flashing their varied tints' was 'brilliant in the extreme', according to the local paper.[96] There were also 'at homes', as in 1910 when the Theomins of

Left

Gramophones were swiftly acquired by the gentry, a decade or more in advance of their poorer brethren. Record shops did not take long to emerge; this picture was apparently taken around 1910.

Photographer unknown, *Evening Post* Collection, Alexander Turnbull Library, F43062-1/2

Below

New Zealand lacked foxes, but hunting was soon modified to match the colonial environment.

James McAllister, James McAllister Collection, Alexander Turnbull Library, PAColl-3054, G-9933-1/1

Dunedin gave a soiree at their town house, the Royal Terrace.[97] Even then, public attention was never far away, and the prospect of gentlemen embarking on a 'series of romps' was frowned upon in some media circles.[98]

The gentry, in short, were doing well. But, holding their financial position was a different matter from surviving wider social change. By the turn of the twentieth century, the settler political world was giving way to one of boards, government bureaucracy and local bodies. This was partly a function of the government reforms of the day, partly the influx of more small-holders with different social ideas, but also an outcome of the increasing scale, maturity and complexity of society. Settler society had been complex in its own way, but the one that emerged in the 1890s took different directions. This ran against the gentry – and it was this, not the land tax, that diminished their social influence, and this, not the changes in land-holding, to which the gentry actually objected.

This explains why the best-organised responses to the change did not coalesce until nearly two decades after the land taxes had been imposed. The loudest protest emerged in 1910, when the younger John Chambers declared that he and fellow pastoralists had 'special duties' that 'included the guiding of public opinions'.[99] Not one to pontificate, he floated a company and got to work. His ideas were based around Herbert Spencer's principles of human competition and freedom from government interference with private property rights. His initial platform was based around the land reforms. Early settlers, Chambers argued, had taken up land 'in the hope and belief that they would be able to hand on the fruits of their labour to their children'. The number who had survived to 1911 'can probably be counted on one's fingers'.[100] He continued:

The compulsory taking of land from one owner, and handing it over to several others, cannot be excused on the plea of public requirements ... and what security has a landowner, or for that matter any property-owner? ... Non land-owners ... appear to have no conception of the sentimental value attached to land long occupied, and on which much labour has been expended ... and are all too ready to value everything in terms of gold, or market value...[101]

Tourism became popular as the twentieth century dawned, sometimes bringing settlers into contact with Maori at a time when contact between the two peoples was rare. This is a travelling party at Te Whati in November 1907. Kathleen Beauchamp stands second from left at the back.

Photographer unknown, Alexander Turnbull Library, F-2584-1/2

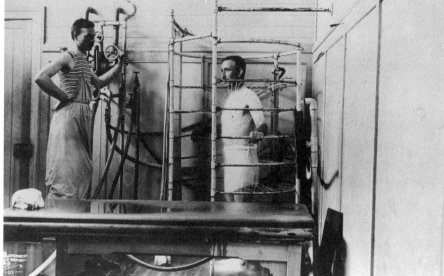

Left above

Steamers and pleasure boats on Lake Wakitipu, April 1910. Walter Peak rises in the background.

Photographer unknown, Alexander Turnbull Library, C-2408-1/2

Left centre

This gentleman 'takes the waters' in Rotorua's Aix Spa around 1903.

Photographer unknown, Alexander Turnbull Library, Tourist Department Album 11, PA1-0-503-7

Left below

A group at Hamurana Springs, Rotorua, on Boxing Day, 1912.

R.G. Marsh, Alexander Turnbull Library, PAColl-3405, F-77256-1/2

West Coasters on an outing near Greymouth around the turn of the twentieth century.

But land was only the beginning; Chambers attacked socialism and free education, recommending private enterprise in local body affairs and concluding that 'wise laws must be consistent with natural law, and with each other...'[102] These were all symptoms of the Liberal period; and he put his money where his mouth was. The group bought and shut down the loudest Liberal voice in the district, the *Hastings Standard*. This was amalgamated into a new conservative newspaper, the *Herald Tribune*. It was a gallant, determined effort by men who had the wealth and political motive to see their case through. But it was to no avail. New Zealand was moving on; the age of 'great men' was passing. The Liberals took the flak, but in a more general sense what was happening was deeper and wider.

Against this changing society the oligarchs changed but did not disappear. Some, such as John Ormond, shifted gears and continued a prominent career with local bodies.[103] He did not even contest the Liberals, pulling out of the parliamentary race in 1890 to the dismay of many observers. 'Mr Ormond belongs to the class of men who are most needed in Parliament,' one newspaper opined. 'If men of his social position ... informed by personal experience of the political history of the colony, will abandon public life at the moment when a state of transition is becoming apparent, it is not difficult to understand the process by which Parliament has deteriorated.'[104] Others, such as William Rolleston and William Reeves, remained important figures in national politics. While, as one historian put it, the gentry and their lifestyle had become 'but one form of rural society' by 1914,[105] they left an enduring core of 'old money' that sat uneasily with the myth of a New Zealand society of financial equals.

Frozen economics

> The London market rules the world, and the great distance of New Zealand from
> this vast city renders it difficult ... to compete with other countries lying closer to
> the British Isles...
> — Editorial, *New Zealand Herald*, 4 November 1890[106]

The economic problems that had caused so much misery during the 1880s were an outcome of the booster period, which provided mechanisms for a few to make a fortune, but had not given the country a basis on which to grow. Once gold, gum, fungus and timber had been exploited there was nothing much to sell beyond wool, and wool markets were depressed by the 1880s. In practice, Vogel's infrastructure was only half the calculation. The country also needed viable export products beyond wool.

The obvious additions were meat and butter, both under active investigation by the 1870s. Enthusiastic pastoralists spent years looking into ways of getting mutton to the lucrative London markets without resorting to salting. Pioneer settler and engineer John Chambers (1819–93) was one of the most active in the field.[107] His early experiments with 'warm' preservation – packing the meat with oats and straw – were unsuccessful. In 1879 Chambers and other Hawke's Bay pastoralists set up a large-scale boiling-down works. But he really wanted to export the meat itself, and perhaps inspired by news that frozen meat had been shipped from Buenos Aires to France that year, developed a blast-freezing technique which he attempted to patent.[108] The cost of freezing by the Chambers method was thought to be about a quarter that of rival systems, but the patent office turned him down because he neglected to submit a specification.[109]

Bluff freezing works.

Photographer unknown, Alexander Turnbull Library,
PAColl-0095, F-91861-1/2

In the end Chambers was beaten to the punch by his South Island rivals. The first cargo of frozen mutton left Otago on board the sailing ship *Dunedin* in 1882, fitted with Bell and Coleman refrigerators. Nobody knew whether the cargo would get through the tropics without thawing, but it reached England in good order after a 98-day voyage.[110] Chambers lost no time founding the Hawke's Bay Freezing Company in October that year. The company had a paid-up capital of £30,000, but the buildings took some years to complete, and the company ran second to the massive enterprise of William Nelson.[111]

Nelson dominated the early industry. He was already active in the field in the early 1880s, and the advent of refrigeration offered opportunity to establish a London-based company on 'a large capital', enough to fund a factory outside Hastings to process and freeze 400, later 800, carcases a day. This was unprecedented, and Nelson 'was subjected to a good deal of quiet chaff' for assuming he could get a regular supply of sheep.[112] The first carcases were frozen in February 1884, and

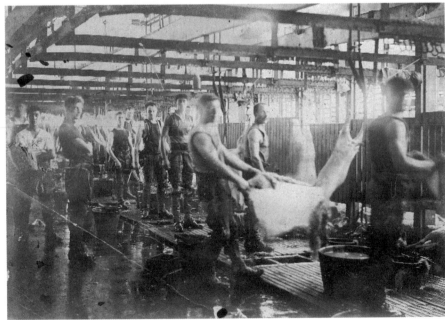

at the end of March around 9000 were loaded on to the *Turakina* in Napier harbour. The refrigerator ship was a novelty — visitors played with snowballs on the deck — and many others reached New Zealand ports over the next few years. During the 1884 season Nelson's works shifted 41,000 sheep and 10 bullocks. In 1891 the capacity was increased sixfold. For Nelson this was a licence to print money, but he lost no opportunity to reduce costs — one coup was wooing the Tyser Line to carry his produce, cutting freight costs from one and a quarter pence per pound to five-eighths pence.[113]

Those with less means pursued dairy products. The introduction of mechanical separators during the 1880s made industrial-scale butter production possible. The push to improve this machinery continued for decades,[114] and the rise of Taranaki can be traced to these developments. Production revolved initially around small co-operative factories, relatively numerous and small-scale because the raw material could not be transported far in carts. Amalgamations followed as transport improved.[115] The thick bush covering much of the district was burned off in a brief orgy of settler arson, opening it up for conversion to dairy farms. Settlements pushed west of Egmont, driving north from Hawera to New Plymouth, often at the expense of Maori reserves.[116]

Managers and staff of the Wellington-based Union Steamship Company, founded in 1875 as an amalgamation of several earlier organisations. It was bought by the Peninsula and Oriental Steam Ship Company in 1917, but retained its original name.

Photographer unknown, Alexander Turnbull Library, F-60016-1/2

These industries helped underpin New Zealand's twentieth-century economy, but were not an instant panacea, nor did they increase the importance of Britain as an export destination. That transition had already taken place in the 1870s, earlier if gold is excluded. Around four-fifths of New Zealand's exports were directly sold on British markets as early as 1876,[117] and part of the reason why New Zealand mutton, lamb, beef, cheese and butter found a market in the 1880s was the existing contacts created by wool, gum, flax and gold sales. Even so, the new

Above

Devon Street, New Plymouth, around the turn of the twentieth century.

William Collis, Alexander Turnbull Library, PAColl-3032, G-6473-1/1

Right

New Plymouth Harbour in 1895. Sail had almost wholly given way to steam by this stage. Lines across the wharf reveal the role of railway in handling New Zealand's burgeoning export trade.

William Collis, Alexander Turnbull Library, PAColl-3032, G-6531-1/1

products were not an overnight sensation, as an editorial in the *New Zealand Herald* lamented as late as 1890. Distance, competition from other suppliers, and the 'uncertainty of its distribution' in England discouraged New Zealand farmers from freezing all their eggs into one basket.[118]

Part of the problem was that British tastes changed relatively slowly, and as late as 1896, meat, butter and cheese exports together still provided only 17 percent of New Zealand's total. Wool held the lion's share at 47 percent.[119] Percentages of total exports sold to Britain also declined during the 1890s and did not trend back to the 80 percent figure until 1913.[120] This appears – at last – to have reflected the rise of frozen produce on the London markets. Meat and dairy products provided 34 percent of New Zealand's exports and wool alone was down to 35 percent.[121] However, the key shift did not come until the First World War. Britain commandeered New Zealand produce from 1915, and by 1919 more than 91 percent of New Zealand's exports were going to Britain, of which more than 90 percent were wool, meat and dairy products. Afterwards, although the commandeer ended, the percentage of New Zealand pastoral products sold on British markets continued to climb, trending to nearly 95 percent of New Zealand's total exports during the mid-1920s. Wool and butter dominated sales,[122] and absolute volumes matched the trend, albeit shaped by the downturn of the 1920s.[123]

Offloading coal on the Wellington wharves around 1908, a grubby job at the best of times. Locomotive coal was imported, and it was not until war exigencies restricted imports that New Zealand Railways was forced to use local grades previously considered unsuitable for the purpose.

S.C. Smith, Alexander Turnbull Library, PAColl-3082, G-20028-1/1

The picture is clear. Britons were not eager for New Zealand meat and dairy during the 1890s, began cautiously adopting them during the first years of the twentieth century – and then, when war came, got them by direction. This happened when British society was suffering the trauma of the most lethal war in history. Tastes were moulded by the New Zealand food products that arrived every day on British tables, coupled with a moral impact. New Zealand food, however odd it was to pre-war tastes, appeared reliably and consistently, replaced similar products from Europe and the Americas, and did so at a time when the world appeared to have gone mad. New Zealand, whose pre-war contributions to Britain had included the outright gift of one of the world's larger warships, could be relied upon in these uncertain times.[124] In effect the First World War became the mechanism by which New Zealand products, particularly butter, were fully introduced to and accepted by Britain – a point that highlights the role that conflict played in shaping New Zealand's twentieth century.

The dark side of unease

New Zealand's character in the two decades leading up to the First World War can best be described as troubled. A new generation of settlers, whose hopes had been cast adrift by the failure of their parents' utopian dreams, struggled with their national image. One outcome was a social inferiority complex, the 'cultural cringe' with its unspoken assumption that anything done locally was, by definition, inferior to the overseas equivalent. This was matched with a 'try hard' ethos, in which New Zealand policy-makers sought to compensate by taking up 'superior' foreign ideals with great zeal. At a personal level, the same national mind-set produced the related ethos of personal overachievement and its flip side, the 'tall poppy' syndrome. All these stood in some tension with each other, and were underpinned by a transfer of patriotic affection to Britain – itself symptomatic of the 'cringe', though also founded in wider colonial factors. Although not the sole characteristics of New Zealand society, this complex array of behaviours and the factors that drove them answer many questions about the general character of twentieth-century New Zealand.

There were benefits. An ethos that demanded compensation for perceived national inferiority helped create an environment in which some people could make genuinely world-beating contributions to their fields. Again, this was not the only factor – there was genuine personal talent, and an explanation for its apparent concentration in New Zealand can also be found in the frontier ethos, the

Auckland's Hobson Street around 1900, from the spire of St Matthew's, looking towards the Cook Street intersection. St James Presbyterian church and spire are visible right of centre.

Photographer unknown, Alexander Turnbull Library, G-2807-1/2

environment that demanded capability simply in order to survive. However, while the cringe helped promote an environment in which people were encouraged and expected to achieve, it also led to assumption that anything done locally was inferior by definition. The only way to circumvent the problem for much of the twentieth century was to achieve overseas — a 'rite of passage' that purchased acceptance back home for talented New Zealand scientists, literati, musicians, military leaders and doctors.

At a general level, the cringe and its various flip sides produced results that have been compared to the phenomenon of the overenthusiastic novice, openly admired as a try-hard but privately ridiculed for naivety. In the 1890s this fed back into attitudes to Empire, driving the idea that New Zealand was the most enthusiastic of Britain's children, 'chief junior' in the wider Empire — an ethos that survived at least until the Second World War. One of the earliest official-level examples of this thinking remains the Seddon government's efforts to obtain a Pacific empire on behalf of Britain, irrespective of Imperial politics.[125] If we accept the arguments of some historians, this mind-set even helped fuel the late twentieth-century notion that New Zealand was a backward ex-colony which demanded radical reform in order to catch up with the real world.[126]

While the cringe, the transfer of nationalist affection to Britain and associated phenomena were not the only arbiters of New Zealand society, they deserve explanation. There has been suggestion that one engine driving New Zealand to Britain was the 'protein industry' that emerged in the late nineteenth century, in which New Zealand domestic industries were effectively run as an extension of metropolitan Britain.[127] However, as we have seen, 'protein' was not a significant economic factor until the First World War, and to this extent, the meat and dairy connections were the sustainer motors, not the starter or booster. In any event, emotions towards Britain were entwined with the wider issues of cringe, tall poppy and national try-hard, all of which flourished for nigh on a century from the 1890s.

The mind-set that generated them had roots in settler ambition and the way in which ideology, greed and event conspired to collapse the ideal of a better Britain. The dream finally staggered to a halt amid the depression of the 1880s, giving a rising generation of settlers pause to think. New Zealand was emerging by this time as an entity rather than a cluster of tiny competing provinces; in the minds of its inhabitants, though, it was not a very good entity, and the rectitude with which successive administrations of the 1880s tried to restore prosperity was perceived by some as punishment for that failure. This also came just as a new generation grew to adulthood, itself a decisive shift. They brought new ideas and a new focus of identity, but amid the sense of failure they looked beyond New Zealand for inspiration. They did not have to look far. Most of the movers-and-shakers of the 1890s had been born in New Zealand — or Australia — and knew Britain only as an ideal, a romanticised home spoken of with the rosy tones of distance by their parents. In the face of the failure of New Zealand to surpass Britain, many turned

'For God's Own Country'. Richard John Seddon (1845–1906), former gold miner, West Coast publican and — by the time this picture was taken — Liberal Premier of New Zealand, wheels away the first sods of the Lawrence–Roxburgh railway. His personal motto seems to have been added later — the term oft left his lips and entered common usage. Much of New Zealand's 'jingo' character emerged during 'King Dick's' 13-year reign as Premier.

Photographer unknown, Alexander Turnbull Library, F-58363-1/2

to that idealised Britain for inspiration. To this mix was added a third factor — new defence thinking, driven by the growing sense of a national New Zealand that emerged as a general outcome of the end of the New Zealand wars, Vogel's deliberate efforts to unify, and the overall growth and ageing of society.

Defence was the catalyst that turned this cluster of concepts into reality. Academic work has shown how fears of foreign invasion from the 1870s onwards crystallised both popular and government thinking towards the notion that New Zealand was a small, vulnerable and lone outpost of Empire. At a time of ongoing economic stringency, when New Zealand had a clear place within the Empire, policy-makers and public alike inevitably looked to Britain for assistance.[128] This came just when military force was supplanting economic power as a measure of strength, drawing defence issues into a complex emotional pattern founded in pre-existing ties to Britain.[129] The results reinforced both the sense of inferiority that followed the failure to become a 'better Britain', and the general mind-set that looked to England for inspiration and leadership. All this was further accelerated by the rise of jingoism, an Empire-wide style of thinking that emerged during the latter decades of the nineteenth century, taking its name from a nonsense term used by G.W. Hunt in a popular music hall song.

Jingoism glorified war, refocused nationalist sentiment at an Imperial level, and popularly redefined Imperial strength around the size and quantity of British military hardware. It was the antithesis of the 'politically correct' ideals of a century later, but similar in that it prescribed a narrow range of acceptable

The last Central Otago gold escort changes horses at Roxburgh, 1901.

J.H. Ingley, Making New Zealand Collection, Alexander Turnbull Library, F-1736-1/2-MNZ

thoughts and behaviour. Jingoism also provided an underlying framework for many of New Zealand's twentieth-century ideals, and its militarist aspects reflected the fact that Britain had last been at war with a European power in 1856. Society had forgotten the realities of the battlefield, and at personal level the jingoes drew on public school traditions of sports-field glory – themselves a metaphor – to emphasise death-defying deeds in battle as a device for social elevation, possibly posthumously. 'Who would not die for England!' poet Alfred Austin wrote, '...Stern to every voice but Hers...'[130]

Social militarism was all the rage across the Empire by this time. The British organised their boys into Brigades, while the Reverend William Booth's Salvationists called themselves an Army.[131] Soon there were Boys' Brigades in New Zealand, and Booth established an 'outpost' of his army in New Zealand during the early 1880s at the behest of Arabella Valpy, drawing wide support and publishing their newsletter, *War Cry*, from their Dunedin base. There were popular songs and musicals about soldiers, one of the best-known lampooning Garnet Wolseley, the 'very model of a modern Major-General'. Naval officers were lauded like twentieth-century pop stars; and when former Australasian Station commander Rear-Admiral Sir George Tryon went down with the *Victoria* off Tripoli in 1893, New Zealand's Parliament paused in respect. Children were often dressed as soldiers or sailors. Composers devised martial tunes, epitomised by the trumpet marches of John Philip Sousa – whose 1911 tour of New Zealand attracted huge attention – or the military-orchestral tone poems of Edward Elgar.

Even country home-owners subscribed to the fenced section with vegetable patch; this impressive example dates to 1905.

James McAllister, James McAllister Collection, Alexander Turnbull Library, PAColl-3054, G-9841-1/1

New Zealand's version of jingoism was particularly intense, as evidenced by the eagerness with which government and people welcomed an opportunity to contribute to Queen Victoria's last 'little war', the struggle that broke out between Britain and Transvaal, along with its ally the Orange Free State, in 1899.[132] New Zealand's First Contingent of 204 men and 11 officers under Major Alfred Robin was rushed into service as the crisis between Britain and the Transvaal blew up. They hastened to South Africa in time for what was later called the first Boer War.[133] This ran far longer than expected, and the first contingent was soon joined by a second, third and then a fourth. There was no shortage of volunteers and Maori too were eager to go. Over 6000 New Zealanders eventually served; as two historians have noted, at a personal level patriotism, jingoism and even the lure of a possible new life in South Africa all played a part in the desire to go.[134] But this response was also symptomatic of a new local image as Britain's 'chief junior'. Public subscriptions to support the war, for instance, raised over £110,000 — about $15.5 million in early twenty-first-century money.[135] Military sentiment ran deep, and when parliamentarian T.E. Taylor tried to question the war, he and his associates were pelted with rotten fruit.[136]

An illustrated history

Opposite above

Sailing for South Africa, January 1900. Jingoism, duty and the notion that wars could only be glorious overrode most fears, at least until the men entered combat.

Opposite below

The 'Ladies Rifle Corps' — colloquially known as 'Wellington Amazons' — with local Wellington militia around 1900. They were recruited by Lady Douglas to raise money for the South African War Patriotic Fund.

Like most ideologies, jingoism carried a dark side of unease. Victory over Napoleon in 1815 had cemented Britain's place as pre-eminent world power, but by the late nineteenth century the laurels were a little wilted, and the ease with which the regiments quashed trouble did not compensate.[137] By the 1870s the naval scales had been reset by the development of steam-driven ironclads; the advantage now went to the nation with the highest industrial capacity, and Britain was not holding ground in the face of German, French and Russian industrialisation. Tension with Russia over the border between Afghanistan and Russia helped prompt fears of a sudden crisis that might plunge the Empire into war. At popular level the British welcomed the idea. 'We don't want to fight,' G.W. Hunt penned in his popular music-hall song, 'but by Jingo, if we do, we've got the ships, we've got the men, we've got the money too.'[138] Braggadocio of this kind put a brave face to the wider public sense of vulnerability. At saner moments, British officials knew these fears were more imagined than real, but this did not deflect public 'panics' based on imagined lack of naval hardware — still less efforts by politicians to capitalise on the feeling. New Zealand's protector, in short, was suffering an inferiority complex, and this fed into New Zealand's perception of itself, helping shape the emerging 'cultural cringe'.

Feelings of vulnerability, bolstered by Empire-wide 'war scares', added depth to this emerging mind-set. New Zealand was 1200 miles from Australia and more than 10,000 from Britain, seeing itself as a lonely outpost of Empire in the South Pacific. Successive New Zealand governments feared that war might leave Britain's South Pacific colonies vulnerable, a feeling that intensified as the New Zealand wars ended and the colonial focus swung from internal to wider issues. The Admiralty disagreed; a Russian fleet coming south would be cut off by British naval forces in Hong Kong, but raids or attacks on shipping were another matter, and the British set up the Australian Station in March 1859 partly for this reason. The Admiralty thought this was an efficient answer; however, these views were not shared in New Zealand where there was wide feeling that only ships on the spot could protect the country against a bolt from the blue.

Efforts to deal with the problem were hampered by penury. Coast defences were mooted as early as 1869, but the cost was prohibitive, and hints that Britain should donate old weapons fell on deaf ears. Whitmore demanded coast defence guns in 1870.[139] Options discussed along the way included 'Whitehead automobile torpedoes' to protect the harbours, but ultimately New Zealand had to rely on Britain — a point rammed home in February 1873 by the *Kaskowiski* hoax. Aucklanders opening the *Daily Southern Cross* were amazed to read that their city had been held to ransom by a captured British warship. Helped by 'mephitic water-gas' and a 'submarine pinnace', the Russian cruiser *Kaskowiski* had apparently slunk into Waitemata Harbour, taken control of the British ship, and demanded £250,000 from authorities. They apparently got away with £131,096.17.6, leaving

a prize crew in the British ship to extort further cash from helpless Aucklanders as the day wore on. 'WHERE IS THE BRITISH NAVY?' thundered the editorial. It was all a fabrication by editor D.M. Luckie, but for a day or two the *Kaskowiski* and its crew of ravening Cossack pirates caused a sensation.[140] The reaction highlighted the mood of New Zealanders, and Luckie pushed his more serious message over the next few weeks. New Zealand lacked any seaborne defence, and the parent Empire was apparently not providing it.

The British lurched on. A fright in 1878 prompted panic warship buying, and Britain seemed on the brink of war with the great bear again in 1884. New Zealand's reaction was sharp: a Russian squadron that appeared off China was thought to pose a direct threat,[141] requests for volunteers prompted a huge response, and an alarmed colonial government placed panic orders for arms.[142] This backgrounded discussions at the 1887 Colonial Conference, where the Admiralty agreed that Australia and New Zealand could pay for five fast cruisers and two torpedo boats to supplement the Australasian Squadron.[143] New Zealand's actual contribution — starting in the 1891–92 financial year — varied between £20,304 and £21,534.[144] But torpedo boats were no substitute for a battle-fleet. The problem was that New Zealand's defence needs were 'blue water' — yet, having failed to become a 'bigger Britain', the colony could not pay for the 'blue water' forces needed to protect vital trade lines. This practical factor added to the social and economic issues that were pushing New Zealand back to Britain during the last decades of the nineteenth century.

However, New Zealand's rush into the arms of the mother country was not a simple admission of lesser status. The idea of a 'bigger' Britain might have failed, but New Zealand still entertained dreams of being a great child — though the first

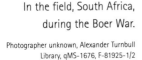
In the field, South Africa, during the Boer War.

Photographer unknown, Alexander Turnbull Library, qMS-1676, F-81925-1/2

strategy for achieving this did not go down well. Liberal thinking revolved around notions of a federated Empire, with the result that Seddon and Joseph Ward found themselves at successive Colonial and Imperial conferences, arguing for such things as a reduction of Dominion trade tariffs and increase in federal defence, in what one historian called a 'minority of one'.[145] Another consequence was a vigorous effort by New Zealand to gain Pacific Island territories as proxy for Britain, in the face of German, French and American expansion. Even Hawaii was coveted. Fiji turned Seddon down in 1900–01, though the Cook Islands and Niue were annexed.[146] However, Britain actually used the islands as a diplomatic bargaining tool, and Seddon's pugnacious efforts to take Samoa in particular were not welcomed by the Foreign Office, whose officials were juggling the delicate balance of European politics.[147]

The decision not to amalgamate with the six Australian states when they federated at the end of the decade was another outcome of this thinking, though it was far from clear-cut. As F.L.W. Wood has argued, all seven Australasian colonies tottered towards union but, in the end, New Zealand tottered away from the other six.[148] Parliamentary opinion was balanced, and abstentions outnumbered individual pro or con voices.[149] Australian-born politicians such as Ward favoured it, and late arguments to join were considered by Royal Commission in 1901. To some extent the decision not to federate was pragmatic; New Zealand's economic star was

The 1st New Zealand Rifles are welcomed home in Dunedin, 23 January 1901.

Photographer unknown, Alexander Turnbull Library, PAColl-6075-02, F-18796-1/2

rising in the late 1890s, whereas the Australian was hammered by drought. Seddon prevaricated, arguably to avoid upsetting anti-federation elements in the electorate. Eventually he began arguing that a federated New Zealand would be run from across the Tasman – striking a chord.[150]

In the broader sense, federation stood at odds with New Zealand's new view of itself. Ties with Britain were more significant; the Australian colonies had far less value by this time as import or export destinations. The decision also had a practical outcome. Instead of being a peer among seven Australasian colonies, New Zealand became the smallest of two.[151] That had disadvantages within the Imperial structure, particularly as Britain treated Australasia – including New Zealand – as a strategic entity.

The Prussia of the Pacific

New Zealand's new self-image as chief of Britain's children emerged just as the Empire was changing to a looser structure. Under British Liberal guidance the colonies became dominions, self-governing internally. The ultimate goal was a permanent alliance between independent nations tied by common ancestry, and New Zealand's rejection of the opportunity to federate with Australia did not mean rejection of Dominion status when it was offered in 1907.[152]

New Zealand's idea of Dominion was, however, a little different from that of the rest of the Empire. New Zealand's response was guided by Joseph Ward, who became Premier on Seddon's death in 1906. Described by his contemporary A.R. Barclay as running an 'indiarubber' government, Ward – Premier and Minister of Defence until 1912 – has generally been dismissed as an impulsive character with a liking for abrupt policy turns,[153] a view echoed by historians who have seen

Ward's activities as little more than a series of headlong rushes to help his beloved Empire.[154] In fact, while Ward stood in the vast shadow of his predecessor, his ideas were framed by the same federal concepts that Seddon had peddled from the 1890s. As Wood has argued, these probably originated as a means of keeping out of federation with Australia, and were unpopular in an Empire moving towards permanent alliance between independent nations.[155]

Even so, Seddon's failure to find support at the Colonial Conferences of 1897 and 1902 did not stop Ward calling for an 'Imperial council' and closer naval links at the 1907 conference. 'There is but one sea around our shores,' he argued, 'and ... with one sea and one Empire, there should in reality be but one Navy.'[156] His proposals were turned down,[157] perhaps predictably in an environment where Britain saw Australia and New Zealand as a single strategic entity, and where Australia — by virtue of a larger economy — held the whip hand. First Lord of the Admiralty, Lord Tweedmouth, grudgingly agreed that Australia might build a small fleet to supplement British forces.[158]

Ward was aware of Admiralty opinion that Australian proposals might be more acceptable if New Zealand co-operated,[159] and his response was a sudden announcement that the New Zealand subsidy would be increased from £40,000 to £100,000 a year, around $12.5 million in early twenty-first-century money.[160] He justified it as an effort to improve general naval defence,[161] which in conjunction

The US decision to send their 'Great White Fleet' across the Pacific in 1908, spurred by Japanese moves into the Philippines, prompted jingoistic fervour in New Zealand. Even the Main Trunk Line was hastened to completion so that a parliamentary delegation could make the journey to meet the Americans in a single day. Here, sailors and crowds mingle in Queen Street during the week-long celebration marking the fleet's visit.

with the timing suggests he had made the offer to torpedo Australian fleet proposals. New Zealand's later treatment by the Board of Admiralty certainly stood out in contrast to the way Australia was handled.[162]

Fresh public panic brewed during early 1909 amid fears that Germany was about to overtake Britain in a new naval race, which at popular level was based around a numbers game associated with 'dreadnoughts' – the new super-battleships of the day. When it looked like the ruling British Liberal party would not authorise six for the 1909–10 financial year, the Conservative opposition led a counter-attack with the catch-cry 'We want eight and we won't wait'.[163] Against this background, Ward abruptly offered Britain a dreadnought, one Sunday in March 1909, without calling either Cabinet or Parliament. The move has been

Right above

School militarism was formalised by the Defence Act 1909, which required schools to run a cadet system. These boys are cadets from the Wellesley Street Normal School.

Photographer unknown, *Auckland Star* Collection, Alexander Turnbull Library, PAColl-2752, G-2929-1/1

Right below

Military camp at Oringi, near Woodville. Bell tents had been characteristic of army camps since the mid-Victorian period, remaining so well into the twentieth century.

S.C. Smith, Alexander Turnbull Library, PAColl-3082, G-20108-1/1

regarded by contemporaries and historians as Ward rushing to the aid of his beloved Empire, and his vague justifications certainly lend some credence to this idea. He told the House that 'prompt action was absolutely desirable – was, indeed, essential – if the moral effect which we had in view was to be secured'. This did not seem credible, and his failure to follow correct procedure was regularly brought up afterwards. Ward tried to get himself off the hook with hints that he had 'confidential information relating to the pressing danger of the situation', but that too was revealed as bluff when the correspondence was published in Australia and cabled to New Zealand.

Reform Party leader William Massey made political capital, and even the Governor-General, Lord Plunket, thought Ward had made an 'error in tactics'.[164] Neither Ward's contemporaries, nor historians since, have questioned the assumption that Ward acted out of personal patriotism.

In fact Ward was again trying to undermine the Australians. His subsidy increase had not had the effect he wanted, so he played his ace. As he later told Plunket, New Zealanders 'would take much greater pride and interest in knowing that HMS "So-and-so" and HMS "Something Else" were *their* ships and a visible tangible object lesson of their Dominion's part in the Empire's defence than in merely paying £100,000 a year in ignorance as to how the money was spent'.[165] Ward explained that he had been thinking of making an offer for some time for these reasons. What he did not say was that his hand had been forced by the annual meeting of Australian Commonwealth leaders in mid-March 1909. On the 18th, Australian Prime Minister Andrew Fisher remarked that Australia and Canada could best help British defence by offering to pay for a dreadnought each, as an indication that the 'relatively rich young Dominions' would be prepared to help the

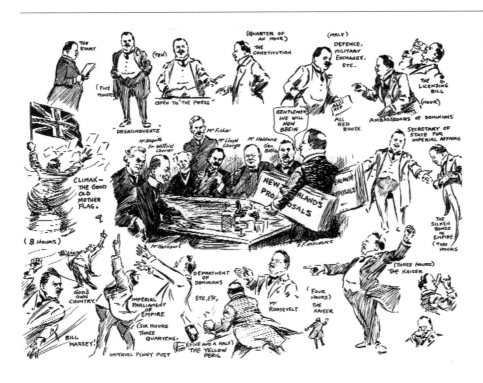

Like Seddon, Ward was quickly lampooned for his wordy pro-Imperial braggadocio. This cartoon hit the nail on the head.

Ercildoune Frederick Hiscocks, Alexander Turnbull Library, PUBL-0200-25 mother country. It was only a talking point, but the remark drew attention.[166] Knowing that an Australian offer would trump his own, Ward made the offer as soon as he heard the news. He could not afford to wait even a day to call Cabinet, in case the Australian government decided to make an announcement before the conference ended.[167]

The gamble paid off. The Australian stock exchange called on the Commonwealth to make a similar offer, sentiments echoed by the Premiers of New South Wales and Victoria who announced that if the Commonwealth government did not make a dreadnought offer, they would.[168] Ward had touched a deep-held sentiment across the Tasman, and had good reason to feel pleased with himself as he left for the Imperial Conference in July 1909. But his strategy quickly unravelled. Although the new Australian government of Alfred Deakin fulfilled its election promises and gave Britain a dreadnought, Australian thinking remained focused on a local fleet and Colonel J.F.G. Foxton was sent along to argue the toss.[169] The Admiralty were keen to settle, and the compromise — degrading the gift ships to battlecruisers and integrating them into Pacific-based 'fleet units' — was geared towards Australia.[170]

It was a slap in the face for the Empire's self-appointed chief junior. Ward was 'rather sorry that the Admiralty has recommended that a [naval] unit be formed for Australia', but realised New Zealand would be denuded of the second-line protection

Crowds waiting to board HMS *New Zealand* at Lyttelton, 1913. The patriotic fervour that swirled around this ship was unparalleled.

Photographer unknown, *The Press* Christchurch Collection, Alexander Turnbull Library, G-2276-1/1

he had expected in exchange for his gift. This forced him to compromise his 'federal' principles and, purely for pragmatic reasons, follow the Australian lead by having part of a fleet unit stationed in New Zealand waters.[171] Although New Zealand's local forces were subsequently administered under legislation passed in 1913, this 1909 arrangement defined the basic shape of the naval force until 1941.[172] The ongoing failure of Ward's policies underlined the fact that his concepts — and by extension those of New Zealand — were out of line. At a time when Britain was beginning to shed its Empire, New Zealand decided to cling ever-tighter to the motherland. The dissonance characterised the relationship for virtually the whole twentieth century.

Red Feds and Massey's Cossacks

Jingoism remained strong as the twentieth century entered its second decade. Thousands flocked to see Ward's gift ship when she came to New Zealand shores in 1913, amid a new outburst of patriotic fervour for the motherland.[173] But the tides of change were already flowing, adding new dimension to this world of blood and Empire. The late nineteenth century was the age of the radical left, a generational reaction to the extremist economic views of the early century. The Communards of Paris showed the way in 1870, and over the next decades there was widespread agitation across Europe and Britain, demanding change on the basis of class unity. British Liberal policies were at least partly geared to meeting these demands. Elsewhere, radicals, reactionaries and anarchists lurked in coffee shops and bars, some planning assassinations or bombings, while others held public meetings to discuss revolution. This was more intense in countries such as Russia, where industrialisation lagged; massive strikes led to an attempted revolt in Russia in 1905, which Tsar Nicholas crushed.[174] While fear overstated the threat elsewhere, such dramatic developments highlighted the fact that working-class society had swung to the left.

New Zealand shared the shift but local radicalism was tempered by the structure of colonial society, which differed from that of Europe. Social mobility and lip-service egalitarianism diffused the feeling, and class unity in the Marxist sense, insofar as it emerged at all, took its lead from colonial structures and values — not European patterns. There was little to compare the 'Red Feds' with the

Socialist Party demonstration at Waihi, in support of striking miners.

Photographer unknown, Nash Collection, Alexander Turnbull Library, PAColl-5792, F-70458-1/2

contemporary Mensheviks led by Leon Trotsky, and New Zealand's labour left was framed within the values of its own society. It was based on small-scale organisations, including early trade unions. Their influence in the labour force was restricted by Reeves' labour legislation, which forced compulsory arbitration, but that was changing by the first decade of the twentieth century under such radicals as Robert Semple ('Battling Bob', as he was called at the time), Michael Savage, Bill Parry and Paddy Webb. They were not as radical as some of their European counterparts and it has been argued that they were less inspired by the teachings of Marx than by moderate labour leaders such as Edward Bellamy.[175]

They were broadly opposed by a new union of farmers, the small-holders created by the Liberals, who defected from the Liberal cause in droves during the first decade of the twentieth century. This group coalesced initially around the New Zealand Farmers Union, formed in 1902 at Kaitaia. This evolved into a new political grouping, the Reform Political League, which emerged to fill the vacuum left by the demolition of Russell's oligarch-based Opposition in 1900. They were led after 1903 by former Tamaki dairy farmer William Ferguson Massey, a bluff figure not unkindly dubbed 'Farmer Bill'. Disillusioned with Ballance's policies, he had become involved in politics as farmers' advocate for the National Association in the early 1890s, and stood for the Waitemata seat in 1894.

This new grouping took time to gain momentum. They made very little headway against Seddon in the 1905 elections, but did better against Ward, though the Liberals won in 1908 despite a swing to the right. Massey renamed the group

Trouble at t'mill; arbitrationists in Waihi after a demonstration, November 1912.

Photographer unknown, Waihi Arts Centre and Museum Collection, Alexander Turnbull Library, F-90377-1/2

Arbitrationists boarding Brakes in Rosemont Road to be driven to their Homes. After Marching down Seddon Street on Monday Nov. 11th 1912.

Strikers at Waihi, led by children,
November 1912.

the Reform Party, garnering support from a fairly wide centre-right base. The main gripe, on which the new party capitalised, was with McKenzie's 999-year leasehold system. In practice this meant that the lessee – irrespective of safe tenure – could not use the land as security on loans, and that proved crippling. Nor could the lessees take advantage of rising land prices, although goodwill on the lease itself was transactable. Ward's efforts to cure these problems were not fast enough to prevent an erosion of his support from the right, but his policies also alienated him from the left. The elections of 1911 left Ward without a working majority, and he resigned the following year.[176]

The results set the pattern for New Zealand politics until the mid-1980s; a centre-right that drew support from the conservative rural farming vote, matched against a largely urbanised centre-left that drew from the workers. Both tended towards the centre, and neither was strictly comparable with overseas equivalents. But in the 1900s the left was regarded as dangerously radical by the conservatives, and the losers during the same period were the Liberals, who by this time represented a centrist party that did not really address the demands of an increasingly diversified electorate. However, even when Massey established a Reform government in 1912, the opposition was at first more Liberal than Labour. Four independent Labour seats expediently sided with the Liberals, but the labour movement of the day was militant rather than political.

Labour militants emerged as a significant force during the later 1900s, particularly on the West Coast where they dominated the Blackball mines and later

Morning of Nov. 12

Black Tuesday — the morning of 12 November 1912. Police attacked striking miners at Miners Hall, Seddon Street. A good number were injured in the scuffle that followed.

Photographer unknown, H.E. Holland Collection, Alexander Turnbull Library, F-44240-1/2

disrupted work on the Otira rail tunnel. The New Zealand Federation of Miners was formed in 1908, the Federation of Labour (FOL) in 1909. They were dubbed 'Red Feds' by their opponents and regarded as communist, but their demands were modest enough — mostly reflecting a living wage and a reasonable old-age pension. Seddon's Old Age Pensions Act of 1898, though later lauded as founding the welfare state, actually provided token payments under such exclusive terms that many could not take advantage of it.[177]

The main issue was the FOL rejection of the arbitration system, and rising tensions finally became effective war in early 1912, when the 1200-member Waihi Miners Union aligned itself with the FOL, but the engine drivers and winders withdrew from the Waihi Miners Union to form their own group. The miners went on strike in protest amid calls to disband the new Engine Drivers Union. At first the dispute merely simmered against the background of a failing Liberal administration under caretaker Prime Minister Thomas McKenzie, but Massey became Prime Minister in July and was able to manoeuvre the Waihi situation into a 'law and order' issue. Police were deployed to the town in September and arrested some of the striking miners for 'obstruction'. The strike dragged on. In November, police raided the Waikino Miners Hall, an armed struggle followed, and two men died — Constable Gerald Wade and miner Frederick George Evans. The strike was forcibly ended and the miners and their families were ordered to leave town. New workers were brought on, employed only if they agreed to abide by the old arbitration system.

It had been a decisive victory for Massey, but as far as the labour movement was concerned this was only the first round. The Waihi experience helped spur the United Federation and the Social Democrat Party into existence. Trouble erupted on the Wellington waterfront, where there was a lockout in late 1913 after a dispute

The sign in the image reads: "IF BLOOD BE THE PRICE OF YOUR CURSED WEALTH, GOOD GOD WE HAVE BOUGHT IT FAIR"

Maritime strikers' protest, 1913. Confrontations followed these strikes, which were broken by force.

over travel expenses. Sympathetic strikes followed in the Huntly coal mines and in other docks. The FOL tried to extend it into a general strike, to which Massey responded by appointing special mounted constables – 'Massey's Cossacks' – to help keep law and order. The strikers did not have the sympathy of the farmers, and the crisis came to a head on 8 November with what has been called the 'battle of the wharves'. In simultaneous operations, the 'Cossacks' took the Auckland wharves, backed by a contingent of farmers and with the cruisers *Psyche* and *Pyramus* providing visible backing. Skirmishing spilled into surrounding streets. Another force of 'Cossacks' tackled the Wellington strikers with a flurry of batons. They were met by revolver fire, but the results were perhaps inevitable. The strike was broken after 58 days, but the labour movement was decisively split. Two-thirds of the FOL resigned.

A general election loomed in 1914. Massey had bare majority, and the Liberal-Labour grouping offered a credible threat. It would have been an interesting contest, but fate intervened. A new international crisis erupted in July, and – as Guthrie-Smith put it – the 'old world crashed and passed away'.[178]

CHAPTER 7

God's Own Country

New Zealand's twentieth century was a roller-coaster of depression, booms, disease and unimaginably lethal wars, through which the settler ideals of security, equality and the quarter-acre dream rode like a ship on a turbulent sea. As a historical entity it was also a short century. Trend and theme seldom match convenient dates, and British historian Eric Hobsbawm has argued that the twentieth century as a world military, socio-economic and political cycle actually began in 1914 and ended with the fall of the Eastern Bloc around 75 years later.[1] His arguments are compelling; and although he wrote from a world perspective, it seems clear that New Zealand shared the broad experience through its Imperial and international ties – and added indigenous twists, including local start and end-points, which generated for domestic reasons.

As elsewhere, the First World War provided a focus for change, a four-year struggle that many historians classify as the first act in a 31-year conflict with a 20-year interval.[2] This was the first time the major industrial nations had fought a full-scale war with each other. It was a mechanism for social change. In New Zealand, shifts that had been implicit suddenly swept into being, along with a sense of social and national unity that overlaid feelings towards Britain and stood in uneasy tension with them, a plural loyalty sometimes called 'double patriotism'.

During the inter-war decades New Zealand matched worldwide swings between 'big' and 'bigger' government, adding twists of its own, underpinned and moulded by the legacy of settler society. It was a heady mix into which idealism, the 'cultural cringe', jingoism and the concept of being 'chief junior' to Imperial Britain fed in complex ways, and were themselves changed by it. It was also a blokeish world in which women and Maori were sidelined – but from which both re-emerged, buoyed by a sea change in attitude as the cycle ended in the 1960s and 1970s. Change when it finally came in the mid-1980s was traumatic – and effectively brought New Zealand's twentieth century to its end.

Ilex at sea, 1913.

Poppies and mud

The First World War stands as a monument to the end of one era and the start of another, soaked in the blood of a generation who never wanted to die, but who were slaughtered in their thousands across the poppy fields of Flanders, at Gallipoli, in Poland, the Alps, and in Palestine among other places. New Zealanders were among them, young men whose lives stretched into an unknown future in 1913, but who — as Laurence Binyon's words remind us — never lived to grow wearied by age.

None of this was anticipated during the glorious northern summer of 1914. Long-standing tensions between Europe's powers seemed quiescent, and even the assassination of Archduke Franz Ferdinand of Austria at the end of June was at first a local affair. But that changed in the face of Europe's volatile combination of alliances, economic rivalries, national competition, personality politics and the legacy of the 1871 Franco-Prussian War.[3] Britain wavered, reluctant to see a German-dominated continent, equally reluctant to get involved in war. But when German forces crashed through Belgium, Britain honoured an 1839 neutrality guarantee and declared war. So did the Empire.[4]

Nobody expected the fighting to last beyond Christmas, but the 'miracle of the Marne' stopped a lightning German push to Paris in October 1914, and the Franco-British and German armies outflanked each other to the Channel. As winter began they dug in. So began three years of soul-destroying trench warfare that — despite the proliferation of other places in which the conflict was played out — remains the enduring image of the First World War. It was also the reality of it for most of the New Zealanders. Comparison has been drawn between First World War trench defences and those the British faced in New Zealand 50 years earlier;[5] but there were differences. The heavy machine gun offered a volume of fire not enjoyed by musket-armed Maori; and the scale of trenches in Flanders was unprecedented.[6] Musket pa were difficult to take by direct attack, but could be flanked or bypassed. By contrast, long multi-layered trenches protected by wire and machine guns could

Crowds outside *The Press* office, Cathedral Square, Christchurch, 1914.

Photographer unknown, Alexander Turnbull Library, F-103409-1/2

not be avoided. It took the British three years to overcome the problem.[7] Until then, fighting devolved to ever-larger artillery bombardments followed by huge infantry attacks, each just successful enough to suggest that a little more effort next time would do the trick.

The armies needed for these brute-force methods were available as another consequence of nineteenth-century change. Rising populations and technical capacity had been matched by a rise in state organisational power, a combined outcome of communications technology, new social structures and the cult of patriotic nationalism. Seddon's reformed public service had led the world, but it was not the only bureaucracy by the first decade of the twentieth century – and wartime governments, in any case, were adept at creating authority. The result was a state ability to direct populations in ways that had been only hinted at during Europe's last big war a century earlier. When combined with the strategies of 'chateau generals' who had yet to find a way around a new tactical problem, the results were industrial-level casualties and a mechanistic dehumanisation of war.

New Zealand contributed principally on land, a consequence of pre-war policies that handed naval defence to Britain and focused local attention on the army. However, there were also air and sea contributions via the Royal Flying Corps, the Royal Navy and Royal Naval Air Service, New Zealand's own tiny naval forces, and in local forces and training establishments, ultimately totalling some 91,941 volunteers and 32,270 conscripts.[8] Total losses in all theatres – heavily skewed towards the division deployed to Flanders – amounted to just over 41,000 wounded and more than 16,500 dead.[9] Of these, 10,245 were killed outright and 3958 died of wounds, while 2351 were listed as dying of 'other causes', including disease. Some 227 others died in New Zealand 'before discharge', some of them casualties of the influenza epidemic of 1918.[10] Hundreds of others died in the 1920s from the after-effects of gas or the lingering results of their injuries, a number not fully captured by official records, although we know that around 3000 servicemen were still being treated in New Zealand hospitals as late as 1920.[11]

The South Canterbury contingent departing Timaru, 21 August 1914.

None of this was anticipated in 1914, when New Zealanders saw war as an opportunity for personal adventure and to show that the loyal Dominion would do its part for the Imperial cause. The Boer War had shown the way, and once again New Zealanders brought up on a diet of jingoism and glory flocked to war, among them Aubrey Tronson who joined 'principally through a pure love of adventure and travel'. He had always harboured an ambition to see London and attributed his enthusiasm for war to his father, and a military descent. Tronson's interest in the military was aroused during boyhood by the Boer War and strengthened by the Russo-Japanese war of 1904–05; when the First World War broke out he was so eager to volunteer that he badgered the recruiting office twice a day for a week.[12]

Haste was demanded for a conflict expected to last only a few months. Legacies of Seddon's Pacific ambitions prompted the government to send a force to take Samoa within a fortnight of war breaking out. The convoy with its light cruiser escort was initially diverted by the British to New Caledonia but finally took the German colony in late August, fortunately without running into the powerful East Asiatic Squadron of Vice-Admiral Graf von Spee, which was at sea – whereabouts unknown.[13]

Plans went ahead for a land contribution in the European theatre. The framework had been laid by the Defence Act 1909 and Defence Amendment Act 1910, which established territorial forces whose training began at school with a new Cadet system. Registration was compulsory, and by mid-1911, three months after the legislation came into force, 21,838 Territorials and 29,991 Cadets had been registered.[14] The army – with a theoretical establishment of 30,000 – was organised under Major-General Sir Alexander Godley, British-sourced commander and nephew of John Godley. They were short on experienced officers, but some 8700 men and 3800 horses left New Zealand late in the year. One of the convoys taking them to Egypt ran foul of SMS *Emden*, a cruiser from the East Asiatic Squadron; the German vessel was defeated in classic ship-to-ship combat by HMAS *Sydney*, one of the escorts.[15]

The men went with the cheers of a nation bored with the dreary round of peace and ignorant of the awful realities of fighting; their enthusiasms, though, were not mirrored in London. Louisa Higginson sailed to England with her friend Mary Collins on board the *Corinthic* in early 1915 in the hope of volunteering for war work. They were surprised by what they saw in the Imperial capital, confiding to the diary then being kept by Mary that they could not understand the apparent lack of English patriotism.[16] By this time Turkey had entered the war against Britain, and as far as Churchill and the British War Cabinet was concerned, this opened up an opportunity to bypass the stalled Western Front, relieving the pressure on the Russians at the same time.[17] Plans to send the New Zealanders on to France were shelved; they got as far as Cairo, and a Turkish thrust into the Syrian desert produced New Zealand's first combat death of the war as early as February 1915, when Private William Ham succumbed to wounds after a tussle at Ismailia.

The Kiwis, it seemed, were in Egypt to stay. Most saw themselves as tourists.

New Zealanders, probably on
Walker's Ridge, Gallipoli,
late April 1915.

Arthur Nelson Field, A.N. Field Collection, Alexander
Turnbull Library, PAColl-1678,
C-10050-1/2

George Bollinger eagerly anticipated seeing the teeming streets of Cairo,[18] though the realities were often disappointing, and Tronson found the city interesting but grubby.[19] Cairo also brought the men into direct contact with Egyptians, with results that highlighted the attitudes of the day towards race. But it is over-simplistic to condemn this as racism – a mistake made by at least one historian.[20] At the time this behaviour was considered normal, and it included violence; Bollinger recorded scuffles in which the New Zealanders appeared to come out worse off.[21] Louisa Higginson thought the Egyptians were rude and rather irritating.[22] Tensions escalated, and all came to a head over Easter 1915 in a major riot, the 'battle of the Wazza'.

However, such performances were sideshows beside the plan to strike Turkey out of the war by taking the Dardanelles and surging directly into Istanbul. The attack was launched in early 1915, separately from land and sea – this latter against the advice of First Sea Lord Admiral Sir John Fisher, who felt the assault had to be combined to succeed.[23] In the event, an attempt to force the Dardanelles with old battleships failed, and the land assault followed against alerted Turkish defenders. Available forces included the Australasian contingents in Cairo, which assembled as the Australia and New Zealand Corps. They landed on 25 April 1915 amid massive confusion. Bollinger saw casualties as they tried to get on to the beach, and the first attack a week later was a dismal failure. So was another in early May across Cape Helles. The campaign degenerated to another hellhole of barbed wire, machine guns, and misery and death.

The New Zealanders made a final effort to take the peninsula in early August, and against all odds, the 760-strong Wellington Battalion under Colonel William Malone reached the objective on Chunuk Bair. But they could get no further. The Kiwis were finally pulled out in December, after eight miserable months that became indelibly etched into the New Zealand psyche. There were 7453 casualties – of whom 2721 were killed outright. Louisa Higginson saw some of the despondent survivors back in Egypt, mourning the lives that had been sacrificed for nothing.[24] It had been a hopeless affair, but it struck a chord with the New Zealand public, and there were informal ceremonies to mark the first anniversary of the landings in 1916 – the start of a tradition which became a keystone of New Zealand's emerging identity.

We must draw a distinction, though, between Gallipoli as the popular birthplace of New Zealand national sentiment, and the more complete way in which this emotion was born of war experience. In this respect Gallipoli was merely the curtain-raiser to an even greater tragedy that began in 1916, when the force was reorganised into a full division for service in the Armentières section of the Western Front, under Hastings pastoral scion Major-General Andrew Russell. The division was one of the largest fielded during the war, and there were plans to add a second in 1917. Maori contributed a Pioneer Battalion, on a voluntary basis but pushed by Maori members of Parliament – notably Maui Pomare of Te Ati Awa – who hoped to elevate the status of Maori in the process.[25] Around 2200 eventually served, mostly from former kupapa.

The net result was that socially significant numbers of young New Zealanders were thrown together under adverse conditions for a far longer period than Gallipoli; and their war became a relatively greater focus of public sentiment and feeling at home. This was the decisive shift. Although Gallipoli triggered feelings of nationalism, the Western Front seared the emotion into the New Zealand psyche. It was a shattering experience. Young New Zealanders, some fresh out of school, fought, bled and died in places that most had not even known as names on a map; Ypres, Passchendaele and the Somme were among them. These tiny villages and the fields between them became irrevocably associated with an endless, inhuman

By the time the New Zealanders reached Ypres – 'Wipers' to the men – it had been on or near the front line for two years and little was left.

Henry Armitage Sanders, gelatin dry plate negative, RSA Collection, Alexander Turnbull Library, PAColl-5311, G-12950-1/2

and dehumanising world of mud, filth, bullets, shells, bombs, mines and the corrupting remains of earlier casualties.

Harry Bourke was conscripted into the Hawke's Bay Company of the Second Wellington Regiment in July 1917. By October he was in France, and on the 12th his company marched to Ypres where they had their first experience of shellfire. Bourke saw the corpses of men and beast, souring his impressions of the landscape. Two days later they were knee deep in mud, forbidden to light fires, subsisting on hard biscuits and cold tinned beef.[26]

Right above

The funeral of Sapper J.F. Haynes, New Zealand Engineers, early May 1917.

Henry Armitage Sanders, RSA Collection, Alexander Turnbull Library, PAColl-5311, G-12761-1/2

Right below

New Zealanders watching the advance on Messines Ridge, 7 June 1917. The tank appears to be a Mk IV.

Photographer unknown, Alexander Turnbull Library, F-11936-1/2

Left above

'Clapham Junction', November 1917. New Zealanders cheer a wounded comrade with jokes from 'New Zealand at the Front'.

Henry Armitage Sanders, RSA Collection, Alexander Turnbull Library, PAColl-5311, G-12979-1/2

Left centre

Hellfire Corner, Ypres Salient.

Photographer unknown, Alexander Turnbull Library, F-51945-1/2

Left below

Meal time in a front-line New Zealand trench, April 1918.

Henry Armitage Sanders, Alexander Turnbull Library, PAColl-5311, G-13087-1/2

New Zealanders advanced on Passchendaele that day, their worst day of the war. More than 1000 were killed and 3000 wounded. The blow was so heavy that, even a quarter-century later and in another war, New Zealand commanders had merely to mention 'Passchendaele' to prompt a rethink of any apparently failing strategy.[27]

The war dragged on, and when the Russian government collapsed during late 1917, German forces swept west. General Ludendorff's campaign of March and April 1918 hurled 43 divisions against 12 British in the Somme, more against the Armentières sector.[28] New Zealanders were swept up in the whirlwind, but Ludendorff's offensive staggered to a halt in July at a cost of around a million casualties. Later in the year, it was the Allies' turn to attack, using new tactics,[29] and for a few weeks the war became a fast-moving struggle that swiftly turned against Germany, who agreed to an armistice on 11 November 1918. It was joyous news.

Temperance, pacifists and influenza

War came home to New Zealanders in letters and casualty lists, in the return of mutilated soldiers from hospitals, in the shortages of imported goods, in the suspicion of Germanic migrants, and in the patriotic quests for funds, gifts and what were called 'comforts' for the troops, small luxuries such as chocolate, cigarettes, cards and clothing to help ease life in the trenches. It struck the hearts of every family with sons or brothers at the front, and that was most of them. Men were still prepared to serve voluntarily late in 1915,[30] but there was growing feeling that the struggle was neither glorious nor likely to have any point at a personal level.

Conscription — when it came in 1916 — was promoted as a way of equalising the sacrifice, and certainly minimised disruption when groups of men volunteered from small areas. It collected around 32,000 for the army, about a third of the total who served, selected by random marble-draw in Wellington. Some, like Bourke, were happy enough to go. Others slipped the net by omitting to register. Others did register but then refused to go — among them a good number of Labour supporters including Peter Fraser. Jingo-era New Zealand treated such dissenters harshly, and many were imprisoned under poor conditions, even stripped of voting rights for a decade. Opposition in the King Country, the only area where Maori conscription was enforced, was organised by Tawhiao's granddaughter Te Puea Herangi, who urged passive resistance.[31]

The struggle affected everyday life in many ways. New Zealand imported virtually all its clothing, textiles, metal, machinery, sugar, tea, liquor, tobacco, paper and books. Forty percent by value came directly from Britain, and availability varied dramatically during the war years. It reached its lowest ebb in 1917 when the Germans launched their second round of unrestricted U-boat warfare in the Atlantic. Prices skyrocketed.[32] Car imports from Britain were restricted, prompting some firms to look to the United States. New Zealand also imported £8000 worth of German goods in 1915, and even in 1917 some £700 worth came into the country, probably through third-party neutrals.

Patriotism was nonetheless the order of the day, and shopkeepers advertised that their products were not German. An Empire Defence Fund was organised to supply New Zealand soldiers with 'comforts', Patriotic Committees raised funds, there were concerts to support the wounded, and drives to raise money for those in Belgium. Overseas charities and aid organisations also sought support from New Zealand. The Over-Seas Club, a London-based organisation backed by *The Times*, sought donations to its Tobacco Fund. 'The brave soldiers in the fighting line are asking for something to smoke,' the advertisement advised. 'Will you help us to supply it?' A typical parcel included 50 cigarettes, a quarter-pound of 'smoking mixture', and matches.[33]

Sectarianism gained surprising ground during the war. New Zealand had never been a particularly religious society; certainly the ill-feeling that flared occasionally between Protestant and Catholic in Britain was little in evidence. However, that changed during the war. The trauma of the struggle undoubtedly had some effect, and so too did external forces such as the Irish Easter Rebellion of 1916. Former Baptist minister Howard Elliott formed the Protestant Political Association in 1917, backed by the Grand Orange Lodge. They were closely tied to the Reform Party and membership flourished, growing by some accounts to

Farewell luncheon for New Zealand soldiers at Trentham Camp, 1916.

Photographer unknown, Kenneally Collection, Alexander Turnbull Library, F-106752-1/2

200,000 by 1919, but they dwindled rapidly after 1921, a move one historian has put down to a combination of British settlement in Ireland and the fact that post-war, Massey's party gained the upper hand.[34]

Temperance also gained new momentum, in part reflecting overseas trends, in part stemming from a feeling that stay-at-homes had no right to live in luxury. Prohibition seemed a very real prospect, and 'six o'clock closing' was introduced in 1917 by way of compromise. It did not seem to curb drinking; and that year some 3116 New Zealanders were arrested for offences under the liquor acts, including drunkenness.[35] Nor did the practice of 'dry' areas make much difference; some 276,510 gallons (1.258 million litres) of alcohol were sent into no-licence districts, most of it beer and stout.[36] This was a rising trend — more than 381,000 gallons of liquor (1.734 million litres), again mostly beer and stout, were taken into no-licence districts in 1919.[37]

This was in line with overseas trends, but the New Zealand edition had a distinct local spin. Six o'clock closing added speed to a growing cult of quantity, reinforcing beer as a currency of New Zealand manhood. 'Sculling' a 'yard glass' became a rite of passage at twenty-first birthday parties. Status was also gained from 'holding' liquor — not apparently suffering the effects of the alcohol — an attitude which translated to the notion that driving after drinking was not merely

District nurses outside their South Durham Street headquarters, Christchurch. Left to right: C. Browne, Sister Constance, M. Palmer, M. Rogers, S. Maude, C. Savory, L. Laing and Tolerton.

Steffano Francis Webb, Steffano Webb Collection, Alexander Turnbull Library, G-5293-1/1

acceptable but helped assert manhood. What all this meant, apart from a rising road-toll, was that most town streets at five minutes past six were briefly filled with intoxicated men looking for a punch-up, and many public bars became male-only swilling venues with concrete floors.

Early closing was only halfway as far as many campaigners were concerned, and in 1919, faced with such intonements as 'alcohol is ... one of the chief causes of cruelty, crime and vice',[38] New Zealanders voted in favour of prohibition by a majority of 3263. However, soldiers overseas tipped the balance and New Zealand remained a nation of drinkers. The army was regarded as 'debauched' in some circles,[39] but in practice it was difficult for the socially pure to threaten Western Front veterans with hell. The soldiers' vote probably saved New Zealand from the violence and black marketeering of the United States, but as late as 1925, 47 percent of New Zealand voters remained in favour of prohibition. Their feeling was not shared across the Tasman. In 1928, for instance, New South Wales residents voted 5:2 in favour of staying 'wet'.[40]

A new killer emerged in 1918, an invisible death transmitted in part by the mass travel associated with the war. So-called 'Spanish' flu became a worldwide pandemic with a death toll estimated at between 25 and 40 million. It reached New Zealand in two waves, the first in July 1918. This produced no more deaths than

Scandinavian picnic at Lowry Bay, 1896. Scenes such as this did nothing to quell the drive for temperance.

Photographer unknown, Petersen Collection, Alexander Turnbull Library, PAColl-5150, F-52226-1/2

the usual winter ills, and authorities only realised it had happened in hindsight. The second was far more virulent. It erupted in Auckland during late October and was carried south 'by rail and shipping'. Within a fortnight there were cases in Bluff, though the 'wave seems to have lessened in virulence as it advanced'.[41] Perhaps a third of all New Zealanders caught it, with fatalities variously quoted at between 6500 and 8600. Official reports make clear that the precise number was unknown partly because there was no way to differentiate between pandemic deaths and those caused by the usual strains of influenza. Many deaths came about from secondary infections, and as an official report noted, several hundred deaths officially put down to pneumonia, bronchitis and pulmonitis 'should have been' attributed to the pandemic.[42] Excluding these, but including deaths attributed to influenza and 'cerebro-spinal fever', some 5471 non-Maori and 1130 Maori died between October and December 1918.[43]

At 226 per 10,000 of population the Maori death rate was more than four times the European, a point that health authorities could not explain beyond the remark that Maori were 'exceptionally liable to attack'.[44] Other sources suggest the official estimate of Maori deaths may have been too low by a factor of about two.[45] The young also fell in disproportionate numbers; almost half those who died were between 25 and 40, 'although only 24 percent of the population are between those ages'.[46]

Popular opinion put the late-1918 outbreak down to cases that arrived in Auckland on board the SS *Niagara* in October. The problem was that this ship – with '100 crew down' – had Prime Minister William Massey and Sir Joseph Ward on board as passengers, and the story went that their pressure to get off prompted the authorities to let the ship dock.[47] However, Auckland health authorities had already noted cases before this ship arrived,[48] and an investigating Commission

could not prove that the *Niagara* had been the trigger. A more crucial issue nationwide had been a 'general disregard of precautionary measures in the initial stages of the epidemic, due to want of knowledge regarding the nature of the disease'.[49] The mechanisms of disease transmission were well known to the medical profession, as was the fact that most people died from secondary infections such as pneumonia.[50] All this was made clear in Public Health Department guidelines:

> ...no form of inoculation can be guaranteed to protect against the disease itself. But the chief dangers of influenza lie in its complications, and ... much can be done to mitigate the severity of the infection and to diminish its mortality by raising the resistance of the body against the chief secondary infecting agents ... The liability of the immediate attendants to infection may be materially diminished by avoiding inhalation of the patient's breath, and particularly when he is coughing ... The risk of conveyance of infection by the fingers must be constantly remembered.[51]

Masks were considered, and the department recommended keeping away from public areas. Disinfection was not extensively required because 'the virus of influenza is very easily destroyed'. If everybody had followed this advice, the spread might have been reduced. Unfortunately there was little popular distinction between viral and bacterial infection, and mechanisms for transmission were misunderstood. Popular thinking was not helped by the profusion of miracle remedies, suffused with scientific terms. These included one ointment that was supposedly able to grow new tissue 'cell by cell', kill 'poison germs', and cure everything from piles to 'scalp disease'.[52] Other products on the market around that time included a 'Violet Ray' generator, for 'radiant health', pluggable into any light socket.[53] Some remedies were promoted – after the event – for supposed anti-flu

'Inhalation chambers' were designed to kill the influenza virus in the throat of those who might have been infected. Although there was some evidence of the rooms being effective, they probably also served to spread the virus.

Photographer unknown, *The Press* Christchurch Collection, Alexander Turnbull Library, G-8545-1/1

properties.[54] The Commission concluded that ignorance and a continuation of everyday life had contributed:

> The infection was largely spread by the congregation of large crowds of people in the various centres in connection with the Armistice Celebrations, race meetings, the 'Carnival Week' in Christchurch ... and the fact that no restriction was placed upon the movements of the people in travelling, even when they had individually been in contact with infected persons.[55]

The epidemic subdued the jubilation that came with the armistice in November 1918. In March 1919 — as the former warring parties negotiated a settlement — the government decided to hold celebrations 'on the second Sunday, Monday and Tuesday after ... the official announcement of preliminary peace having been signed'.[56]

Right

Influenza and disabled soldiers highlighted the need for hospitals and care in New Zealand. This is a maternity hospital around 1920.

Photographer unknown, *The Press* Christchurch Collection, Alexander Turnbull Library, PAColl-3031, F-55156-1/2

Below left

Christchurch medicine depot during the influenza epidemic, December 1918. 'Stimulants' on sale at the Central Medicine Depot included small bottles of brandy, whisky and stout.

Photographer unknown, *The Press* Christchurch Collection, Alexander Turnbull Library, G-8542-1/1

Below right

A 'medicine department' in the Wellington Town Hall, where tonics were prepared for influenza victims.

Photographer unknown, *New Zealand Free Lance* Collection, Alexander Turnbull Library, C-16207-1/2

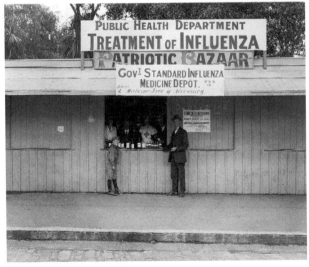

Anzac Day processions in Wellington, 1920. Celebrations began as an essentially spontaneous event in 1916. By 1920 they were popular tradition, soon picked up by government as a day of national remembrance.

Photographer unknown, Alexander Turnbull Library, G-116483-1/2

Dominions and jazz

Like most Western states, New Zealand left the war with an intrusive administration.[57] In many respects it was inevitable. Exigencies such as the British 'commandeer' prompted the government to establish a Board of Trade, authorised to control prices and prevent profiteering. Wartime censorship boosted pressure to legislate everything from films to drinking times and places – and added a requirement for state apparatus to administer them. Few wartime measures were dropped afterwards. In this New Zealand reflected a world trend, and parties of left and right embraced big government as a means of guiding, improving and asserting national power; filtered in New Zealand's case by the idea of being a 'chief junior' within the Empire. It has been argued that both trends helped define New Zealand as an entity.[58]

To some extent the expansion of the state, by definition, meant intervention – but it was couched as a reframing of existing ideals, in effect movement along the small–large government continuum. Wartime promises to look after returned soldiers did not reflect an ideological sea change among a generally conservative government and, in 1921, conservative MP Sir Francis Bell declared that government should not start 'poking its nose in ... to provide employment'.[59] But amid criticism that he had broken the government 'pledge to the soldiers',[60] he did endorse larger public works schemes. This was more Vogelian than Fabian, highlighting the point that the left-right split was operating at the 'big' end of the big-versus-small government spectrum, rather than the 'small'. From that position, successive governments of all colours could lean to the socialist left, as the New Zealand Labour Government of 1935–49, espousing more direct intervention, or to the conservative right in the fashion of earlier Reform governments, with a focus on indirect support through works schemes in particular.

Ward left the coalition in 1919, hoping to lead the Liberals into victory by seizing ground held by a still-radicalised Labour party. But his proposed state-owned bank, nationalised coalfields and freezing works, all funded by new overseas loans, were rejected by the electorate. He was not helped by the Protestant Political Association, which lobbied against the Catholic Ward in particular.[61] The result was a crashing defeat; even Ward lost his seat, remaining in the wilderness for nearly nine years. However, Labour were also spurned – their 40-hour week and plans to nationalise banks, shipping, factories and farms were too radical for a basically conservative populace, and Massey's Reform Party came to power with 43 seats and 36 percent of the vote, much of it from the rural farming sector.

The inter-war years were the first great age of the farmers, the group born of the dairying and frozen meat revolution of the 1880s and nurtured by the Liberal land reforms. War turned them into a broad class whose products were snatched up by the British market. Pastoral industries provided 91.2 percent of all exports in 1919,[62] and even after the 'commandeer' ended in 1920, these products held disproportionate sway.

The economic strength of the farming sector was further reinforced during the

William Ferguson Massey (1856–1925), 'Farmer Bill', lifelong champion of the New Zealand farmer, was the son of an Irish tenant-farmer and followed his family to New Zealand in 1870, aged 14. By the 1880s he was a self-employed farmer, but he had political ambition and became president of the Mangere Farmers Club in 1890, then provincial leader of the Auckland Agricultural Association. He entered Parliament in 1894 on the National Association platform, and presided over the decline of the Liberals and the rise of the small-holder as a key force in New Zealand.

Herman John Schmidt, Schmidt Collection, Alexander Turnbull Library, PAColl-3059, G-1533-1/1

1920s by the first of two pastoral revolutions. Superphosphate, mainly sourced from the guano mountains of Nauru, was initially spread by hand or with 'blower' trucks. Tractors appeared in number: internal combustion engines registered on farms rose from 13,981 to 18,321 during the decade. Much of the mechanisation was focused on the dairying sector. In 1920, there were 26,678 cream separators and 8806 milking plants. By 1928 there were 45,246 and 18,049 respectively. Most were electrically driven, reflected by the rise from 640 electric motors on farms in 1921 to 10,806 in 1928.[63] Improved productivity helped embed the role of the rising farming class in New Zealand's economy, and the technology – notably telephone – also had a social spin-off. Rural party lines were adopted early and spread rapidly, linking otherwise disparate holders together. Their new prosperity, translated into lifestyle and new consumer products, helped cement common ground. This new breed of farmers were middle-holders rather than small-holders, and just under 41 percent were on properties of between 100 and 640 acres by 1930.[64] They focused on dairy, lamb, beef and wool, but did not quite overwhelm the big sheep runs – a few still operated in back-country Hawke's Bay and Canterbury. In these places old money still held sway.

A good number of New Zealanders wanted in, and newspapers of the period were flooded with advertisements asking for rural land. 'Wellington city property,' one request read, 'Exchange for sound Dairy or mixed farm.' Hicks and Bull of Wanganui wanted 'land to sell' to clients in the Manawatu district.[65] The door was not opened to many. In 1919, there were 116,059 New Zealanders in pastoral occupations, including dairying. By 1929 there were 124,451.[66] But they gained power; pastoral products never fell below 91 percent of New Zealand's total exports in the 1920s, peaking in 1924, 1925 and 1929 at 94.2 percent.[67]

Pomp of government: the Legislative Council chamber, Massey on the left.

Photographer unknown, Alexander Turnbull Library, F-31486-1/2

Under this circumstance it was perhaps understandable that returned soldiers were thanked with land. Many were settled into country areas, others into towns. Some 6363 had been helped into urban properties by the end of the 1919–20 financial year, aided by maximum advances of £1000 each – though as an official report remarked, 'already the soldiers are selling the houses at a profit to civilians or men not entitled to benefits under the Discharged Soldiers Settlement Act...'[68] Most sought further profit from the rural boom, and the prospect of quick wealth on the back of rising property prices lured others into orchards, market gardens,

small sheep runs and dairy farms. By the end of the 1919–20 financial year, more than 365,000 acres had been set aside for returned soldiers, some from existing runs, others from new land carved out of previously unsettled back-country. This was done in part by state loan; government forked out over £8.6 million to 12,415 soldiers by the end of March 1920, around $663 million in early twenty-first century money.[69] Many were eager to accept, mortgaging themselves to the hilt in the hope that land values would continue to spiral upwards.

The relationship between government, economy and farming sector bore fruit in many of the public works of the period. Roads had been a bug-bear for years, and rural mechanisation added to the 30,000-odd cars already on New Zealand's roads by the late-war period, wearing down roads built to handle horse traffic. Only about 40 percent of the national network was even metalled, and wartime production helped focus the crisis. Lobbying fermented during 1918 around the

'Good Roads Association'.[70] Part of the problem was that cars and trucks moved further than horses, straining a system based around separate local Road Boards funded by local users. Several Taranaki counties tried to toll 'foreign' vehicles,[71] setting a precedent which others looked likely to follow by the early 1920s. Voices of complaint from the Good Roads Association were joined by others from the Automobile Association and Farmers' Union, and J.G. Coates proposed a 'Main Highways Bill' in 1921. County interests managed to delay it 12 months, but it was passed at the end of 1922 and came into being in April 1924, establishing a Main Highways Board and designating some 6000 – later 10,000 – miles of road under state control. Rebuilding and sealing these was a gargantuan task, and by 1929 some £59.5 million had been sunk into New Zealand's roads, outstripping rail for the first time. A further £49 million (about $357 million in early twenty-first-century money) had been spent on vehicles.[72]

Right above

Motor-buses were increasingly common on New Zealand's roads in the 1920s. This US-built REO Speed Wagon was owned by the Bell Bus Company of Wellington.

Photographer unknown, F.R. Just Collection, Alexander Turnbull Library, F-71431-1/2

Right below

New Zealanders took to cars in the 1920s like ducks to water. The initial uptake was white-collar and in the wealthier farming sector, and they proliferated in rural service towns.

S.C. Smith, Alexander Turnbull Library, PAColl-3082, G-48844-1/2

Left above

National transport services drew
attention to the state of roads
that had never been designed for
motor traffic. This is the H.C.
Baulf 'Auckland Star' service car,
between Frankton and Te Aroha
around 1924.

Left below

A service car owned by Napier's
Aard Motor Services gets a pull
on the Wairoa road, mid-1920s.
Founder G. Woodcock reputedly
coined the name to get his
company listed first in the phone
book.

Above

Sealing was expensive and labour intensive; here, road-builders rake out asphalt.

Photographer unknown, Tyndall Collection, Alexander Turnbull Library, PAColl-0866, F-104338-1/2

Above right

Putting the first coat of seal on the Paekakariki–Paraparaumu road, around 1930.

Photographer unknown, Alexander Turnbull Library, F-61963-1/2

Hydro-electricity was the other big state money-soaker, driven in part by demand from the rapidly electrifying dairy sector, but also by a proliferation of electrical appliances in general. Government acquired national water rights in 1903, and the first state power station at Lake Coleridge was in operation by 1915, supplying up to 4500 kilowatts to Christchurch. It was clear as war progressed that more would be needed. Plans to reticulate the North Island were proposed in 1918 by Chief Electrical Engineer Evan Parry. He envisaged stations generating 150 watts per capita at Mangahao, north of Wellington; Waikaremoana, near Wairoa; and Arapuni on the Waikato.[73] Despite opposition from Hawke's Bay, priority went to the Mangahao scheme, which was finished in 1924. The Arapuni station was last, mainly because it required a high dam that seemed likely to bloat the price to £3 million — around $221 million in early twenty-first-century money,[74] and demand had to top 27 megawatts to make the station economic. Teething problems with the dam delayed completion of the first stage until 1932.[75]

Massey's New Zealanders still defined themselves as double patriots, though this had subtly changed into a near-bipolar view that ranked local sentiment as highly as Imperial. As before, however, the pro-British sentiment was not reciprocated. Although seeking new trade ties with her former colonies, the mother country had been pushing her children out of the Imperial nest for some time. New Zealand, like the other Dominions, had separately signed the Treaty of Versailles, and then been a founding member of the League of Nations, where New Zealand was entitled to a separate voice. Massey had gone along under protest. His vision of Dominion partnership differed from Britain's intention of turning its empire into a commonwealth of independent nations. Partly for this reason Massey did not push New Zealand's independent role in the League of Nations.[76] Patriotism to Massey — and indeed to many New Zealanders — still meant loyalty to Imperial Britain. Schools still lined their children up, pseudo-military style, to salute the Union Jack or sing 'God Save the Queen'. 'Our country' was New Zealand, but 'our nation' remained Imperial Britain.

This attitude stood alongside a heightened sense of local nationalism, a feeling that was in part a consequence of a more intrusive government, which by definition treated New Zealand as a nation. It also reflected front-line experience. During the war, New Zealand soldiers were treated as distinct by soldiers of other nations, including the British. Shared battlefield camaraderie reinforced the trend, and by the 1920s the idea of New Zealand as a nation stood in uneasy tension with the concept of New Zealand as 'junior partner' within Empire. The oppositions remained a key tension for decades, and even in the late 1940s, when the British Empire was a faded glory, Peter Fraser was still trying to rationalise the concept in the Commonwealth context as 'independence with something added'.[77]

Left

Tuai hydro-electric station power-house under construction near Lake Waikaremoana, 1929. Early consumers were apparently told that power would be virtually free once the capital cost of the system had been paid for.

A. Hardcastle, Alexander Turnbull Library, C-14298-1/2

Below

The power-house on Lake Coleridge, one of the first buildings in New Zealand to use ferroconcrete, was formally opened with half of the planned six 1500-kW turbo-generators in November 1914.

Photographer unknown, Alexander Turnbull Library, Making New Zealand Collection, F-564-1/4-MNZ

Engineers inspect the Arapuni Dam, November 1930. An initial fill in 1929 produced cracks in the landscape around the head of the lake, traced to the weight of water, and the lake was drained while engineers dealt with the problem. The headrace was finally sealed and the station opened in 1932. Predictions that the 27-mW station would be overkill were soon dashed, but the station had been designed with expansion in mind. When completed in 1946 the enlarged station had a capacity of 162 mW, then the largest in New Zealand.

E.C. Lackland, *Evening Post* Collection, Alexander Turnbull Library, C-27085-1/2

Defence policy during the period broadly reflected this bipolar thinking. Britain began pressuring the dominions to build their own navies after the 1923 Imperial Conference, and New Zealand received its first oil-fired cruiser in 1924. However, plans to acquire a second fell foul of Massey's intention to part-fund the Singapore naval base instead. His offer of £100,000 per annum for two years went down well with Australia and India, but Canada saw little sense in the strategy and Britain's minority Labour Government also disliked the idea. Singapore went on hold and Massey came under pressure to use the £100,000 for a second cruiser in the local naval division.[78] The New Zealand Parliament approved it in October but, almost simultaneously, the British government was defeated in a general election and the incoming Conservatives restarted Singapore.

Massey wavered towards the cruiser, but wondered about taking out a loan for a £250,000 one-off grant for the base. The debate was inherited by his successor, J.G. Coates.[79] There were more calls for a third cruiser in early 1926,[80] but Coates was also pressed by the British to contribute £225,000 per annum to Singapore. The motive was financial, and while Coates refused to take over two sloops in New Zealand waters, he told the House in late 1926 that he would be guided by the Admiralty during the coming Imperial Conference. Here he 'sought the advice of Admiral Hotham',[81] attended meetings with other Imperial leaders at Downing Street, and went on to the Admiralty, the War Office and the Air Ministry.[82] As a result Coates decided to cancel a third cruiser but replace the existing ships. Meanwhile, he committed £1,000,000 to Singapore, by instalment – some $72.9 million in early twenty-first-century money.[83]

On wider matters Coates, colourfully dubbed the 'Jazz Premier' by Labour member and war veteran John A. Lee,[84] proved very different from the autocratic and conservative Massey. New Zealand's main problem was an indifferent economy. The United States partied that decade, buoyed by the second industrial revolution and the European debt mountain, but Britain was in dire straits. A generation had died in the war, the Victorian inheritance had been spent, and the 1920s were years of unrelieved gloom. New Zealand joined this glum Imperial world when the 'commandeer' was cancelled. Some £44,344,503 worth of beef, mutton, lamb and other meat had been despatched under terms of the guaranteed purchase by the end of the 1919–20 fiscal year[85] – $323.5 billion in early twenty-first-century money – along with 2,898,294 crates of cheese worth £19,106,866,[86] 1,874,912 boxes of butter valued at £8,143,100,[87] £175,970 worth of the mineral scheelite, and wool worth £2,031,092.[88]

This cash cow came to an abrupt halt in 1920–21, contributing to a dive in New Zealand property prices that left many owners unable to repay mortgages. Exports picked up as the decade wore on, in part an outcome of a British drive to trade with its dominions rather than other nations. Dairy produce was in particular demand, but prices were never high, and apart from a slight surge in 1926–28 the decade consisted of an erratic lurch from one downturn to the next. Some economists have argued that New Zealand's whole inter-war period was depressed,[89] and there seems a good deal of truth in that. Massey's government met the situation with conservative policies, and there was a call for flat-rate income tax in 1924, accompanied by an abolition of land taxes. Coates, though sharing Forbes' attitudes to direct intervention in social policy, saw succour in a vigorous public works programme. He became Minister of Railways in 1924 and restarted a raft of pre-war proposals that included reconstructing the Auckland approaches, building a deviation out of Wellington and putting a new station in near Palmerston North. In an atmosphere where cars had made inroads into short-haul travel and were digging into the longer routes, he called for new operating efficiencies and higher speeds.

J.G. Coates (1878–1943, standing at left) at the Mahina-a-rangi meeting house, Ngaruawahia.

Photographer unknown, Alexander Turnbull Library, F-59948-1/2

To some extent this neo-Vogelism paid off; goods travelling by rail rose by about 1.8 million tons per annum over the decade, and passenger numbers doubled.[90] This policy — and other programmes Coates inherited — outlasted his administration. Public works spending hovered around 21–22 percent of state spending during the war, dipped slightly in 1919, then began a steady climb to a high of 31.4 percent in 1931,[91] before plunging drastically in the face of George Forbes' efforts to trade out of the depression. However, direct social spending remained minimal, apart from education, which absorbed around 10 percent of the state budget. Health budgets stood at around 3 percent of state spending in the first decades of the century, then plunged to under 2 percent through the 1920s.[92]

An ageing J.G. Ward returned to politics in 1928. He stands here with his son Vincent Aubrey Ward.

Photographer unknown, Alexander Turnbull Library, F-123686-1/2

Social welfare payments included war, old age and widows pensions, along with epidemic funds and a variety of annuities, and the net total in 1922, the peak year, amounted to 9.8 percent of all state expenditure.[93]

In the end, however, neither new public works nor a bungled effort to hijack prices on the London dairy market managed to pull the New Zealand economy out of the doldrums. Seventy-two-year-old Sir Joseph Ward re-emerged as leader of a United Party coalition in 1928, promising to cure all with new borrowing. Figures such as £70 million were bandied about after an address Ward gave in the Auckland Town Hall. In fact the plan was to borrow £7 million a year for a decade, and Ward's error has been put down to his failing eyesight and difficulty reading his speech notes.[94] Ward's United party was elected as a minority government in November, but the decrepit ex-Liberal was not up to the job. His absences from the House became longer, his declamations vaguer, and his land-tax was a political disaster. He made his last appearance in September 1929 with the claim that every New Zealander who wanted work would soon have it. This apparently reflected his misunderstanding of the £7 million loan, and Forbes had to issue a formal denial.[95] Ward was persuaded to resign in May 1930, handing the reins to Forbes, and the old Liberal warhorse died eight weeks later.

By then, New Zealand's fortunes had turned for the worse. The US stock market crashed in late 1929, bursting the United States bubble and starting a chain of events that brought the Western world to its knees. Produce prices collapsed, and New Zealand — reliant on dairy and produce markets in London — entered a slide that continued until the bleak winter of 1933.[96]

MR HAWKER ARRIVES FROM BLENHEIM
WITH 2 PASSENGERS - MESSRS. PERANO
AND MC ARTNEY. NELSON 13.11.21. F.M.JONES.

Puritans and parties

Life in New Zealand between the wars differed from that of the jingo world of 1914. Trends that had been quietly bobbing along were refocused, re-energised and remixed by the conflict, particularly the ethos of social purity – which as one analyst has noted, became entwined in the new ideals of the post-war period.[97] In part, this change reflected a crisis of confidence brought on by the strains of war. The more zealous advocates of social purity feared society was about to collapse in the face of unrestrained irreligious activity, seeing sexual misbehaviour and drunkenness around every corner. Protestant churches railed against contraception, joined by Baptists and Methodists as the decade went on. Family life was exalted through what we might call the cult of domesticity. Much of this extended previous idealism – the family, for instance, had been evangelised in British cities and towns from the mid-nineteenth century.[98] However, all emerged in full flower after the war, a lurch to the safe and well-understood by a generation traumatised by events they had been unable to control or avoid.

Many institutions changed under these pressures. Racing was a particular target. Totalisator machines had been subject to criticism since the 1880s, generating petitions to Parliament in 1903 and 1907 – the last running neck-and-neck at 36,311 for and 36,471 against.[99] Ward's Gaming and Lotteries Act of 1908 compromised: off-course bookmaking was legalised and the totalisator entrenched, giving the government a percentage of the turnover. However, the system was a disaster and the moral evangelists prevailed in 1911 when bookmaking was made illegal. This did not reduce betting, and estimates suggest that illegal bookmaking up to 1946 topped £24 million. The ultimate answer was a government-run Totalisator Agency Board (TAB), established in 1949.[100]

The evangelists found another expression in Plunket, founded by asylum administrator Dr Truby King in 1907. His hygiene advice helped reduce the infant mortality rate, but his philosophy also drew upbringing into the framework of the socially pure, adding elements of racial destiny and patriotic fervour. His

Opposite above

New Zealand burst into the age of aviation with several spectacular cross-country flights by rival air transport companies. This is the DH-9 of the Canterbury (NZ) Aviation Company in 1921 after an early flight to Nelson.

Frederick Nelson Jones, F.N. Jones Collection, Alexander Turnbull Library, PAColl-3051, G-28554-1/2

Opposite below

The public welcomes Charles Kingsford Smith at Wigram after his flight across the Tasman in September 1928.

Photographer unknown, Alexander Turnbull Library, PAColl-4273-3, F-30845-1/2

Above left

Francis Chichester's de Havilland DH-60G Gypsy Moth is unloaded at Wellington.

Photographer unknown, Alexander Turnbull Library, PAColl-0614, G-32441-1/4

Above right

Francis Chichester (1901–72) made the first east–west solo crossing of the Tasman in 1931. In 1967 he became the first to complete a solo circumnavigation of the world in a yacht.

Sydney Morning Herald, Alexander Turnbull Library, C-27086-1/2

prescription for new mothers involved large doses of discipline, obedience and regular bowel movements. This last, it appeared, was the way to avoid tendencies to vice, and mothers were intoned and exhorted to enforce their infants' toilet habits by the clock, to keep the children clean, and, in general, to conform.

Conformity was certainly the name of the game during the inter-war decades. New Zealand social norm was built around a narrow spectrum of acceptable thoughts and actions. Those who did not match up were defined as 'abnormal' and in need of 'correction' — a mind-set that led, among other things, to some left-handers being forced to write with their other hand at school. This reduction of humanity to a uniform machine extended to thought, following the lead of thinkers such as Carl Jung who portrayed the psyche as a mechanistic system. The mind-set ultimately devolved into eugenics, a world phenomenon that New Zealanders expressed in the absurd claim that the Dominion was 98.5 percent British — a remark that ignored Maori, Chinese, Irish and Scandinavians among others.

Above left

Wanganui bookmaker Sidney Blain on the job before the First World War.

Photographer unknown, Tesla Studios Collection, Alexander Turnbull Library, PAColl-3046, G-16693-1/1

Above right

Crowds highlight the huge popularity of racing during the inter-war period.

John Reginald Wall, J.R. Wall Collection, Alexander Turnbull Library, PAColl-3065, G-17834-1/11

Right

Night races.

Photographer unknown, Alexander Turnbull Library, C-27176-1/2

This new society also found new places to live. 'The homes of the town-workers,' John Mulgan wrote of these years, 'ate wide into the country, red-roofed, with their small gardens, concrete paths, and modern sanitation...'.[101] Facilitated by car and mass transport, the new suburbs spread from inner-city Auckland, Wellington, Christchurch and Dunedin in particular. Some, like Johnsonville, were old villages; others were laid out from scratch. They brought a new look to the New Zealand urban landscape. Villas were passé; architects and draughtsmen sought alternative inspiration in the Americas, and California bungalows went up alongside English cottage-style homes in the burgeoning suburbs,[102] interleaved with occasional Spanish Mission. Later they were joined by daring flat-roofed, speed-lined modernist styles, pastel-stuccoed expressions of the art-deco age. In a few suburbs these styles predominated. All were set amid wide streets with roadside trees — often one to each berm — with space for parks, small shopping centres, and schools.

Left above

Quarter-acre paradise, early 1920s style, complete with Dodge and Hupmobile. House, garden, berm and car defined the classic Kiwi suburban home for the rest of the century — only the details changed.

Henry Norford Whitehead, H.N. Whitehead Collection, Alexander Turnbull Library, PAColl-3068, G-4610-1/1

Left below

Early bungalows brought twentieth-century styles to New Zealand.

Steffano Francis Webb, Steffano Webb Collection, Alexander Turnbull Library, PAColl-3061, F-3904-1/1

Social utopia did not seem far away as garden beautification societies competed
to make the neatest and most attractive properties. 'Scientific' home management
was the order of the day.[103] Rooms gained new names; the verandah became the
porch, parlour the living room, and many homes featured a 'sleeping porch' –
designed to maximise fresh air by putting the slumbering home owner outside. As
in the settler era, cleanliness had a moral dimension, helped in a physical sense by
new technical advances that brought easy-clean materials to home interiors,
notably chrome, ceramic and tiles in the bathrooms.[104]

These developments, sieved through the filter of apparent scientific certainties, stood against the other forces of the 1920s and 1930s. A new youth lifestyle emerged with the Hollywood movie culture. This was the other reaction to wartime trauma; the lucky ones had come out alive and intended to live life to the full. Others had been children during the war and had no intention of suffering like their fathers or elder brothers. Their culture was spread by radio, popular magazines and cinema, giving New Zealanders fresh impressions of life outside New Zealand and the British Empire. It was a world of temptation. Early Hollywood output was riddled with nudity and unsubtle innuendo, ranging from 'what the butler saw' kinescopes to dancing girls in D.W. Griffiths' *Intolerance* of 1916. Films also brought implicit sex, epitomised for many by screen vamp Theda Bara ('Arab Death'), whose performances pushed the boundaries of moral sensibilities.

Lawn tennis, 'dates', outdoor picnics, parties and the Charleston combined with the latest New York or Parisian fashions to create a new culture of youth and freedom. The main sources of inspiration were not surprising given the similarities between the New Zealand and American frontiers since the colonial period. Indeed, some Californian architecture had been in vogue across New Zealand since before the First World War. Parks and gardens were 'Americanised' with date palms. Shops and businesses reflected the culture in their window displays and range and style of products. Telephones became widespread for the first time and fuelled new ways for people to communicate and relate to each other.

Wellington expanded during the inter-war years as new public transport and motor cars made suburban life practical. This is Wilton in 1932, looking towards the Karori Cemetery. Otari Native Plant Museum stands on the left, established in 1927 by Leonard Cockayne and Director of Parks and Reserves J.G. MacKenzie.

Photographer unknown, *Evening Post* Collection, Alexander Turnbull Library, PAColl-0614, G-88436-1/2

This lifestyle was backed by new consumer products. Cars — made common by the invention of the production line — poured into New Zealand, finding a ready market among white-collar workers, professionals and the rising farming class. Numbers rose from around 100,000 at the end of the First World War to nearly 300,000 by the end of the 1930s,[105] and they were joined by trucks, tractors and buses. New Zealand effectively motorised during the period. Some commercial trade was still carried on by cart, but for the average family, transport in the late 1920s meant either taking the bus or train, or getting their own car. Around one in eight families had one by the 1930s, and garages vied for sales. 'The invincible Talbot,' intoned one Christchurch advertisement in 1928, offering a tourer for £575 and a saloon for £685.[106] These were significant sums — $41,972 and $50,001 respectively in early twenty-first-century money — but New Zealanders were prepared to pay them.[107] Many preferred American cars, such as the Dodge 'Victory Six', a snip at £465 ($33,425), which was sold on the basis of safety features such as hydraulic four-wheel brakes,[108] or a 'turret-top' all-steel body.[109] In 1928, some £2.9 million ($211.68 million) worth of cars were imported from the United States and Canada, against just £800,000 ($58.39 million) worth from Britain.[110]

This was the age of mass-produced and disposable consumer goods. Poorer families could afford to buy products that had been luxury items 20 years earlier, including electric kettles, toasters, ranges and hotplates, water heaters, refrigerators, washing machines with electric wringers — even glow-in-the-dark 'radium' switches for those wanting to turn on the light without groping.[111] 'Pinnacles of perfection,' one advertisement for Moffats 'Gold Medal Electric Ranges' declared.[112] Electricity also brought voices and music from afar. In this golden age of wireless, 'Stellar Altair' five-valve radios promised 'wide reception with true microphone reproduction' through an 8-inch speaker, with 'spin type tuning' for 'easier, quicker tuning'.[113] Other goods were gimmicky, such as the Roycroft 'Billiards & Dining Table Combined' that could be picked up for £45 'complete with cues, balls and marking board' — or easy terms of £2.10.0 down and 7/6 weekly.[114] Many of these products came from the United States; imports from America hovered between £5 and £8 million — roughly $359.41 and $575.06 million in early twenty-first-century money — for much of the 1920s, and in 1926 were nearly half that imported from Britain.[115]

Below left

Clean, controllable heat made all the difference in the kitchen, and it did not take long for marketing to capitalise on the benefits of gas and electricity over coal. This is a Wanganui Gas Company display in 1923.

Frank J. Denton, Tesla Collection, Alexander Turnbull Library, PAColl-3046, F-21467-1/1

Below right

Radio transmitters going up on Mount Victoria in 1927. Most homes had a valve receiver in that golden age of wireless; and most boys dreamed of building crystal sets.

Photographer unknown, Alexander Turnbull Library, PAColl-0614, G-997-1/2-EP

None of this went down well with the social purists. Dancing was too sexual, movies too corrupting, popular magazines and books too explicit. As late as 1937 *Truth* was declaring that 3,000,000 books annually were pouring into the country and 'contaminating the mental outlook' of youth with 'sewer literature'.[116] Again, this attitude had its origins in jingo society, refocused by war and technology. Regulations were already in force to restrict literature by 1913, and in 1917 attention swung to movies. The Minister of Internal Affairs circularised local bodies about 'the exhibition on hoardings and in the vestibules of theatres and other places of objectionable posters'. If municipal authorities were not prepared to 'exercise their powers in this matter', Government 'may consider it necessary to find some other means of coping with what is an undoubted evil, and which is calculated to undermine the morals of the juvenile population of the Dominion'.[117] The battle continued after the war, reinforced in May 1921 by an Order in Council banning any document inciting violence or sedition.[118]

Right

Motorcycles came of age in the 1920s. This is a well-packed Clyno and sidecar around 1920. The limed road is noteworthy.

Photographer unknown, *The Press* Christchurch Collection, Alexander Turnbull Library, PAColl-3031, G-8536-1/1

Below

Hodson's Pioneer Motor Service, Ridgway Street, Wanganui, selling various brands of fuel during the 1920s.

Frank J. Denton, Alexander Turnbull Library, PAColl-3046, F-21107-1/1

Left

Chummy motoring: a couple with
their Austin 7 around 1929.

Photographer unknown, Bill Main But Is It Art?
Collection, Alexander Turnbull Library, PAColl-2489,
C-15900-1/2

Below

New Zealanders were not slow
when it came to buying cars.
American varieties initially stood
alongside English cars.

Samuel Heath Head, S. Head Collection, Alexander
Turnbull Library, PAColl-3049, G-12090-1/1

Right above

Cars soon supplanted horse and buggy, opening up the tradition of the Sunday drive and weekend picnic for many families.

H.N. Whitehead, Alexander Turnbull Library, PAColl-3068, G-4667-1/1

Right centre

Cars at a sports meeting, 1920s. New Zealand's tradition of geriatric motor vehicles did not flourish until later in the century, but some older models still poke through the masses here.

Photographer unknown, Alexander Turnbull Library, PAColl-0866, F-104319-1/2

Right below

Cars at a race meet near Stratford in 1927.

John Reginald Wall, J.R. Wall Collection, Alexander Turnbull Library, PAColl-3065, G-17853-1/2

It was a largely male society. A blokeish world with its emphasis on alcohol, rowdiness and a professed indifference to the visceral had existed before the war as a part of labouring culture and the overall frontier environment. But the shared experiences on Gallipoli and the Western Front pushed the phenomenon in new directions and gave it new strengths, welding it to the family ethos and the rising world of dairy and sheep farmers. In many respects this became the definition of New Zealand culture as a whole for the next 60 years.

These traditions drew together to create an image of resourceful, independent, egalitarian, straight-talking, rugby-playing, hard-living outdoorsmen. This ideal drew inspiration from the 'working-class' ethos of the settler period. New emphasis on rugby and outdoor sporting pursuits was one of several factors driving the popularity of weekend hunting and tramping. What had been a way of life for hill-country shepherds emerged as a popular recreational activity, one also shared by women – but inevitably imaged around the 'good keen man'. From this also emerged the twentieth-century image of the gumbooted, laid-back 'Kiwi farmer' and the laconic 'she'll be right' attitude. Fred Dagg, Wal Footrot, and the imagery echoed in some advertisements of the late 1990s all stem from a frontier ethos brought together and refined by the traumatic lens of Gallipoli and Flanders.

New Zealand's bloke culture had its own customs, mostly to do with alcohol. The most prominent was 'shouting' – buying drinks for others in the group in even numbers. Beer was sold in jugs over the bar and 'chugged' in seven-ounce glasses. It was also watered, a temperance-driven strategy that fostered consumption in quantity. Bloke culture had its own jargon – often derived from drinking, but also reflecting other facets of hands-on pastoral life. It was a white sub-culture, and it was wholly male. Even husbands tacitly behaved as single men when with their fellows, and wives were expected to be submissive stay-at-homes.

This ethos was reflected in sport; the inter-war years were the golden age of rugby. There were All Black tours of Australia in 1920 and 1922; and in 1924 a new team – including legendary fullback George Nepia – took on Britain, France and British Columbia. They played 32 games and won all of them, giving the team the epithet 'Invincibles'. Another tour of Australia followed in 1926, South Africa in 1928, Australia again in 1929, 1932, 1934 and 1938, and the British Isles and Canada in 1935.[119] War stopped the formal tours but did not dim the enthusiasm, and 'friendlies' were occasionally organised at army level, as in North Africa where a team drawn from 2 NZ Division played another drawn from the South African force – an event requiring its own air cover. International matches were backed by grassroots popularity, fostered by strong inter-provincial rivalry based around the Ranfurly Shield. This had been established in 1902 as a gift from the Governor-General of the day, and came into its own in the 1920s. At this social level, rugby was part of the social flattening of the inter-war period, simultaneously a leveller that brought together people from all walks of life and a mechanism for exalting the heroes of the field as a national elite.

The legendary George Nepia (1905–66), fullback with the 1924 'Invincibles', seen here in 1928.

S.P. Andrew, Alexander Turnbull Library, F-18732-1/1

The 'Invincibles' return, 1925.

Photographer unknown, Alexander Turnbull
Library, C-21948-1/2

The cultural cringe and its flip sides found new expression as the century aged. In the new environment, New Zealanders could be the best of the best – but only overseas – and the result was a disproportionate number of New Zealanders in high places outside the country, particularly in the arts and sciences, epitomised by the pioneers, Katherine Mansfield and Ernest Rutherford. A list of names and barebones biographical information published in the 1965 *Encyclopedia of New Zealand* occupied more than 30 pages of close-printed text, listed by country.[120] By then there were prominent New Zealanders from Argentina to Zambia, where Leonard Bean became one of nine Permanent Secretaries in 1960.[121] Most expatriates flourished in Britain, where there were high-achieving Kiwis everywhere from the armed services to the arts, photography, ballet, government offices, medicine, the sciences, academia and literature.

The reasons for going were not solely cringe-related. New Zealand, as a small country, simply did not offer opportunities for the ambitious. However, the issue of acceptance as an achiever within New Zealand was also a factor. Perhaps the key question is why there was such a disproportionate number of authors, poets and scientists among the migrants. Britain's community of talented expatriate Kiwi writers was well known – their numbers during the century included Dan Davin, Geoffrey Cox, Alan Mulgan, Hector Bolitho and Dorothy Eden. Scientists included anthropologist Raymond Firth. Medical men were also prominent, notably in the field of plastic surgery, among them Sir Robert Macintosh, George Maloney, James Murdoch and Arthur Mowlem. Not all went 'home'. William Pickering (1910–2004) went instead to the United States, where he became a leading space scientist.

New Zealand meets South Africa on the Titirangi putting green: Murray (New Zealand) putts while plus-four-clad Locke (South Africa) looks on during a 1930s challenge match.

Weekly News, Alexander Turnbull Library, 2336-MNZ

Above left

Deerstalkers in the 1930s.

Photographer unknown, Alexander Turnbull Library,
F-1768-1/2-MNZ

Above right

A record head shot in the
Whitcombe watershed, Westland,
around 1938. 'Many good heads
have come from this part of the
back-country', the original caption
remarks. 'But it is not every
stalker who has the endurance to
carry the head out to civilisation'.

G.G. Atkinson, Alexander Turnbull Library,
F-1352-1/4-MNZ

Left

Deer hunter at White Rock, South
Wairarapa, in 1921.

Leslie Hinge, Leslie Hinge Collection, Alexander
Turnbull Library, PAColl-3050, G-16902-1/4

To some extent this pattern was skewed because New Zealand's first and most prominent achievers were a writer and a scientist – Katherine Mansfield (1888–1923) and Ernest Rutherford (1871–1937) respectively. Others followed their lead, but there were also cultural issues. While the gentry had pretensions to art and mind, the 'bloke' culture that had grown to dominate by the early twentieth century was superficially anti-intellectual. Work gangs had little time for the finer arts; and as twentieth-century conformity emerged, the rewards of being exceptional diminished. Settler literature had been neither snobbish nor wholly fictional; authors typically wrote often lurid accounts of their experiences. Populist literature included pot-boiler fiction, serials, detective stories and romances, but there was almost nothing considered great literature by the 'high-brow' in-crowd. For a young Kathleen Beauchamp it was only in the opiate-riddled, sexually relaxed and generally dissipated Bloomsbury set of London that she could find an environment of like-minded literati with whom she could relate. She left her name behind in New Zealand.[122]

Rutherford's situation was different. When the 'father of modern physics' graduated he tried initially to find work as a teacher, then moved to Trinity College, Cambridge in 1895. His professional career led him from McGill University – where he did the work that won him a Nobel Prize in 1907 – to Manchester University, and in 1919 he became Professor of Experimental Physics at Cambridge, a post he held until his death in 1937. Rutherford helped define the theoretical basis of

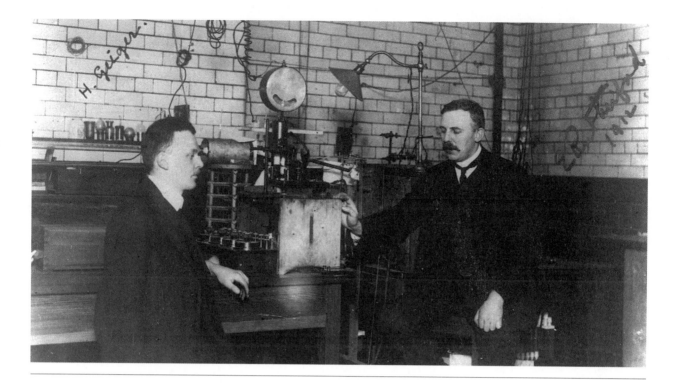

Ernest Rutherford (1871–1937) and Hans Geiger (left) in the Manchester University physics laboratory, 1912.

twentieth-century atomic theory, and at popular level remained best known for what he regarded as a party-trick – splitting the atom. His career encapsulated the paradox of the expatriate game; in practice, Rutherford became an Englishman. He visited New Zealand just four times during the twentieth century, yet he – like Mansfield – remained a celebrated national hero in New Zealand.

The brain drain was not all one-way. Anti-Semitism in Germany and Austria prompted a wave of emigration by those who could afford it during the 1930s, among them many of Europe's top scientists and intellectuals. Some came to New Zealand, including Karl Popper (1902–94), one of the giant philosophers of the twentieth century, who picked New Zealand for its distance. He taught at Canterbury University from 1937 to 1946 and produced one of his best known works, *The Open Society and its Enemies*, in New Zealand. As an Austrian he did not subscribe to New Zealand's cultural cringe, though it subscribed to him. Local recognition of his genius, outside academia, had to wait until he moved to England in the wake of the Second World War.

Sugarbags and conservatives

There was food in New Zealand at this time, but the trains did not always load it. Rain fell that winter on empty docks. Did we hear, perhaps for the first time, the voice of a people that has recognised an injustice, that has perceived the possibility of disorganisation in its midst? Economists and old men told us that all this had happened before and would pass away, but this comfort was of philosophic form and our natures were sensuous and unsuited to philosophy.

– John Mulgan, *Report on Experience*[123]

The 'Great Depression' of the early 1930s seared itself into the psyche of a generation, a time of hardship and hopelessness that defined mid-century New Zealand. Those who lived through it were determined that the pain should never be repeated, and many of the decisions and policies that followed in the 1940s and beyond were specifically moulded by that determination. It was the 1980s before a generation came to power that was not, directly or indirectly, shaped in mind and deed by the experience.

The depression was a world phenomenon, which some historians argue was the low point of a Kondratieff cycle — a generations-long swing in the fortunes of capitalism.[124] This is debatable, and in any event the immediate causes for the crash of 1929 are well known.[125] Part of the problem was the second industrial revolution, itself accelerated by the First World War, which introduced widespread mass machine production, entrenching the multinational corporations that had been expanding in the previous decades. These removed the 'averaging' effect of many small companies that had been crucial to the success of the nineteenth-century capitalist system. Another part of the problem was war reparations levelled against Germany, coupled with the fact that the United States emerged in 1918 as a creditor to Europe. This affected the system of world payments and helped keep Britain poor, which in turn became a problem for New Zealand. Another problem was greed, particularly in the United States where banks cashed in on the local boom, lending without adequate security for overpriced properties and throw-away consumer goods. When the New York stock exchange crashed in late 1929, destroying a good deal of the paper wealth on which speculative prosperity hung, the edifice burst. It took down the United States economy and, with it, the capitalist world. As Eric Hobsbawm and others have noted, there is no explanation for the crisis without America.[126]

New Zealand's main difficulty was its status as primary producer, selling into a single market. Exports stood at £54.9 million in 1929, around $400.5 million in early twenty-first-century money, of which £40.4 million went to the mother country, but quantities and prices plunged as the British economy dived during 1930.[127] Unemployment rose. Unrecoverable debts soared. In 1929, there had been 687 bankruptcies over debts totalling £233,000. In 1930, 752 people and companies went belly-up for debts totalling £471,000.[128]

Something had to be done, but as Guthrie-Smith remarked, the 'harassed government' had lost its sources of income.[129] Forbes sailed for the Imperial Conference in August 1930 with no cure to hand other than the 'sanity and sobriety' prescribed by visiting banker Sir Otto Neimeyer, meaning fiscal restraint.[130] This provided a background to cancelling several railway projects, throwing 1700 men out of work. In his absence the government passed an Unemployment Act, but Forbes returned in January 1931 to declare that the dole would be paid only to those who worked for it — which in the absence of a vigorous export sector meant make-work. Forbes also declared that the state books had to be balanced, announcing reductions in relief wages and the salaries of all public servants.[131] The people, he insisted, must return to the land, a remark that, as one historian has noted, made no sense when produce prices had plunged and the farming sector was in crisis.[132] Guthrie-Smith's own net income from Tutira station plunged from an unprecedented high of £5722 in 1929 to a £4276 loss in 1931. He was not alone, and remarked that by 1933, 'New Zealand sheep-farmers everywhere were temporarily bankrupt'.[133]

Forbes' efforts were patently counter-productive, but most people remembered the halcyon days of 1913, and Forbes — at best an unimaginative, dour and conservative politician — was simply reflecting a worldwide effort to return to those times. In practice, of course, this effort to revive a lost golden age through renewed evangelism of the old doctrines was racked with problems. The third decade of the twentieth century was a new environment, with its mass production, war reparations, large corporations, different social mores and new technology. The philosophy of capitalism was unchanged, but the detail of its operation had moved on. These difficulties were eventually realised, but in the meantime, as John Mulgan later put it, economists 'gained the status of witch doctors'.[134]

The crisis was compounded by a summer drought in early 1931 — and then, just when it seemed New Zealand's fortunes were diving to rock bottom, Hawke's Bay was laid to ruin by a massive earthquake. It was New Zealand's most lethal calamity, with twice the casualties on a per-capita basis than the 1979 Erebus DC-10 disaster.[135] Victims ranged from six-week-old David Tripney to 92-year-old

Napier's Hastings Street could have been mistaken for a war zone in this classic image of the Hawke's Bay quake on the morning of 3 February 1931. A fireman, possibly Fire Superintendent W.J. Gilberd, walks away as a blaze rips through the ruined town centre. Although often captioned 'ten minutes after the quake', a comparison with other photos and available records shows that it was actually taken about 45 minutes later. Lack of water pressure — spurred by damage to the pipes, combined with power failure — hampered fire-fighting efforts.

Arthur Bendigo Hurst, P.T.W. Ashcroft Collection, Alexander Turnbull Library, F-139885-1/2

Gilbert Brown.[136] At one early stage authorities feared that up to 300 had died.[137] The toll was finally settled at 256 — though despite an outstanding effort, two people were never accounted for.[138] Over 400 were hospitalised with serious injuries. At least 2500 were cut, bruised, scratched and shocked, a toll never fully evaluated because few bothered to report trivial injuries. Damage stretched from Gisborne to Wanganui. Napier and Hastings were devastated.

For some the scenes of death and ruin were all too familiar. Former soldiers drew on reserves of emotional strength forged a dozen-odd years earlier in the trenches, making a difference in the minutes and hours after the shocks. The Western Front also laid important groundwork for post-quake organisation — in Hastings one wartime unit was even resurrected; and people fell back on the wider bonds built during the conflict. They were joined by civilians whose own responses were shaped by the organisation around them. 'Too much cannot be said of the splendid spirit of the Napier people,' a reporter wrote. 'There is something in big catastrophes that brings out the best in everyone, as did the Great War, and the way in which people are forgetting themselves to others strikes the stranger forcibly. Property is nothing. Fatigue and personal feelings do not count.'[139] Another contemporary account wrote of the way 'neighbour helped neighbour' and 'for the time being, at least, there is a greater human understanding of each other than ever there was before. May it continue!'[140] Many worked on despite personal loss, among them Constable Tripney who knew his wife and infant son had been killed but 'continued to work ... with rescue and search parties'.[141] At least one miscreant, under arrest in the police cells, did what he could to help and then turned himself in again.

Not everyone stood up to the strain. Some collapsed into what E.F. Scott called 'an attack of excitement hysteria'.[142] Others were effectively shell-shocked. One woman escaped from a collapsing store in Hastings only to see two friends crushed by the falling building. For some hours she and several others wandered 'aimlessly about the streets, which were piled up with wreckage. We were all dazed, and could only sit there and half realise what had happened. The most terrible feeling was that of helplessness.' She was found by a friend who 'took her to a place of

Below left

Napier hospital — the only hospital in Hawke's Bay — was wrecked by the quake. Staff hastened to get patients and equipment out, setting up tents in the nearby Botanical Gardens.

Photographer unknown, Williams Collection, Alexander Turnbull Library, F-29566-1/2

Below right

Hastings was almost as heavily hammered as Napier. However, although both the borough power-house and most of the water pipes were damaged, they were not completely wrecked and there was enough water for fire-fighters to extinguish blazes before they spread.

S.C. Smith, Alexander Turnbull Library, PAColl-3082, G-47684-1/2

refuge'.[143] Still others put on a brave face; W. Olphert thought the 'people of Napier were wonderfully cheerful',[144] but Agnes Bennett thought those she found on the Marine Parade the day after the quake were wrapped in 'an expression of dumb misery ... even the children seemed toneless and wearied...'.[145] For still others the quake brought out the worst. 'A ghoul was seen stealing a wristwatch off a dead man lying on the pavement,' a horrified Dorothy Campbell wrote to her aunt, 'while articles of clothing were removed from living, wounded people. Houses were robbed while the owners were doing rescue work, goods & money were stolen from shops.'[146]

Left and below

Emergency depots in Hastings. Many survivors were evacuated in the days that followed.

Sydney Charles Smith, S.C. Smith Collection, Alexander Turnbull Library, PAColl-3082, G-47882-1/2

Sydney Charles Smith, S.C. Smith Collection, Alexander Turnbull Library, PAColl-3082, G-48308-1/2

Napier reborn, seen here in 1934.

The war continued to dominate thoughts during the days and weeks afterwards. 'Scenes reminiscent of the war time in France,' read one caption in the 1931 book *Hawke's Bay – Before and After*.[147] Others compared the destruction of the Napier nurses' home to the effects of shellfire.[148] The favourite comparison was Ypres, probably because it was well known. Dorothy Campbell heard former soldiers declare that damage had been greater than several months' shelling.[149] Others found the exodus that followed reminiscent of war-torn France. 'The traffic on the road to Palmerston North was tremendous,' one reporter wrote. 'Cars, lorries, everything on wheels seemed to be there. They were full of furniture, bedding, mattress, babies prams, and all sorts of household utensils. It was a flight.'[150] Mary Hunter was driven south by a Feilding dairy factory manager at night, in a convoy of 'thousands of cars almost touching each other', though she saw 'almost as many going to Napier'. The lights of the vehicles 'looked like a fiery serpent when we got to the bends in the road'.[151] Hunter's estimate was no exaggeration. The 70,000-odd residents of Hawke's Bay owned just over 10,500 vehicles in 1931,[152] but literally tens of thousands of other vehicles drove in during the two days after the disaster to bring aid or evacuate refugees. Some 27,000 cars passed through Waipukurau in 13 and a half hours on 5 February alone.[153]

Forbes did not change his attitudes in the face of the disaster. A rehabilitation loan offered by the Bank of England at peppercorn rates was turned down, and so was an offer by the Mayor of San Francisco to raise a Mansion House Fund.

Crowds await election results on the corner of Mercer and Willis Streets, Wellington, in late 1931. Labour increased its support by 45,000 votes that year, and Forbes' wildly unpopular United Party seemed set to lose, but a coalition deal with J.G. Coates' Reform Party kept them in power. The cost was a heavier defeat in 1935.

William Raine, Alexander Turnbull Library, F-66497-1/2

Contemporary estimates put earthquake losses at £3,685,450,[154] while a 1997 study suggests £3,402,500.[155] Both were far in excess of the £1.5 million granted by government under the Hawkes Bay Earthquake Act, of which £1,250,000 was earmarked for businesses and the rest to local bodies. This 'feeble start' represented all that the Forbes administration was prepared to provide,[156] and a study has shown that it did not stave off the depression. Construction work in Hawke's Bay rose from the usual average of around 6 percent of the national total in 1930 to 13 percent in mid-1934, then fell to the usual 6 percent in 1935, with a net effect equal to about 2 percent of pre-quake GDP.[157] Specific employment figures are not available,[158] but one analysis suggested up to 600 jobs were created,[159] while a more convincing 1997 study identified 300 new jobs in 1932–33.[160] The earthquake was associated with a brief spike in unemployment, but there was no sustained reduction of unemployment afterwards.[161]

George Forbes (left) and British Prime Minister Ramsay MacDonald.

Photographer unknown, Alexander Turnbull Library, F-41881-1/2

The quake, in short, simply compounded the miseries of the Depression. New Zealand generally continued to slide through the year. National unemployment soared from 8000 to 27,000 during February 1931, in part a combination of the quake and changes in seasonal work. But it compounded the sense of calamity, and the Labour Party took up the cause, calling for industrial action if wage cuts were enforced. Three thousand workers marched on Parliament in March to support the call.[162] Late that year, Forbes suggested the crisis had reached such dimension as to demand wartime unity, proposing an all-Parliament government. Labour refused, but Coates — though he disliked Forbes — agreed, and a United-Reform coalition was announced in September. Labour increased its support in the election that year to the tune of 45,000 votes, but held just 24 seats against the 51 that went to the United-Reform juggernaut.

Coates became Minister of Unemployment, then Minister of Finance after 1933 — positions that, with a little post-fact help from Sidney Holland,[163] led to him becoming one of New Zealand's most hated politicians for 60 years. To some extent, such criticism is unfair. Coates had been an advocate of efforts to build private-sector prosperity through government construction and management of infrastructure, and he continued to hold these views into the 1930s — even setting

Right above
Mount Victoria Tunnel, Wellington, under construction around 1930.

Photographer unknown, Alexander Turnbull Library, PAColl-5448, G-25094-1/1

Right below
Depression-era hut in the Waimarino plains.

Samuel Heath Head, S. Head Collection, Alexander Turnbull Library, F-41332-1/2

up a think-tank in 1933 that included such left-leaning economists as W.B. Sutch and R.M.R. Campbell. But history should not rehabilitate him too far. He was also of a mind with his Prime Minister and others in Cabinet when it came to balancing the books irrespective of the social cost.

New Zealand's books were certainly in trouble by 1932. National export receipts plunged from their 1929 high of £54.9 million to £34.9 million in the 1931–32 financial year.[164] With puritanical zeal the Coates-Forbes administration slashed state wages by 20 percent between 1931 and 1932. Pensions were cut 30 percent. Public works expenditure was cut by three-quarters, and hospitals were plunged into a funding crisis, forced to re-use disposable equipment and cut back on patient food.[165] The National Expenditure Adjustment Act of 1932 slashed bank deposit rates. Compulsory arbitration was cancelled, giving employers power to reduce wages and conditions. This orgy of Calvinist rectitude was meant to facilitate growth, but in fact it merely succeeded in taking money out of a depressed economy, intensifying the depression.[166] As Guthrie-Smith remarked, 'every legislative enactment seemed to hinder not help'.[167]

The social cost was staggering. Children, often barefoot, were sent to school with Chelsea sugar-sacks as their only protection from winter rain. Once inside, many clustered around the classroom stove, their only source of warmth that day. Some had to work, outside school hours, on milk or paper runs – often still in bare feet. Every penny brought into the household counted, and even so, meals were often reduced to bread and butter, sometimes with jam if the family were lucky. Malnourished children grew into unhealthy adults, which fuelled the rejection of so many New Zealanders as medically unfit for military service a few years later. It was a time of making do or doing without. Buckets, pots, pans and spades were repaired. Worn wallpaper, furniture and paint were lived with. Luckier families fell back on their 'quarter acre', using domestic chickens and vegetable

J.G. Coates, as Prime Minister in the late 1920s, tried to use public works to stimulate the economy, but Forbes slashed budgets, and projects such as this Wellington reclamation slowed to a crawl.

Photographer unknown, Alexander Turnbull Library, F-91142-1/2

gardens to supplement diets that might otherwise have fallen below subsistence. The garden as defence against starvation was well recognised; suburban garden clubs encouraged householders to cultivate their quarter-acre, and there was even a competition in 1933 to find the best garden kept by an unemployed house-holder.[168]

Some of the unemployed became swaggers, roaming the roads in the way of their grandfathers 50 years earlier, hoping they might find work on farms here and there. However, rural outlook was worse than the urban because the drop in producer prices meant the full weight of depression fell on the countryside. Droughts in February 1932 prompted South Canterbury farmers to ask government for free rail transport as an offset, threatening to otherwise 'cut the throats' of their sheep and 'fill up the gullies with the carcases'.[169] The Farmer's Exchange Committee declared the same month that farms could become profitable if costs were slashed 30 to 40 percent – and as that was impossible, the only answer was dropping the exchange rate.[170] Marginal farms fell into ruin, including many of the remaining soldiers' settlements. Their owners simply abandoned them to the banks, leaving behind their spirits with the magpies and the macrocarpas, unable to make ends meet in a world of depressed produce prices.

As a recipe for prosperity, the Coates-Forbes plan was a failure. Britain began clawing back from depression in 1933, pushed in part by a building boom.[171] The

Willis Street, Wellington, around 1930. Cars and electric trams jam the road, underlining the alacrity with which New Zealand picked up twentieth-century transport.

S.C. Smith, Alexander Turnbull Library, PAColl-3082, G-1792-10XB

United States economy began picking up the same year in the face of Franklin Delano Roosevelt's 'new deal';[172] but it was 1934–35 before New Zealand began showing signs of life. In part this was because the downturn hit primary producers hardest, but New Zealand's problem was also philosophical. The idea that people chose unemployment out of laziness was hard to break, and while relief schemes under the Unemployment Act of 1930 were not so soul-destroying as the prospect of a daily queue at the local post office, they were punitive enough. Many unemployed came under Scheme 5, designed to subsidise local bodies that would, in turn, give the men work. Rates were miserly – 14 shillings a day sustenance and 17 shillings relief for single men, graduated upwards for married men with children.[173] This was partly a function of government penury, partly deliberate as a means of deterring bludgers. In practice the scheme prompted a new wave of impoverishment as businesses and local authorities sacked their employees and rehired them under the relief scheme.[174] Huge numbers of New Zealanders ended up in that position, and payments under the scheme totalled £4.2 million in the 1933–34 financial year.[175]

Some families were ripped apart as the breadwinners travelled to up-country work camps, there to face leaky tents, thin blankets and poor sanitation. Some of the tasks were useless make-work, as when men were made to drag ploughs.[176] Others laboured in drains, often waist-deep in water, never able to dry their clothes in the winter. The work was mindless, pointless and soul-destroying; yet it was often a case of doing it or starving. There was never enough money and many families relied on charity to make good the difference. The Auckland City Mission doss house, during a seven-month period in 1932, apparently provided 37,000 beds and 102,080 meals to hungry New Zealanders.[177]

Looking seawards over New Plymouth during the early 1930s.

John Wall, Alexander Turnbull Library, PAColl-3065, 13054-1/1

A World Land Speed Record attempt gave New Zealand brief distraction from the rigours of depression in February 1932. An Australian syndicate backed by Sydney businessman Fred Stewart picked Ninety Mile Beach as the venue on which to race their Napier-engined *Fred H. Stewart Enterprise*. Designed by Don Harkness, the car was driven by well-known racer Norman 'Wizard' Smith. They based themselves at Hukatere with a declared intention of cracking 300 miles an hour (480 km/hr) over the flying mile. Cooling problems forced Smith to add a heavy locally fabricated radiator. Then they discovered the tyres were falling prey to toheroa shells. In the end Smith failed to reach the syndicate's goal but did break the world ten-mile record with a speed of 164.084 mph (264 km/hr).

Smith's wife was on hand to wish him good luck before a record attempt on 3 February 1932.

The plight of those with paid work was often also miserable. While some historians have argued that falls in wages were offset by falls in the consumer price index (CPI),[178] such claims are misleading, not least because the all-groups CPI represents an average 'basket' of goods. A better indicator at the lower end of income is food, which for poorer families was often a significant part of the household budget. Here the picture is different. Food prices initially fell faster than the CPI, but from 1932 were rising faster — in other words, the relative price of food rose through the Depression. Nor was this the only problem. At a time of retraction, high-paid workers invariably went first. Government also introduced direct unemployment taxes, followed by a sales tax that yielded £1.8 million in 1933.[179] The average per head in 1932 was £11.9.4, but by 1935 it was up to £15.18.4, most of the increase a result of the unemployment levies.[180] All this was

G.G. Martin's butchery, Cuba Street, Wellington.

Gordon Burt, Gordon Burt Collection, Alexander Turnbull Library, PAColl-4118, G-15384-1/2

coupled with a near-total lack of job security, a direct outcome of depression retractions at both state and private level. Nobody knew when their job might disappear, or if they would find themselves facing a take-it-or-leave ultimatum over pay cuts.

National morale was not helped by the fact that New Zealand's rich appeared to be staying that way. Old money had not disappeared, new money had emerged with new industries, and some of those who had it were unafraid to flaunt it. 'Here in Remuera,' John Mulgan wrote a little later, '...lived the aristocracy. Their daughters were lovely and satirical, drinking surreptitious gin in the half-empty cabarets.'[181] Landscape designers such as Alfred Buxton were in demand during the 1920s and 1930s, setting up impressive gardens around back-country estates, often blending 'arts and crafts' stylings with more traditional New Zealand forms. Some large suburban homes too were given massive and impressive surrounds.[182]

Many held government responsible for the 'ill-starred necessities' of depression.[183] As one historian remarked in 1965, 'so much legislation that hurt so many people had never before been crammed into so brief a period'.[184] Hungry crowds stoned the Dunedin relief depot in April 1932 after the mayoress insisted on distributing food only after investigating each case. A few days later there was a mob attempt to break into the hospital, deflected by baton-wielding police. Riots followed in Auckland after a meeting to protest wage cuts, only stopped after ratings from HMNZS *Philomel* and firemen took to the fray. Queen Street was spattered with glass, and many shops were looted. John A. Lee, who was there, thought most of the rioters were 'so hungry, with families as hungry' that they had no choice but to make a 'desperate bid for food'.[185] There were more riots the following month in Wellington, where protesters were forbidden to congregate in Basin Reserve and stampeded into town, followed by a crowd, shattering windows as they made their way along Lambton Quay. In Christchurch, a tramway strike was brought to an end with batons.[186] Government responded with a punitive Public Safety and Conservation Act – but, as one historian has pointed out, the tensions ebbed, as if New Zealanders had gone to the brink but then pulled back.[187]

By September some 73,650 New Zealanders were unemployed, of whom 67,110 were on relief schemes.[188] More followed into 1933, reaching a high of 79,435, a figure not exceeded until the early 1990s.[189] Coates was widely – though wrongly – believed to have proclaimed that the needy could 'eat grass',[190] and in these desperate times some sought radical alternatives. The Soviet Union had sailed on apparently unaffected, and in Hastings there was even a 'communist' revolt among relief workers. In fact the apparent success of the Soviets was illusory; the collectivisation of farming resulted in mass famines in 1932–33.[191] However, the fact that some New Zealanders seriously considered such alternatives indicates the degree to which Forbes' policies had undermined society. In 1932 New Zealand was one of the half-dozen longest-standing free democracies in the world. New Zealanders had fought and died to preserve it in the First World War, yet by 1932 dissent simmered from Kaitaia to Bluff. The following year the proto-fascist New Zealand Legion emerged as a pressure group.

Patea co-operative dairy factory.

The marriage rate fell with the economy; in 1929 it stood at 7.8 per 1000, but by 1932 it was down to 6.81.[192] People simply could not afford to get married and have children. Curiously, crime dropped during these crisis years. Some 37,214 offences were reported in 1930 on a national population of 1,506,800, but by 1935 the figure was down to 33,168 offences.[193] This was the reverse of what might be expected during times of hardship, as both the nineteenth-century British pattern and the New Zealand experience of the 1984–99 period makes clear.[194] However, we do not have to look far to find the explanation; as the Hawke's Bay quake revealed, society of the 1930s had been shaped by the trauma of Flanders into something with real community spirit and genuine altruism.

The depression ground on. Coates toyed with plans to settle the unemployed on small farms in 1933, but there seemed no end in sight, and as Lee put it, New Zealand's youth wanted more than to be just 'clothed and fed'.[195] New Zealand was facing a moral crisis of unprecedented dimension, but the opportunity to reject Forbes' policies was postponed with the general election, put off from 1934 to 1935. Fortunes looked a little brighter as the world started to pick up. Coates began retracting the most draconian measures in 1934, but the people remained miserably unhappy with the government, an unease expressed in a desire for new political

Wellington Railway Station under construction in 1934. This steel-framed building was the largest single building in New Zealand at its time, and proposed as early as 1929. Construction on reclaimed land posed technical challenges.

Photographer unknown, *Evening Post* Collection, Alexander Turnbull Library, F-90785-1/2

The Reverend Colin Graham Scrimgeour (1903–87), Methodist minister and champion of the Depression-era underdog. Known as 'Uncle Scrim', his radio programmes revealed him to be a staunch opponent of the puritanical Coates-Forbes government. He is seen here in 1938 broadcasting for 2YA.

Dorothy [?], Kenneally Collection, Alexander Turnbull Library, F-135748-1/2

structures. There was talk of implementing proportional representation as an alternative to the 'First Past the Post' system, but it was 'urged upon the Government in vain'.[196] By this time Labour had emerged as a credible opposition. Radical leader Harry Holland died in late 1933 and was succeeded by Michael Joseph Savage, an Australian by birth who led the conservative faction of the party and whose warm persona contrasted with that of his predecessor.[197]

During 1935 Coates made cautious plans for new social spending, including introducing milk in schools. However, he reflected only one aspect of the United-Reform coalition, and too much water had flowed under the bridge for these tidbits to overcome a cynical electorate. Government directives to quash dissent resulted in Post Office staff zealously jamming the Reverend C.G. Scrimgeour's popular 1ZB radio programme, moments before he was due to explain why everyone should vote Labour.[198] The incident did Forbes no favours. Labour, by this time, had successfully shed the radical image. Policies formulated by Walter Nash and Peter Fraser, presented by the kindly Savage, offered a 'Way out of Chaos to a Land fit for Heroes'. Labour's new platform was built around conventional capitalism with a friendlier face, facilitated by state direction of the economy.[199] Their manifesto of 1935, penned by Walter Nash, promised prosperity and work for all; and in the election that November, Labour won 53 seats to the government's 19, throwing the Coates-Forbes coalition into complete disarray.

There was a little cash left in the Consolidated Fund, and Savage gave it to the unemployed as a Christmas bonus. To the hungry victims of the Depression it was like a gift from heaven.

CHAPTER 8

The quest for security

The impact of the first Labour administration on New Zealand is difficult to understate. C.G. Scrimgeour compared it to the sun shining 'for the first time in years'.[1] Although he had a particular axe to grind with Forbes' social policies, many New Zealanders were demoralised by 1935. They looked to Labour for rescue, and Labour delivered. Savage gave New Zealanders what they wanted in the avuncular manner — as one historian put it — of a kind uncle.[2] And what the people wanted was clear: secure employment, security of accommodation through their own quarter-acre section, and enough surplus money to make life comfortable.

None of this was achieved overnight — indeed, New Zealand did not approach the ideal until after the first Labour administration was gone — but the journey itself was as important, and in the late 1930s it was enough for most New Zealanders to know they were on the way. It was a moral recovery rather than economic. Positive attitudes counted, and by 1939 the national mood was optimistic. The joy of the age was encapsulated in the Centennial celebrations of 1940, a dramatic combination of fairground attraction and industrial displays in Rongotai, near Wellington. People had hope for the first time in years, and Savage was upheld as a national saviour, his portrait hung alongside that of Christ in many working-class homes. Two generations of devoted Labour supporters followed, establishing the shape of New Zealand politics until the 1980s.

Michael Joseph Savage (1872–1940), seen here around 1935, remains one of New Zealand's historically best-known — and best-loved — prime ministers. Born near Benalla, Victoria, he was working on the Victorian gold mines around 1900 when he met Paddy Webb, establishing the Political Labour League. Webb left for New Zealand, and Savage followed in 1907, joining the New Zealand Labour Party when it formed in 1916. More moderate than some of his peers, he became leader in 1933 when Harry Holland died. He presented a warm family persona, building popularity for the party in a way that drier colleagues such as Peter Fraser could not. New Zealand mourned when he died in 1940.

Photographer unknown, Alexander Turnbull Library, C-8866-1/2

Radical conservatism

Despite the fears of the conservative farming lobby, the arrival of Labour's former pre-war radicals into power did not send New Zealand lurching uncontrollably to the left. Picking up where the Liberals left off, as Savage put it, was conservative by definition.[3] The key shift was a change in the unwritten social contract between taxpayers and government. Savage and fellow Cabinet members Walter Nash, Peter Fraser and Robert Semple sought a new balance between nineteenth-century capitalism and the realities of the second industrial revolution, leavened with doses of Fabianism, to create the 'land fit for heroes'[4] that New Zealanders had been promised after the First World War. Capitalism would be harnessed, not destroyed.[5]

Labour was helped by the fact that economic restoration was under way and Coates' public works policies provided infrastructure on which to build. Farm output had fallen to a low of £49.2 million in the 1931–32 financial year, improved in 1933–34, and by 1935–36 was almost back to 1929 levels. Factory output followed a similar pattern.[6] Total trade per head, which had plunged to just over £39 in 1932, climbed away after 1933 and returned to its 1929 levels late in 1936.[7] Various public works schemes were already under construction when Labour came to power, including Wellington Railway Station, the largest building in New Zealand to date.[8] Labour took the credit for this 'temple of transport' when it was completed in mid-1937.[9]

In these respects Coates was, as one historian has noted, closer to Labour than he was to Forbes;[10] and while Labour sought to maximise prosperity in a way rejected by the Coates-Forbes coalition,[11] aspects of their approach did not require radical policy changes. Repackaging and humanising was enough, as when the Unemployment Act 1930 was replaced by virtually the same thing in 1936 – now called the Employment Promotion Act.[12] The effect is illustrated by what Minister

Walter Nash (1882–1968), speaks to reporters on election night 1935. The former Kidderminster sweet-shop owner was one of the key movers behind Labour's economic policies. Secretary of the Labour Party from 1922 to 1932, he held a variety of ministerial posts and was Deputy Prime Minister 1940–49, Prime Minister in the second Labour Government in 1957–60, and retired from politics in 1963.

of Works Robert Semple did for the work camps. These were still needed in 1936, but by mid-year most had been given recreation facilities, including in some locations cinemas, accommodation was radically improved, and a new piece-work system effectively doubled the relief rate.[13] At a stroke, and at relatively low cost, the camps became places where New Zealanders could live with dignity and receive reasonable returns for their efforts.

Labour's economic methods were more radical, based on centralising authority and insulating New Zealand from the vagaries of overseas markets.[14] This was a dramatic change and Walter Nash worked 18-hour days to develop the initial plan with input from Coates' former adviser William Sutch.[15] Yet the goals were again conservative and, as we will see, the strategy was broadly maintained for the next four decades by both centre-right and centre-left. Savage launched the plan as soon as Parliament met in March 1936. The Railways Board, Transport Co-ordination Board, Unemployment Board, Broadcasting Board, Dairy Export Control Board and Mortgage Corporation were abolished and their functions transferred to ministerial portfolios.[16] The Reserve Bank, founded as a semi-private organisation by the Coates-Forbes administration in 1934 on Neimeyer's recommendation, was nationalised and its lending limits eliminated.[17] Nash, meanwhile, organised his Primary Products Marketing Bill, designed to let the state buy dairy products at the average price of the past eight to ten years. Semple worked up a three-year public works plan on a £17 million budget — $1479 million in early twenty-first-century money — covering roads, bridges, railway construction and new airfields. This was orthodox, though with a focus on mechanisation to save labour and avert humiliating make-work schemes. Semple symbolised the change by using one of the bulldozers to push a pile of wheelbarrows down a bank.[18]

Robert Semple (1873–1955) was an early radical, West Coast agitator, and the power-house behind the Miners Union formed in 1907. Nicknamed 'Fighting Bob' or sometimes 'Battling Bob', he was imprisoned for conscientious objection in the First World War, joined the Labour Party and was elected to Parliament in 1918, lost the seat at the next election, then regained Wellington East in 1928. As Minister of Works in 1935 he set about replacing labour-intensive wheelbarrow gangs with bulldozers.

Photographer unknown, *Evening Post* Collection, Alexander Turnbull Library, F-105128-1/2

321

John Alexander Lee (1891–1982),
novelist, soldier and *enfant
terrible* of the Labour Party. He
played a lead role in selling a
renewed RNZAF to Cabinet, and
as Under Secretary to Walter
Nash was also responsible for
implementing Labour's housing
policy. However, he fell out with
Peter Fraser over monetary policy
and was expelled from the
party in 1940.

Photographer unknown, Alexander
Turnbull Library, F-49375-1/2

Despite their intention to introduce more State control, Nash's first budget of August 1936 was surprisingly orthodox. The only radical idea was a proposal to borrow £5 million from the Reserve Bank to fund new state housing schemes. Yet new homes had become urgent. Nearly a third of all mortgages were foreclosed during the Depression and there had been little new construction.[19] By the end of the decade many families were feeling the squeeze, and at a time when the nuclear family remained a mainstay of society, Labour intended to do something about it. Other works included improvements to the railway system, restarting the long-stalled East Coast line and implementing ultra-modern electrified commuter rail in Wellington.[20]

Labour-market reforms followed. The cancellation of compulsory arbitration in 1932 had triggered an avalanche of unilateral reductions in wages and conditions, and unrest followed. Some 108,605 working days had been lost that year, more than double that of the year before.[21] New Minister of Labour H.T. Armstrong introduced a bill in April 1936 to restore arbitration, guarantee minimum wages, and create a 40-hour working week.[22] Compulsory unionism for those covered by Arbitration Court awards followed, a more radical move that put a good deal of power into the hands of the 'Black Prince', Fintan Patrick Walsh (1894–1963), who by 1937 was president of the Seaman's Union, secretary of the Wellington Clerical Workers Union, and president of the Wellington Trades Council among other posts.[23]

These shifts won some praise in the United States, which was looking for 'experiments that have been successful' which 'might be adapted to American requirements'.[24] Britain was less applauding, but the fact remains that Labour's policies worked in New Zealand. Morale recovered, and growth began to absorb the pool of unemployed. There were around 20,000 men on work schemes when Labour came to power; by 1938 this had dropped to 2735. Total unemployed fell from 56,502 in January 1936 to 29,899 in March 1938, although the figure fluctuated as seasonal work came and went, and the pool still had to be fully absorbed when the Second World War broke out.[25]

Michael Savage meets supporters
during the 1938 election
campaign. New Zealanders had
not forgotten their suffering
under the Forbes-Coates coalition;
Labour was returned with an
increased majority that year.

Photographer unknown, C.A. Jeffery Collection,
Alexander Turnbull Library, F-517934-1/2

Wellington Railway Station in 1939. This 'temple of transport' was the largest single building in New Zealand when it was completed.

Electric Multiple Unit at Khandallah: in 1938 Labour restarted the long-delayed Tawa rail deviation out of Wellington, which reduced the Johnsonville stretch to a branch, but instead of ripping it up, the government decided to introduce an ultra-modern commuter service, fostering the suburbs along the line. At policy level it was part of the general promotion of the quarter-acre section and the New Zealand dream. Services began in 1938. The unit seen here was the first of six ordered for the initial run, in original blue paint with 'streamline'-style silver flash and wheel spats. Later orders dispensed with the spats and were finished in NZR red, but were virtually identical. Some of the 1946 batch, delivered in 1949, remained in service into the twenty-first century.

'Is this the New Zealand home for the future?' reads the original caption. Perhaps not this 'streamline' style, but state houses were home for thousands of Kiwis under the first Labour Government.

Marching, as a competitive sport for women, was a curious New Zealand phenomenon. This is the Woolworths marching team in 1935.

Photographer unknown, *New Zealand Free Lance* Collection, Alexander Turnbull Library, C-16178-1/2

Right centre

Forwards of the combined Thames, Waikato and King Country teams meet the Springboks in 1937. The South Africans won this particular game 6–3.

Weekly News, Making New Zealand Collection, Alexander Turnbull Library, F-2320-1/2

Right below

Swimming, 1930s.

Photographer unknown, Alexander Turnbull Library, F-67401-1/2

Labour's welfare reforms – 'applied Christianity', as Savage put it[26] – took longer to organise. Early steps included improving existing benefits and implementing a programme of state housing for the poor. Families who had been jammed cheek-by-jowl with uncles, cousins and other relations could expand into their own 'quarter-acre'. Government took reform further during 1937–38, reorganising benefits into an encompassing system, including health care and low-cost state houses. While this was sometimes viewed as the start of a slippery slope to welfare dependency, the aim at the time was to provide a safety net for those few unfortunates unable to support themselves. Labour always envisaged the system as a backstop in an economy of near-full employment, and at a time of rising prosperity people were thrown out of the system rather than into it. This was reflected in costs; welfare spending between 1937–38 and 1938–39 followed a slowly ascending curve, but this was mainly driven by growth in old-age pensions, including a restoration of pre-Depression pension levels.[27]

Primary education came in for attention during Labour's second term. The entry age was dropped to five – a reversal of Depression measures when it was raised to cut costs – and government-funded milk was made available to all primary schools. The practice continued into the mid-1960s, but the eventual notoriety of tepid 'school milk' did not offset the value of this service in its earliest years. Some schools also received apples. Dr C.E. Beeby was appointed Director General of Education to reform the national school system on a secular basis.

These innovations helped transform the country, and Labour destroyed the opposition in the process. A National Party emerged in 1936 from the wreckage of United-Reform, but Labour won the 1938 elections with an increased majority – some 55 percent of the vote – and forged on.[28]

Children line up for porridge at the Sunlight League's Christchurch health camp, January 1936.

Photographer unknown, Alexander Turnbull Library, C-16182-1/2

Children and teacher pose for the photographer in a new upstairs classroom at Newtown School in June 1939, the day it was opened by Minister of Education Peter Fraser. Wider corridors opened the classrooms to 'sun and air', both considered essential for children. The classroom was a product of Labour education reforms, implemented in the late 1930s and organised by Dr C.E. Beeby.

Photographer unknown, Alexander Turnbull Library, PAColl-0614, F-96818-1/2

Above

This Lockheed Electra 10, one of half a dozen ultra-modern monoplanes brought into main-trunk services in 1937, captured the excitement of the age as New Zealand emerged from a depression that had been as much one of morale as of economic stringency.

Photographer unknown, *Evening Post* Collection, Alexander Turnbull Library, PAColl-0614, G-32345-1/4

Right

Michael Joseph Savage opens the Social Security and Health Departments building on Aotea Quay, 27 March 1939. He referred to the new approach to public welfare as 'applied Christianity'.

Photographer unknown, *Evening Post* Collection, Alexander Turnbull Library, G-49203-1/2

American and British interests pioneered flying-boat routes into New Zealand during 1937–38. Plans were also pushed ahead to set up a trans-Tasman service under the aegis of Tasman Empire Airways Ltd (TEAL). Here, Captain J. Burgess brings *Aotearoa* into Wellington in January 1940, with officials bound for the Centennial celebrations. By 1941, *Aotearoa* and her sister-boat were the only long-range aircraft in New Zealand, perforce swapping some passenger duties for urgent war work.

The MLC building on Wellington's Lambton Quay around 1940.

Art deco and appliances

The 1930s were the great age of art deco, then called modernism. By the late 1930s the styles were woven into virtually every design, particularly the bulbous cars which had shaken off the last vestiges of their ancestry as coaches. Their spread in New Zealand was helped by the recovery of the late 1930s. 'Step up to the V8 class', buyers were urged in one advertisement for 'Built-in-New Zealand' Ford saloons.[29] Local manufacture was a particular selling point at a time when government was urging 'buy New Zealand'. The country had yet to adopt television – picked up in Britain and Germany at the end of the 1930s – but radios with 'streamline' design features began appearing on mantelpieces.

Coal stoves and candles of earlier years had been almost completely supplanted with gas and electrical appliances by 1939. The Hawke's Bay Electric Power Board promised cooking for 'as little as 8/- a month' with its electric ovens. 'Stop wasting money on antiquated cooking methods ... You'll know what it means to cook more enticing meals in a better, cleaner, cheaper and easier way than you have ever done before.'[30]

Other technology had to be sold as a concept. 'Come on the telephone,' one advertisement declared. 'The telephone, for social and domestic purposes. A swift and reliable messenger. Always a comfort and convenience.'[31] Refrigerators were

Grocery shopping, late 1930s style.

another new appliance waiting for a use. Automatic washing machines remained in the future, but manufacturers lost no time finding ways of easing the load on wash day. In 1935 consumers were urged to say 'goodbye to washing-day drudgery' with the aid of 'oxygen charged suds'. The 'gentle, cleansing oxygen bubbles' were guaranteed to 'do the work for you'.[32]

Kiwis needed less persuasion to go to the movies. Cinema gained sound at the beginning of the 1930s, then burst into glorious colour – *The Wizard of Oz* and *Gone with the Wind* made a splash like no film before.

Food gained new sophistication. Cheese was sold in handy pre-packaged slices, 'Pixie segments … . So tasty … so handy!'[33] Although the age of convenience food was still half a century away, customers at any grocery were advised to try 'Dr William's Health Loaf' and Vienna bread, or 'Morah Cooking margarine' produced by Abels Ltd of Auckland. The Dominion Compressed Yeast Company of Christchurch and Auckland offered consumers the 'Malt that Makes the Difference' – DYC Mellowed Malt Vinegar; 'bottled in the scrupulously hygienic modern plant of the Dominion Yeast Company', this 'product of sun-ripened grain' was available in screw-top bottles from most grocers. A pound of Roma 'Dust Freed' Tea was another addition to any shopping basket.[34]

Art deco and appliances

Modernist window display, Wanganui DIC.

Art deco and appliances

Gas oven and hot water made this kitchen one of the more up-to-date of its day. Many New Zealanders were able to afford such facilities by the late 1930s; all that is missing from the line-up is a refrigerator. 'Odourless' models using freon rather than ammonia were on sale, but manufacturers were still selling the concept. 'Leftovers normally thrown away during hot spells can be kept and made up into delicious salads and cold dishes', one advertisement declared. 'You'll never worry again when friends drop in unexpectedly', trumpeted another. Most fridges could be bought for around £40, but whether householders had that to spare in the wake of the Depression was another matter — it amounted to around $3500 in early twenty-first-century money.

Art deco and appliances

Ngata and Ratana

For Maori, the twentieth century brought opportunity and challenge. There was opportunity in the sense that although Maori as a percentage of total New Zealand population did not change, absolute numbers rose from 42,113 in 1896 to 52,723 in 1911 and 83,326 by 1936,[35] not including Maori of part-European descent who were living as Europeans.[36] However, the new century was also a challenge in the sense that jingo society was monocultural and exclusive, though its racism was not that of other countries. Maori had been thought of as 'better natives' by the British, an attitude that reflected into settler society, and there were even turn-of-the-century efforts to suggest that they were Aryan.[37]

This contrasted with attitudes elsewhere. A 'gruelling game' between Maori and Springboks at Napier's McLean Park in September 1921 focused many of these issues.[38] One Springbok was disgusted at 'thousands of Europeans cheering on [a] band of coloured men to defeat members of their own race'.[39] This assertion – published in the local newspaper – met a vigorous rejoinder from one correspondent, who pointed out that the Springboks had been royally entertained by Maori and 'if they so despised the Natives why did they accept their hospitality as they did?'[40] An editorial declared that New Zealand could 'take pride in the fact that this noble people, so far from being exterminated by war or disease, are a virile and increasing community'. But, the paper warned, Maori would in future 'find it more and more difficult to maintain his racial purity' – leading to a future subsumed by 'the newcomers'.[41]

Such sentiment summed up the general attitude of the day. In fact, Maori and jingo societies were still effectively segregated – most Maori lived rurally. Yet

Ohinemutu around 1874.

Maori had no option but to find ways of engaging jingo culture if they were to improve their position. Early twentieth-century strategies for doing so continued approaches begun in the nineteenth. The Kotahitanga (Parliament) movement promoted Maori unity and rights under the Treaty of Waitangi. Rangatira such as Te Heuheu Tukino picked up the sceptre during the 1890s, and for a while — as one historian notes — a sense of 'Maoriness' seemed about to overtake tribal feeling.[42] However, the movement faded in the face of resurgent tribalism. The Kotahitanga was effectively defused by the Maori Councils Act of 1900, and in other respects overtaken by the Young Maori Party, an ostensibly political movement which originated among some Te Aute old boys. These people, all highly educated and 'Europeanised' Maori, sought to push the cause from within the framework of jingo society. Theirs was not strictly a political party — indeed, it had been originally known as the 'Association for the Amelioration of the Conditions of the Maori Race'.[43]

Prime movers included Te Rangi Hiroa (Peter Buck), Apirana Ngata and Maui Pomare. They had been active in the late 1880s while still at school, and developed their thinking the following decade. It was another bold effort, but did not last at political level. Pomare joined Reform in 1912, and Ngata became a Liberal. However, the strategy of engaging jingo society itself was more successful; Young Maori supporters worked to promote Maori both through the public service and by parliamentary representation.

The strategy of high-level engagement was also taken up by Eastern Maori MP and former kupapa James Carroll, as Native Minister during the first decade of the

Ohinemutu, early one morning in March 1907.

Photographer unknown, Hislop Album, Alexander Turnbull Library, C-2498-1/2

century. He slowed the process of land sales, but his efforts stood in opposition to other movements, and accusations that he continued to act as a kupapa during his parliamentary term never completely evaporated. For all that, Carroll was less controversial than Pomare, who became a pariah for what arguably amounted to an imposition of settler values,[44] including an effort to get rid of practices such as hui and tangihanga. But this is not to underrate his other achievements, as during the First World War when he took charge of Maori recruitment for the government, formed a committee and went out to collect volunteers. A Pioneer Maori Battalion was eventually formed, and while the practical benefits of serving in the hellish conditions of Flanders were dubious in hindsight, it was a significant step forward by the standards of the day. There were hopes that a good performance on the front might enhance Maori status back home afterwards. In the event these hopes were dashed, but this was not through want of trying.

Apirana Ngata (1874–1950) of Ngati Porou became perhaps the most successful of Te Aute graduates. After leaving the school he attended Canterbury University College, where he graduated BA (Hons) in political science in 1893. Later he studied for an MA and was given an honorary doctorate in 1948. He became involved in politics through Te Aute Old Boys Association, which became the Young Maori Party. Ngata himself remained Liberal until 1928. He prodded Coates, Native Minister in 1921, into establishing the Maori Purposes Fund Board, designed to promote Maori cultural activities. From this flowed the Maori Arts and Crafts Act of 1926, and a Board of Ethnological Research to refocus academic attention on Maori language and culture. To some extent this was predicated on the notion that Maori culture had to be recorded for posterity before it disappeared, and this was not an entirely unfounded assumption. It had become clear by the 1920s that Maori were not doomed to extinction, but whether traditional culture would survive was less obvious. Te Puea Herangi followed suit at Turangawaewae, supporting carving and organising touring concert parties.

Prefects of Te Aute College in 1880 – Britishers even down to morning coats, cricket bats and fob watches, epitomising settler ideas of 'integration'.

Photographer unknown, Athol Williams Collection, Alexander Turnbull Library, F-61582-1/2

Above far left

Wairoa-born James Carroll (1853–1926) fought with government forces against Te Kooti in 1871 and was twice Acting Prime Minister. A leading member of the Liberal party, Carroll was Minister of Native Affairs under John Ballance and slowed, though he did not halt, the flood of Maori land sales during the period.

Photographer unknown, General Assembly Library Collection, Alexander Turnbull Library, F-136-35mm-D

Above left

Apirana Turupa Ngata (1874–1950), Ngati Porou leader and Te Aute graduate who, as member for Eastern Maori from 1905 until 1934, championed the Maori cause.

William Henshaw Clarke, General Assembly Library Collection, Alexander Turnbull Library, PAColl-0838, F-94-35mm-D

Left centre

Tama te Kapua meeting house, Ohinemutu.

Photographer unknown, Alexander Turnbull Library, 47253-1/2

Left below

Food preparation at Ohinemutu.

Photographer unknown, Alexander Turnbull Library, F-56337-1/2

Children from Tokomaru Bay
School visit Wellington Zoo
in 1943.

John Dobree Pascoe, John Pascoe Collection,
Alexander Turnbull Library, PAColl-0783, F-846-1/4

To this was added a government-backed Te Arawa effort to promote Rotorua as a tourist Mecca. The town had been founded by government in the early 1880s to take advantage of local thermal attractions, a strategy which Te Arawa eagerly engaged at every level. Although this raised tensions with other tribes — who felt Te Arawa were getting unfair advantage — it did help raise the profile of wider Maori cultural issues. The Rotorua Carving School, established with Ngata's help in the late 1920s, was intended to educate a new generation in traditional methods, and some graduates moved on to Turangawaewae to start their own carving school. One result of these initiatives was new emphasis on the physical aspects of Maori culture, notably traditional carving, art, poi dances and songs. By the 1930s, Maori motifs had entered mainstream art and design, as in rebuilt Napier where some buildings featured Maori motifs, adapted to modernist styles.[45] However, other aspects of traditional culture, including hui and tangi, were not promoted with such vigour, arguably because it was more difficult to assert these in the wider post-jingo environment of moral evangelism and renewed attention to Christian doctrine. To some extent there was also indifference. Ngata successfully had the Maori language adopted as a university subject in 1923, but very few students took it up.

Ngata went on to back an effort by Arawa to claim the lakebeds in the Rotorua region.[46] He also became Minister of Maori Affairs during the Depression and pushed for funds to build meeting houses, money to improve Maori welfare, and

The infant room at Auckland's Horo Horo School.

money for cultural events and promotions. He often got it, despite general government penury and an attitude of individual self-help as first port of call. Ngata also slowed, but did not stop, the ongoing process of land sales. However, a 1933 investigation uncovered evidence of false accounts and misappropriation in the Native Department, and while Ngata was not involved, he felt obligated to resign his portfolio. But he continued to push Maori matters privately, and was a prime-mover behind the Maori Battalion a few years later.

These efforts to promote Maori from within the framework of post-jingo society were paralleled by Maori efforts to promote their own cultural framework. King Mahuta tried working with government along these lines on the advice of Henare Kaihau, during the first decade of the century. Perhaps the key leader of the period was Te Puea Herangi (1883–1950), of Tainui, who rose to particular attention through her opposition to conscription among her people. Afterwards she moved to Ngaruawahia where she established Turangawaewae marae, which by the end of the decade had become a focus for nationwide Maori sentiment. She developed a close association with Coates, whose plans for assisting Maori through agriculture coincided with hers, and maintained a relentless effort to support, develop and promote Maori until her death in 1950.

Religion, ultimately, provided the mechanism for the most successful Maori association with post-jingo society. Te Kooti's spiritual successor, Rua Kenana, led a new millenarian movement at Maungapohatu in the depths of the Urewera during the first years of the twentieth century. He was tolerated by government, but dogged by ongoing accusations of sly-grogging, and the Government finally sent armed police to arrest him on that pretext in April 1916. It was a pseudo-military operation, a move which some historians suggest was the last battle of the New Zealand wars.[47] However, a more likely reason for the disproportionate government reaction was rumour that Rua had German connections – enough, at a time of frothing anti-German sentiment, to prompt decisive steps.

A new and enduring religious movement emerged after the war, founded by Tahupotiki Wiremu Ratana. The Rangitikei ploughman received divine revelations in 1918; and as the Mangai (mouthpiece), attracted a substantial following in the early 1920s, focusing a sense of Maori unity. Specifically why this happened has been debated; Ratana was not rangatira but, like Te Kooti, drew power from his adaptation of Christian teaching, including faith healing,[48] and it has been argued that his teachings struck a chord at a time when Maori had been doubly dislocated by both war and the influenza epidemic.[49] Former servicemen, in particular, expected better than they had received. Followers were often affiliated with other denominations, but the duality was not considered a problem and Ratana soon became a focus for a Maori renaissance. The movement was swiftly politicised; Ratana took up the long-neglected Treaty of Waitangi as his sword and went to see King George V as early as 1924 to protest Maori treatment. Later he launched a petition calling for ratification of the treaty, accumulating over 30,000 signatures, which he presented to Parliament in 1932.[50]

Ratana then turned to politics. His son almost dislodged Maui Pomare in the 1922 election, and from this flowed a strategy to put Ratana members into all Maori seats. Ratana fielded four candidates in 1928; and Eruera Tirikatene became an Independent Ratana member for Southern Maori after a by-election in 1932. Ratana had been attempting to woo political leaders in the hope of finding allies in the House, and approached Holland with the offer to deliver 38,000 Ratana supporters to the Labour camp if Labour took up Maori causes, including ratifying the Treaty of Waitangi and addressing a range of land grievances. Holland agreed. When Labour became government, Ratana visited Savage to remind him of the agreement. As a result, the two Ratana members voted with Labour, joined by a third in 1938. By this time up to half of all Maori were associated with the movement.

Labour made good on the promises, allowing Maori to draw equal benefit from the new welfare state established during the late 1930s. Health and education was extended to Maori, helping establish the basis for the post-war Maori population boom. There was also new focus on the Treaty of Waitangi – in part literally when the remains of the original document were put on display at Waitangi for the centenary. In the 1943 election all four Maori seats went to Ratana-Labour members, an arrangement that held good until the 1980s.

Te Puea Herangi (1883–1950).

William Archer Price, William A. Price Collection, Alexander Turnbull Library, PAColl-3057, G-1920-1/2

Commonwealth conundrums

New Zealand's curious double patriotism flourished through the 1920s and 1930s, pushed by an ongoing – and reciprocated – trade focus on the mother country. The influx of American goods and movies during the 1920s coloured but did not dislodge these links; and while the 'buy New Zealand' emphasis refocused attention on the New Zealand part of the calculation, it is debatable whether this reflected nationalism at the expense of Imperial ties. The relationship Labour developed with the League of Nations provides a clue. Savage pursued closer ties, and New Zealand was elected to the League Council in 1936.[51] Some historians have argued that this reflected a partially independent foreign policy,[52] a point highlighted by Savage's criticism of British 'appeasement', including New Zealand's refusal to recognise Italian-conquered Abyssinia.[53] New Zealand stood alone in the Commonwealth on this issue, but on closer analysis the target was fascism, which the Savage administration – like Winston Churchill – regarded as a threat. The British government seemed disinclined to act, so New Zealand did, and to this extent the policy was in line with pre-war Liberal policies. It reflected New Zealand's ideas about what was best for Empire – whether Britain and the rest agreed or not – and by the 1930s one of the mechanisms for pursuing international policies was the League of Nations.

This argument is given weight by the fact that when war broke out in September 1939, Savage threw New Zealand's lot in with that of Britain. It was the British, not New Zealand, who shifted relative to fascism. Nor did dissent from the Imperial line reduce ties; British links through the inter-war period were reinforced as Britain turned to the Dominions as trading partners. Of the £58.4 million in

Bristol Fighter F2B of the New Zealand Permanent Air Force in 1928. These First World War vintage fighter-bombers were the backbone of the NZPAF for much of the inter-war period.

Photographer unknown, *Evening Post* Collection, Alexander Turnbull Library, PAColl-0614, G-8669-1/4-EP

goods exported by New Zealand in 1938, £48.9 million, roughly $37.9 billion worth in early twenty-first-century money went to Britain, and the majority of imports – nearly three-quarters – came from Britain.[54] The whole has to be seen in context of the British-driven conversion of Empire to Commonwealth in the 1930s. Here, New Zealand was dragging the chain, and there were tensions between national identity and Imperial loyalty that no other Dominion experienced.

All this was a legacy of jingoism, sustained past its use-by date in part by the dairy, meat and wool trade, in part by the 'cultural cringe', in part by habit. People still spoke openly of 'home', meaning Britain, even if they had not been born there. The Union Jack was saluted at schools, the national anthem remained 'God Save the Queen' – 'God Defend New Zealand' was the 'national hymn' – and overseas travel invariably meant a pilgrimage to the United Kingdom. This dichotomy was not a problem at everyday level. The real difficulty, as always, came when government faced the problem of reconciling Pacific defence with that demanded of the European situation, though it was not quite a rerun of pre-war liberalism. This time, New Zealand penury was matched by British weakness. Technology and lateral thinking offered prospects; and in January 1936 Labour's *enfant terrible*, John A. Lee, submitted a report calling for a modernised local air force.

Lee followed that in March with the argument that naval policy was subservient to British whim. The country was isolated by ocean, he argued, and even disruption of trade would not 'afflict us with hunger'.[55] This was untrue; New Zealand had effectively mechanised its farms on the basis of imported fuel. These ideas were discussed by Cabinet in May, where there was talk of concentrating all spending on air forces. An air force pandered to nationalist sensibilities and addressed the Commonwealth issues New Zealand saw as crucial. As Savage told the House while discussing a separate air service in 1936, 'the general European situation is not one to make us feel that we can afford to be indifferent to defence matters'.[56] Air also had modernist connotations at a time when Labour were eager to bring new technology into the country. At a practical level it was a means of reducing defence expenditure, driven by a need to economise in order to fund the social programme.

Tensions between national and Imperial priorities simmered through 1936. Lee swung to the former. So did the services, though perhaps for different reasons. British estimates of the likely scale of attack on New Zealand had not changed in 30 years, and New Zealand's Director of Air Services, Wing Commander T.M. Wilkes, believed 'the previously accepted scale ... can no longer be regarded as a maximum'. Warning that Singapore reinforcements might have to come via the Cape of Good Hope if the Mediterranean situation deteriorated, he argued that a 'fairly strong naval force' might overwhelm local defence, destroy local shipping, bombard the main centres, and occupy Auckland. It might take six months to repel them. A secret appendix – 'The case for a Japanese invasion of New Zealand' – argued that Japan could 'launch a limited overseas attack without warning' and the strength of Singapore might force Japanese planners to seek targets further south.[57]

These oppositions forced a compromise. The whole Cabinet favoured an air force, but the Cabinet Defence Committee thought naval expenditure was the way to go. When the British government offered to send an officer to report on the New Zealand air defence situation in August,[58] Cabinet clutched the straw, deciding to take no decisions until the British officer had made his report. Imperial sentiment had won; and Wing Commander Ralph Cochrane wrote his report during the journey to New Zealand, indicating he had no intention of taking local need into account. 'The rapid strengthening of the defences of Singapore and the decision of the United Kingdom government to press forward with its programme of rearmament,' he wrote, 'promises an increasing measure of security.'[59] An air force would operate in conjunction with 'the general naval dispositions' and 'local forces and defences'.[60]

Cabinet acceptance did not resolve tensions within New Zealand, nor allay perception of a Japanese threat, particularly as Britain could not maintain its 'main fleet to Singapore' strategy.[61] This became explicit in 1938, and Cochrane proposed air reconnaissance from Fiji. This contributed to a New Zealand government decision in May 1938 to request a Pacific Defence Conference. It was held in Wellington 11 months later, attended by British, New Zealand and Australian

HMS *Achilles*, victor at the Battle of the River Plate in December 1939 and – with her sister ship *Leander* – one of the mainstays of the New Zealand naval effort during the Second World War. After a lengthy refit during 1943–44 she joined the British Far Eastern Fleet and took part in the naval campaign against the Japanese homeland in early 1945.

Photographer unknown, Alexander Turnbull Library, F-49007-1/2

The funeral procession of Michael Joseph Savage, April 1940. He died after a long battle with cancer, and the public outpouring of grief afterwards was without parallel in New Zealand's history.

William Hall Raine, W.H. Raine Collection, Alexander Turnbull Library, G-21743-1/1

delegates, each with their own agenda.[62] What emerged was a plan for a New Zealand and Australian patrol line from Port Moresby to Tonga, using aircraft based on Port Moresby and Suva. Cabinet accepted most of the recommendations in May, but nothing had been implemented by September when Europe, for the second time in a quarter-century, plunged into war.

Savage extended the 'fullest assurance of all possible support' to the mother country.[63] To the people he was more direct. 'Where Britain goes,' he declared, 'we go.'[64]

Total war

...to-night we are facing dangers such as we have never known in these islands ... at this critical hour we must face the future with good heart and deep determination to do all and give all in the struggle for our country...
— Peter Fraser, 8 March 1942 [65]

The Second World War ultimately drew in every New Zealander able to work or fight[66] – and the effort continued, through domestic rationing and occupation forces, well after the fighting ended. It was a total war in every respect, an extraordinary effort that allowed a country of just over 1.7 million people to make a disproportionate contribution. This commitment certainly surprised the Germans. 'Why are you New Zealanders fighting?' Field Marshal Erwin Rommel demanded of Brigadier George Clifton in mid-1942. 'This is a European war, not yours! Are you here for the sport?'[67] Clifton saw that his captor was genuinely puzzled and struggled to explain, 'never having previously tried to put into words the ... self-evident fact that if Britain fought then we fought too'.[68]

Clifton's experience encapsulated the whole issue. At popular level the motives were emotional, a concrete expression of the double patriotism that all New Zealanders lived and breathed – and it was unique, a true New Zealand sentiment that few outside could visualise or understand. These sentiments were also felt in New Zealand government circles. At this level, however, there was also a deep streak of pragmatism, even a cynical acceptance of the realities. Labour had resolutely stood against fascism, even when that took New Zealand down a different road from mother country and Commonwealth.

All these issues joined the immutable reality of the economic relationship. In 1939 New Zealand relied absolutely on the mother country for prosperity. If Britain fell, New Zealand's future would have been bleak. On a more subtle plane, the country had also just faced a difficult battle to renew state loans – Bernard Ashwin

Peter Fraser (1884–1950), Minister of Education in the late 1930s and Prime Minister 1940–49. Although initially Marxist, he became a 'right-wing' socialist during the First World War, a platform he held throughout his political career. He was certainly the right man at the right time in 1940, proving himself an effective war leader who did not hesitate to champion New Zealand's cause with Britain. Afterwards, however, his reputation as energetic 'cold warrior' did Labour few favours.

Photographer unknown, Alexander Turnbull Library, A20185, F-5064-1/2

classified British proposals as 'severe' and effectively 'putting in a receiver'.[69] The new loans were due in 1940 and it seems likely that Savage had a little quid pro quo at the back of his mind when he leapt behind the Chamberlain government. Nor did joining Britain in what, in 1939, seemed to be a limited European conflict seem a large step.

These factors continued to drive New Zealand's participation, which grew into an encompassing totality as the war itself developed. It was not a smooth journey. Pre-war dissonance between local and British defence priorities was intensified as the conflict deepened, though what followed was not a simple shift by New Zealand from British to Pacific priorities. The local defence scheme laid out during the 1939 Pacific Defence Conference relied on air power, but the teeth were drawn by the decision to hand the RNZAF's 30 bombers over to the RAF.[70] This proved a problem in 1940 when German raiders appeared in New Zealand waters. Sea forces alone could not find them, and the only long-range aircraft in New Zealand by 1940 were two passenger flying boats and a handful of airliners.[71] Fraser's efforts to get patrol bombers were rebuffed, and as he told new British Prime Minister Sir Winston Churchill in June 1940:

> ...we wonder if it is fully realised in the United Kingdom how helpless this Dominion is against attacks from seaward. As you know, the whole of our defence measures were built on the assurance that in time of potential trouble in these waters adequate naval forces would be available. They are not... . We believe we are the only Dominion in this situation, and we are reminded every day that we would not have been in this situation had we not, voluntarily and unasked, decided to release the Wellingtons...[72]

a U.S. Ships Dance

Opposite above

Although Fraser and leading members of his War Cabinet had been conscientious objectors in the First World War, they did not hesitate to have objectors imprisoned in the Second. Harold Hansen, Bernard Giles, Tom Smith, Colin Clark and Jack Hammerton stand behind the wire at the Hautu Detention Camp, 1943.

Photographer unknown, A.C. Barrington Collection, Alexander Turnbull Library, PAColl-3955, F-37726-1/2

Opposite below

WAAF wireless operators ready for a training flight. The de Havilland in the background was one of several airliners impressed for war service.

William George Weigel, Weigel Collection, Alexander Turnbull Library, PAColl-5469-007, C-23048-1/2

Above

An Infantry Mk III Valentine tank from the merchant *Akaroa* being transferred to the floating crane *Hikitea*, 1943. Although obsolescent by European standards, the Valentine was adequate against Japan's tanks, and some were deployed to the Solomons.

John Dobree Pascoe, John Pascoe Collection, Alexander Turnbull Library, DA-01791, F-70-1/4

When Churchill demurred, Fraser — who had a Japanese threat at the back of his mind — proposed sending a New Zealand minister to America 'in the hope of strengthening the security of the Pacific'. This was not to push an independent line but a way of 'reinforcing the representations already made to President Roosevelt...'.[73] Churchill disagreed; he was already treading a delicate line between the hawkish Roosevelt and isolationist Congress, and feared a New Zealand move might be misinterpreted as an attempt to influence domestic US politics. The crisis was brought to a head when Britain had to bow to Japanese pressure to close the Burma Road, through which Chiang Kai-shek's armies were supplied.[74] Fraser reacted in no uncertain terms; appeasing Japan was 'no more likely to be successful in the Far East than it was in Europe'.[75]

The War Cabinet considered the situation so threatening that by August 1940 there was talk of holding the Third Echelon back.[76] Churchill wanted part of this force in Britain, and finally told Fraser that if, 'contrary to prudence and self-interest', the Japanese attacked Australia or New Zealand, 'I have the explicit authority of Cabinet to assure you that we should then cut our losses in the Mediterranean and proceed to your aid, sacrificing every interest except only the defence of ... this Island on which all depends'.[77] Churchill made the same assurance to Roosevelt, though he was concerned by the 'disastrous military possibilities'.[78] It was the concession Fraser had been looking for; he dropped his plan to send a delegation to Washington and suggested they might set up a diplomatic post. Churchill agreed. These moves have invariably been interpreted as an assertion of nationhood,[79] but it seems clear that Fraser's plans were geared within the framework of Commonwealth. Even his threat to send an independent minister, which New Zealand was legally entitled to do, was couched within those parameters.

Tensions with Japan continued, driven by British and United States support for China. The fall of France left its Indo-Chinese colonies unprotected, and by early 1941 it seemed clear that a crisis was brewing. Early in the year, the New Zealand government invited General Sir Guy Williams to help develop anti-invasion precautions. His recommendations included a range of harbour-defence booms and minefields, and after a vigorous dispute, 200 mines were finally laid off Auckland in March.[80] Other minefields followed. In August the War Cabinet decided to train the Home Defence Forces 'to the standard of overseas troops'. Nash gave Churchill a shopping list that included 38,000 rifles and bayonets, 582 anti-tank guns, 2500 Bren guns, and 170 M3 light tanks,[81] while Coates discussed war material with US representatives without success.

The Pacific crisis burst in December. Popular fears of a Japanese invasion were exaggerated, but there were already shortages of fuel and industrial goods as a result of the European war, and German raiding vessels had shown that even inter-island connections could be threatened. War with Japan prompted more extreme

Gun drill on a Fairmile launch. The RNZN ran a comprehensive and ongoing anti-submarine campaign in New Zealand waters, later extending coverage up into the islands.

John Dobree Pascoe, John Pascoe Collection, Alexander Turnbull Library, PAColl-0783, F-490-1/4

measures. Because local coal production only just met needs,[82] rail travel was limited to 100-mile (160-km) journeys with no guarantee that return travel would be possible. Some people panicked, 'besieging petrol service stations' in an 'attempt to exchange whatever December and January coupons they held for precious benzine'.[83] Government withdrew some coupons,[84] then banned petrol sales altogether on 15 December in an effort to prevent stocks running dry.[85] The sense of crisis was fuelled by reverses in North Africa, where 2 NZ Division pulled the 8th Army's irons out of the fire outside Tobruk, but suffered heavy losses in the process. Long casualty lists appeared in New Zealand papers alongside news of Japanese successes in the Pacific.[86]

Japan conducted a small but sustained submarine campaign into the South Pacific through the first year of the Pacific war.[87] *I-20* was off Fiji in January 1942. *I-29* entered Cook Strait in February, looking for troop transports, and Pilot Fujita Nobuo reconnoitred Port Nicholson with a float-plane. *I-25* arrived in the South Pacific during March, encountering the armed merchant *Tongariro*. *I-21* made a similar sortie in May, when Lieutenant Isumo Ito took a floatplane over Auckland 'and observed some small boats which he thought were fishing craft lying in the harbour'.[88] A submarine attack on Sydney prompted precautions against similar raids in New Zealand.[89]

Women outside the Westfield Freezing Works, Otahuhu, September 1943, after a visit by Eleanor Roosevelt. Women joined the workforce in very significant numbers during the Second World War. Some worked the farms, others took up office jobs, ticket collecting and other tasks left vacant by men.

John Dobree Pascoe, John Pascoe Collection, Alexander Turnbull Library, PAColl-0783, F-573-1/4

Invasion was a separate matter. The British Chiefs of Staff thought Japan might deploy a brigade group — a few thousand men — but New Zealand's Chief of General Staff, Lieutenant-General Sir Edward Puttick, thought a range of scenarios more likely,[90] and Fraser warned Churchill that British assessments were an 'attempt to think in terms of the past'. He added: 'if this line of thought is persisted in we must brace ourselves to meet the fate of Malaya and with infinitely less reason or excuse'.[91] In January 1942 government ordered full mobilisation. By this time 27,000 men were in training, many for a new armoured brigade which government decided to retain in New Zealand. A total of around 50,000 men were under arms, and some 18 battalions, nine rifle regiments and four field regiments were in formation. A further 17,500 — including married men with children — were called up in March. Newspapers warned men to 'place their private and business affairs in order immediately'.[92]

The total number in the forces — including 61,368 overseas, but not the Home Guard — amounted to '...7.6 percent of the total population and 38 percent of the men within the age groups from which they were drawn'.[93] They were backed by limited but largely adequate equipment including several batteries of six-inch guns, and artillery that included three dozen 25-pounders and fifty 18-pounders.[94] There was consequently no government clamour for the return of forces serving in the Middle East,[95] but as Fraser remarked, '...the success of anti-invasion operations depends to the greatest extent on air superiority, without which our land forces and coast defences will be at the worst possible disadvantage'.[96] The problem was that New Zealand had no modern fighters, and in early 1942, over 100 de Havilland DH 82 Tiger Moth trainers were nominated for combat duties.[97] These were moves of desperation. Fraser put the issue to Churchill:

> ...no reasonable security against carrier-borne air attack can be provided unless the limited air striking forces available are provided with fighter protection. In addition [we] ... consider that some fighter protection in the form of interceptor aircraft is essential for the protection of at least the two main ports of Auckland and Wellington...[98]

Britain could provide just 18 fighters.[99] An alarmed Fraser protested,[100] but the British could only promise to 'do our best to help in consultation with the Americans'.[101] Superficially, this fuelled a swing to the United States, but it seems clear that Fraser was more concerned with asserting a New Zealand place within the British relationship with the Americans. In the end the United States accepted the 'heavy responsibility ... for the defence of Australia, New Zealand, and sea approaches',[102] but only because US military chiefs had decided that they needed 'New Zealand and the Fiji islands', which '...together with Australia, must be held and used as bases for an offensive against Japan'.[103]

This brought change to New Zealand in more ways than one. Although Hollywood had given New Zealand audiences a window on America, the Marines and GIs who arrived in Auckland and Wellington during mid-1942 were effectively foreigners. Disputes over women and Maori often flared to violence, notably the 'battle for Manners Street' which has been dismissed by one historian as largely myth,[104] but which actually occurred, and generally for the reasons attributed at the time.[105]

New Zealand's problem was meeting its self-imposed contribution. The Air Force – including pilots for British air services – headed the priority list issued by the War Cabinet in 1942, followed by the Navy, local industry and finally the army. Raising a second division for Pacific service during 1942 meant a manpower crisis was inevitable, and it was triggered by the 1943 mutton season. The prognosis for the 1944–45 season was worse and it was clear that one of the divisions would have to be disbanded. It was not an easy decision because Fraser and his administration wanted to 'ensure that when the future of the Pacific is being considered after the war we ... are in the most favourable possible political position'.[106] The matter went beyond tactical considerations, and New Zealand was groping for direction:

How can New Zealand best serve? (a) By maintaining and expanding its air forces? (b) By maintaining its present naval strength? (c) ... its Division in Europe (d) ... its forces in the Pacific zone? (e) By maintaining and if possible expanding its production of food supplies, particularly butter, cheese and meat?[107]

'All the sorrow in the world', the original caption reads, 'finds expression in the mother's last embrace'. Men of 28 (Maori) Battalion leaving for war.

John Dobree Pascoe, John Pascoe Collection, Alexander Turnbull Library, PAColl-0783, F-831-1/4

The question is whether this was an assertion of New Zealand within the framework of Commonwealth, or whether the approach had changed to what F.L.W. Wood called a 'small power rampant',[108] an assertion on the world stage. Wood's observation runs at odds with the point that New Zealand, in Churchill's words, was 'with' Britain 'from the moment when ... war was loosed upon the world'.[109] The paradox has attracted extensive analysis,[110] but is explicable in context of Fraser's concept of New Zealand within Commonwealth as 'independence with something added'.[111]

New Zealand's handling of its expeditionary force was consistent with this line. The government was determined to have it treated as a national unit. One of the strategies was to make the force answerable solely to the New Zealand government. There would be no more Gallipolis or Passchendaeles. However, this was not understood by Middle East Command, a problem compounded by the fact that 2NZEF's commander, Major-General Bernard Freyberg, was still a serving British officer, and treated as such by his superiors. There was a sharp intra-service spat within Middle East Command during 1940 as a result.[112] The Crete debacle of late May 1941 brought several related issues to the fore. The island was lost because Middle East Command lacked air power and heavy equipment – issues well in evidence before the battle began.[113] New Zealand did remarkably well despite the odds.[114] However, although the New Zealand government demanded 'a full appreciation of the question of air support',[115] neither Fraser nor the War Cabinet recommended withdrawing the division from North Africa.

New Zealand gun position in the Olympus Pass. The Second New Zealand Division fought gallantly during the Greek campaign in April 1941, but at that stage in the war the forces Britain could deploy stood little chance against the might of the Wehrmacht.

Sir John White, Alexander Turnbull Library, DA 14657, F-14657-1/2-DA

Still fuming over Crete,[116] Fraser went to press his grievances in London and clamour for other support. Churchill was eager to oil the waters, particularly as Australia was threatening to withdraw from North Africa, but Fraser never used 2 NZ Division or New Zealand's other forces in Europe as a bargaining counter. There were points during the North African campaign when 2 NZ Division could have been withdrawn – for example, after the victory at El Alamein in October-November 1942. However, government also demurred from withdrawing it after Axis forces had been driven out of North Africa in May 1943. Instead, after much debate, the division went to Italy.[117] Here too there were break points – such as the fall of Rome in mid-1944, where there was discussion of a withdrawal, but the New Zealanders went on to the end.[118] The contribution to the RAF, Royal Navy, Royal Marines and merchant marine was also kept up. In other words, although Fraser's government pursued a more energetic international policy during the last two years of the war, it was not at the expense of the pro-British war effort. The failure of collective Commonwealth security in the early war years did not destroy long-term faith in the institution. New Zealand continued to step forth, as Churchill put it, to the 'rescue and liberation' of the old,[119] pushed – in Fraser's words – 'to the fullest extent of our capacity'.[120]

The 'rampancy' of 1943–44 still has to be explained, but in many respects this was the Pacific-versus-Europe tension writ large. The issue had dogged New Zealand's defence policy-making for decades, and came to a head during the desperate years of 1942–43 when the failure of pre-war collective security hit home. To this was added an apparent failure of the usual quid pro quo associated with war contributions. Despite providing disproportionate forces, producing virtually all the food for the Pacific war effort, and providing base facilities for US

Peter Fraser attends a United Nations Conference on International Organisation session, San Francisco, 21 June 1945.

Photographer unknown, Alexander Turnbull Library, 42356-FO, F-160156-1/2 troops, New Zealand was excluded from the 1943 Cairo agreement on post-war Pacific affairs. So was Australia, and there was a direct link between the Pacific carve-up in the Cairo Declaration and the Australian-initiated Canberra Pact – with its assertion of Australasian interests.[121] Yet it is difficult to place the responses that followed in anything other than the context of Commonwealth. As in Seddon's day, Fraser's government was flexing its international muscles but remained very much within the British framework, and if the Canberra Pact can be called rampancy it was short-lived. New Zealand sprang back into Commonwealth structures after the war. To Fraser, the Commonwealth was an 'association of independent democratic nations',[122] and within that New Zealand had 'independence with something added'.[123]

Marching into history

They were mature men, these New Zealanders of the desert, quiet and shrewd and sceptical. They had none of the tired patience of the Englishman, nor that automatic discipline that never questions orders to see if they make sense. Moving in a body, detached from their homeland, they remained quiet and aloof and self-contained. They had confidence in themselves, such as New Zealanders rarely have, knowing themselves as good as the best the world could bring against them ... Everything that was good from that small, remote country had gone into them – sunshine and strength, good sense, patience, the versatility of practical men. And they marched into history.

– John Mulgan, *Report on Experience*[124]

Major-General Bernard Freyberg (1889–1963) and his ADC Jack Griffiths (left) watch German paratroopers descend over Maleme airfield, western Crete, 20 May 1941. This classic image of the general, much reproduced, was taken by Freyberg's PA John White, and captures one of the few occasions when Freyberg wore a 'tin hat'.

Sir John White, Sir John White Collection

Peter Fraser visiting New Zealand
forces in Britain, mid-1941.

Between 1939 and 1945 New Zealanders fought in virtually every theatre of war from the Arctic to the Pacific Islands. And they fought on to the end; New Zealand forces fired the last shots of the Italian campaign in early May 1945, and a few months later HMNZS *Gambia* was targeted by a kamikaze that dived on her minutes after the Japanese surrender was meant to come into effect.[125]

Achieving this world-spanning effort within New Zealand's limited resources was not easy. Pilot training programmes and RNZAF got first call on available manpower.[126] Equipped with US aircraft, the RNZAF deployed a number of fighter and bomber squadrons into the Pacific, and although New Zealand forces were excluded by the US from front-line work in 1944, the RNZAF continued to support Australian mopping-up operations in the Solomons until the end of the war.[127]

At sea, the New Zealand Naval Division – Royal New Zealand Navy after late 1941 – operated from the South Atlantic to the Mediterranean, Pacific and Indian Oceans, making a direct contribution to the war effort and offering indirect protection for New Zealand's world-spanning trade links. The service also ran a sustained campaign into the Pacific islands from 1942 until the end of the war and maintained extensive coastal defences around New Zealand throughout, including minesweeping and anti-submarine patrols. Much of the effort was framed within the structures of the Royal Navy, allowing New Zealand's naval forces to fight with the British Pacific Fleet off Japan in 1945.

The largest direct contribution, as in the First World War, was on land. Structures of Commonwealth allowed New Zealand to participate in the Mediterranean and related theatres, from Greece to Crete, Egypt, Syria, Libya, Tunisia and Italy. Unit battle honours read like a tour itinerary, a testament to the duration and intensity of the campaigns into which the Second New Zealand Expeditionary Force (2 NZEF) and its component Division was deployed between 1940 and 1945.

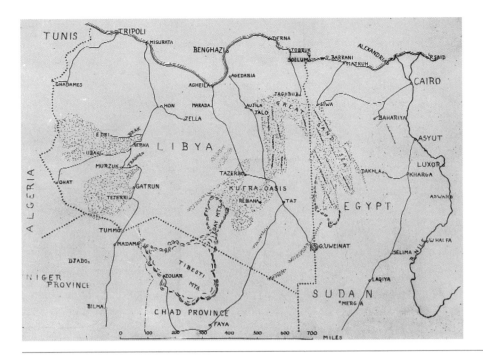

Part of the North African theatre.

Maadi, Cairo, Maleme, Canea, Benghazi, Tobruk, Syria, Minqar Qaim, El Alamein, Tripoli, Medennine, Tebaga, Mareth, Takrouna, the Sangro, Cassino, Florence, Rimini, the Senio, the Gaiana, Venice and Trieste all held places in the hearts and minds of the New Zealanders who fought there. And as John Mulgan put it, the soldiers 'carried New Zealand with them' as they went.[128]

Other participation was by proxy through British services. Kiwis were prominent in the RAF from the outset as a result of pre-war service schemes. New Zealanders fought in the skies during the Battle of Britain – many led by Air Vice Marshal Keith Park, who had been with the RAF since 1919 and when Britain's darkest hour came was in command of No. 11 Fighter Group, covering southeast England. Seven New Zealand bomber squadrons were also formed within the RAF, at the insistence of the New Zealand government, but the squadrons were never fully 'Kiwified' by comparison with similar units developed for the Canadians and Australians. Later commanders included Air Vice Marshal Arthur 'Mary' Coningham, who served prominently in North Africa. New Zealanders also served with the Royal Navy, Royal Marines and the British Merchant Marine. More than 150 went down with HMS *Neptune* off Tripoli one stormy night in late 1941. Others worked in defence establishments, as engineers or technicians, and others made scientific contributions, including – directly – to the atomic bomb.[129]

This effort drew in a high proportion of New Zealand's young men and women. Around 105,000 New Zealanders served on land with 2 NZEF between 1940 and 1945, one in 17 of New Zealand's total population, and a high proportion of military-age men. Casualties amounted to 6829 killed, 16,543 wounded and 8395 taken prisoner. Over 6000 other New Zealanders served with the RNZN, others with the RN and Royal Marines. Others served with the RNZAF, and more than 500 were with the RAF when war broke out, largely a result of the 1937 short-service scheme. More followed, and by December 1943, 2537 Kiwi airmen had become casualties, plus 59 who died in Canada during training. A significant proportion were with the bomber squadrons – put into brutal figures, the 1680 New Zealanders killed while serving with Bomber Command during the Second World War made up 47 percent of the fatalities suffered by New Zealand airmen with the RAF and RNZAF worldwide, and 52 percent of Kiwi air casualties in the whole of the European, Middle Eastern and Southeast Asian theatres.[130]

All these people went knowing what had happened to their fathers in the First World War, but there was no shortage of volunteers. They were motivated by a range of attitudes including lingering jingoism, pro-Imperial feeling and family sentiment. 'I will never regret that I am able to do what I can,' one RNZAF volunteer wrote, 'to prevent, even in the smallest and most indirect way, the war ever coming to New Zealand.'[131] In 1939 there was also the fact that, as one soldier remarked, nobody 'knew, or could possibly realise, the magnitude of the coming struggle'.[132] Between October 1939 and May 1940, the war was fought low-key at sea and in the skies – a 'phoney war' that might yet have been resolvable by diplomacy.[133] Early battles such as the naval engagement off the River Plate, where a squadron that included the New Zealand light cruiser *Achilles* came up against the *Graf Spee*, were met with First World War-style fervour in New Zealand.[134] However, even after the war had turned into a long struggle, New Zealanders continued to join up.

Training at Baggush, mid-1941. Exercises were made as realistic as possible, to the point of detonating mines to simulate shellfire. The result, as General Archibald Wavell put it, was 'one of the best trained disciplined and fittest divisions I have ever seen'.

Photographer unknown, War History Collection, Alexander Turnbull Library, DA-02096, F-2096-1/4-DA

Like their fathers, most servicemen played tourist when they could. Henry Miller, sailing to join the RAF in 1940, was entranced by his first sight of foreign shores, discovering Bermuda was an island paradise filled with Americans. 'The Americans think a terrible lot of us and are always wishing they could do anything for us,' he wrote. When he got to England he had time to see London, a 'dirty place and very smelly', though he thought it would be 'wonderful during peacetime when there would be no blackout'.[135] Soldiers in Egypt were within easy striking distance of exotic and spectacular destinations such as Karnak, Luxor, the Valley of the Kings and the pyramids. Those with more leave went further afield. Palestine was within easy striking distance by rail, crammed with places known to many through Sunday School or church. Later, formal tour parties were organised to Rome – the 'eternal city' remained a popular destination for New Zealand forces from its fall in June 1944 until the end of the war.

New Zealand's forces earned a significant reputation in the field, though the realities have been debated by some historians. By the 1980s, many truths had been buried beneath layers of myth, nostalgia and time. A second generation of war historians looked to cut through those layers, but efforts to demythologise over-compensated.[136] To some extent this reflected general 1980s thinking, which portrayed New Zealand as a small, hide-bound former colony that needed to play catch-up. Perception of the war, in short, suffered from the 'cultural cringe'.

Such argument diminished a wartime achievement that was, in fact, well-founded. Kiwi aviators put up a noteworthy performance in the RAF and Fleet Air Arm. Apart from Park's command of the key air battles, there were personal heroics

Night barrage at El Alamein, October 1942. New Zealand forces played a key role in the two-week battle that broke the *Panzerarmee Afrika*.

Photographer unknown, Alexander Turnbull Library, F-115568-1/2

such as A.C. Deere's exploits before and during the Battle of Britain and James Ward's climb on to the burning wing of his Wellington to extinguish the fire.[137] As a report noted in 1943, 'New Zealanders have earned the reputation of taking part in every operation worth while on every fighting front where the RAF operates.'[138] The performance at sea, particularly with the Fleet Air Arm, was no less spectacular. New Zealanders joined a risky and difficult attack on the *Tirpitz* in late 1944, and later played a significant part against Japanese air forces in the Pacific.

The RNZAF gained a solid reputation among New Zealand, Australian and American forces in the same theatre.[139]

Perhaps the greatest debate has swirled around the performance and capability of the Second New Zealand Division, the principal combat force deployed to the European war. Again, the evidence of the day paints a clear picture. Middle East Commander in Chief, General Archibald Wavell, told Fraser in mid-1941 that 2 NZ Division was 'one of the best trained disciplined and fittest divisions I have ever seen'.[140] Their performance won respect from their enemies. Rommel regarded the New Zealanders as 'among the elite of the British Army',[141] and by 1944 the Germans were issuing official warnings about the force and its 'dangerous' commander.[142]

Friendly opinion was glowing. 'New Zealand Division,' US Middle East Intelligence reported in June 1942, 'is by far the best fighting unit in the Middle East.'[143] Lieutenant-General Bernard Montgomery offered fulsome praise. 'The Battle of Egypt,' he wrote in December 1942, 'was won by the good fighting qualities of the soldiers of Empire. Of all these soldiers, none were finer than the fighting men of New Zealand... . The Division was splendidly led and fought magnificently.' In a reference to the role divisional commander Lieutenant-General Sir Bernard

Bringing the wounded down from Takrouna, May 1943. The 28 (Maori) Battalion distinguished itself on this Tunisian peak as the North African campaign drew to a close.

Dr C.N.D. D'Arcy, War History Collection, Alexander Turnbull Library, DA14028, F-14028-1/41/4

Freyberg had played in the army battle at El Alamein he added, 'Possibly I myself am the only one who really knows the extent to which the action of the New Zealand Division contributed towards the victory.'[144] Lieutenant-General Richard McCreery, last commander of the 8th Army, was of the opinion that 2 NZ Division's 'splendid fighting qualities' had 'achieved successes that have often been decisive to the operations of the Army as a whole'.[145]

Such widely sourced sentiments cannot be entirely dismissed as wartime overstatement. The fact that the division was explicitly given the difficult jobs, including the attempt to hold Crete, a lead role holding back the *Panzerarmee Afrika* in mid-1942 after the Germans surged into Egypt, and being sent to lead the early 1944 attempt to crack Cassino, suggests that the reputation was genuine. The real question is how that came about. Although New Zealand styled itself the 'Prussia of the Pacific' in the early years of the twentieth century, building a self-professed tradition of combat excellence from the foundations of the Boer War, the idea that New Zealand had become a nation of expert militarists does not seem credible. Mistakes were made, and some New Zealand commanders were aware of their early inexperience.[146]

Four factors seem to have set 2 NZ Division apart. First was enthusiasm and potential – a mix largely founded in the legacy of a rugged, physical, do-anything frontier ethos and its successor, the 'Kiwi bloke' do-it-yourself all-rounder. This was filtered and expressed through the egalitarian ethos, a thinking that allowed the men to focus less on protocols than on getting the job done. The result was a unique skill and mind-set that was well suited for the battlefield – and this was noticed. As Freyberg remarked in March 1941:

> I am back with the NZers [sic] after twenty-six years absence. I find in them qualities of heart and mind that in my youth were not apparent to my unskilled eye. I believe that there is a higher standard of talent and character in the ranks of the men of the New Zealand division than any troops I have seen.[147]

This was not something to be wasted, but it might have been if the division had been led by an average British officer, or one who did not have a charter laying out his powers and lines of responsibility of the divisional commander. The differences between the colonial ethos and that of the British army were clear.[148]

New Zealand forces landing on Nissan Island, part of the Green Islands Group, in early 1944.

Photographer unknown, Alexander Turnbull Library, PAColl-4164, F-44747-1/2

New Zealand soldiers in Cassino, March 1944. This picture was probably taken before the main battle for the town, but does reveal something of the conditions.

George Kaye, War History Collection, Alexander Turnbull Library, F-5499-1/2

In the event, however, the division was led by an extraordinary officer. Freyberg, a career British soldier who been brought up in New Zealand, has received his own share of historical debunking;[149] but the realities again seem clear.[150] Freyberg, personally, seems to have been the second factor behind the New Zealand divisional performance in the war. He gave them leeway in minor matters – part of a skilful strategy to bring them together. 'A difficult old cuss at times,' one officer opined. 'But we'd do anything for him.'[151] New Zealand battlefield superiority became reality under Freyberg.[152] His tactical abilities were among the best in the British army. During the North African campaign, he was one of the few general officers to understand the implications of new technology, in which tanks, infantry, artillery and aircraft had to work together.[153]

Composition, size and equipment contributed to the mix. The division was the only fully motorised infantry force in North Africa, and by the second battle of El Alamein had become one of a handful of light divisions – two-thirds infantry, one-third armour, with artillery and armoured 'cavalry' in support. It was larger than an equivalent British unit. The final factor was that the division also had the knack, as Freyberg put it, of 'sitting over the vital point at the vital time'.[154] He made this observation of the desert war, but it also seems true of the Italian campaign, though this was not wholly chance.[155] For much of the 1941–43 period, 2 NZ Division made up a significant proportion of the 8th Army – usually one of six divisions,

War's end: G. Hammond (Hawke's Bay), C.H. Thompson (Christchurch), W.G. Warner (Wanganui) and B.S.N. Berry (Dannevirke) in Trieste, May 1945. The dash by 2 NZ Division to Trieste during the last hours of the war in Italy, there to face Yugoslav communist forces, remains one of its more spectacular achievements.

Photographer unknown, War History Collection, Alexander Turnbull Library, DA9389, F-9389-35mm-DA

and at one stage in June 1942, one of only two that remained intact. As its reputation grew, British commanders deliberately used the Kiwi force for the hard tasks.

The results were decisive. New Zealand soldiers turned the battle for Tobruk into victory in December 1941, hampered the German advance into Egypt six months later, led the advance at El Alamein that defeated Rommel's *Panzerarmee Afrika* in the field of battle, and were in the vanguard of the breakthrough battle at Tebaga Gap that opened the way to victory in Africa in May 1943. They repeated the performance in Italy between 1943 and 1945. During that 20-month campaign, New Zealanders made significant inroads into the toughest fortifications ever developed during the war, contributed to the drive north of Rome, and were instrumental in the destruction of the German armies in Lombardy in April 1945. Finally they led the dash to Trieste and the first confrontation of the Cold War.[156] It was an enviable record.

As in the First World War, the experience of the Second focused, honed and recast New Zealand's long-standing social ideals, including egalitarianism, job security and home ownership. For those overseas — a socially significant proportion of New Zealand's youth — there was exposure to other cultures, along with the experience of the war itself. Battlefield comradeship became a binding force in post-war New Zealand, adding to and shaping existing ties and cultural norms. The servicemen also had ideas about the kind of society they wanted to live in. 'We spent a lot of time,' John Mulgan wrote in 1945, 'talking about the world after the war. Some of this discussion was organised by the Army on highly creditable lines, but as usually happens, the basic conclusions were arrived at more crudely and personally.'[157] Soldiers from all nationalities shared the experience. Most wanted simply to 'feel well and happy in themselves', and as Mulgan put it:

> Most of the men that I knew asked for very little beyond this. Every sensible man wants a home and the woman that he wants to live with and room for his children to move in. And besides that he wants some work to do. It doesn't matter at all what the work is, whether it is making roads or making books, although it is better if it is work that he can do satisfactorily or with belief...[158]

The role of 2 NZ Division in defining New Zealand's future hopes was significant, largely because this force drew such a disproportionate percentage of the total who served into a single, integrated and proud unit. It was deployed into the field for six years, developing a social environment of its own – described by one officer as 'home'.[159] In part this environment derived from divisional leadership. Freyberg had the knack of focusing the strengths of his men and, in consequence, their values. It seems clear that 2 NZ Division encapsulated the usual comradeship of the field in ways that could not be matched even in the Pacific's 3 NZ Division or in the New Zealand squadrons of the RAF, which between them made up New Zealand's other big contributions to the war. This fed back into post-war society on two levels: in a general social sense through the experiences shared by tens of thousands of New Zealanders in the division, and specifically because many of those in the divisional officer corps were professionals in civilian life, returned to their normal work after the war, and became significant movers-and-shakers in fields ranging from education to the judiciary. Some entered Parliament – notably Robert Muldoon, a corporal with 9 Brigade in 1944–45.[160]

This service thinking added a dimension to the general shifts in thought, behaviour and attitude that war brought to every New Zealander. They had come out of the Depression, been briefly offered hope by the Labour Government, and then been plunged into total mobilisation, the threat of starvation or invasion, renewed shortages, blackouts and devastating family loss. These developments extended the exigencies of the Depression. At the same time the war opened the eyes of both service personnel and civilians to the wider world, epitomised for many New Zealanders by the arrival of American troops in 1942. These experiences helped define new expectations. The joyous crowds that surged into the streets to celebrate victory over Europe in May 1945 and – six months later – the surrender of Japan, were also symbolically marking the end of an era and expressing their hopes for a new and brighter future.

CHAPTER 9

Slices of heaven

The safe, secure, conservative world that New Zealanders had sought for so long finally came to reality in wake of the Second World War — a reality that British journalist Austin Mitchell whimsically classified as the 'half-gallon, quarter-acre, pavlova paradise'.[1] This paradise, as Gordon McLauchlan once noted, was also superficially 'passionless'.[2] Yet the popular image of a dull, grey suburban world should not be taken as criticism. New Zealanders had struggled, suffered and even died to achieve a prosperous, stable, family-oriented society since the settler period. The closest approach to this ideal came after two world wars and a depression — a turbulent time of loss, sacrifice and drama. Life since 1914 had been far too interesting, and by the late 1940s most New Zealanders wanted a peaceful life. The 'passionless' aspirations of the 1950s and beyond were deliberate.

Climbers watch the Ruapehu crater lake during the 1945 eruption.

Bruce Valentine Davis, B. Davis Collection, Alexander Turnbull Library, F-698- 35mm-B

Devon Street, New Plymouth,
1948.

Nor, beneath the surface, was their world entirely uninteresting. The 1950s started with a bang: the 1951 waterfront strike was New Zealand's most serious industrial issue since 1913. The settlement that followed did not entirely resolve the tensions, which simmered on beneath the surface. The arts flourished, pushed by deliberate policy. For virtually the first time, New Zealand had local voices of its own. There was also social dissonance. Like the settler and jingo societies from which it developed, the pavlova world had in-built contradictions, notably the ongoing tensions between moral evangelism and partying. It remained a quintessentially white, blokeish and conservative society. Maori, though moving to the towns and cities in ever-greater numbers, remained essentially second class; and the social issues that flowed from their move were not effectively addressed. Other perceived problems ranged from drunken brawling to teenage rebellion. Although by later standards there was little to choose between the political parties, the issues that did emerge were closely fought and drew often heated attention from the electorate.

From the wider historical perspective these undercurrents did not diminish the triumph of the age. For 30-odd years from the early 1950s, more New Zealanders enjoyed a better life than they could have had in previous years, and their world – which we might with due reference call 'pavlova-era' New Zealand – survived for the active adult lives of those who built it. This remarkable longevity was achieved in part because this society was artificially preserved past its 'use-by' date, in part because its success diminished the motive to change.

A nation for heroes

> The object of all economic activity is the satisfaction of human needs. But it is
> sometimes forgotten that human beings have needs and desires apart from those
> which can be satisfied by purely economic means. It is proposed now to open up
> this aspect, and to indicate forms of national development which, while not
> economic, must be given due place...
>
> — Organisation for National Development, 'Interim Report on Post-war Reconstruction and National
> Development', July 1944[3]

New Zealand's pavlova era emerged from long-standing hopes and dreams,
brought to reality by policies that evolved through the war, founded in a drive to
get New Zealand back on its feet. The country was still in economic trouble in
1939, highlighted by the foreign loan crisis that year, and 1940 looked likely to
bring fresh financial difficulties. The war changed that, and Fraser's War Cabinet
consciously took the opportunity to cure the problem. The effort was facilitated by
the internal belt-tightening that went with the war, which the electorate stoically
accepted in a way not possible during peacetime. British purchase of available
produce, plus war production, created an income that Fraser's War Cabinet used to
repay foreign debt. This had peaked in 1931 and been slowly pegged back since,
but still stood at 51.8 percent of total state debt in 1939. By 1945 that had plunged
to just 20.4 percent, and successive governments continued the policy, bottoming
the external debt in 1953, when it was at a historic low in percentage and absolute
terms.[4]

Government turned its attention to the wider future as the war drew to a close.[5]
The Organisation for National Development laid out a comprehensive vision for the
post-war period in 1944.[6] The mistakes of 1919–21 would not be repeated. What
followed was driven by the wartime sectoral compact between state and unions,
to some extent a reflection of the personal friendship between Fraser and Walsh,
and by Treasury advice under its wartime secretary, Bernard Ashwin. 'The Labour
movement,' Walsh wrote in a 1944 paper, 'is interested in improving its conditions
and in raising the real standard of living' to the benefit of 'the whole country'.[7]

It worked. New Zealand was ideally placed to grow in the new post-war world,
and not alone in the desire to avoid the pitfalls of 1919. Agreements reached at a
series of international meetings in Bretton Woods – attended by Walter Nash – laid
the foundation for post-war co-operation. The pace was accelerated by the wool
boom of the early 1950s, fuelled by the Korean War. Greasy wool prices rose from
37.98 pence per pound in 1949–50 to 87.47 pence per pound the following year.[8]
Export returns soared; in 1945 they were £62 million, by 1950 they were £183
million and the wool boom pushed them to £248 million in 1951. They continued
to climb, reaching £277 million in 1957,[9] albeit eroded somewhat by inflation.[10]

New Zealand was able to meet post-war demand for its products with the help
of the second agrarian revolution. Giant discing and aerial topdressing brought

marginal land into production in the early 1950s and sent lowland prosperity soaring. Tiger Moths buzzed the hills – particularly in Taranaki, Tauranga, Auckland, Northland and Hawke's Bay – replaced in the 1960s by de Havilland Beavers and other agricultural aircraft, even DC-3 airliners.[11] These helped make smaller properties viable; by 1954, there were around 90,000 farms in the country, of which 64 percent were less than 200 acres. Little remained of the old oligarch land holding – there were just six properties of more than 50,000 acres.[12] But some old pastoral patterns remained; sheep were concentrated on the east coasts of both islands, the Manawatu and Waikato; cows and cattle in Taranaki, the Waikato and Auckland.[13]

The economic power of the farmers belied their numbers. By the mid-1950s, around a quarter of the workforce were in manufacturing, and nearly 56 percent of all New Zealanders were in the so-called 'tertiary industries' – building construction, power supply, transport, finance, domestic service, administration and the professions.[14] Most of this was supported by prosperity that derived from the 18 percent who worked on the farms. High prices for lamb, mutton, butter, wool and beef made the 1950s the most prosperous years New Zealand had enjoyed. Downturns, as in 1957–58, were the exception, and New Zealand soared very high on world prosperity rankings – though, in perspective, this was partly a function

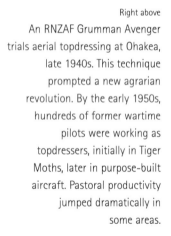

Right above

An RNZAF Grumman Avenger trials aerial topdressing at Ohakea, late 1940s. This technique prompted a new agrarian revolution. By the early 1950s, hundreds of former wartime pilots were working as topdressers, initially in Tiger Moths, later in purpose-built aircraft. Pastoral productivity jumped dramatically in some areas.

Photographer unknown, Evatt Collection, Alexander Turnbull Library, PAColl-5546, F-106439-1/2

Right below

Larger aircraft were also used for topdressing. This is a Lockheed Lodestar of Gisborne-based Fieldair.

Photographer unknown, Agriculture Department Collection, Alexander Turnbull Library, C-27177-1/2

of the fact that other nations were down in wake of the most destructive war of recent history. Even so, New Zealand's average growth between 1955 and 1973 amounted to around 4 percent per annum,[15] far in excess of what was achieved during the 1973–99 period.

All this provided a foundation for the 'nation of heroes' promised a generation earlier. Government backed it with a comprehensive and expanding welfare state – though this was not the profligacy it might seem. In 1950 there were 38 registered unemployed in New Zealand, and the figure stayed below 100 until 1956. All of them, the joke went, were known by name to the Prime Minister. To some extent this understates the level, because seasonal work accounted for several thousand who worked only periodically but did not register. Even so, the figure was orders of magnitude less than the 342,000 unemployed in Britain – 2 percent of the workforce – in 1949.[16] Prosperity was rising, and under this circumstance government could afford to be inclusive and generous. There were big rises in health spending, which had been hovering at 4–6 percent of state expenditure since the early 1930s. It climbed to 11.6 percent in 1958, and by the early 1960s was around 15 percent.[17] Public works expenditure also climbed, topping more than 20 percent of state spending in 1949, rising to nearly a third in 1956. It did not drop much below 20 percent until the early 1970s.[18]

Loading timber at Tauranga for Australian housing, early 1950s.

Photographer unknown, *New Zealand Free Lance* Collection, Alexander Turnbull Library, C-23029-1/2

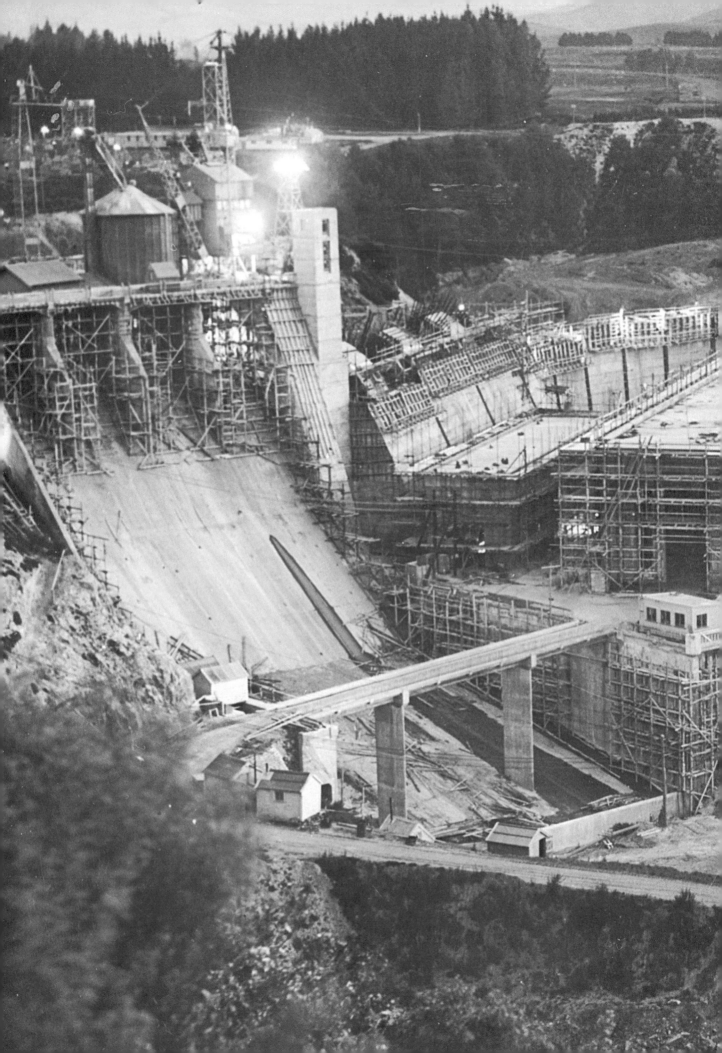

Karapiro Dam under construction, 1946.

Photographer unknown, Alexander Turnbull Library, 29435-1/2

Specific direction was guided by the consensus vision laid out during the last year of the Second World War by the Treasury, unions, the Economic Stabilisation Commission and the Organisation for National Development among others. The latter's 1944 report included a call for 'long-range plans' to build roads, hydro-electric stations, bridges, railways, airfields, housing, factories, water systems, drainage, hospitals and schools.[19] This vision was broadly implemented, leading to a 30-year arc of infrastructure projects ranging from large-scale highway sealing and urban motorway systems to flood-control schemes — notably in the Manawatu and Wairarapa — and world-scale hydro-electric development.[20] Some of these schemes broke new ground, notably the High Voltage Direct Current link from Benmore to Haywards, designed to bring power from a new rolled-earth dam at Benmore to the North Island. Nobody had built a DC transmission system of the scale envisaged by State Hydroelectric Department Chief Engineer M.V. Latta, but it was done with Swedish help. By the late 1990s the cable was carrying up to a third of the North Island's power.[21] These projects were in turn dwarfed by the Upper Waitaki power development of the 1970s, one of the largest hydro schemes in the world, including 58 kilometres of canals, designed to boost the Waitaki River hydro output to 7640 gWH per annum.[22]

South Island 'hydro-towns' such as Roxburgh and Twizel were matched in the North Island by 'timber-towns' such as Kawerau and Tokoroa, built to house workers harvesting the maturing radiata forests of the central North Island — some of which were legacies of Depression-era make-work schemes. These towns were homes to hundreds of 20-something New Zealanders, many of them with young families. Some flourished; Turangi, built as a tourist town, developed a life of its own fairly quickly. Others did not. Otematata, established to house the Benmore workforce, had a population of 3993 by 1966 — but at the expense of Roxburgh Hydro, which provided many of the houses.

Sorting peas at Wattie's, 1948. The Hastings-based company produced military rations during the war. This fare was not suited to the post-war civilian market, but owner James Wattie swiftly sought new lines. Much of the produce came from company-owned farms on the nearby Heretaunga Plains.

Photographer unknown, *New Zealand Free Lance* Collection, Alexander Turnbull Library, PAColl-5469-023, F-160227-1/2

However, all was not rosy in this emerging utopia. An electorate that had supported Labour through the late 1930s and the war emergency of 1942–43 was less happy to find wartime hardships continuing. Labour's first hurdle was the Cold War. New Zealanders had been in on it from the outset, facing down Tito's troops in Trieste at the end of April 1945. The last New Zealand soldier killed during the European war fell to a Yugoslav bullet.[23] Fraser proved an enthusiastic 'cold warrior', perhaps over-enthusiastic; his reintroduction of conscription in 1949 was unprecedented, but less unpopular than the continuation of wartime rationing so that produce could be sent to a hungry Britain. Perhaps more crucial from the electorate viewpoint was the fact that in other respects Labour seemed merely to be offering more of the same. At the very moment when the long-promised bright future was upon New Zealand, it seemed Labour had no new ideas with which to guide the people into it.

This apparent intellectual exhaustion needs explanation, and it is hard to go beyond the point made by Bill Parry in 1947. Labour had won. Everything they had fought for was in place. The political war was over in every sense.[24]

Yet post-war problems remained to be tackled. The main popular gripe by this time was the delays finding homes for returned servicemen and their families. This assumed near-crisis proportions in the late war period, a legacy of the Depression when extended families had crammed into single homes out of necessity. Then war came, taking many householders out of circulation. Even so, housing was 'already far short of requirements' as early as 1944, and planners expected that skilled builders would be 'required in record numbers', calling for training schemes. Demand for everything from furniture to 'floor coverings, stoves, utensils, linen, gardening implements, and all the other supplies which go with the establishment of homes', was expected to be 'acute'.[25]

A National Airways Corporation DC-3 at Paraparaumu in 1953. Air travel came into its own after the Second World War, still an expensive luxury but increasingly affordable. Passenger numbers rose dramatically during the 1950s. Around 150,000 New Zealanders flew in 1948, more than double that by 1953, and in 1964 passenger numbers rose to one in three New Zealanders. Post-war services were initially operated by the RNZAF, then taken over by the new National Airways Corporation. DC-3s were the backbone of the fleet until the mid-1960s.

Photographer unknown, Alexander Turnbull Library, F-58295-1/2

Large-scale housing projects began in 1944, and 70–80 percent of all construction in the country during 1945 was on new homes. But it was still not enough.[26] Extended families lived cheek-by-jowl, even using tents as extra bedrooms, and after wartime sacrifices the people expected better. Fraser's government staggered through the 1946 election, framing their responses within the ideals they had fought to achieve, but the writing was on the wall. 'It's YOUR money they're spending on SUPER-DUPER CARS FOR MINISTERS' National Party posters declared in the build-up to the 1949 elections, capitalising on the car-hunger among voters.[27] What finally did the damage was the housing crisis. 'We will house ALL the people QUICKLY!' another 1949 National slogan screamed.[28] The party came into power in that year's election with a 12-seat majority.[29]

Prime Minister Sidney Holland distanced his party from the Forbes-Coates coalition, but while National electioneering had focused on state retraction, his new government did not actually make fundamental changes. The withdrawal of state control from urban land prices, cancellation of rationing and opening up of state housing to private purchase were mere tid-bits. The big pillars of Labour's 1930s initiatives, including state control of produce marketing, remained untouched – and emphasis on home ownership, this time via state loans, essentially extended what Labour had begun with its state housing schemes. The difference was that where Labour provided the houses on a socialist basis, National did so within a private framework – but the net result, in which government

Opposite above

Post-war rail: a Ka-class locomotive hauls the Daylight Limited across the Hapuawhenua viaduct, Main Trunk Line.

Photographer unknown, Alexander Turnbull Library, F-20339-1/2

Opposite below

Tasman Pulp and Paper Mill under construction near Kawerau, September 1955.

E. Woolett, Alexander Turnbull Library, A41 844, F-34603-1/2, Archives New Zealand/Te Whare Tohu Tuhituhinga O Aotearoa Wellington Office, AAQT 6426/11

Above

Forestry housing under construction at Kaingaroa, central plateau.

Edward Percival Christensen, National Publicity Studios Collection, Alexander Turnbull Library, A2397, F-34608-1/2, Archives New Zealand/Te Whare Tohu Tuhituhinga O Aotearoa Wellington Office, AAQT 6401, A2397

money underwrote the quarter-acre paradise by one mechanism or another, was much the same. National also extended the welfare state in other respects, as did Labour when it came back in the 1957 election. This pattern dominated politics for a generation, and there was often little to choose between the two parties. Although issues were bitterly disputed, they did not reflect particularly deep philosophical divisions. The so-called 'black budget' of Labour finance minister Arnold Nordmeyer in 1958, for instance, doubled duties on tobacco, alcohol and cars – and could easily have been a United-Reform measure.[30]

There was nothing unusual about these approaches by both sides of the political spectrum. New Zealand's welfare system was upheld as a model alongside some of the Scandinavian systems, but this was the great age of John Keynes. Planning was in vogue around the Western world as the victorious powers sought to avoid the pitfalls of unregulated economies, looking instead to build a practical environment within which to promote their market system.[31] The attitude of the New Zealand electorate was certainly clear. Politics were split almost exactly between National and Labour – the parties each typically attracted between 41 and 47 percent of the vote until the early 1980s, with around 10 percent going to Social Credit after 1954. Labour leaned left, National leaned right, but by comparison with the politics of other days, they were remarkably similar. Elections were usually fought over detail, not thrust of ideology. When the pattern did change, it was at the expense of both parties – the razor-tight election of 1981 slashed support for Labour and National, and they were separated by just 0.2 percent of the vote.[32] Such fortunes betrayed a society that sought stability. Who delivered it was less critical, and for a conservative electorate in the 1950s and 1960s this usually meant centre-right National, leavened on occasion with Labour's centre-left brand of essentially the same thing.

Opposition leader Walter Nash (left) with Prime Minister Sid Holland, at the ceremony to open the new Rimutaka tunnel in November 1955. Rain did not deter smiles for the camera. The two men knew each other well, and although political debates were often bitter, there was actually little to choose between mid-century Labour and National if viewed from the wider context of history.

Graeme Ayson, *New Zealand Free Lance* Collection, Alexander Turnbull Library, F-65448-1/2

This did not mean that the issues of the day were less intensely argued. Many of the problems that successive governments had to tackle during the post-war decades stemmed from an unprecedented baby boom. This was another phenomenon that New Zealand shared with the world, and had its origins during the war; the non-Maori birth rate hovered around 16–17 per 1000 in the 1930s, began climbing during the conflict, reached 25–26 per 1000 in 1946 and stayed around the 24–25 per 1000 mark until the mid-1960s. The phenomenon was facilitated by a fall in marriage age. Post-war couples typically married in their early twenties, and were also urged to marry for romantic reasons, which differed from the 1920s when mothers were expected to marry as duty. Arguably, this was a consequence of attitudes that were changing from an emphasis on family as a cog in the machine, to family as a social experience. Maori rates were even higher, climbing from 23.22 births per 1000 in 1927 to 46.64 ten years later. To a large degree this reflected the Labour-led push to improve Maori health, and the rate did not drop below 40 births per 1000 until 1964.[33]

The 'baby boom' put rolling pressure on services and facilities, starting with schools and going on to universities, jobs and, ultimately, pensions. The rising birth rate also extended the post-war housing crisis, complicating efforts as successive governments actively sought to cure it.[34] In 1954 just on a third of all new privately owned houses were built with state support, some 5402 in total, and though National focused on supporting private owners, state rental housing was still some 17.8 percent of all new construction.[35] But it was not all plain sailing. The legacy of wartime restrictions, and even issues such as friction between Housing Minister W.S. Goosman and the building industry, made the construction effort fractious.[36] Plans floated in 1953 called for 206,000 houses to be built nationally within the next decade, and differential interest rates were set for state loans to induce would-be owners to build rather than buy. The policy eventually spanned the political spectrum; Labour came to power in 1958 and implemented 3-percent state loans.

Returned servicemen joined others in the building industry during the last years of the war, helping build the homes government knew would be needed. Work initially focused on the greater Wellington environs, including the Hutt Valley, and South Auckland. This is part of Naenae under construction in September 1944.

John Dobree Pascoe, John Pascoe Collection, Alexander Turnbull Library, PAColl-0783, F-1171-1/4

Suburban rail under construction, Hutt Valley, 1944. Two-storey state houses march into the distance behind.

Photographer unknown, *Evening Post* Collection, Alexander Turnbull Library, PAColl-0614, C-27127-1/2

Right centre

Suburban dreams, late 1944. Eighth-acre sections, curved streets, concrete footpaths and berm defined New Zealand's post-war urban landscape, the shape of the pavlova paradise.

Photographer unknown, *Evening Post* Collection, Alexander Turnbull Library, PAColl-0614, F-35249-1/2

Right below and below

Ian Holmes and his family outside one of more than 5500 state houses built by the Labour Government in the Hutt Valley. These homes were widely used to settle returned soldiers and their families after 1945.

Alexander Turnbull Library, F29452-1/2 John Dobree Pascoe, John Pascoe Collection, Alexander Turnbull Library, PAColl-0783, F-1168-1/4

Most of the new houses went up in 'dormitory' suburbs, conceived around the combination of car and quarter- or eighth-acre sections. The first and largest were in South Auckland and greater Wellington. Nicknames such as 'Nappy Valley' (Wainuiomata) and 'Stork's Gully' (Stokes Valley) left no doubt as to their role. By 1954, some 41.7 percent of all New Zealanders were living in the four main centres, out of a total town-dwelling percentage of just over 70 percent.[37] These suburbs also introduced new lifestyles. Shopping centres had been features of a few late pre-war suburbs, and came into their own in the post-war period — as did the supermarket. The antecedent was the 'Four Square' grocery, the ubiquitous chain-store that was almost synonymous with the 1950s, but supermarkets with their vast range of products and total self-service ethos were a different phenomenon. New Zealand's first opened in the early 1960s and by the end of the decade these self-service stores on steroids were widespread, dislodging older grocery outlets.

The experience was not all positive. Multi-unit state housing zones became ghettos for lower socio-economic groups. These included youthful blue-collar workers and their families, and a rapidly urbanising and detribalising Maori, whose economic position did not improve much with the shift to town.[38] Social problems were evident as early as the 1960s, made worse as the pavlova society stagnated the following decade.[39] Efforts to cure these perceived problems underpinned the development of second-stage suburbs during the early 1960s, such as Hastings' Flaxmere, which was intended as an 'elite subdivision'.[40] Unfortunately it did not work. Some of the new suburbs in provincial centres such as Hastings, Hamilton, Napier and Wanganui generated reputations as troubled communities, prone to crime, littered, some homes reversing pride in the quarter-acre by planting an inverted car on an uncut front lawn. Reputation was often worse than the reality, but concerted efforts by local authorities, residents' associations and community groups to address the difficulties were often ineffective. So were schemes to eliminate the problem in other suburbs by 'pepper-potting' — putting state houses in among privately owned dwellings in newer suburbs.

State housing in upper Champion Street, Porirua, early 1960s.

Photographer unknown, *New Zealand Free Lance* Collection, Alexander Turnbull Library, F-51884-1/2

Conformity was the name of the game in pavlova-era New Zealand, imposed in part through state suburbs by the repetition of housing plans; but there was also an expected conformity of lifestyle. This is Naenae around 1960.

Photographer unknown, silver gelatin print, *New Zealand Free Lance* Collection, Alexander Turnbull Library, PAColl-6303-08, C-9624-1/2

Pavlova world

I have had visions and dreamed dreams of another New Zealand that might grow into this future on the foundations of the old. The country would have more people to share in it ... Few would be rich, none would be poor. They would fill the land and make it a nation.

— John Mulgan, *Report On Experience*[41]

New Zealand's society of the 1950s and 1960s brought together many of the ideals, hopes and dreams that had been sought by the settlers, and at its ideal best was a secure world, framed around a comprehensive welfare state, full employment, private home ownership, and suspicion of any new trend that might upset the apple-cart. And although there were dark sides, that ideal was approached more closely than we might imagine. The quarter-acre paradise was pushed by policy, demanded by the people, built by deliberate intent. Increasingly urbanised New Zealanders spread into the burgeoning suburbs. Yet this did not diminish the populist image of a nation built around blokeish farmers. Indeed, the conservative, true-blue, prosperous farming sector was the key pillar that made everything possible.

Most mid-century New Zealanders felt they had earned it. Two generations of misery had, at last, given way to prosperity and comfort. Most of the adults of the 1950s and 1960s remembered family loss in wake of the First World War, going to bed hungry or darting to school with bare feet in winter rain during the Depression,

New housing eventually went up around most towns and cities in post-war New Zealand. Hamilton expanded by a third, topping 6100 acres by the mid-1950s. This is Hillcrest in mid-1955. 'Beyond this', the original caption reads, 'are stretches of open country that are even now marked in red as "residential" and "industrial" on town-planning maps in the Hamilton City Council offices'.

Photographer unknown, Alexander Turnbull Library, F-51824-1/2

and most had endured the hardships of the Second World War. When good fortune finally came, largely as a result of their own efforts, mid-century New Zealanders embraced it as due return.

The period is often portrayed as a dull, grey world of boring people and limited lives. This is not wholly true, though certainly society was conformist, and though Truby King's ideals were tempered for young mothers by the less Calvinist thoughts of Benjamin Spock, society in general was restrained. It was also an age of regularity. The weekday usually ended on a Friday, for men at least, with a hasty 'scull' at the pub, less hasty after six o'clock closing was abandoned by referendum

Left
Lylian Shuker in the kitchen of her Titahi Bay home. Fashionable Swedish Modern stylings brought angled cupboards, Formica surfaces and print fabrics to interior design.

Duncan Winder, Duncan Winder Collection, Alexander Turnbull Library, F-1045-1/2-DW

Below
New architectural styles produced a new 'look' by the 1960s. Concrete paths, 'Morrie Thou' and close-cut lawns typify the image of suburban New Zealand.

Duncan Winder, Duncan Winder Collection, Alexander Turnbull Library, F-2508-1/2-DW

in 1967, after which Kiwi blokes were allowed to continue the swill until the unheard of hour of 10 p.m. Women stayed at home, often all week, often on Saturday as 'rugby widows' forbidden to enter the sacred halls of men's society. It was a reversal of wartime hopes. 'Rosie the Riveter' made a brief appearance during the Second World War when over 30,000 women did everything from tractor driving to ticket collecting. But when the men returned, women were pushed aside. Women in the 1950s were usually expected to be submissive home-makers, responsible for the front garden with its flowers and shrubs and, later, able to drive the second car. A few women found jobs, often part-time, but increasingly full-time as the pavlova era moved on, but for many even the 1960s were years of dull, often lonely, domesticity.

Right above

Auckland families relax at Mission Bay, early 1950s.

Photographer unknown, *New Zealand Free Lance* Collection, Alexander Turnbull Library, C-27126-1/2

Right below

Mission Bay from Bastion Point, October 1952.

Edward Percival Christensen, Alexander Turnbull Library, A-28502, F-18973-1/2, Archives New Zealand/Te Whare Tohu Tuhituhinga O Aotearoa Wellington Office, AAQT 6401, A29867

The pavlova world was not all positive. Large-scale punch-ups in city back-streets were well known but seldom reported. Some people felt stultified by the regulations that limited access to overseas goods; or by the superficial ethos of conformity. Many found ways of subverting it; life, beneath the surface, was sometimes more varied than the ethos might suggest. Most men resented the drinking laws. Others saw threats to society from all quarters.

Government fear of communism added spice in the 1950s. Peter Fraser embraced the Cold War, and even the Holland administration feared 'reds' might lurk in New Zealand bedrooms. This had its effect on foreign policy, but there was also an internal consequence, and New Zealand's minuscule Communist Party – with its even tinier band of genuine communists – received undue attention. So did government officials with apparent left-leaning tendencies, including William Sutch, part-architect of New Zealand's mid-1930s socio-economic changes. This tarring came back to haunt him later. However, none of this attracted much public attention, and there was little of the witch-hunting hysteria that accompanied US anti-communist rhetoric. Nor was there any real substance behind most of the allegations, as officials such as Alister McIntosh realised.[42] The historical reality, missed at the time, was that communism had originally emerged in response to circumstances that did not exist in New Zealand. It had been spread by conquest

Beachgoers at Days Bay, Eastbourne, 1950.

S.C. Smith Collection, Alexander Turnbull Library, PAColl-3082, G-47360-1/2

through eastern Europe and parts of Asia during the 1940s, circumstance again not shared by any South Pacific nation. In any case, by the 1950s New Zealanders were enjoying one of the highest standards of living in the world. They generally had what they wanted; there was no need to have a revolution.

At a time of rising prosperity, even ordinary working-class families had the time and money to go to the beach, have picnics, and travel the country. Yet that did not mean ostentation. New Zealand holidays were an extension of home; a switch from suburban house to the beachside bach, or perhaps a motel — where the same rituals of home cooking, cleaning and regular meals were repeated. Some took their homes with them, packing clothes and children into the car and towing a caravan to one of the camping grounds that sprang up after the war.

New Zealanders played harder than they worked. Prosperity and full employment, coupled with the occasionally abrasive but generally successful populist compact between government and union after 1951, produced a working environment where watersiders ran systems of 'spelling' — taking unauthorised breaks — and where government servants operated on 'glide time', which some-times meant 'gliding' at both ends of the day. Yet when all these people got home of an evening they worked with demoniac intensity on do-it-yourself home projects, fearlessly assembling furniture, repainting, re-roofing, or adding extra rooms to the family home. Weekends did not slow the pace. Saturday mornings echoed to the roar of the rotocut as men harvested the quarter-acre lawn, often going on to dig the vegetable patch or work on their car. They were frequently joined by their wives who tilled the flower beds. Saturday afternoon was reserved for organised sport: rugby in winter, cricket in the summer, beer afterwards in the sports club regardless of season. Sundays were less devoted to church than in the 1920s, more to family. The day often included a 'Sunday drive' or picnic, perhaps leavened with an ice-cream in a cone from a corner dairy — often 'hokey-pokey', New Zealand's own flavour.

Mourere motor camp in 1953. Cars, caravans and camping grounds allowed pavlova-era New Zealanders to take their lifestyle with them.

W. Walker, Alexander Turnbull Library, A 29864, F-27534-1/2, Archives New Zealand/Te Whare Tohu Tuhituhinga O Aotearoa Wellington Office, AAQT 6401, A29864

Eating out usually meant self-catering, taking picnic lunches to beach or riverbank. An American import, the barbecue, was sometimes translated into a 'sausage sizzle' or, more often, into fish and chips on the beach. 'Bought food' was less common. Dairies stocked hot pies, and there were daytime sandwich bars serving Eccles and butterfly cakes, Neenish tarts, milkshakes, tea and filter coffee. Milkbars were popular evening venues for a teenage youth. But for adults or families, dinnertime options beyond the ritual Friday take-home packet of 'greasies' were spartan. Most hotels operated a dining room, but broadly there were two choices in the 1950s – silver service or the pie cart. Part of the reason was licensing laws that prevented many restaurants serving liquor – though occasionally teapots did not contain what they appeared to. But tastes also played a part. Even cordon bleu was daring in pavlova-era New Zealand, and many Kiwis were reluctant to explore culinary options beyond traditional meat-and-two-veg roasts, steak, chips, and the pie cart repertoire of beans, eggs and sausages on toast.

Pressure to change the licensing laws built during the 1950s, but it was not until 1960 that the Holyoake government began seriously considering reform. The Licensing Amendment Bill of 1961 increased the number of licences that could be issued. Other amendments during the decade opened up opportunities for 'family restaurants', large-scale eating houses often attached to public bars, typically offering steak, salad and chips, with pavlova-style desserts to follow.

The pine-clothed slopes of Powhaturoa rise before this family and their Mk I Zephyr near Atiamuri, August 1955.

Photographer unknown, *Evening Post* Collection, Alexander Turnbull Library, PAColl-0614, F-164517-1/2

Lack of a cafe culture helped contribute to New Zealand's post-war reputation as a cultural desert, but the impression was also founded in the idea that 'culture' referred exclusively to the higher arts, something which New Zealand generally lacked as the war ended. Although art was gaining local ground – notably in the work of Peter McIntyre and Frances Hodgkins, among others – late-1940s Kiwis hoping to make good in opera, on stage or as writers still had to do so overseas, typically in Britain. This created the misleading image of a dull country. In fact, at the populist level, New Zealand enjoyed a vigorous and exciting cultural life. Sport was a mainstay of male social activity, and cinema flourished. Matinees and evening features were the reality of New Zealand's cultural life, a mass opiate that made the transition in the 1950s to cinemascope, more colour and, in some cinemas, 3D. By their very popularity, these were the true expressions of New Zealand's mid-century cultural life.

So-called 'higher' arts also emerged during the 1950s, pushed in part by deliberate decision. 'In making her way toward national maturity,' a 1944 report on New Zealand's post-war direction declared:

it is essential that New Zealand's own voice and character should not be drowned in the flood of machine-made music, exotic literature, and imported films ... New Zealand's own voice, her national consciousness, and the sense of nearness of her people to the higher forms of culture, can best be developed through a policy of positively searching out and promoting the development of such talent as may appear anywhere among her people...[43]

This meant overcoming the cringe, but there were clear signs that this was happening. Amateur operatic and dramatic societies went from strength to strength. The Auckland Community Arts Service brought opera to the city in the early 1950s, and in 1954 the New Zealand Opera Company was established, largely at the behest of Donald Munro. Ballet emerged from the Auckland Light Opera Club with support from the Auckland Community Arts Service in 1953. By the early 1960s, New Zealand Ballet was performing to packed houses, and in 1970 it sent dancers to the widely promoted 'Expo 70' in Japan.

Literature engaged pavlova society at its dominant edge – blokes and beer. Local production was nurtured by Christchurch-based Caxton Press, a pre-war company founded by Denis Glover and John Drew, pioneering the 'slim volume' format by which local poets could get their work into print. Another vehicle for verse was *Landfall*, founded by Charles Brasch. All met surprising success. A.R.D. Fairburn's *Collected Poems* shifted around 6000 copies, high by world standards, and Alistair Campbell's 1950 *Mine Eyes Dazzle* went into a second edition. Populist literature did even better. War literature was significant in pavlova New Zealand, including novels such as Errol Braithwaite's *Fear in the Night* of 1959. Jim Henderson's memoir *Gunner Inglorious* apparently sold around 90,000 copies in hard and soft-cover form. However, the path to populist fiction was bush-bashed by Barry Crump, a deer-hunter turned raconteur whose *Good Keen Man* of 1960 was published by A.H. and A.W. Reed, evidently shifting more than 80,000 copies in its first decade in print.[44]

Yachting in Keneperu Sound, March 1952.

Above right

The argument for six o'clock closing boiled down to family values versus alcohol, epitomised by this 1948 poster.

Artist unknown, Alexander Turnbull Library, Eph-A-ALCOHOL-Hours-1948-01

Left

Hotel bar, 1950s style.

Gordon Burt, Gordon Burt Collection, Alexander Turnbull Library, PAColl-4118, G-15560-1/2

Above left
John Dobree Pascoe, John Pascoe Collection, Alexander Turnbull Library, PAColl-0783, F-1262-1/4

Above

Shopping centres sprang up through the new suburbs of the 1950s. These are the Hutt Valley Consumers Co-operative Society stores at Naenae, built with voluntary labour.

Photographer unknown, Alexander Turnbull Library, 7680, F-116976-1/2, Archives New Zealand/ Te Whare Tohu Tuhituhinga O Aotearoa Wellington Office, AAQT 6403, 7680

Right

Wave of the future: Wardell's self-service 'super market', May 1956.

E. Woollett, Alexander Turnbull Library, A45368, F-34159-1/2, Archives New Zealand/Te Whare Tohu Tuhituhinga O Aotearoa Wellington Office

This book and its sequels made Crump a New Zealand icon for a generation. And books with titles like *Bastards I Have Met* were certainly more likely to sell in quantity to a culture that exalted blokeish masculinity than slim volumes like Anton Vogt's *Love Poems*. However, the surprising success of the 'high-brow' literati suggests they also struck a chord with the people, and Crump's appeal highlighted the path. Poets and writers successfully engaged pavlova society, some mixing pubs with poetry and popularising the medium to an unprecedented degree during the 1960s and 1970s. Pavlova-era New Zealand proved itself to be not merely literate but keenly so; and on this basis, this world could hardly be called dull or unimaginative. 'Bloke books' were only part of a brisk market that was well-filled by writers ranging from good keen Kiwis to thoughtful academics. Some writers shone out as truly extraordinary – notably Janet Frame (1924–2004), whose 1957 book *Owls Do Cry* established her as one of New Zealand's leading novelists.

When it came to numbers, however, literature ran second place to practical living. New Zealand's most popular tome of all time was the *Edmonds Cookery Book*. Originally a promotion for a Christchurch-based baking-powder manufacturer, the recipe book became a pillar of New Zealand domestic culture. The De Luxe version went through 38 editions between 1955 and 1995, totalling some 2,556,000 copies.[45]

All this was played out to a backdrop of rising lifestyle and increasing affluence, both adding lustre to life that belied the stereotypical dullness of the period. As in the 1920s there was a rapid uptake of new technology. The 1950s and 1960s brought a wave of increasingly sophisticated gadgets to the domestic scene, including electric eggbeaters, transistor radios, hairdryers and stereo record players. They were not cheap. A Leonard refrigerator of 1957, offering eight and a half cubic feet of storage space, retailed for £123.10.0, around $4500 in early twenty-first-century money.[46]

Cars were in high demand. Although New Zealand motorised rapidly in the 1920s, vehicles remained unaffordable for most blue-collar workers. That changed after the war when rising relative wages made cars more affordable, though they were still not cheap. By the late 1950s registrations were running at around 50,000 per annum, double that of late 1930s figures. The majority were British: Vauxhalls, Austins, Hillmans, Humbers and the ubiquitous Morris Minor and its successors. A lot of New Zealanders, it seemed, had the money around to buy a 'Morrie Thou',

Above left

Technology marched on during the 1950s, bringing a wide range of consumer goods to shop floors — albeit limited by foreign-exchange regulations. These refrigerators and radiograms were on sale in Napier's 'Melody House', around 1959.

John Wright

Above right

All-in-one entertainment, 1950s style: a Columbus valve radio with built-in monophonic record player and storage cupboards.

Gordon Burt, Gordon Burt Collection, Alexander Turnbull Library, PAColl-4118, F-15789-1/1

which was available in various models. They were joined by Holdens, Australian cars that became New Zealand's motoring gold standard. These big, robust vehicles were ideal for New Zealand conditions, epitomised by the HQ of the early 1970s that was used by everybody from back-country farmers to real estate agents.

However, while more cars were being built and sold than ever, foreign exchange restrictions left demand soaring well above supply. Prices were theoretically fixed, waiting lists long. A few families took advantage of the 'no-remittance' licensing regime by which those with money overseas could use it to bring goods in. New Zealanders purchased 1998 cars that way during 1955. By 1960 the figure was up to 4482 and five years later it topped 14,116.[47] Shortages fuelled a brisk second-hand market, and in the early 1950s even pre-war cars were selling for up to half their original value.[48] Newer cars were even more valuable. A 1954 two-door Morris Minor was advertised in 1957 for £525 — about $19,500 in early twenty-first-century money.[49] There was cash to be made for those quick enough off the mark. 'As new,' another advertisement that year declared about a 1956 Humber, '£850 for quick sale.'[50] New cars were frequently advertised as a safe investment. 'Available only on overseas funds,' one dealer declared as late as 1972, 'these models protect your re-sale value!'[51] The market was liberalised that year, but a car-culture based around 15- or 20-year-old vehicles held sway until the mid-1980s.

Television arrived late by world standards. Part of the delay was financial, part of it cultural. Successive governments felt New Zealand did not need it, and during the 1950s television was — wrongly — thought to be the death-knell of cinema and — rightly — considered likely to change styles of social interaction. In any event,

Skating on Lake Ida, mid-1950.

K.V. Bigwood, Alexander Turnbull Library, F-34514-1/2, Archives New Zealand/Te Whare Tohu Tuhituhinga O Aotearoa Wellington Office

building the system sopped up precious foreign exchange, and for all these reasons, television arrived well after it had in Britain and the United States. The first broadcasts took place in 1960, three evenings a week: first in Wellington, then Auckland, broadcast separately, then Christchurch. Dunedin followed in 1962. The provinces took a little longer, but by the end of the decade virtually the whole country had television, supported by a network of private translators that helped extend coverage. Kiwis took to it like ducks to water. Sets were licensed after 1961, and by the following year there were 65,000 of them, a figure that more than doubled in 1963 and topped more than half a million by 1968. Every family had to have one, although early sets were expensive and some consumers turned to hiring as a cheaper option.

Initial basic programming – featuring the *Flintstones* as prime-time Saturday viewing – was followed by more sophisticated offerings. Selwyn Toogood's popular quiz *It's In the Bag*, which ran to more than 500 radio shows in the ten years from 1954, made the transition to television in the late 1960s. Other local shows included *Country Calendar* and Peter Read's *The Night Sky*, broadly modelled on Patrick Moore's English equivalent, which began broadcasting in 1963. Chef Graham Kerr introduced New Zealanders to different styles of cooking. Music shows such as *Happen Inn* and *C'Mon* catered for a new generation of 1960s youth, though how well they addressed the needs of that generation remains debatable. But it was 1970 before a national network emerged and, despite various proposals, colour did not arrive until 1973 – later in the regions – although that was no bad thing because it allowed New Zealand to adopt the technically superior PAL system.

Salmon fishers at the mouth of the Rangitata River in 1958.

Photographer unknown, *New Zealand Free Lance* Collection, Alexander Turnbull Library, C-27124-1/2

Right above

Ford Mk I Zephyr under assembly at the Ford Motor Company plant in Lower Hutt, August 1951. The welded all-steel body is being steam-cleaned before going on to an acid-cleaner, essential to de-grease the metal before painting.

Edward Percival Christensen, Alexander Turnbull Library, A 25216, F-30407-1/2, Archives New Zealand/Te Whare Tohu Tuhituhinga O Aotearoa Wellington Office, AAQT 6401, A25216

Right centre

Broadway, Matamata, in March 1954: pre-war cars still feature, highlighting the car-hunger that created a culture of 20-year-old cars and high-value second-hand vehicles.

Edward Percival Christensen, National Publicity Studios, Alexander Turnbull Library, A 34 703, F-32717-1/2, Archives New Zealand/Te Whare Tohu Tuhituhinga O Aotearoa Wellington Office, AAQT 6401, A34703

Right below

Racing on the Levin circuit around 1956.

Photographer unknown, B. Davis Collection, Alexander Turnbull Library, F-811-35mm-E

More cars demanded more roads, and in the main centres the spread of new 'car' suburbs quickly overloaded existing systems. In Wellington the problem was compounded by the fact that the Hutt Road, seen here, already occupied most of the available space around the edge of the harbour. This picture was snapped over Ngauranga at the height of the morning rush hour in December 1962. In the event, road improvements were matched by rising traffic volumes.

Photographer unknown, *Evening Post* Collection, Alexander Turnbull Library, PAColl-0614, F-55130-1/2

Above

The New Zealand National Orchestra rehearsing in July 1951, before a concert with Yehudi Menuhin.

W. Walker, Alexander Turnbull Library, A 24 029, F-34512-1/2

Left

The Auckland Community Arts Ensemble touring 'La Serva Padrona' in 1953.

Steele Photography, D. Munro Collection, Alexander Turnbull Library, PAColl-0230

Above

The Riverslea School float at the Blossom Festival, Hastings, 1958. Greater Hastings Incorporated came up with the idea of a spring promotion in the late 1940s, in part to push Hastings' interests over those of nearby Napier, and the first Blossom Festival was held in 1950. It struck a national chord, and at its peak in the mid-1950s these festivals attracted up to 50,000 visitors from around New Zealand. Special trains were laid on, many welcomed by Highland dancers at the Hastings railway station. The festival's key to success was its correlation with contemporary ideals and values — a link that also contributed to its decline in the 1960s as society changed. The last old-style festival was held in 1973, but they were revived, in different format, in the late 1990s.

New Zealand Free Lance Collection, Alexander Turnbull Library, C-27125-1/2

Right

Edmund Hillary. His 1953 conquest of Everest and epic 1958 crossing of Antarctica made him one of New Zealand's best-known and most popular figures.

Photographer unknown, John Pascoe Collection, Alexander Turnbull Library, F-F-20196-1/2

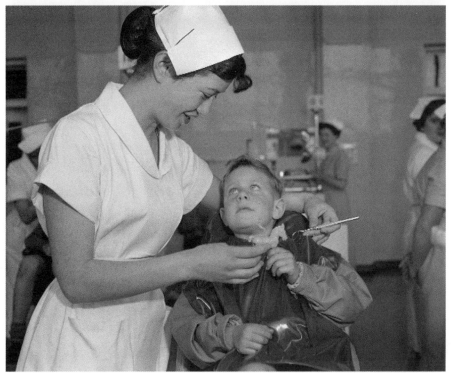

Back-country hunters. New Zealand literature came of age through the engagement of this rugged 'bloke' culture with popular writing. This party was photographed in the 1930s, but the imagery survived for decades.

School dental clinic, 1954. Visits to the 'murder house' were feared by generations of schoolchildren, even threatened as punishment by some teachers. Yet they made a significant impact on New Zealand's dental health.

Equality and conformity

Pavlova society refocused attention on New Zealand's other settler-age ideal — equality. In theory, the people of 1950s 'Godzone' were social and economic equals, all enjoying much the same standards of living, opportunities and incomes. This pleasant ideal was fuelled by the rise and spread of working-class suburbs and the new prosperity of the age. To a large extent it was even true; a mid-1970s study of socio-economic groups in Auckland suburbs revealed that 31.3 percent could be classified as 'middle class' and 54.5 percent as 'lower middle' or 'working' class.[52]

However, the same study also identified a rich elite of 5.7 percent and an impoverished underclass of 8.5 percent,[53] and in practice the gulf between very rich and very poor was larger than ever throughout the period. The division was racially based. Many Maori, both rural and new urban, remained poor, a situation that persisted to the end of the century. They were joined by Pacific Islanders during the 1970s. Unemployment in these socio-economic groups was endemic, and while the welfare state of the day meant they did not suffer Depression hardship, their lives invariably bumped along the poverty line.

This contrasted with extraordinary wealth at the top of the pavlova world. The gap between rich New Zealanders and the average family in the 1950s and 1960s was greater than that between the typical family and the poor. A few farmers became very wealthy indeed on the back of the wool boom and second-stage pastoral revolution. Elsewhere, old money still held sway; and there was also a class of new industrial and commercial rich who emerged in spite of — and in some instances, because of — depression and war. A 1936 list of New Zealand's ten richest people includes three brewers, three car dealers and one dairy magnate. Four of the ten were also beneficiaries of old money, filtered through death duties

Prime Minister Walter Nash, seen here in Sydney in March 1958, felt obligated to tell reporters why he wore two wristwatches when travelling — one was set to New Zealand time, the other locally.

Photographer unknown, *Evening Post* Collection, Alexander Turnbull Library, PAColl-0614, F-76226-1/2

— indicating that rich families, once they had made their pile, usually found ways of keeping it.[54] They were joined in the pavlova era by beneficiaries of the twentieth century revolution. Car makers — notably the Todd family — topped the rich list in 1966, followed by cinema magnate Sir Robert Kerridge (1901–79), a crop of brewers, a timber miller, and a significant number of businessmen who had founded their wealth in the construction and food processing, packaging and transport industries. There was one investor.[55]

Left

A Napier house, mid-1960s. Ranch-slider doors broke with tradition in this 'sliding age'. By the 1970s, wood framing had given way to aluminium.

Duncan Winder, Duncan Winder Collection, Alexander Turnbull Library, F-875-1/2-DW

Below

Kenepuru under construction in April 1963. A suburban section with modest house typified home for most New Zealanders by this time.

Photographer unknown, *Evening Post* Collection, Alexander Turnbull Library, PAColl-0614, C-27161-1/2

Rich new farmers and wise 'old money' families usually did not display their lucre in spectacular ways. There were exceptions,[56] but in general pavlova-era displays of wealth were restrained, even disguised. The rich might buy a new car – but it would be a top-range Holden rather than a Rolls-Royce. Others bought several cars of the same make, colour and model. In short, although all New Zealanders were not financially equal, most behaved as if they were. There were exceptions: a few 'old money' families acted as if they were superior, but in a general social sense New Zealand was a nation of peers. As late as the 1960s, Prime Minister Keith Holyoake had his home address and phone number listed in the Wellington phone directory; ordinary New Zealanders could – and did – ring him up.[57] Norman Kirk was another who felt he should be personally accessible to the electorate. In the 1950s, Sydney Holland occasionally fell in with other commuters while walking to Parliament from his Prime Ministerial residence in Thorndon.

Like its inter-war predecessor, pavlova society frowned on dissent. School-children were dressed in strictly policed uniforms and made to march to 'Colonel Bogey' as late as the 1970s, exhorted to ready themselves for army life. This was 1939 thinking, already out of date as the Vietnam War came to its unpopular conclusion – though explicable because schools had to appeal to parents whose own formative years had been during the Second World War. This was accompanied by a surprising degree of institutionalised violence. Section 59 of the Crimes Act 1961 permitted teachers to use 'reasonable force', but it was questionable whether such practices as routinely strapping classes of eight year olds about the legs and threatening them with a three-foot blackboard ruler could be called reasonable.[58] A 1972 study of a Christchurch high school revealed that canings were meted out for behaviour typical of children – a pattern that had not changed in 80 years. But none was recorded for vandalism, assault and drug-abuse, and it has been argued that the purpose was classroom control rather than actual discipline.[59]

Pavlova conservatism had its effect on youth culture. Parents in the 1940s had frowned on their daughters jitterbugging with GIs, but the rock 'n' roll of the 1950s posed a moral threat in another order of magnitude. Musically, rock 'n' roll was closer to big band jazz than the 'rock' of the 1960s, but it differed enough to be picked up by a youth who were reacting to the stringencies of war, and was leavened with newer styles such as doo-wop. By the early 1950s New Zealand had its own population of teenagers who frequented milkbars and conducted themselves badly. Getting the real Chuck Berry songs in New Zealand was hard, but local bands filled the gap and by the late 1950s New Zealand even had its own rock 'n' roll hero, Johnny Devlin – better than Elvis, because he was accessible.

Teenagers gained notoriety as a sub-culture in 1953 when nearly 60 adolescents were arrested at Lower Hutt's Elbe Milk Bar for various sex offences. None of the girls became pregnant, but that merely compounded the scandal because they had clearly been able to obtain contraception. Amid ministerial-level talk of 'terrible laxity', the Holland administration asked a committee led by Oswald Mazengarb to investigate the whole affair. The report that emerged – sent by government to

Steam at Tawa railway station, 1972. Urban rail in Wellington, Auckland and Dunedin played a significant role in the growth of outer-city 'dormitory' suburbs through the mid-to-late twentieth century.

Photographer unknown, *Evening Post* Collection, Alexander Turnbull Library, PAColl-0614, F-20370-1/4

every householder in 1954 — blamed 'oversexed' adolescent girls and lack of domestic guidance, citing mothers' absence at work.[60] This was a curious explanation at a time when most New Zealand wives were actually at home, but the whole reaction was somewhat overwrought. While one historian has argued that there probably was a sexual revolution of sorts among New Zealand's youth in the 1950s,[61] it remains unclear whether this differed from the sexual revolution half a generation earlier when GIs flooded into the country, or the sexual revolution of the 1920s that accompanied post-First World War youth culture. However, there was a high level of public attention to the issue in pavlova New Zealand, and to this extent the problem was more extreme.

If the youth culture of the 1950s and its supposed delinquents had been a threat to pavlova society, that of the 1960s was a positive menace. Here, perhaps, was the real difference between inter-war culture and that of the 1950s. The Bodgies of the 1950s with their motorcycles and distinctive clothing gave way to a youth movement inspired by overseas trends. The way was led by the Beatles, and New Zealand's own 'mop tops' soon emerged — a charge led by Ray Columbus and the Invaders. All were viewed with suitable shock by the older generation. The Rolling Stones toured in 1965, their bad-boy stage image somehow epitomising the whole ethos. The Stones and similar bands that came later in the decade made the Beatles look innocuous. Sympathy for rock was, it seemed to many older New Zealanders, indeed sympathy for the devil.

Opposite above

Odlins timber yard, Petone, mid-1960s.

Duncan Winder, Duncan Winder Collection, Alexander Turnbull Library, F-1598-1/2-DW

Opposite below

The Hawke's Bay Farmers Co-operative store in Dannevirke. Department stores came into their own during the 1960s.

Duncan Winder, Duncan Winder Collection, Alexander Turnbull Library, F-900-1/2-DW

Left above

The roll-on-roll-off inter-island ferry *Wahine* goes down off Seatoun after striking Barrett's Reef in a storm, 10 April 1968.

Photographer unknown, *Evening Post Collection*, Alexander Turnbull Library, PAColl-0614, F-1149-35mm-28

Left centre

Survivors coming ashore at Seatoun wharf. Half the lifeboats were unusable as a result of the list, and rescue vessels — including the rail ferry *Aramoana*, tugs, a naval launch and the university research launch — were hampered by 70-knot winds. The *Aramoana* launched lifeboats, some of which were themselves swamped in high seas, and the sloop *Tahi Miranda* was wrecked during the rescue effort.

Photographer unknown, Alexander Turnbull Library, PAColl-0614, F-148061-1/2

Left below

Safe at last. More than 500 were rescued from the *Wahine*, and none went down with the ship. Nevertheless, 51 lives were lost. Some drowned when the S1 lifeboat was swamped; others died after being cast ashore south of Eastbourne.

Photographer unknown, *Evening Post* Collection, Alexander Turnbull Library, PAColl-0614, F-1161-35mm-20

Yet rock music, television and the youth culture of the early-to-mid 1960s did not destroy New Zealand's post-war society. Nor did the *Little Red Schoolbook*, a controversial and subversive effort to educate teenagers about sex. Some people railed against what they considered threats to community standards, but although campaigners such as Patricia Bartlett struck genuine chords in some sectors, the general effort to preserve the social purity of the 1920s was overwrought enough to be self-discrediting. Nor could it make headway against a new society. By the 1960s the world had moved on, and even regulated, exchange-controlled New Zealand could not shut itself away. The historical question is whether these new trends really changed New Zealand's pavlova society – and it seems clear that at first they did not. The fundamental ideals of mid-century New Zealand were resilient, accommodating the teens of the 1950s as they became adults in the 1960s. Aspects of life changed, new ideas flowed, some things could be done or talked about without society frowning – but pavlova society did not collapse.

Colony to nation?

New Zealand's double patriotism remained a force to be reckoned with through the 1950s, though this did not prevent changes in foreign policy. Some historians have argued that international relations during the pavlova era were a separate issue from continued economic and emotional adherence to Britain,[62] and in part this is true. New Zealand had always had regional defence issues, and British withdrawal from its world defence obligations could not be ignored. This contrasted with attitudes to the British economic withdrawal, where successive New Zealand governments, manufacturers and producers studiously pretended that the British drive to join the Common Market from the late 1950s did not matter. Only a few voices rang out in warning – notably W.B. Sutch, who saw undiversified adherence to British markets as colonial and dangerous.[63] Time proved him right, but in the mid-1960s he was a lone voice in the wilderness.[64]

The desire to hold on was predictable. Pavlova thinking was drawn in large part from the ideals of the 1920s, including the sentiment of Empire. Under this circumstance Imperial ties had to be preserved. Schoolchildren still saluted the Union Jack, and 'God Save the Queen' was sung before the national hymn, 'God Defend New Zealand'. The 'overseas experience' meant Britain, and those who went elsewhere were thought not to have properly travelled. When the new Queen toured New Zealand during 1953 she was feted wherever she went.

The question, then, is not whether New Zealand made the transition from colony to nation – for in the social sense it did not – but why it did so in the international field.

The answer seems clear; there was no choice. New Zealand adhered to a Commonwealth structure immediately after the war, but such views were increasingly out of step with a world that was becoming ever-more polarised between the two superpowers, and where the nations of Oceania occupied a key geographical position relative to the Pacific – not the other zone of contention in Europe.[65] The local issues that had always stood at such tension with European ones gained new importance. Old habits nonetheless died hard; New Zealand policy-makers recognised the change as it began but initially saw the Commonwealth as a credible third player, despite once again being in a minority. Peter Fraser argued alone for a Commonwealth of the New Zealand concept in 1949, within which he viewed New Zealand as an independent nation.[66] Sentiment was backed with action; frigates and aircraft were sent to back British forces in the Mediterranean from 1950 to 1951, by way of helping deflect a possible Soviet threat to British interests in the region.[67] The big event of the early 1950s was the Korean War, which New Zealand joined at sea and on land, again within the British framework. Cabinet decided to move after consulting Field Marshal William Slim; a 2000-odd-strong Army contingent joined a British Commonwealth contribution, and New Zealand naval forces operated under British command in Korean waters.[68]

However, Korea was also a harbinger of change. United States efforts to 'contain' communism led them to conclude a favourable peace treaty with the Japanese, which set alarm bells ringing in Australia and New Zealand, where memory of 1942 was too close. The prospect of alliance with the United States against a re-armed Japan was raised by the Australians when Secretary of State John Foster Dulles visited Canberra in February 1951, and after a painful gestation the ANZUS pact came into force in April the following year. It promised consultation in event of war in the Pacific, but as one historian has observed, was more to bolt the door against Japan than swing away from Britain.[69] Indeed, ANZUS accepted that New Zealand and Australia had military obligations outside the Pacific area, and as late as 1955, Holland was describing the United Kingdom as having 'a great deal to offer as an ally'.[70] Pacific policies were also framed within the British ambit. New Zealand supported the Colombo Plan as a means of defeating Asian communism through economic means and gave arms to support the French in Indo-China during 1952.

Keith Jacka Holyoake (1904–83) entered Parliament in 1932 as Reform member for Motueka, lost the seat in the 1935 election, but returned as National member for Pahiatua, his home district, in 1943. He was made deputy leader of the party in 1947 and briefly became Prime Minister in 1957 when Holland retired. He became Prime Minister once again in 1960 and led New Zealand through that turbulent decade. His conviction that the office made him a servant to the people led him to list his home address and phone number in the Wellington directory. He retired from politics in 1972 and became Governor-General.

Photographer unknown, Alexander Turnbull Library, C-10579-1/2

Willis Street, Wellington, 1969.

Photographer unknown, *Evening Post* Collection,
Alexander Turnbull Library, PAColl-0614,
F-16394-1/4

Southeast Asia continued to drive shifts in New Zealand perception, helping guide the policy of forward defence which, itself, demanded alliance ties with nations that shared New Zealand's strategic views – essentially, Australia and the United States. After the siege of Dien Bien Phu in early 1954, New Zealand Minister of External Affairs, T.C. Webb, agreed with US and British proposals for new collective security arrangements in Southeast Asia. If the strategically important and resource-rich nations in Southeast Asia fell to communism, he argued, 'Australia and New Zealand would be gravely threatened'.[71] As a result, New Zealand joined the Southeast Asia Collective Defence Treaty and Pacific Charter, which created the South East Asian Treaty Organisation. A state of emergency was declared in Malaysia in 1948 in response to activity by 'communist terrorists'. To Holland, it had become 'increasingly clear' that the 'security of South East Asia, and ... Malaya, are of special significance to New Zealand'.[72] Cabinet discussed withdrawing 14 Squadron from Cyprus early in 1955. However, the struggle was still framed within British structures; during a meeting in London, Holland couched the move in terms of relieving the British defence burden in Malaya.

They left one jump ahead of the Suez Crisis of 1956. This set the seal on Britain's decline as a first-rate power, and in its wake Britain began actively moving away from world obligations and collective Commonwealth security. The change continued into the 1960s, accelerated by a British White Paper of 1966 that foreshadowed a reduction in British defence interests in the Far East. The same year, New Zealand and Australia joined the Asian and Pacific Council (ASPAC), a loose association that included Japan, Malaysia, Thailand and South Vietnam. New Zealand gained observer status with the Association of Southeast Asian Nations (ASEAN), formed in 1967.

None of this was achieved without a good deal of argument. Some voices pushed the line that New Zealand should sink or swim on its own.[73] In the broader sense, however, these policies were a reaction both to rising regional defence imperatives and to British withdrawal, both of which were beyond New Zealand's control and could not be ignored. In practice the Cold War was impossible to avoid, so dominating that by the 1970s international analysts framed all their thoughts around it,[74] and even major third-player developments were portrayed as shifts in the superpower balance rather than anything new.[75] New Zealand was integrally aligned with the West from the outset, and the geographical position in Oceania, coupled with the progressive British admission of second-line status, essentially dictated orientation with American – and Australian – interests.

The practical transition was complete when the government decided to deploy 550 troops and RNZAF units into Vietnam, attached to Australian units. This was wholly independent of any British ties, and in July 1965 the service airlifted No. 161 Artillery Battery to Bien Hoa. Although it was later announced on television, the moment of departure was kept secret to avoid protests by the Progressive Youth Movement – even the aircrew believed they were only going to Singapore until shortly before the first flight. RNZAF Bristol Freighters operated on a weekly basis into South Vietnam between 1968 and 1971.

New Zealand kept British ties via the Five Power Defence Arrangement (FPDA), and other arrangements including officer exchange. However, by the mid-1970s, the hoped-for special Commonwealth arrangement was gone. Even hardware was not always procured from Britain, and the decision by the Muldoon administration to send a frigate into the Middle East to help the British naval recovery of the Falkland Islands in 1982 was a last salute to tradition. Politically, New Zealand's international disengagement from Empire was complete by the early 1980s. Despite the fond ties of memory, Britain had become, in practice, but one ally among several. The question was whether people, society and economy could follow.

Snakes in paradise

...economics is not money, or wealth, or resources, but people; their hopes, their fears, their reactions to stimuli or adversity...

– Robert Muldoon[76]

Although the British withdrawal from its Pacific and Far Eastern interests – coupled with efforts to join the European Economic Community (EEC) from the late 1950s – prompted a New Zealand response at foreign policy level, New Zealand remained heavily committed to the British meat and dairy market. Some 65.5

percent of all exports went to Britain in 1952, down from the levels of the previous 50 years, but still under the ambit of wartime bulk purchase arrangements. These were renewed in 1944 and 1948 for butter and meat, but all ended in 1954, at which point New Zealand returned to the open market.[77] This forced a return to exchange controls after a brief taste of freedom. Large-scale British exports continued, but at volatile prices – contributing to another exchange crisis in 1957–58 – and although the percentage of New Zealand's exports sold to Britain fell to 50.8 percent of New Zealand's total exports by 1965, New Zealand was still one of the two least diversified exporters in the OECD, beaten only by Iceland.[78]

New Zealand's response to the threat of Britain joining the EEC was to pursue the British harder, seeking access to the European market, a reaction at least partly driven by the fact that it was too late to change tack. A 1961 list of 'desired goods' New Zealand wanted to sell into that market included butter, cheese, milk products, beef, sheep meat and fruit. By 1967 this had been cut back to butter, cheese and sheep meat, and the actual access arrangements of 1972 allowed just butter and cheese.[79] This was not a diplomatic failure; Britain made a case to the EEC to no avail.[80] It was obvious from early on that the writing was on the wall for New Zealand's one-stop export shop, and W.B. Sutch warned of the consequences.[81] Few listened; at the time, Sutch was a voice in the wilderness, and no new policies followed a wake-up call in 1967, a foreign-exchange crisis that forced a near-20 percent devaluation of the dollar.[82]

Norman Kirk (1923–74) presides over a press conference in his office after returning from an Asian tour, 1974. The camera crew is noteworthy: the age of TV politicians had arrived.

Photographer unknown, *Evening Post* Collection, Alexander Turnbull Library, PAColl-0614, F-21519-1/4

The main problem was that pavlova society had been too successful. It had brought to reality the society New Zealanders had sought since before the First World War, and there seemed little reason to question either the thinking or mechanisms behind it. This included the image of Britain as 'home', and the point that by the 1960s British markets had taken everything New Zealand could supply for two generations. The issue was not that New Zealand policy-makers and businessmen neglected to consider the consequences of the failure of the British market, but that they reacted to it by trying to find ways of preserving the old, familiar and comfortable. In a psychological sense it reflected a fundamental insecurity, the 'colonial cringe' writ anew. Such thinking was also expressed in the ostrich-like reluctance to diversify – in effect, a subconscious denial of change. Ultimately, faced with a threat to the umbilical cord, New Zealand sought solace in the bosom of Mother England.

Yet not everybody had this view. It has been argued that Labour leader Norman Kirk – reflecting a significant portion of his own party and similar views in the electorate – took a nationalist perspective. Kirk apparently hoped to take the country in a new direction. As Opposition leader in early 1972 he had criticised Common Market access provisions, declaring that New Zealand was living in a 'fool's paradise' and calling for diversification.[83] Once in power he began implementing the vision, evidenced by his foreign policies that oriented New Zealand as a small nation on the world stage.[84] His aims included nationalising the oil companies and breaking with Britain,[85] and the brief economic buoyancy of the early 1970s helped convince the Kirk administration that their policies might lead New Zealand into a new future, adapting the pavlova society to suit and sailing high in world rankings. Terms of trade rose, and the dollar was revalued 10 percent in late 1973.

However, Kirk reckoned without the decision by the Organisation of Petroleum Exporting Countries (OPEC) to raise the price of oil that year, itself a downstream consequence of British withdrawal from the Middle East. The shift hammered Western economies and burst New Zealand's brief prosperity bubble. Inflation had re-emerged in the late 1960s and was fuelled by the oil shock. Government efforts to control it began as early as October 1973 with measures to spread price stabilisation across all sectors.[86] By 1974, New Zealand faced problems, but how Kirk might have tackled them longer term is a moot point. The popular prime minister, dubbed 'Big Norm' by his supporters, and subject of wide adulation – even a pop song – died in office in August 1974.

A shocked nation went into mourning and Kirk went into legend. He had gained popular adulation and, like Savage, had been precipitately snatched away. The tantalising question always remained: where would New Zealand have gone

Wallace Rowling (1922–95), Prime Minister after Norman Kirk's death, announcing new wage restraints late in 1974. Minister of Finance Bob Tizard sits behind him.

had he remained in power? The immediate problem for Kirk's successor, former Finance Minister Wallace (Bill) Rowling, was the economic tightening of 1974–75, but he never had opportunity to find longer-term answers. Labour was swept from power in the 1975 election, largely because National Party leader Robert Muldoon promised a universal superannuation benefit at age 60, set at 80 percent of the median wage, no strings attached.[87] Pensioners were reputedly queuing up to vote for him.

As Prime Minister, Muldoon – Minister of Finance in the previous National Government – again took up the reins of the economy. He had rescued New Zealand from the shocks of 1966–67, and apparently hoped to do so again in 1975. Nor was this out of line with what the electorate apparently wanted. His own background, a child of the Depression, Second World War serviceman, and rising National party star during the 1950s and 1960s, struck a chord with others of the same generation. He dominated New Zealand politics from 1975 until a snap election in 1984, and was one of New Zealand's most powerful historical figures, able to push his policies against opposition, genuinely concerned for the people, a man honest to his convictions, a prime minister of similar stature to Seddon, Massey or Savage.[88]

How Muldoon kept the trust of the electorate while implementing policies that were increasingly out of step with world trends remains a key historical question. To some extent he failed; Labour gained more votes in the 1978 and 1981 elections. But despite increasing isolation from the right wing of his own party,[89] and the attempted 'Colonels Coup' of 1980, Muldoon kept an iron grip on the caucus, and his grassroots supporters – 'Rob's Mob' – stuck with him through thick and thin. Muldoon's longevity was also a function of the executive powers of government, which he aggrandised to himself, combined with an abrasive style. He was extraordinarily astute, quick in debate, and backed his points with in-depth and

Robert Muldoon (1921–92) on the campaign trail, April 1975. One of New Zealand's best-known politicians, Muldoon served with the Second New Zealand Division in Italy while completing his accountancy qualifications. He entered Parliament in 1960 as National MP for Tamaki, a seat he held until 1991. By 1967 he was Minister of Finance, rescuing New Zealand from crisis that year. He became Prime Minister in the landslide National victory of 1975, well aware of the problems New Zealand faced, but his combative and abrasive political style polarised popular opinion, disguising his genuine concerns for ordinary New Zealanders.

Photographer unknown, *Evening Post* Collection, Alexander Turnbull Library, PAColl-0614, F-22486-1/4

accurate data, allowing him to dominate the caucus and brow-beat leading public servants. His arguments were legendary, and he extended this approach to his enemies – notably journalists, cartoonists and academics. One analyst considered him a 'political thug',[90] but while there were elements of Seddon-like thuggishness about his approach, Muldoon also remained brutally honest. He invariably did what he said he would. Few were prepared to stand up to him, and as his biographer notes, some colleagues did not frankly criticise Muldoon until he was gone from power. A few waited until he was dead.[91]

This combative public persona contrasted with that of the private Muldoon, who genuinely and deeply cared for the society in which he lived. He was also loyal to his supporters, notably the slice of middle New Zealand who backed him into power in 1975, and this proved his undoing. He preserved their society for them as best he could, against all odds and well past the point where a man of lesser conviction and ability might have given up. His biographer has argued, convincingly, that although the voices for liberalisation were growing by the late 1970s, the human cost of disentangling New Zealand from 40-plus years of intervention was not acceptable to Muldoon. Depression-era experience had left him acutely aware of the pain that governments could bring, and he was determined to minimise the hurt at all cost.[92]

This cost proved significant, in part because Muldoon inherited an invidious situation. By 1975 New Zealand had survived Britain's entry to the EEC and exporters were diversifying, but it was a late effort, undermined by the oil shock. Inflation was rising. New Zealand's had been below the OECD average between 1954/55 and 1968/69,[93] but in 1975 the all-groups consumers price index (CPI) stood at over 14 percent. By 1976 it was nearly 17 percent.[94] This spurred lobby groups such as CARP, the 'Campaign Against Rising Prices', and bargaining to keep wages up gave new weight to the unions. Other difficulties were of Muldoon's own making. The pension scheme had to be paid for, and suggestions that it might be scarcely more expensive than Labour's compulsory actuarial system were soon scotched. Muldoon nevertheless honoured the promise, and pension payments that stood at $140 million in 1975 soared to $926 million three years later. By 1984 – when Muldoon went out of office – pensions stood at some $2.5 billion.[95] This was in part caused by inflation, in part by rising numbers of elderly as the wartime generation retired. All had to be paid for out of the consolidated fund.

Muldoon's policies for handling these issues were more sophisticated than some of his successors were prepared to admit. To survive, New Zealand's pavlova society had to be modernised, and while he extended the interventionist state with

Fire sale at McKenzie's Wellington branch, 1975.

Photographer unknown, *Evening Post* Collection, Alexander Turnbull Library, PAColl-0614, F-22834-1/2

one hand, he also pushed change with the other, including some of the reforms for which later governments either took the credit or were blamed. Muldoon's first act in 1976 was to implement Treasury recommendations to liberalise aspects of the financial sector. Then when he was told that it was cheaper to import pillow-cases, towels and sheets than to import cloth for local industry to make them, implemented reforms designed to allow those imports, and then 'gradually worked through the whole range of industries'.[96] Railway reform – completed in 1993 when the taxpayer-owned asset was sold – began in 1979 as a Muldoon-era initiative.[97] The local body restructuring of the late 1980s was actually part of a 15-year process initiated by the Kirk administration. Muldoon put his stamp on it, as did his successors.[98]

However, Muldoon also introduced new forms of intervention. In the hope of boosting the farming sector and export earnings, Muldoon initiated a Livestock Incentive Scheme, low-interest rural loans and a Supplementary Minimum Payments system. He intended this to be a short-term measure to keep the farmers on their feet while they developed new markets. Other measures included state supplements to freezing workers' wages in 1978. New sickness and domestic purposes benefits, the latter introduced in 1975,[99] joined the queue for state cash. Although superficially contradictory, this policy mix had a consistency as an attempt to manage change. As his biographer argues, Muldoon found the alternatives unacceptable because of the likely social and political cost.[100]

Primary school pupils learning cardio-pulmonary resuscitation, 1974.

Photographer unknown, *Evening Post* Collection, Alexander Turnbull Library, PAColl-0614, F-21968-1/4

Left above

Holden Monaro at speed,
circa 1975.

Photographer unknown, *Evening Post* Collection,
Alexander Turnbull Library, PAColl-0614,
F-22558-1/2

Left centre

All Blacks in action against
Scotland at Eden Park, 14 June
1975. They won the game 24–0.

Photographer unknown, *Evening Post* Collection,
Alexander Turnbull Library, PAColl-0614,
F-22740-1/4

Left below

Rugby lost none of its popularity
during the extended pavlova era;
these boys are playing probably in
the Wellington region during the
1977 season.

Photographer unknown, *Evening Post* Collection,
Alexander Turnbull Library, PAColl-0614,
F-28181-1/4

Voices of change

The economic upheavals of the early 1970s were only one of several pressures nudging New Zealand away from its pavlova paradise. To this was added the 'generation gap' that emerged as the first post-war generation grew to adulthood in the 1960s, knowing nothing of the depression and war that had influenced their parents. Their world was the safe, warm, comfortable, conservative society of the 1950s, and it was to this that they reacted. In a general sense this was an international phenomenon. Beatniks, drop-outs and hippies 'happened' across the world from Monterey to Chelsea in 1967's 'summer of love'. New Zealand lagged – in part because of the strength of New Zealand's post-war culture – and it was the end of the decade before this new thinking really took hold.

The New Zealand variety drew general inspiration from overseas, but in specific form can be traced to Jerry Rubin's 'yippie' movement, to the Haight-Ashbury district of San Francisco, and to the populist expressions of this thinking in rock festivals such as Woodstock. Much of the new youth philosophy was founded in anti-war sentiment, ironically adopting some of the superficial features of contemporary US army field life in the process, including illicit drug-taking. New Zealand's incarnation also added elements of British counter-culture, with its folkish and idealised view of pre-industrial life. These views were sometimes mixed with selected and misunderstood elements of Indian tantric philosophy, taken out of its original strict caste context and re-interpreted to suit the 'free love' ideas of a generation that, once again, believed it was the first to discover the opposite sex.

To the 20-somethings of the counter-culture, a life of 'dropping out' with the aid of various illegal pharmaceuticals may have seemed like the wave of the future, but many leaned on conventional society for survival. New Zealand's 'hippies' could live what some imagined to be a pre-industrial lifestyle in Coromandel, Northland or Karamea because they could get modern antibiotics, obtain an unemployment or sickness benefit, and rely on wealthy parents to prop up their bank accounts. Some became self-sufficient with the help of the welfare system and high-yield varieties of traditional foods. They could 'space out' to Bob Dylan, Jethro Tull, Pink Floyd, Joni Mitchell, Moody Blues, Jimi Hendrix, Steeleye Span, England, Fairport Convention and Yes because they bought records and owned radios, stereo amplifiers, cassette decks and turntables. The music itself was produced with sophisticated recording technology, and the defining sounds were created by the Moog synthesiser, fuzz-tone electric guitars and the Mellotron – all exploiting the technical developments of the 1950s.[101]

The 'counter-culture', in short, was less radical than some of its adherents liked to think, certainly in New Zealand. Most 'hippies' eventually re-entered mainstream society, but while the counter-culture itself was short-lived as a mass movement, we should not understate the impact of its thinking. Sexual liberation filtered into the mainstream at worldwide level, fuelling a wider swing away from the tighter society of the early twentieth century. Nudity re-emerged on stage, introduced to

New Zealanders in 1972's *Hair*. New clothing and hair styles gained mainstream status as commercial enterprise latched on to the youth dollar and restyled its products accordingly. Short-back-and-sides were out for 1970s New Zealand men, replaced by longer styles even among white-collar professionals. Women's hair styling became even more adventurous.

This thinking joined an emerging matrix of post-colonial values, which gained ground worldwide during the post-war years in part as a reaction to the institutionalised atrocities of Nazi Germany, and in general as a product of de-colonialism. Opposition to nuclear weapons and emphasis on conservation were added in the 1960s, all outcomes of practical concern and youth disillusion with an ever more militarised and industrialised twentieth century. The mind-set of bigger-is-better had won the Second World War for the Allies and soared on through the 1950s, peaking with the moon race. But there were limits. First World pollution and Third World hunger were significant problems by the 1960s, and New Zealand's youth shared the rising tide of opposition to the extremes of mid-century thinking. Attention was focused by the controversial 1969 proposal to raise the level of Lake Manapouri by over 30 feet, drowning most of the islands and natural beaches and giving extra capacity to the massive underground power station being built on its shores. The Save Manapouri campaign quickly became a national effort, drawing in a wide cross-section of the population and devolving to an election issue in 1972. The incoming Labour administration of Norman Kirk honoured promises not to raise the lake.

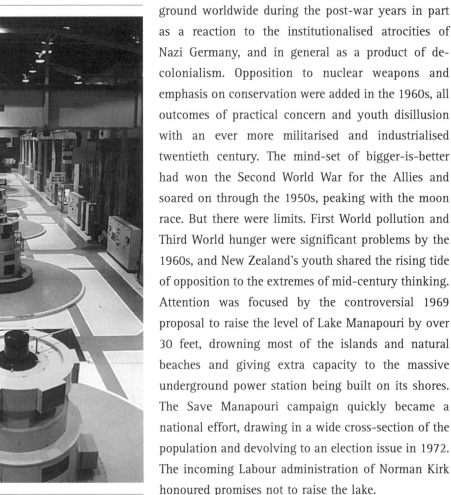

The underground power-house at Manapouri. The decision to build a station implied a rise in lake level, prompting deep controversy in the early 1970s. From a technical viewpoint the station was an unalloyed triumph, a power-house deep underground fed by fall from the lake above, venting through pipes into Doubtful Sound. A new water race opened in 2002, increasing the capacity.

Matthew Wright

To this was added an explicit rejection of war, fuelled by the fighting in Vietnam, which was a politically inspired and foreign struggle very different from the Second World War. It was also in every living room every night. New Zealanders first learned of their involvement – initially, an artillery battalion – when Prime Minister Keith Holyoake announced it on television. The same medium brought images so graphic by the standards of the day that the wisdom of showing them in New Zealand was debated at official level. Such pictures fuelled the campaign against the struggle, both in New Zealand and elsewhere, a drive that became an emotive push against war itself.

Post-colonial thinking emphasised self-determination, opposed discrimination, and tried to improve the rights of minority groups. However, the ideals were only slowly adopted at mainstream level. This was particularly so in New Zealand where pavlova society preserved older thinking with only lip-service change – the reversion of women to the home is a case in point. A rare exception was populist opposition to nuclear weapons. New Zealand servicemen had observed British bomb tests in the 1950s,[102] but public opposition grew during the 1960s, reaching the point where the Kirk government despatched frigates to formally support a protest flotilla sailing to Mururoa Atoll in 1973, where the French had started atmospheric testing.

Successive governments of the 1960s and 1970s, though working towards change, evidenced by new legislation for equal pay, reform of the marriage laws and the formation of the Waitangi Tribunal, were not moving quickly enough for the Vietnam generation. Perhaps for this reason, post-colonial thinking was taken to an emotional extreme in some circles. It became de-colonialism, reversing the targets of old thinking without changing the framework within which the concepts were expressed. In a social sense there were similarities between the extreme post-colonialists of the late twentieth century and the moral evangelists of a century

Youth values of the late 1960s differed from those of their parents. For the first time since the nineteenth century a generation emerged that had not known world-encompassing war, and their values changed accordingly. The shift was highlighted by the Vietnam War, which attracted opposition from the new generation. Anti-war protests were a harbinger of wider social shifts later in the century.

Photographer unknown, *Dominion Post* Collection, Alexander Turnbull Library, PAColl-7327, EP-Ethics-Demonstration-Vietnam-01

High inflation during the 1970s raised pressure on wages, and unions were determined to make sure that increases kept pace. One outcome was street protests. Here, unions take part in a march to restore free wage bargaining.

earlier. Both phenomena were a reaction to prevailing society, characterised by a polarisation of opinion and alliances between otherwise disparate lobby groups. Post-colonial thinking was certainly a feature of some New Zealand campus environments by the early 1980s, where some students displayed an unprecedented level of thin-skinned and humourless anger at the world in general, and at any who apparently disagreed with their narrowly defined world view in particular.

Re-contact: Maori urbanisation and revival

New Zealand's majority society was ferociously monocultural for much of the twentieth century. The issue reflected both attitude and demography. Maori comprised just 5 percent of the population in 1936, some 87 percent lived in the country,[103] and as a people they were effectively segregated.[104] As we have seen, efforts by the Young Maori Party, Apirana Ngata and other leaders to bring change had effect, but the main arbiters behind Maori reassertion in the late twentieth century appear to have been population recovery, backed by a shift in general attitude initially triggered by the Second World War.

Maori population began growing again in the 1890s, but the rate of increase remained slow until the mid-1930s, when it began increasing dramatically. A Maori population that had stood at 82,000 in 1936 increased to 201,159 some 30 years later. Perhaps more crucially this also represented an increase from 5 to nearly 8 percent of the total.[105] This was due to two factors. The birth rate rose in the 1930s to around 45 per 1000, and stayed there until the mid-1960s – indeed, it did not drop below 30 per 1000 until 1973. This was combined with a sharp fall in the death rate, which had stood at around 15–20 per 1000 during the late 1930s and fell sharply in the late 1940s – an improvement that can be largely credited to a Labour Government drive to improve sanitation. The death rate dropped below 10 per 1000 in the 1950s and continued to drop until the late 1960s, when it hovered around four to five per 1000. This was two-thirds the non-Maori death rate, though to some extent the comparison was deceptive because Maori were younger on average.[106]

To this was added the social effect of the Second World War. Maori were closely involved with 2 NZ Division; 28 (Maori) Battalion was used as an elite unit,[107] and pulled the divisional irons out of the fire on several occasions.[108] There was even talk of raising a second unit for Pacific service.[109] Afterwards, many veterans felt that they had suffered for the country – and expected more than they were getting. Although even settler society had considered Maori a superior 'native', Maori were still discriminated against, often in subtle ways. Some bars would not serve Maori, credit arrangements differed, and job opportunities were usually less. However, the real arbiter of change was less the field performance of the battalion than the work of the Maori War Effort Organisation. There were two results. War work pushed Maori into the towns, bringing the two peoples into real, effective and growing contact for the first time in 80 years. The drive also submerged elements of tribal feeling. Tribal structures did not disappear, but where earlier initiatives by Maori had been diffused by old rivalries, the post-war arrangement was one of unprecedented unity. Many Maori moved into the larger towns to work in factories and service industries.

By 1945, around a quarter of all Maori lived in towns, and this number exploded over the next two decades. The big shift came between 1951 and 1966, when rural Maori population dropped from 70 to 38 percent of the total. Rural numbers continued to trend down afterwards, falling to 19.8 percent by 1986.[110] This has been put down to snowballing – a shift pioneered by a few who were then joined by relatives and friends, drawn by the apparent opportunities of the urban environment.[111]

This urban drift was the effective arbiter of detribalisation. While ties back to whanau and hapu were maintained in some respects – as in a return to the country for tangihanga – the shift generally broke old links. New forms of leadership had to be found, new social ties and connections forged, new ways of applying customary practices in an urban setting developed. These took time to emerge, and in the interim there was a sense of separation. Even use of Maori as a language fell away – a legacy in part of a mid-century notion that Maori people could integrate better if they spoke English – and a new generation emerged in the towns and cities who, in many cases, did not speak it. New social structures included gangs and a sub-culture highlighted by author Alan Duff's *Once Were Warriors*. The gangs were not welcomed by pavlova society.

This was not the only issue. Many Maori found work in fields ranging from freezing works to construction. These were not always well paid and usually the first to go in a downturn. Others found work as labourers, or with state organisations; Maori were over-represented in state employment such as the Railways or the Ministry of Works, under-represented in white-collar private enterprise and skilled professions.[112] Just 6.56 percent of Maori, in 1956, worked in professional or managerial circles, as opposed to more than a quarter of non-Maori. It took time to adapt to urban life. The practical result was that Maori entered the pavlova urban world at its lower end and usually stayed there.[113] Maori were more liable than European to live in second-class housing – itself, thanks to the emerging state suburbs, often clustered – and the result was an effective ghettoisation. However, proposals to 'pepper pot' Maori housing around European were disliked by both peoples.[114]

The wider problems that Maori faced were only sporadically addressed by government. The Maori Social and Economic Advancement Act of 1945 helped, as did the decision to drop the term 'native' in 1947. Some officers of 28 (Maori) Battalion became public servants in the newly organised Department of Maori Affairs after the war, extending the general approach taken by Ngata. But the state moved with a glacial pace and it was the early 1960s before steps were taken to address the issues that went with Maori urbanisation. Despite hints at an integrated future in the Hunn Report, and the Maori Welfare Act that followed in 1962, it was clear that government was paying only lip service to Maori needs. By this time more than 100,000 Maori were living in Auckland alone. Nearly half were under 30, nearly half in unskilled employment. Maori also formed a disproportionate part of the jail population.[115]

This was new, and to a significant extent reflected dislocation, expressed in part through new rules of behaviour and new attitudes. These were symptomatic of the failure of pavlova society to properly engage Maori at all levels; and of Maori to engage the pavlova world. In the longer term it was an outcome of the effective marginalisation and segregation that had begun a century earlier. The issue was also highlighted and to some extent perpetuated by a failure of the education system. Specialist Maori schools focused on agriculture, which was not relevant to the urban environment. General schools were not geared for a detribalised urban population and the syllabus was seldom relevant. In 1963, for instance, 93.3 percent of Maori boys left school without any qualifications, by comparison with 67.4 percent of European. Just 2.6 percent of Maori school leavers went on to full-time higher education, compared with 14 percent of Europeans.[116] Unqualified Maori had little option but to find unskilled work – perpetuating the cycle.

To this was added the fact that, pushed in part by urban flow, Maori society, language and culture were on the wane by the 1960s. The percentage of Maori speakers plunged, particularly among the burgeoning youth, pushed in part by elders who felt that Maori were better off speaking English if they wanted to live in an urban world, in part by the cultural centrism of the dominant pavlova society, and in part by the general ethos of conformity. In this environment any language other than English was effectively a form of dissent.

Yet Maori as a language did not vanish, nor did the culture. As before, the people proved resilient, able to adapt to the new environment. Dissatisfaction found expression in protests, and by the 1970s there were strident calls for equality. The Kirk administration made 6 February a public holiday and renamed it Waitangi Day as a move towards biculturalism, but while this line of rapport was arguably cut short by Kirk's demise in 1974, in a general sense it reflected both emerging post-colonial attitudes and a growing need to address Maori issues. Arguably government should have done this much earlier, but in practice – given mid-century attitudes – action was not really feasible until an improving demographic position made it possible for Maori to effectively capture government attention. It has also been argued that agitation was facilitated by urbanisation during the 1950s and 1960s.[117]

Land protest grew in the wake of the 1967 Maori Affairs Amendment Act and new rating legislation, which seemed likely to strip Maori of much of their remaining land because it had been abandoned to urban drift, and hapu could not afford to pay accumulating rates.[118] Protests culminated in a spectacular land march down the length of the North Island in 1975. This was not led by radical youth, but by a respected kuia, Whina Cooper (1895–1994), and attracted enormous attention. Cooper, born Josephine Te Wake, was one of a new generation of Maori leaders, a long-standing campaigner for Maori interests.[119] She led 50 followers from Te Hapua in March 1975, and thousands flocked to join the march as they reached Auckland. Core supporters went on to Wellington amid a blaze of publicity. Soon afterwards, Ngati Whatua began a 17-month occupation of Auckland's Bastion Point, and there was other action to recover land lost at Raglan during the Second World War. In 1979, Matiu Rata resigned his Northern Maori seat to found the Mana Motuhake party, designed to promote Maori rights.[120]

Protests gained new momentum during the early 1980s. There was a second Bastion Point occupation and eviction in 1982. Meanwhile, groups such as the 'Waitangi Action Committee' drew new attention to the Treaty of Waitangi. Decried as a 'fraud',[121] the Treaty was certainly on the back-burner in pavlova circles at the time. The Waitangi Tribunal had been formed in 1975, but it could only handle contemporary grievance and was viewed by many as toothless. Attention swung to active protests at the Waitangi Marae on Waitangi Day, reaching the point where it became difficult for ceremonies to continue. There were arrests, and the court cases that followed were used as a forum to air the issues. Government listened, giving the Waitangi Tribunal power to hear retrospective claims in 1985, identifying where Treaty principles had been breached and making recommendations.[122]

The following year a court ruling required government to take account of Maori claims in the state asset sale programme.[123]

This was an effective shift, of which the more important aspect was the ability to claim retrospectively; Maori had been shabbily treated by colonial authorities and had never been allowed to express the problem, still less heal the wounds. Claims became a mechanism for doing so, and far more than could be heard in a reasonable time flooded in. However, the system required the Tribunal to identify breaches of Treaty 'principles', which had not been envisaged by officials in 1840 and had to be deduced. Some commentators have argued that the Waitangi Tribunal did so by means of 'instrumental presentism' – evaluating past events in terms of late twentieth-century values, rather than the factors that applied at the time.[124]

To some extent this reflected the judicial aspects of the settlement process, a function of the timelessness attributed to law,[125] and it was perhaps appropriate for the required purpose. However, the historical work done for the settlement process was also used in some cases as a contribution to general historiography; and this was less satisfactory. As more than one commentator observed, there were differences between the purpose-driven work done for the 'industry' and the enquiry-driven analysis required of abstract historical enquiry.[126] It was important not to confuse the two.

10

Extreme decades

New Zealand's twentieth century as a social and political phenomenon came to an end in the 1980s. The shift, fashionably, has usually been pinned to 1984 and a Labour Government that implemented a series of socio-economic reforms. The truth is less clear-cut; from the wider historical perspective it seems clear that the process of change actually began in the 1960s, and while there can be little doubt that the so-called 'Rogernomes' of 1984–90 and their National successors put a distinctive stamp on developments, these reforms were in fact overlaid across deeper trends.

For this reason it is an overstatement to call the changes of the reform period revolutionary. Nonetheless, by 1999, when a newly elected Labour Government declared the experiment over, the classic age of the Kiwi farmer was essentially finished. Echoes still resounded, but the close-knit, socially flattened, blokeish, conservative world of farms and urban quarter-acres that emerged from the crucible of the First World War had essentially run its course.

By the early twenty-first century New Zealand stood at the beginning of a new phase – founded, as always, in the past, but yet to reveal its own historically important forms and vectors. The old pattern lay behind, its problems forgotten, its ideals and priorities fading into the warm glow of pleasant memory.

Thinking big

The Muldoon administration faced serious challenges as the 1980s dawned. Oil prices were rising in the wake of the Iranian revolution. Inflation remained high, debt was spiralling and growth was not what it had been. The government proposed to cure all these issues with a strategy dubbed 'Think Big'. It was twentieth-century Vogelism: projects built with borrowed money, that would provide 400,000 jobs, flood capital into the economy, and build a basis for the future. While there were obvious political motives associated with the lead-up to the 1981 election, the main rationale was energy self-sufficiency – the spot price of imported crude rose from $12.88 a barrel in March 1979 to $41.50 in December 1981, with dire effect on New Zealand's balance of payments.[1] In any case, New Zealand had been committed by the Kirk administration to compulsory purchase when the Maui gas field began producing in 1979, and the gas had to be paid for whether used or not. The huge upper Waitaki hydro-electric scheme was also about to come on line, transforming New Zealand's power calculations.

The three-leg strategy that emerged was designed to improve New Zealand's energy position via a synthetic fuel plant, and direct use of Maui gas; to take advantage of an expected electricity surplus to add a steel plant and expand the Tiwai Point aluminium refinery; and to generally boost the economy through a raft of development projects including the rebuild and electrification of the Main Trunk Line, and fresh incentives to boost the farming sector. From an engineering standpoint 'Think Big' was innovative. The synthetic fuel plant was the first in the world to use the zeolite-catalyst method,[2] and early estimates suggested New Zealand could be made 50 percent self-sufficient in petrol as a result.[3]

In the event the early 1980s brought an oil glut, the 400,000 jobs never eventuated, and government was lambasted for myopia. However, while 'Think Big' did not deliver as advertised, much of the criticism was caught up with the general demonisation of Muldoonism, ignoring the point that 'Think Big' was framed within the mind-set of a protectionist state that had survived 40 years. It was a logical extension of that style of thinking. The energy elements stemmed from arguments batted back and forth during the 1970s amid Middle Eastern oil restrictions and the general issue of a dwindling world oil supply, a real concern in the 1970s.

The other big issue of 1981 was a long-planned tour by the Springboks. It was political at every level. South Africa's white minority government had been an international pariah for years, and official Commonwealth condemnation extended into the sporting arena, enshrined in the Gleneagles Agreement of 1977. The problem for New Zealand rugby players and supporters was that the Springboks offered the only credible challenge on the field. Rivalry had been ongoing for years. A 1949 tour of South Africa by the All Blacks went 4–0 in favour of the Springboks. The All Blacks achieved a three to one series victory in 1956, and the tussle continued with successive tours into the 1960s. However, all this went ahead against the background of South Africa's unpalatable racial policies, and eventually the political issues became overwhelming. An All Black tour of South Africa in 1967 went ahead amid controversy. The Kirk administration cancelled a proposed return visit by the Springboks to New Zealand in 1973; and the All Black tour of South Africa in 1976 led to the Gleneagles Agreement.

These wounds were reopened when the New Zealand Rugby Football Union Council decided to organise a tour for 1981. Muldoon, according to his biographer, could 'see nothing but trouble' coming from it.[4] However, he refused to cancel the tour and made a national television appeal calling on the NZRFU to 'think well' before committing.[5] With just five months to an election in which the stakes seemed evenly balanced, Muldoon was probably trying not to alienate part of the electorate, but the result was that the tour went ahead amid a divisive atmosphere of public protest, rhetoric and invective on a scale New Zealand had not seen since 1913.

University students contributed some of the loudest voices. In a campus environment of thin-skinned and angry indignance towards the world in general, framed around emerging post-colonial thinking, it was not difficult for a few to whip up an emotive opposition to the tour. The same thinking also prompted the attitude that failure to join the protests equated to racism – and racists were defined as an inferior breed of humanity. In a wider sense this youthful hypocrisy had less to do with opposing racism than it did with intellectual bullying and the definition of narrow 'in' and 'out' social groups in the student community, but it gained disproportionate attention, obscuring the fact that protesters as a whole came from a much wider slice of society.

Protesters managed to stop a test match in Hamilton, where police protected them from the irate crowd, and violence escalated as the tour went on – though it never reached 1913 levels. Police were eventually armed with so-called 'Minto bars', long batons which were used in late July against protesters in Wellington's Molesworth Street, outside Parliament. The more strident voices of the anti-tour movement succeeded in upping the ante to the point where, by August, even a small-scale protest in a rain-soaked Napier, which included women pushing prams, was met by police in riot gear, backed by dump-bins. The struggle ended at Eden Park, where the All Blacks won the tour two tests to one, while police battled protesters outside and a light aircraft dropped projectiles onto the pitch.

It had been an emotional, divisive year, and feelings ran high afterwards. A group was assembled late in 1981 by one university history department to document the tour, but one meeting degenerated into a slanging match;[6] and in an environment where any view other than an anti-tour, anti-government line was apparently dismissed as racism, conclusions of intellectual worth were unlikely to emerge.

An angry crowd hurls eggs and water-bombs as Robert Muldoon and his wife, Thea, leave an election meeting in the Dunedin Town Hall, November 1978.

Photographer unknown, *Dominion Post* Collection, Alexander Turnbull Library, PAColl-7327, EP-NZ-Obits-Muldoon-001

All this masked the key historical issue, which was that a wide cross-section of ordinary New Zealanders had taken to the streets in numbers. They ran the gamut from retired clerks to mothers with babes-in-arms. Many participated to show that New Zealand people upheld international opposition to apartheid, but they were joined by a more vigorous element apparently keen on having a punch-up with police. At social level, the protests were a metaphor for New Zealand's internal frustrations. The true battle-lines were between old and new, between the over-stretched norms of the pavlova society and the changing world outside New Zealand's cosseted shores, framed through the emerging ideals of post-colonialism.

At this wider level change could not be regulated out of existence, and the popular response to the 1981 Springbok tour was less safety valve than gauge. Muldoon was re-elected by a whisker in the election that year,[7] an electorate decision perhaps influenced by the apparent civil disobedience of the protest movement. Muldoon himself credited electorate support for Think Big,[8] but the writing was on the wall, and his administration limped into a third term with the tide of change swirling around it.

Opposite above

Protesters march against the Springbok tour, central Wellington, early July 1981.
The tour divided New Zealand in a way not seen for generations.

Photographer unknown, *Evening Post* Collection, Alexander Turnbull Library, PAColl-0614, F-1602-35mm-25

Opposite below

Anti-Springbok tour protesters and police in Sydney Street East — later Kate
Sheppard Place — near Parliament, mid-1981.

Photographer unknown, *Evening Post* Collection, Alexander Turnbull Library, PAColl-0614, F-1391-35mm-20

Above

Elements of the anti-tour movement escalated tensions to the point where both
police and protesters armed and armoured themselves. The resulting violence
was of a scale unseen in New Zealand since the industrial disruptions of 1913.

Photographer unknown, *Evening Post* Collection, Alexander Turnbull Library, PAColl-0614, F-1392-35mm-11A

Beating the cringe: films, songs and stories

New Zealand's mid-century literature, music and film reflected a search for identity, a drive to find a 'New Zealand' image and escape the prison of the cultural cringe. Literature led the way, and a 'New Zealand' voice emerged after the Second World War through the engagement between literature and popular culture. Other arts took longer. Movies languished for decades; Rudall Hayward's populist *wanderjahr* from Northland to Bluff in the 1920s, making local movies for local people – epitomised by shorts such as *Natalie of Napier* – was a false dawn. Just five movies were made locally in the three decades from 1940. Part of the reason was financial, part the notion that anything New Zealand produced would be inferior.

That changed in the mid-1970s. The renaissance was led by *Sleeping Dogs* (1977), an adaptation of C.K. Stead's novel *Smith's Dream*. The break with the 'cringe' finally came with Geoff Murphy's *Goodbye Pork Pie* (1981), a quintessential road movie set in classic New Zealand, which was comparable with anything else in that genre on a world stage. It also became a New Zealand icon, the imagery still valid and instantly recognisable more than 20 years later, when a music video paid homage to the image of the rebel-in-a-Mini. A full-length cartoon, *Footrot Flats – A Dog's Tail* (1985), celebrated mid-century rural New Zealand, arguably

Lampshades, glass barrels and acetylene containers provide instruments for this 'Scratch' orchestra from Auckland performing at the Wellington Teachers College, 1974.

gaining popularity because that culture was dying as the film came out. The 'splatter' comedy *Bad Taste* (1988) started the career of Wellington film-maker Peter Jackson. By the 1990s New Zealand was producing movies the equal of any overseas, and the local voice was clear in *Once Were Warriors* (1995), *Topless Women Talk About Their Lives* (1997) and *Savage Honeymoon* (2000), the last poking gentle fun at Auckland's 'Westie' sub-culture. Maori priorities were explored by *Whale Rider* (2003), an adaptation of the Witi Ihimaera novel, which met unprecedented international success.

A reputation for top-rate production values, spectacular scenery, and a favourable exchange rate prompted interest from United States producers in the 1990s, and by the turn of the century, New Zealand — like Yugoslavia before it — had become a regular location for Hollywood stars and film-makers. Local talent was also making a splash. Jackson's rise to international prominence continued with *Brain Dead* (1992) — a brilliant homage both to splatter movies and the classic New Zealand of the pavlova era, notably the lawn mower. Jackson's ranking as one of the world's greatest film-makers was cemented at the end of the century by his epic three-part adaptation of J.R.R. Tolkien's classic novel *The Lord of the Rings* (2001–2003).

Beating the cringe: films, songs and stories

A dose of culture: Robert Muldoon shows his earplugs to Steve Gilpin, Don Martin and Kevin Stanton of Mi-Sex, June 1980. The band invited the Prime Minister to attend a concert in response to Muldoon's comments that rock music was not cultural. 'About as much culture as the rugby league test on Sunday', he quipped afterwards — obviously well aware of the double meaning.

Photographer unknown, *Dominion Post* Collection, Alexander Turnbull Library, PAColl-7327, EP/1980/1962/28

Beating the cringe: films, songs and stories

Music, like film, lagged when it came to local voice. Douglas Lilburn penned orchestral pieces with local flavour from the 1940s, but there were practical and financial barriers to performances in mid-century New Zealand and audiences were limited. Local jazz and swing bands were more popular; and the baby boomers picked up on rock music, but it took a while for local bands to play their own compositions, longer still for a 'New Zealand' sound to emerge. Ray Columbus and the Invaders paved the way; Fourmyula's 'Nature' of 1969 was an early exploration of local sound. But there was still a feeling that serious musicians only existed overseas, and local bands had to 'make it' elsewhere — usually Sydney or Melbourne, ideally London. Dragon, Split Enz and Th' Dudes, among others, made the trans-Tasman journey in the late 1970s.

The local scene was transformed that decade, helped in part by new drinking laws that turned pubs into practical concert venues. Split Enz pioneered the push back into New Zealand, and others followed, building a clear local voice during the 1980s. The Swingers' 'Counting the Beat' was the third-best selling song of 1981.[9] Songs such as Split Enz' 'Six Months in a Leaky Boat', or DD Smash's 'Devil You Know' were quintessentially New Zealand. In 1984, Dalvanius Prime's Patea Maori Club released 'Poi E', which became the best-selling song in New Zealand that year, beating Stevie Wonder, Bob Marley and Bruce Springsteen among others.[10] Dave Dobbyn, meanwhile, went on to write the soundtrack for *Footrot Flats*, of which 'Oughta Be in Love' and 'Slice of Heaven' became classics in their own right.

By the mid-1980s New Zealand was producing regional styles, including the 'Dunedin sound' epitomised by The Chills and Netherworld Dancing Toys. The ultimate power-band of the era was The Gordons, who anticipated thrash-metal by nearly two decades and carried a raw energy that left overseas punk in the shade. By the 1990s, although some shops insisted on maintaining separate 'New Zealand' sections, local music had become an integral part of New Zealand's taste, and bands such as Pacifier and the Datsuns were maintaining the international profile pioneered 30 years earlier by Split Enz. It was a case of getting to Broadway the hard way. New Zealand music had come a long, long way from its colonial roots.

Split Enz.

Wellington Newspapers Ltd

Disengaging paradise

Faced with falling standards of living, rising unemployment and a burgeoning welfare bill, Muldoon turned to ever-more draconian legislation in an effort to preserve the pavlova world. Much of this was personally directed, and as Muldoon's biographer remarks, by 1982 there was a 'widely held view' that Cabinet had 'become largely unaccountable to the caucus' – which could not 'check the Prime Minister and Finance Minister'.[11] It was clear from Muldoon's calls for a new Bretton Woods agreement that he hoped rescue might come by external readjustment. Meanwhile, social discontent simmered. Music became an outlet for a restless people, and Muldoon received a popular ribbing in 1980 when he suggested that rock music was not cultural. The Knobz responded with the gently satirical 'Culture' – and Muldoon apparently saw the joke, accepting an invitation to attend a rock concert. The songs of the early eighties were more direct. 'There Is No Depression in New Zealand', Blam Blam Blam's take on the national plight, soared high in the 1981 charts on the back of anti-Springbok tour protests.

Muldoon remained reluctant to implement the strategy recommended by the Treasury to address the immediate economic issues. Instead he turned to tighter controls, implementing a wage-and-price freeze in mid-1982,[12] and tackling unemployment via work schemes. All this was stop-gap. New Zealand's overseas debt had risen from $1436 million in 1976 to $7764 million in 1983.[13] This represented a near-three-fold increase once corrected for inflation,[14] highlighting the fact that New Zealand was living beyond its means.[15] New arrangements with Australia – Closer Economic Relations (CER) – hinted at improvements in 1983, but they were not enough, and Muldoon accepted recommendations from the Treasury to end supplementary minimum prices (SMPs). By now he faced dissent within the ranks, although calls for free-market reforms by new MPs elected in 1981[16] were not regarded as serious by many at the time.[17]

Thea and Robert Muldoon during a press conference in the 'Beehive' theatrette, 15 June 1984.

Photographer unknown, Alexander Turnbull Library, PAColl-7327, EP/1984/2786

The end came suddenly. A working majority of one had given Muldoon problems since the 1981 election,[18] and in mid-June 1984, Marilyn Waring and Mike Minogue crossed the floor to support a private 'Nuclear-Free New Zealand' bill. A meeting on the evening of 14 June left Muldoon and senior members of caucus convinced that their only option was an early election, and an apparently alcohol-fuelled Prime Minister made the announcement to stunned journalists late in the evening.[19] The notion that he had precipitately called the election after one too many drinks at Bellamy's became one of the supposed truths of this tumultuous period. But it was actually a myth; Muldoon discussed the options extensively during the evening with available members of caucus, including the President of the National Party who came down from Auckland for the purpose;[20] and Muldoon's biographer has argued that diabetes, medication, frustration and exhaustion contributed to Muldoon's demeanour when he faced the cameras.[21]

In the event, Labour won the election largely because the conservative vote was split by the recently formed New Zealand Party.[22] New doctrine called for the removal of all barriers and regulations, widening the tax base, and reducing government in favour of private enterprise. This reflected prevailing international ideas which were in resurgence around the West by the late 1970s, in part spurred by the oil shocks, in part a reaction to the worldwide bloating of welfare states, and in part a product of ongoing ideological tensions between communism and capitalism. The New Zealand approach was nicknamed 'Rogernomics', a play on the 'Reaganomics' of contemporary United States, and a choice that itself high-lighted one of New Zealand's differences with the world. By contrast with America, the New Zealand version got the first name of its chief architect, Roger Douglas.

The agenda was laid out in a briefing paper prepared by the Treasury in August 1984,[23] matching ideas that a small 'think tank' of intellectuals, businessmen and politicians had been tossing around for some years.[24] This was combined with a more explicit drive to incorporate new popular thinking towards the environment, including prevailing anti-nuclear sentiment, and a legislative trend that focused on individual rights. By old standards this integration of economic conservatism and humanitarian liberalism was a curious mix, but it reflected world trends of the day – particularly the conceptual alliance between monetarism and individualism and the broad swing away from inclusive, controlling government. As always, however, the New Zealand incarnation differed in the specific from overseas examples.

New Zealand was certainly in a mood for change, but the economic side of the reforms came as a surprise, in part because it was the opposite of what Labour had previously stood for, in part because the snap election prevented the party issuing a full manifesto, and in part because other events competed for attention in 1985. These included the sinking of the Greenpeace protest vessel *Rainbow Warrior* in Auckland harbour by French government agents. One man died. Public imagination was also captured by the 'nuclear ships' row that erupted when the government forbade nuclear power and weapons in its waters. This mirrored a

populist worldwide swing against all things nuclear. However, New Zealand was well ahead of the pack both at popular and policy levels – no other government in the main alliances had yet moved to a full ban. It came at a price. In the mid-1980s the Cold War was entering its last dangerous spasm, and the United States formally suspended the ANZUS alliance.

Over the next few years the 'Rogernomes' restructured New Zealand government, and by extension society, around concepts of free-market enterprise and a minimalist state. Tasks previously conducted by government were devolved to communities – the proliferation of boards, councils and authorities were whittled back by about 80 percent.[25] State activities such as New Zealand Railways, the Forest Service, which was just starting to reap a commercial return, the Post Office and State Coal Service were restructured into 'corporate' entities, shedding staff and premises along the way.[26] This had significant effect on rural communities, particularly as the Post Office began closing branches previously kept open in back-country districts for social reasons.

Disengagement from 'fortress New Zealand' added to the changes. Much of this was overdue adjustment for the loss of the British markets, and SMPs were being withdrawn by the Muldoon administration – but now their loss came on top of the general retraction of services.[27] The combined withdrawal created rural impoverishment unseen for 60 years.[28] By 1986, some farmers were talking about abandoning the back-country.[29]

The picture in the cities was different. The removal of the regulatory regime unleashed demand for everything from cars to cellphones, money pent up by old rules flooded into the pockets of consumers, and for a while, city-dwelling New Zealanders celebrated. The image of the mid-eighties as an urban lifestyle party of youthful hedonism, awash with fat expense accounts, champagne, caviar, over-priced and undersized nouvelle cuisine, 'brick' cellphones and fast cars, is small exaggeration. New Zealand's 20-something Generation Xers soared into the 'yuppie' age of conspicuous consumption. This was a world of chrome-and-glass office towers and pastel interiors. It was a world of big hair, bad behaviour and bold clothing styles. The lifestyle was aided and abetted by liberalisation of the drinking laws, which helped contribute to a new 'cafe culture', well entrenched by the end of the decade.

This urban culture contrasted sharply with pavlova ideals and behaviour,[30] though perhaps not general aspiration. However, the particular expressions of the period were new, and there is no single explanation for the pace of adoption. To some extent this mid-eighties lifestyle matched what was happening overseas. It was generational, a response by young adults to a childhood that had been insulated from hardship by the pavlova world and its overseas counterparts. However, in New Zealand the 'yuppie' period was also a reaction to freedom. As one commentator has remarked, New Zealanders had been penned up for three generations behind protectionist walls. Now the restrictions were gone, and nobody knew quite how to behave. The result was a kind of naive, adolescent excess.[31]

Opposite

Downtown Wellington was transformed in the late 1980s. Chrome and glass towers soared where old Edwardian buildings had once stood. In part a function of new earthquake regulations, the building boom was further fuelled by the so-called 'yuppie' period, as investors threw money into property. The reforms also freed up retail shopping, opening up imports and giving New Zealanders their first taste of such freedoms since the early 1950s.

Matthew Wright

Helicopter in Queenstown, February 1985. Even then, as the 'reform period' began, there was a sense of vibrancy about life in the tourist town which differed from the rest of New Zealand — but which the main centres soon shared.

Matthew Wright

This social whirl was accompanied by a wide-eyed money-culture. It was an age of financial novelty and of financial innocence. Money became a commodity to be transacted, and many New Zealanders also plunged into the share market. Every businessman had a stock-broker, it seemed, and there was status to be gained from ringing that broker on a cellphone during a champagne-drenched working lunch. 'Corporate raiders' emerged, companies whose function was simply to buy and sell the stocks of other companies — including, at times, those of other raiders. For a few heady months it seemed that financiers had found a way of making money with money, and soon everybody wanted a piece of the action.

The edifice came unstuck when the stock market crashed, just three months after the reformers were re-elected in August 1987. It was a worldwide phenomenon, but the New Zealand market was more heavily hit than some. It stood at a total value of $45 billion before the crash, lost $9.9 billion in one day, and was down to $24.2 billion by the end of the year.[32] The problem, one observer suggested, was that New Zealanders were market cowboys.[33] Others have argued that ethical standards slipped.[34] Wealth certainly did; by late 1991, for instance, the local share market was valued at just $14.5 billion.[35] The average Kiwi's large-scale flirtation with stocks and shares was over, and it hit most in the pocket. Many lost retirement savings, a few their homes. Businesses fell on hard times, an unprecedented number of bankruptcies followed, and the government initiated a Ministerial Commission of Inquiry in 1988.[36]

Douglas continued reforming.[37] His 1988 budget laid out a programme of state asset sales thought likely to bring $14 billion.[38] However, even after Telecom was sold for $4.25 billion, the return on public assets that had taken taxpayers a century or more to build up was just $8.3 billion.[39] The wake of the stock-market crash had not, it seemed, been the best time to sell, and growing popular unease with the policy was reflected by ructions within the Labour Party. The administration

The Ohaaki thermal power station
north of Taupo, completed in
1989.

Matthew Wright

went into the 1990 general election with its third prime minister in 18 months. A
last-minute 'growth agreement' with the unions was launched amid suitable
mugging for the cameras,[40] but proved ineffective as a vote-buyer; Labour slumped
to just 29 seats. To some extent this was a reaction to the political confusion of the
previous 18 months, but in a wider sense was also a popular vote against
Rogernomics.

However, the incoming National Government continued the policies –
extending them into the social sphere and labour market. The new administration
also had to tackle several inherited problems. The Bank of New Zealand was in
trouble.[41] Then the New York credit rating agency Standard and Poors signalled a
possible reduction in New Zealand's ranking.[42] Government debt had risen from
$21,879 million in 1984 to $44,347 million in 1990 – though not all of this was
caused by the reforms. One component was an absolute rise in health costs.
Another was rising pension costs, a legacy of Muldoon's 1975 scheme. However, a
part of the increase was also a rising welfare bill, itself caused to some extent by
the restructuring. By 1991, labour-force unemployment rates had reached levels
similar to those of the Great Depression, more than double those of the mid-
1980s.[43] Unemployment benefit payments that had stood at $195.2 million in 1984
had risen by 1991 to $1.4 billion.[44] This time it was not a shared phenomenon; by
1991 many world economies were booming, but New Zealand's shrank that year
by 0.8 percent.[45]

Finance minister Ruth Richardson's so-called 'Mother of all Budgets' cut
welfare support and introduced direct charges on taxpayer-funded health services
and medicines. These moves shaved 0.9 percent off the external debt,[46] but the
social and political cost was high. Government popularity plunged to record lows
while protesters burned effigies of Richardson and Social Welfare minister Jenny
Shipley. Richardson – whose policies were publicly dubbed 'Ruthenasia' – received

police protection,[47] previously unheard of in a country where prime ministers once had their home addresses and phone numbers in the telephone directory. Polls showed that trust in politicians had dropped to just 4 percent by 1992, down from 32 percent in 1975.[48]

Unemployment peaked nationally that year at 11.2 percent, some 172,600 individuals,[49] a historic high that exceeded even the depression of the 1930s. A stroll down Wellington's Lambton Quay – the 'golden mile' of New Zealand retail – revealed empty shops, temporary shops and yellowing sale signs.[50] Crime soared, in sharp contrast to the experience of the 1930s depression. Some 37,214 offences were reported in 1930 on a national population of 1,506,800. This dropped to 33,168 offences in 1935 – around one in 40 Kiwis committed crimes at that time. By contrast, rates climbed in the later period from 349,193 reported crimes in 1980 to 1,049,915 in 1994, on a national population of just over 3,325,900.[51] This was 15 times depression figures and could not solely be explained by the inclusion of traffic offences in the statistics.[52]

Sales of taxpayer assets continued, and the national railway system was sold just before the 1993 election to another consortium of US interests and merchant bankers Fay Richwhite. The price of $328 million was little more than had been spent rebuilding the Main Trunk Line a few years earlier.[53] By this time the electorate was in a mood for change, but National kept power with a reduced majority in the 1993 election. Labour, it seemed, had not been forgiven and

Minister of Finance Ruth Richardson meets Ken Douglas of the Combined Trade Unions, 20 November 1990.

John Nicholson, *Dominion Post* Collection, Alexander Turnbull Library, PAColl-7327, EP/1990/4080/30

frustrations were expressed instead in the vote for a new electoral system. The idea of changing New Zealand's traditional First Past the Post (FPP) system to proportional representation had been bandied about since the mid-1980s. Provision was made for a referendum in the Electoral Act 1993, and it went to the poll that year. The result favoured mixed-member proportional (MMP) representation, which under the circumstances was essentially a vote against the existing system – and against the reforms.

This was put to the test in the first MMP election of 1996, when the more extreme elements of the main parties spun off in the hope of getting representation. A relatively new party, New Zealand First, held the balance of power – choosing, after some weeks, to support a National coalition. The reforms continued, and support for both New Zealand First and National crashed in the 1999 election. Labour, with the help of a resurgent Alliance party – itself the spiritual descendant of mid-1930s Labour – came to power with the declaration that the experiment was over. New Zealanders, incoming Prime Minister Helen Clark declared in a widely reported speech, were 'weary of radical restructuring'.[54] The policies that followed underlined the point,[55] and key departments began moving away from what one commentator called 'narrow and prescriptive analysis', to a more 'reflective' and 'open minded' perspective that 'acknowledges the wider significance of social factors'.[56]

From the historical viewpoint the years from 1984 to the end of the century had certainly been significant, and included government changes at least as dramatic as those implemented by the Liberal administration in the 1890s, or the Labour

The Reverend Richard Randerson (left), author Patricia Grace, and then Black Power president Rei Harris show their support for MMP in 1996.

Phil Reid, *Dominion Post* Collection, Alexander Turnbull Library, PAColl-7372, EP/1993/3398/14

Government of 1935–40 — whose concepts of state intervention were broadly undone by the Rogernomes. What it had all meant was not immediately obvious. Contemporary analysts — some with axes to grind both for and against the changes — saw the reform period in absolute terms, identifying the government as solely responsible and classifying what happened as everything from essential medicine to a 'con' driven by theoretical ideology.[57] Opinions remained polarised even a few years later; New Zealanders, another commentator explained in 2003, had been 'flagellating ourselves at the altar of economic orthodoxy' — a push for 'purity' for which, in practice, country and people had paid heavily.[58] External opinion was blunt. New Zealand's 'radical free-market reformers', one Australian magazine declared, had been 'peddling damaged goods'.[59]

In short, New Zealand's experience as a 'free-market laboratory'[60] had not gone down well with a wide swathe of the people. However, the reforms had to be considered in context of the last third of the twentieth century. They added detail and direction, but in a wider sense both the dislocation and the intensity of emotion that went with them were also functions of the disengagement both from Britain and from the mid-century state. By the 1980s New Zealand had failed to adapt to the changing world, particularly the loss of British markets, and 40 years had bloated the 'cradle to grave' welfare state into a corpulent beast well removed from its origins.

The bloat was compounded by the sinking economy of the late 1970s, which threw people into the system. This contrasted with the situation during the infancy of the cradle-to-the-grave state 40 years earlier when prosperity was rising and people were thrown out of it. By the 1970s the state support system was more comprehensive than that of the late 1930s, including welfare payments, indirect

Westport fishing boats, mid-1997.

Matthew Wright

support in the form of deliberately overstaffed departments, notably Railways, subsidies, grants, rebates and a universal no-fault accident compensation system. After two generations, some New Zealanders viewed welfare as a lifestyle option, and many availed themselves of state padding in various ways. To this was added the walls of 'Fortress New Zealand', which by the early 1980s included subsidy schemes for farmers, work schemes to entice employers to hire youth, and make-work subsidies for local councils. Change was needed, and any change was likely to be difficult under the circumstances.

Whether the particular changes then implemented by the Rogernomes were the only way is another matter. At the time the approach was sold as the sole strategy – there was even an acronym, TINA, 'there is no alternative'. Such affirmations disguised the fact that there were other approaches, including the path taken by Australia, or strategies suggested by some businessmen.[61] Most commentators agreed that there had been elements of crusading zeal about the reforms, and there were also signs that some directions had been a product of conviction rather than analysis. While leading Chicago School economist Frederich Hayek influenced some New Zealand policy papers of the day,[62] the leading reformers – as one observer noted – had apparently not read his works.[63] Books by New Zealand's main movers-and-shakers of the period, the commentator suggested, displayed 'intellectual shallowness', masked by 'cocksure arrogance'.[64]

Jazz band at a Masterton wine-and-food festival, February 1995.

Matthew Wright

Right above

Not everything changed during the reform period. The tower blocks are new, but the camping ground under Tauranga's Mount Maunganui, seen here in January 2003, reflect the classic mid-twentieth-century holiday experience.

Matthew Wright

Right below

Rotorua Museum, former bath-house and a town icon.

Matthew Wright

To this extent the reforms of the 1980s were unique; even the radical shake-up implemented by the Liberals 90 years earlier had pegged back from pure application of theory. Some historians have considered a coup,[65] policies forced on an unwilling electorate by a small group of politicians with the aid of the three-year parliamentary mandate.[66]

Yet even this point does not fully convey the complexity of what happened. In a broader sense, New Zealanders were in a mood for change by 1984, welcoming freer access to imported goods, easier overseas travel, a less regulated lifestyle and opportunity to keep up with overseas trends and fashions. At its best, new-libertarian New Zealand was an exciting, urbanised nirvana of cafes, late-night clubs and shopping malls – all essential medicine for a populace starved of consumer goods. Liberalisations were also necessary to set New Zealand up to compete well on the world stage; and other relaxations allowed New Zealanders to enjoy lifestyles previously envied as available only to those overseas. The reforms forced the export sector to diversify, shocking producers away from failed reliance on a few bulk products.

But popular support did not extend to the rapid-fire sale of key taxpayer-owned assets, pension claw-backs, and the imposition of 'user pays' on services already funded by the taxpayer. The problem was that the reforms were presented as a package, and opposition was often defined either as rejection of all change, or as advocacy of continued Muldoonism, an approach demonised by the reformers.[67] Much of the message was also couched around nineteenth-century concepts of inevitability and linear progress; the reforms were 'advanced' and 'sophisticated', keying into both the 'high-tech' imagery of the day and the popular view of change, itself founded in nineteenth-century shibboleths. The combination of all these factors made constructive debate difficult.

Finally the electorate tired of change. Arguments that prosperity had failed to emerge because the reforms had not been pushed hard enough were becoming difficult to sustain by the 1990s. By then New Zealand had pushed further, harder and faster than most nations. However, the average annual growth rate between 1984 and 1999 was 0.5 percent. This was no better than typical 1970s figures, worse than 1950s levels, and below that of unreformed countries such as Australia.[68] Taking housing out of the equation, the net wealth of the average New Zealand household fell by half between 1978 and 2003. The cause was debt rising faster than assets, an issue masked by a rise in house prices.[69] While a few individuals caught the wave and made fortunes, many did not; and the fact that the pie did not grow much implies that the new rich became so by impoverishing the poor, though the mechanisms were not direct. In 1997, for instance, a third of Maori women reported that their families could eat properly only occasionally. By 2000–01, 22.6 percent of the population were surviving on less than three-fifths of the average income. This included 29.1 percent of all children, 32 percent of all Maori families, 40 percent of all Pacific Island families, and 66.3 percent of all solo-parent families.[70]

These were different figures from those of the classic pavlova era, and many problems of poverty had also re-emerged by the turn of the century, including 'Third World' diseases such as tuberculosis. An OECD report also showed that New Zealand had one of the world's highest rates of youth suicide, teen pregnancies and drug use.[71] Structural unemployment, the emergence of a new and conspicuous elite, an apparently permanent state of 'recovery', seemingly endless reforms and political upheaval did not make a populist mix in 1990s New Zealand.

It also obscured wider historical trends, including the decades-long disengagement from Britain, and other world changes that New Zealand reflected. In the end, the reforms coloured, sometimes facilitated and certainly detailed the way New Zealand developed, but did not much alter the broader momentum. Like most trends these wider shifts were also multi-faceted, complex and could not be wholly explained by any single factor; the reforms, in this broader sense, joined other socio-economic, political and technical forces operating to change New Zealand during the period.

Complex change also flowed from the information revolution of the 1990s, which introduced New Zealanders to the world. Cellphones, email, faxes and the Internet all had an impact on thinking, ideas, behaviour and attitudes. Television expanded from two channels to three, then four, and finally dozens as satellite TV and cable appeared. The Internet promised further change, not as the super-shopping mall envisaged in the failed 'dot com' boom, but as a medium of its own.

All this contributed to the popular reduction of complex concepts to eight-word 'sound bites' and exciting visuals. There were signs by the turn of the century that this was becoming entrenched. New Zealand teen-speak by this time had more than a passing resemblance to Californian 'valley speak' – a vacuous dialect lampooned more than a decade earlier by American composer Frank Zappa.[72]

The last decades of the twentieth century also brought new attitudes to violence. The First and Second World Wars had helped mould a particular kind of society, marked by strong social bonds between peers, an understanding of the realities of war, and a genuine abhorrence of fighting. This had dissipated by the 1980s in the face of a new generation who had experienced neither that nor the later Vietnam conflict. The peace movement was increasingly emotive and 'greened', contrasted at mainstream level by popular movies and television that portrayed cartoon-like 'action heroes' in gladiatorial spectacles, trivialising the personal consequences of warfare. This became the pre-eminent image of conflict for a new generation. It was an international trend that New Zealand shared, and which almost certainly licensed a new level of violent crime. The advent of games in which contestants actually shot each other with dye-loaded airguns did not help. Nor was the acceptability of violence as entertainment the only social change. To this could be added the rising popularity of illicit drug use – drugs that broke new boundaries of medical risk with each generation.

Lake Rotoiti.

Matthew Wright

New Zealand's view of its past gained local focus during the pavlova era, matching the emerging local voices in arts and music. At popular level there was a persistent cringe-based conception that real history existed only in Britain. As late as the 1980s, it was feasible to complete a degree in history without touching New Zealand.

Yet there were historians who saw New Zealand as something more than a barnacle on the mother country; and it was perhaps no coincidence that the two first works along these lines were written at the end of the 1950s, as New Zealanders struggled with the concept of dual nationhood.

Keith Sinclair and W.H. Oliver's respective one-volume accounts of New Zealand's past – *A History of New Zealand* and *The Story of New Zealand* – were classics. They were also very different, both steeped in the framework of New Zealand's mid-century self-view as an emerging nation, but tackling it from contrasting angles. Sinclair's stayed in print for more than 40 years, progressively updated – and an edition was even published after his death in 1993. Both Sinclair and Oliver went on to lustrous careers as leading historians.

Another distinctive historical voice of the period was Dick Scott, whose book *The Parihaka Story* (1954) was one of the first to highlight the treatment of the south Taranaki Maori community in the wake of the wars. A second book on the subject, *Ask That Mountain: The Story of Parihaka* (1975) ran to nine editions. Scott penned numerous other popular histories. His *Winemakers of New Zealand* (1964) highlighted a youthful industry at a time when most Kiwis were obsessed with beer, and when much local wine was deprecatingly called 'Dally plonk'. That book, too, was long-lasting and republished as *Pioneers of New Zealand Wine* (2002).

They were joined by others in the 1960s and 1970s, notably Michael King (1945–2004), who chose writing as a full-time career in a country where even part-time work pumping petrol usually provided more lucrative income. Although academically trained to the highest level, King did not subscribe to the often petty jealousies of the academic world; and he wrote in a way that was readily accessible to the wider public. He did not hesitate to tackle the shibboleths of New Zealand's past, virtually pioneering the study and popularisation of Maori history and biography even at risk of alienating himself. With such works as *Being Pakeha* (1985), *Pakeha* (1991), and *Being Pakeha Now* (1999), King also advocated the point that by the late twentieth century, Europeans were effectively also an indigenous New Zealand group.

Michael King (1945–2004).

King was a voice of reason during the last decades of the century, and his writings offered wisdom at a time when post-colonial sentiment threatened to distort the view New Zealanders had of themselves. His death in a motor accident came just months after he had written a new and thoughtful general history of his country and its peoples.

These general changes reflected a shift from the cult of the individual as a cog of the nation state, to a new general theme of individual determination, a change that reflected broad trends of the late twentieth century, but which developed a characteristic New Zealand stamp. The new cultural norm was highlighted by a change in the values of the dominating culture – which was neither settler, jingo nor pavlova, but becoming broader and more inclusive. New Zealand's reform period helped facilitate that trend, but it was a two-way street and the reforms were also a reflection of this new thinking. In these respects, New Zealand of the late twentieth century was moving on from its mid-century state-controlled paradise in ways that far exceeded the ability of any government to influence.

The change was highlighted by a revival of mid-century imagery in advertising – one promotion showcased the icons of mid-century New Zealand, including steam train, school trips, Chopper bicycles, and traffic department Veloxes. Another contrasted an indolent and self-centred 'new money' Y-generationer, perhaps a banker, with images of hard-working, self-sacrificing, hard-playing, Kiwi blokes – judged from a heavenly bar by a digger, a rugby player and a farmer. It was a nostalgic appeal to a romanticised past amid a new and seemingly dangerous world.

Yet, despite an unprecedented combination of new rich, new poor, new language and new attitudes, some of the basic tenets of New Zealand thinking were not altered. Prevailing ideals were still shaped by the concepts on which New Zealand society had been founded – house-ownership, the quarter-acre section, lip-service

Swimmers at Days Bay, Eastbourne, early in 2002.

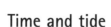
Matthew Wright

egalitarianism and, ideally, employment security. These underlying concepts remained strongly held as the twentieth century came to an end. Indeed, by 2003, 87 percent of New Zealand's net household wealth was tied up in the brick-and-mortar of housing, up from the 65 percent it had been in 1978.[73] Figures released in late 2002 showed that 7 percent of all retired couples over 65 still had an average mortgage debt of \$42,000.[74] As always, the legacy of New Zealand's colonial past continued to shape the unknown future.

Time and tide

The new course on which New Zealand society was set became clear during the 1990s. Like all trends it was complex and multifaceted, founded in the past, but laying new ideals over old, notably the cult of individual freedom, coupled with significant retightening of attitude towards behaviour. These were not contradictions but different aspects of the same phenomenon, a change away from a society that emphasised conformity and nation-state, to one that focused more on individual rights and self-determination – but within a new ethos of conformity, defined in part by a pluralist emphasis on the rights of identifiable groups. These built-in oppositions were not unusual; as always, society remained complex, with in-built tensions and inconsistencies. Thinking sometimes reflected opposing goals. The implications echoed through everyday life, and could be seen in fields as diverse as race relations, education, social services and medical care.

The retightening that had begun to underpin many social relations by the turn of the century was evident in attitudes to behaviour and language, including a redefinition of which words were offensive. The shift was distinct, even radical. In March 1972, Germaine Greer had been arrested by Auckland police for saying 'bullshit' in public, but by 2003 this expletive, when used to mean 'nonsense', was openly published in mainstream newspapers,[75] and even appeared conversationally on prime-time television drama. Like the settler-era intensifier 'damn', it had ceased to be offensive in turn-of-the-century New Zealand. But other terms had become unacceptable. New-speak idealism demonised words associated with colonial-era prejudice, replacing them with abstract euphemisms. Automatic email systems, designed to protect recipients from what one software manufacturer called 'profanities' – a word with clear evangelistic overtones – were sometimes zealously set. This Orwellian mind-set reflected a general social tightening. Many things could not be done on stage any more, still less in public; and ideally they were not even to be thought.

All this was symptomatic of changing attitudes, often framed as a reversal of older prejudices. As always, these ideas were taken to an indignant extreme in some circles, including by some historians. The presentism of 'politically correct' thought and terminology was also clear, as was the point that valid intellectual insight could not be gained by disguising the realities of the past with the euphemisms of the present. To this extent, new thinking carried in-built tensions, and there were surprising parallels with the moral evangelism of a century earlier. In both cases, a few overzealous enthusiasts identified some aspects of ordinary

Russell from Flagstaff Hill, with a human vista very different from the old Kororareka days, though many old buildings remain, nestled here and there in the township.

Matthew Wright

human behaviour as unacceptable, and used that extreme to create a narrow definition of acceptable thought. This fed back into mainstream society where it was picked up and used to redefine normality. In many respects this provided an overdue correction for earlier problems, but in other respects it created fresh injustice. There was also a backlash, and a working balance seemed hard to find.

This was not the only comparison; 1880s evangelism had been adopted by disparate groups drawn together by common struggle against mainstream society. Similar alliances could be seen in the 1990s. For all these reasons there seemed good reason to consider that, by the 1990s, New Zealand's twentieth-century social cycle was over and a new phase was beginning. Whether the new world would be 'blokeish', as the twentieth century had been, or something different, was unclear. Certainly the trends to pluralism suggested something different.

As always, these trends overlaid deeper patterns from the past. As we have seen, nineteenth-century British settlers came to New Zealand with ideals of equality, looking for security of livelihood, of accommodation, and insulation from the instabilities racking Britain. This provided the key to much that followed. Settler society swamped Maori, marginalising and almost extinguishing their culture. The settlers looked to build a bigger and better Britain, but when that ambition failed in the 1880s, their children turned back to their idealised homeland – now armed with a built-in inferiority complex and its flip side, the 'leading the bloody world' syndrome.

This set the pattern for New Zealand's twentieth century, to which was added both the internal search for security and the external pressures of the most militarised century the world had yet seen. The First World War acted to refocus the ideals of the 1890s, but the post-jingo society of the 1920s did not provide the security its people sought. New thinking had to be stirred into the mix for it to work; and the Labour Government of Michael Joseph Savage had only just begun to do that when the world was hurled into a new war. As a result it was the 1950s

Left above
Arrowtown, autumn 2002.
Matthew Wright

Left below
The Frankton Arm, Lake Wakitipu.
Matthew Wright

before New Zealand's twentieth-century society blossomed. It was built on the colonial ideals of security and egalitarianism, coupled with the pro-British focus and the social restraint of the moral evangelists. As a society it was remarkably successful, surviving nearly 40 years and weathering severe social storms on the way. Small wonder that successive governments wanted to preserve it, but the world moved on and New Zealand failed to engage the new thinking at its peril.

Much of what happened from the 1970s to the end of the century reflected the disengagement from these mid-century ideals. It was a slow process, marked by a push, first, to the most protectionist state outside the Eastern Bloc; then a push to become the world's most deregulated state. In many respects this was, once again, the problem of eager New Zealanders rushing in where wiser heads feared to tread, drawing admiration for guts, but suffering consequences that were avoided by the

Vineyards in Hawke's Bay's
traditional sheep country reveal
a diversified late-century
economy.

Matthew Wright

less zealous. The social fallout of the reform period from the mid-1980s was significant, in part because it also reflected the real consequences of the disengagement from Britain, a shift which had started decades earlier, in part because the protectionism that had gone before had masked so many social difficulties, but in part also because the speed, nature and intensity of the reforms was itself socially disruptive.

To this extent, New Zealand's twentieth century was counter-productive at both extremes of the pendulum. However, this extremism was also an integral part of the twentieth-century cycle, a monocultural and male-dominated era that was changing by the 1990s. New ideals offered a way out of the self-defeating 'cringe', and the potential for moving into a new multicultural and inclusive environment seemed clear. By this time it also seemed clear that New Zealand's former settler society had itself become indigenous. Most of New Zealand's white population had been born locally. Their late twentieth-century New Zealand world was not transplanted British society, nor inherited American, but had unique characteristics that had a clear identity and life of their own. New Zealand was their country too; their fathers and grandfathers had fought and died for it. This society and people, a people we could justifiably call Pakeha, stood alongside a resurgent Maori culture, and alongside other cultures that were also gaining ground as New Zealand became a wider multiracial, multicultural world. How they would all meet the challenges ahead was not clear, but the evidence of history showed that it would not be through lack of trying.

Notes

Introduction

1 Keith Sinclair, *A History of New Zealand*, Penguin, Auckland, 1959, revised Pelican edition 1988; W.H. Oliver, *The Story of New Zealand*, Faber and Faber, London, 1960.

2 Michael King, *The Penguin History of New Zealand*, Penguin, Auckland, 2003.

3 Keith Sinclair, *A History of New Zealand*.

4 James Belich, *Making Peoples*, Penguin, Auckland, 1996; James Belich, *Paradise Reforged*, Allen Lane, Auckland, 2001.

Chapter 1: The first settlers

1 R.P. Suggate (ed.), *The Geology of New Zealand*, Vol. II, Government Printer, Wellington, 1978, p. 741; Stevens, Graeme, and McGlone, Matt, and McCulloch, Beverley, *Prehistoric New Zealand*, Heinemann Reed, Auckland, 1988, p. 90.

2 C.M. Lees, V.E. Neall and A.S. Palmer, 'Forest persistence at coastal Waikato, 24,000 b.p. to present', *Journal of the Royal Society of New Zealand*, No. 28, Vol. 1, March 1998, pp. 55–81.

3 See R.P. Suggate (ed.), *The Geology of New Zealand*, Vol. II, pp. 736–41; Malcolm McKinnon (ed.), *The New Zealand Historical Atlas*, Bateman, Auckland, 2000, Plate 7; Brian Enting and Les Molloy, *The Ancient Islands*, Port Nicholson Press, Wellington, 1982, esp. Ch. 1. For the cultural implications of the end of glaciation see also Jared Diamond, *Guns, Germs and Steel*, Vintage, London, 1998.

4 W.H. Oliver, *The Story of New Zealand*, p. 27.

5 See, e.g., Gary J. Cook and Thomas J. Brown, *The Secret Land: People Before*, StonePrint Press, Christchurch, 1999; John Tasker, *Secret Landscape*, Kanuka Press, Hastings, 2000; John Tasker, *Myth and Mystery*, Tandem Press, Auckland, 1997.

6 Described in M.P.K. Sorrenson, *Maori Origins and Migrations*, Auckland University Press, Auckland, 1979, pp. 41 and 44.

7 King, *The Penguin History of New Zealand*, pp. 39–40, 46.

8 Matthew Wright, *Town and Country – The History of Hastings and District*, Hastings District Council, Hastings, 2001, p. 11.

9 King, *The Penguin History of New Zealand*, p. 44.

10 K.R. Howe, *The Quest for Origins*, Penguin, Auckland, 2003, p. 171.

11 David Simmons, *The Great New Zealand Myth*, A.H. & A.W. Reed, Wellington, 1976; Howe, pp. 161–64.

12 King, *The Penguin History of New Zealand*, p. 49.

13 J.D.H. Buchanan (ed. D.R. Simmons), *The Maori History and Place Names of Hawke's Bay*, A.H. & A.W. Reed, Wellington, 1973, p. 5.

14 Richard N. Holdaway, 'A spatio-temporal model for the invasion of the New Zealand archipelago by the Pacific rat *Rattus exulans*', *Journal of the Royal Society of New Zealand*, No. 29, Vol. 2, June 1999, pp. 91–105.

15 Richard N. Holdaway, Richard G. Roberts, Nancy R. Beavan-Athfield, Jon M. Olley and Trevor H. Worthy, 'Optical dating of quartz sediments and accelerator mass spectrometry 14C dating of bone gelatin and moa eggshell: a comparison of age estimates for non-archaeological deposits in New Zealand', *Journal of the Royal Society of New Zealand*, Vol. 32, No. 3, September 2002, pp. 463–505.

16 Nigel Prickett, *Maori Origins – from Asia to Aotearoa*, David Bateman, Auckland, 2001, p. 26.

17 'Pollen shows Maori here for 1400 years', *Evening Post*, 18 January 2000.

18 Patrick J. Grant, *Hawke's Bay Forests of Yesterday*, private publication (Waipukurau), Havelock North, 1996, p. 218.

19 See, e.g., Howe, pp. 27–59.

20 For a delightful account of this voyage see Erik Hesselberg, *Kon Tiki and I*, Allen and Unwin, London, 1950.

21 Howe, pp. 153–54.

22 See, e.g., Garry R. Law, 'Multiple settlement in Eastern Polynesia', in Douglas G. Sutton (ed.), *The Origins of the First New Zealanders*, Auckland University Press, Auckland, 1994.

23 Geoffrey Irwin, *The Prehistoric Exploration and Colonisation of the Pacific*, Cambridge University Press, Cambridge, 1992, p. 108.

24 Howe, p. 68.

25 Ibid., pp. 115–21. This is the inverse of Thor Heyerdahl's theory.

26 See Ben Finney, 'Experimental Voyaging and Maori Settlement', in Douglas G. Sutton (ed.), *The Origins of the First New Zealanders*, pp. 52–76.

27 Jeff Evans, *The Discovery of Aotearoa*, Reed, Auckland, 1998, p. 27. See also Belich, *Making Peoples*, p. 36; Nigel Prickett, *Maori Origins*, p. 23.

28 Patrick J. Grant, 'Climate, Geomorphology and Vegetation', in Douglas G. Sutton (ed.), *The Origins of the First New Zealanders*, p. 183.

29 See, e.g., Prickett, *Maori Origins*, p. 23.

30 Ibid., pp. 16–18.

31 Patrick J. Grant, 'Climate, Geomorphology and Vegetation', p. 166.

32 King, *The Penguin History of New Zealand*, p. 51.

33 Prickett, *Maori Origins*, p. 25. See also H.B. Elliott, B. Striewski, J.R. Flenley, J.H. Kirkman and D.G. Sutton, 'A 4300 year palynological and sedimentological record of environmental change and human impact from Wharau Road swamp, Northland, New Zealand', *Journal of the Royal Society of New Zealand*, Vol. 27, No. 4, December 1997, pp. 401–18.

34 H.S. McGlone, A.F. Mark and D. Bell, 'Late Pleistocene and Holocene vegetation history, Central Otago, South Island, New Zealand', *Journal*

of the Royal Society of New Zealand, Vol. 25, No. 1, March 1995, pp. 1–22.

35 Marcus J. Vandergoes, Sean J. Fitzsimons and Rewi M. Newnham, 'Late glacial to Holocene vegetation change in the eastern Takitimu mountains, western Southland, New Zealand', *Journal of the Royal Society of New Zealand*, Vol. 27, No. 1, March 1997, pp. 53–66. The point about carbon dating is that it only works with carbon, in the New Zealand context usually burnt wood, shell, bone or fibre. Human evidence such as stone tools are dated 'by association', i.e. by being found in the same location, which is implicit but not guaranteed proof of age.

36 H.S. McGlone, A. Anderson and R.N. Holdaway, 'An ecological approach', in Douglas G. Sutton (ed.), *The Origins of the First New Zealanders*, p. 148.

37 Michael King, *Nga Iwi o Te Motu*, revised edition, Reed, Auckland, 2001, p. 15.

38 McGlone, Anderson and Holdaway, 'An ecological approach', p. 147.

39 Noted in King, *The Penguin History of New Zealand*, p. 49.

40 Janet Davidson, *The Prehistory of New Zealand*, Longman Paul, Auckland, 1984, p. 129.

41 McGlone, Anderson and Holdaway, 'An ecological approach', p. 149.

42 Ibid., p. 139.

43 Noted in King, *The Penguin History of New Zealand*, p. 49.

44 Belich, *Making Peoples*, pp. 35–36.

45 Atholl Anderson, *Prodigious Birds – Moas and Moa Hunting in Prehistoric New Zealand*, Cambridge University Press, Melbourne, 1989, p. 176; Margaret Orbell, *Hawaiki – a New Approach to Maori Tradition*, University of Canterbury, Christchurch, 1985, p. 59.

46 Buchanan, p. 43.

47 Philip Houghton, 'A Vigorous People', in John Wilson (ed.), *From the Beginning, the Archaeology of the Maori*, Penguin, Auckland, 1987, p. 36–42.

48 Anderson, *Prodigious Birds*, p. 179; Davidson, *The Prehistory of New Zealand*, p. 57; Belich, *Making Peoples*, p. 35.

49 Cited in McGlone, Anderson and Holdaway, 'An ecological approach', p. 152.

50 Davidson, *The Prehistory of New Zealand*, pp. 166–67.

51 Anderson, *Prodigious Birds*, p. 181.

52 Beverly McCulloch and Michael Trotter, *Digging Up the Past, New Zealand's Archaeological History*, revised edition, Penguin, Middlesex, 1997, p. 50.

53 Patrick J. Grant, 'Climate, Geomorphology and Vegetation', p. 166. This is not Grant's argument.

54 Beverley McCulloch, illus. Geoffrey Cox, *Moas – Lost Giants of New Zealand*, HarperCollins, Auckland, 1992, pp. 41–43.

55 Anderson, *Prodigious Birds*, p. 98.

56 Ibid., p. 100.

57 McCulloch, *Moas – Lost Giants of New Zealand*, pp. 54–55.

58 Anderson, *Prodigious Birds*, pp. 178–187.

59 McCulloch and Trotter, p. 51.

60 Anderson, *Prodigious Birds*, p. 184.

61 McCulloch and Trotter, p. 53.

62 See, e.g., R.N. Holdaway and T.H. Worthy, 'A reappraisal of the later Quaternary fossil vertebrates of Pyramid Valley swamp, North Canterbury, New Zealand', *New Zealand Journal of Zoology*, Vol. 24, 1997, pp. 69–121.

63 King, *The Penguin History of New Zealand*, p. 66, suggests 150.

64 Anderson, *Prodigious Birds*, pp. 171–76.

65 Anderson, *Prodigious Birds*, p. 157.

66 Garry Law, 'Coromandel Peninsula and Great Barrier Island', in Nigel Prickett (ed.), *The First Thousand Years*, Dunmore Press, Palmerston North, 1982, p. 56.

67 Davidson, *The Prehistory of New Zealand*, p. 40.

68 David Lewis and Werner Forman, *The Maori: Heirs of Tane*, Orbis, London, 1982, p. 24.

69 Anderson, *Prodigious Birds*, p. 178. As Anderson notes, suggestions that moa survived into the European period can be discounted.

70 John Wilson (ed.), *From the Beginning, The Archaeology of the Maori*, Penguin, Auckland, 1987, pp. 73–84.

71 Anderson, *Prodigious Birds*, p. 176.

72 Davidson, *The Prehistory of New Zealand*, pp. 134–35.

73 See Atholl Anderson, 'Canterbury and Marlborough', in Nigel Prickett (ed.), *The First Thousand Years*, p. 89.

74 See, e.g., N.L. Elder, *Vegetation of the Ruahine Range: An Introduction*, Royal Society of New Zealand, Wellington, 1965.

75 Argued by Patrick J. Grant, *Hawke's Bay Forests of Yesterday*.

76 See, e.g., Ash, Cunningham, 'The Indigenous Forests of East Coast – Poverty Bay, Hawke's Bay', and N.L. Elder, 'Maori Cultivation and the Retreat of Forest', talk given 9 October 1956.

77 Grant, *Hawke's Bay Forests of Yesterday*, pp. 219–24 provides a summary.

78 See also, McKinnon, Malcolm (ed.), *The New Zealand Historical Atlas*, Bateman, Auckland, 1997, Plate 12.

79 Stevens, McGlone and McCulloch, pp. 118–19.

80 Davidson, *The Prehistory of New Zealand*, p. 41.

81 King, *The Penguin History of New Zealand*, p. 71.

82 James R. Goff and Bruce G. McFadgen, 'Nationwide tsunami during prehistoric Maori occupation, New Zealand', *ITS 2001 Proceedings*, Session 3, No. 3-1, pp. 469–76.

83 Atholl Anderson, 'North and Central Otago', in Nigel Prickett (ed.), *The First Thousand Years*, p. 124, notes the distinction between lowland 'archaic' sites and 'classic' habitations on defensible headlands.

84 As argued by Brian Fagan, *The Little Ice Age – How the Climate Made History*, Basic Books, New York, 2000, pp. xiv–xv.

85 See Lewis and Forman, p. 21.

86 Douglas G. Sutton (ed.), *The Archaeology of the Kainga*, Auckland University Press, Auckland, 1990, second edition 1994, p. ix.

87 Davidson, *The Prehistory of New Zealand*, p. 147.

88 Sutton (ed.), pp. 33, 47.

89 Davidson, *The Prehistory of New Zealand*, pp. 184, 188.

90 McGlone, Anderson and Holdaway, 'An ecological approach', pp. 152, 160.

91 King, *The Penguin History of New Zealand*, p. 41.

92 Philip Houghton, *The First New Zealanders*, Hodder & Stoughton, Auckland, 1980, p. 77.

93 See, e.g., Eric Schwimmer, 'The Maori

Hapu: A generative model', in *Journal of Polynesian Studies*, Vol. 99, No. 3, September 1990.

94 McGlone, Anderson and Holdaway, p. 156, following Parsonson.

95 Houghton, *The First New Zealanders*, p. 96.

96 See, e.g., Angela Ballara, *Taua*, Penguin, Auckland, 2003, pp. 71–73.

97 Davidson, *The Prehistory of New Zealand*, p. 181.

98 Buchanan, p. 17.

99 Houghton, *The First New Zealanders*, p. 115.

100 Ibid., p. 117.

101 Davidson, *The Prehistory of New Zealand*, p. 128.

102 Kevin Jones, 'Skill with Stone and Wood', in John Wilson (ed.), *From the Beginning, the Archaeology of the Maori*, pp. 57–72.

103 Houghton, *The First New Zealanders*, pp. 126–27.

104 Robert McNab, *Historical Records of New Zealand*, Vol. II, Government Printer, Wellington, 1914, 'Tasman's Journal', p. 18.

105 See, e.g., H.R. Trevor-Roper, 'The General Crisis of the Seventeenth Century', *Past and Present* No. 16, 1959; Andrew Sharp, 'More blood out of Stone; what was the crisis of the aristocracy?', *Historical News*, March 1969, pp. 6–8; Michael Cullen, 'Lawrence Stone, the Manors and other ruins', *Historical News*, March 1969, pp. 8–10; Robert Ashton, 'Aristocracy in Transition', *Economic History Review*, Vol. 22, 1969; Robert Hexter, 'The English Aristocracy, its Crises, and the English Revolution, 1558–1660', *Journal of British Studies*, Vol. VIII, 1968.

106 See, e.g., Fagan, pp. 101–12.

107 Theodore K. Rabb, *The Struggle for Stability in Early Modern Europe*, Oxford University Press, New York, 1975, pp. 116–45.

108 Grahame Anderson, *The Merchant of the Zeehaen – Isaac Gilsemans and the Voyages of Abel Tasman*, Te Papa Press, Wellington, 2001, pp. 31–32; see also 'Mar di India', print of c1630 map in author collection.

109 Philip Edwards (ed.), *The Journals of Captain Cook: Prepared from original manuscripts by J.C. Beaglehole for the Haklyut Society, 1955–1967*, Penguin, London, 1999,

pp. xlviii–xlix; map between pp. lxii and lxiii.

110 Anderson, p. 32.

111 Edwards (ed.), p. lvii.

112 McNab, Vol, II, 'Resolution of the Dutch East India Company', p. 3.

113 McNab, Vol. II, 'Tasman's Instructions', p. 11.

114 Anne Salmond, *Two Worlds*, Viking, Auckland, 1991, p. 73.

115 Ibid., p. 20.

116 Ibid., p. 21.

117 Ibid., p. 78.

118 King, *The Penguin History of New Zealand*, p. 96.

119 McNab, 'Tasman's Journal', p. 21.

120 Ibid.

121 Ibid., pp. 21–22.

122 Ibid., p. 22. This translation differs from that used by Grahame Anderson; see e.g., Anderson, p. 92.

123 McNab, 'Tasman's Journal', pp. 22–23.

124 Ibid., p. 23.

125 Ibid.

126 Graeme Anderson, p. 100.

127 McNab, 'Tasman's Journal', p. 26.

128 Ibid., p. 29.

129 'Gereduceedre Kaart vant Zuid-Land', print in author collection.

130 Beaglehole, J.C., (ed.), *The Journals of Captain James Cook on his Voyages of Discovery*, Vol. 1: 'The Voyage of the *Endeavour*', Cambridge University Press, London, 1968, page c.

131 McNab, Vol. II, footnote p. 84.

132 Beaglehole (ed.), 'Friday May 27th to Friday July 29th', p. 1. Cook's original spelling and capitalisations have been preserved.

133 McNab, Vol. II, 'The Lords of the Admiralty to Lieutenant Cook', 30 July 1768, pp. 54–55.

134 Beaglehole, 'Additional Instructions for Lt James Cook', p. cclxxxii.

135 Cited in Salmond, *Two Worlds*, p. 124.

136 Cited in Beaglehole (ed.), p. 169.

137 Bruce Biggs, 'Does Maori have a closest relative?', in Douglas G. Sutton (ed.), *The Origins of the First New Zealanders*, pp. 96–97.

138 Beaglehole (ed.), 'Monday 9th October 1769', p. 169.

139 Cited in Beaglehole (ed.), p. 169, n. 2.

140 Salmond, *Two Worlds*, pp. 126–27; Beaglehole (ed.), p. 170.

Chapter 2: Agents of change

1 McNab, Vol. I, 'John Thomson to Henry Dundas, 22 November 1792', pp. 584–85.

2 Anne Salmond, *Between Worlds*, Viking, Auckland, 1997, p. 205.

3 McNab, Vol. I, 'The Plan', p. 47.

4 McNab, Vol. I, 'Lord Sydney to the Lords Commissioners of the Treasury, 18 August 1786', pp. 50–51.

5 McNab, Vol. I, 'Governor Phillip to Under-Secretary Nepean, March 1 1787', p. 71.

6 Salmond, *Between Worlds*, pp. 207–8.

7 Ibid., p. 250.

8 McNab, Vol. I, 'J.M. Haite and W. Fenwick, Chatham Rope Yard, 10 June 1818'.

9 McNab, Vol. I, 'Governor King to Earl Camden, 30 April 1805', p. 254.

10 Alan Moorhead, *The Fatal Impact*, Hamish Hamilton, London, 1966, pp. 3–8. While the term was coined by Moorhead, the idea was widespread well before then.

11 Belich, *Making Peoples*, pp. 145–47.

12 Peter Adams, *A Fatal Necessity*, Auckland University Press, Auckland, 1977, pp. 39–40.

13 F.E. Maning, *Old New Zealand*, Golden Press reprint, Auckland, 1987, p. 213.

14 McNab, Vol. I, 'Governor King to Earl Camden, 30 April 1805', p. 254.

15 A.N. Brown Diary, cited in Bronwyn Elsmore, *Like Them That Dream*, Reed, Auckland, 2000, p. 19.

16 Cited in Dom Felice Vaggioli, *History of New Zealand and its Inhabitants*, trans. John Crockett, Otago University Press, Dunedin 2000, p. 131.

17 McNab, Vol. I, 'Government and General Orders', 9 November 1814, p. 428.

18 McNab, Vol. I, 'Extract from the Report of the Committee delivered to the Annual Meeting held May 4, 1819, at Freemason's Hall, Great Queen Street: Australasia Mission', p. 434.

19 Ibid.

20 King, *The Penguin History of New Zealand*, p. 141.

21 Ibid., p. 440.

22 McNab, Vol. I, 'Mr Marsden's Queries to the Settlers of the Bay of Islands, Nov. 5 1819', p. 439.

23 Judith Binney, 'The Expansion of the

Missions', in *New Zealand's Heritage*,
Paul Hamlyn, Auckland, 1971, Vol. I,
Part 11, p. 282.

24 Adams, p. 43.

25 Maning, pp. 106–7.

26 McNab, Vol. I, 'Governor King to Earl
Camden, 30 April 1805', p. 254.

27 McNab, Vol. I, 'Commissioner Bigge's
Enquiry', p. 540.

28 Belich, *Making Peoples*, pp. 153–54.

29 McNab, Vol. I, 'Commissioner Bigge's
Enquiry', p. 539.

30 Cited in Judith Binney, 'The
Expansion of the Missions', in *New
Zealand's Heritage*, Vol. I, Part 11,
p. 282.

31 McNab, Vol. I, 'Commissioner Bigge's
Enquiry', p. 540. See also, McKinnon,
The New Zealand Historical Atlas,
Plate 28.

32 McNab, Vol. I, 'Commissioner Bigge's
Enquiry', p. 561.

33 Wright, *Town and Country – The
History of Hastings and District*,
p. 20.

34 Graeme Hunt, 'Ignorance lets Tuia
spread her poisoned gospel', *National
Business Review*, 8 September 2000.

35 For discussion of how the land courts
could be used, see, e.g., Stephen
Chrisp, 'The Maori occupation of
Wairarapa: orthodox and
nonorthodox versions', *Journal of the
Polynesian Society*, Vol. 102, No. 1,
March 1993, pp. 39–70, especially
pp. 49–50.

36 R.O. Crosby, *The Musket Wars*, Reed,
Auckland, 2000.

37 See, e.g., Vaggioli, p. 51.

38 Also noted in R.C.J. Stone, *From
Tamaki-Makau-Rau to Auckland*,
Auckland University Press, Auckland,
2001, pp. 56–57.

39 Ballara, pp. 74–163.

40 Ballara, p. 55.

41 See, e.g., McKinnon, *The New
Zealand Historical Atlas*, Plate 11.

42 Wright, *Town and Country – The
History of Hastings and District*,
p. 20.

43 Fagan, pp. 138–39, 150.

44 Ibid., p. 117–18.

45 Grant, 'Climate, Geomorphology and
Vegetation', pp. 169–70.

46 Fagan, p. 151.

47 Noted in ibid., p.34.

48 H. Guthrie-Smith, *Tutira*, third
edition, William Blackwood & Sons,
London, 1951, p. 61.

49 Diamond, pp. 54–59, 148–49.

50 Crosby, p. 90.

51 Noted in Crosby, pp. 59–60.

52 Vaggioli, p. 51.

53 Belich, *Making Peoples*, p. 158.

54 McNab, Vol. I, 'Ralph Darling to Sir
George Murray, 22 September 1830',
p. 712.

55 Crosby, pp. 73 and 80 and plates.

56 Argued by Judith Binney, 'The
Expansion of a Competitive Society',
in David Hamer, 'Towns in
Nineteenth Century New Zealand,' in
D.A. Hamer (ed.), *New Zealand Social
History*, Papers from the Turnbull
Conference on New Zealand Social
History, 1978, University of
Auckland, Auckland, 1978, p. 93.

57 Crosby, pp. 227–28; See also,
McKinnon, *The New Zealand
Historical Atlas*, Plate 29.

58 Belich, *Making Peoples*, p. 158.

59 Crosby, p. 90.

60 McKinnon, *The New Zealand
Historical Atlas*, Plate 29.

61 Ibid.

62 Crosby, p. 357.

63 Judith Binney, 'The Expansion of the
Missions', p. 283.

64 Ballara, p. 455.

65 See, e.g., Wright, *Town and Country*,
pp. 32–44.

66 Patricia Burns, *Fatal Success – A
History of the New Zealand
Company*, Heinemann Reed,
Auckland, 1989, p. 136.

67 WTu MS 1232, Donald McLean
Journal, 18 April 1851.

68 Ballara, pp. 454–57.

69 Adams, pp. 21, 25.

70 McNab, Vol. I, 'Darling to Murray,
22 September 1830, enclosure',
p. 713.

71 McNab, Vol. I, 'Letter from Baron de
Thierry to the Editor of the Sydney
Gazette, 17 December 1837', p. 726.

72 Belich, *Making Peoples*, p. 198.

73 McNab, Vol. II, 'Commissioner Bigge's
Report', pp. 587–96.

74 McNab, Vol. II, 'Depositions of J.
Swan', p. 588.

75 Correspondence in McNab, Vol. II,
pp. 578–601, esp. Solicitor Maule to
Treasury, 23 April 1832, pp. 600–601.

76 Oliver, *The Story of New Zealand*,
p. 41.

77 Adams, pp. 66–67.

78 Ibid., p. 70.

79 Cited in Matthew Wright, *Hawke's

Bay – The History of a Province*,
Dunmore Press, Palmerston North,
1994, p. 24.

80 Binney, 'The Expansion of the
Missions', p. 285.

81 Elsmore, p. 75.

82 Burns, p. 27.

83 Cited in Claudia Orange, *The Treaty
of Waitangi*, Bridget Williams Books,
Wellington, 1987, p. 20.

84 Cited in A.H. McLintock, *Crown
Colony Government in New Zealand*,
Government Print, Wellington, 1958,
p. 23, n. 3.

85 Orange, p. 21.

86 Adams, p. 76.

87 But see Orange, p. 21, also Appendix
2, p. 258.

88 McNab, Vol. I, 'Baron de Thierry',
pp. 724–28.

89 Adams, p. 79.

90 Cited in McLintock, *Crown Colony
Government in New Zealand*, p. 25.

91 Cited in ibid., p. 26.

92 Orange, p. 25.

93 Jack Lee, *The Old Land Claims In
New Zealand*, NHPS, Kerikeri, 1993,
pp. 33–34.

94 Orange, pp. 24–25.

95 McNab, Vol. I, 'J. Stephen esq. to
John Backhouse, 12 December 1838',
p. 742.

96 Burns, p. 133.

97 McLintock, *Crown Colony
Government in New Zealand*, p. 48.

98 See Orange, pp. 28–29.

99 McNab, Vol. I, 'Marquis Normanby to
Mr Attorney-General, 30 May 1839',
p. 740.

100 McLintock, *Crown Colony
Government in New Zealand*, p. 48.

101 McNab, Vol. I, 'G.J. Pennington, Pro-
Secretary, to James Stephen, esq.,
22 June 1839', pp. 745–46.

102 Argued by McLintock, *Crown Colony
Government in New Zealand*, p. 48.

103 McNab, Vol. I, 'Marquis Normanby to
Captain Hobson, 15 August 1839',
pp. 731, 734.

104 McNab, Vol. I, 'Marquis Normanby to
Captain Hobson, 15 August 1839',
p. 731.

105 Ibid., p. 734.

106 Ibid.

107 Ibid., p. 735.

108 McNab, Vol. I, 'Captain Hobson to the
Under Secretary of State, Colonial
Department, August 1839', p. 750.

109 McNab, Vol. I, 'Marquis Normanby to

Captain Hobson, 15 August 1839', p. 731.

110 E. Jerningham Wakefield, *Adventure in New Zealand*, ed. Joan Stevens, Golden Press, Auckland, 1975, p. 35.

111 Cited in J.G. Wilson (ed.), *History of Hawke's Bay*, A.H. & A.W. Reed, Wellington, 1939, p. 144.

112 McLintock, *Crown Colony Government in New Zealand*, p. 50.

113 Ibid., p. 58, n. 6.

114 WTu MS-Papers-1983, Busby, James, 'Three documents by or relating to James Busby, 1840'.

115 R.M. Ross, 'Te Tiriti o Waitangi', in Judith Binney (ed.), *The Shaping of History*, Bridget Williams Books, Wellington, 2001, p. 100; see also Orange, p. 40.

116 King, *Nga Iwi o Te Motu*, pp. 33–34; see also King, *The Penguin History of New Zealand*, p. 160.

117 King, *The Penguin History of New Zealand*, p. 160.

118 Ross, p. 100.

119 WTu-MS-Papers f-76-048 – Colenso, William, 1811–1899: letter from James Busby to William Colenso and other papers, letter by Waka Nene and others (fragment).

120 Vaggioli, p. 96.

121 For discussion see Oliver, 'The future behind us' in Andrew Sharp and P.G. McHugh (eds), *Histories, Power and Loss*, Bridget Williams Books, Wellington, 2001, pp. 26–27.

122 Belich, *Making Peoples*, p. 194.

123 Cited in Alan Ward, *A Show of Justice*, ANU Press, 1974, p. 88.

124 William Colenso, *The Authentic and Genuine History of the Signing of the Treaty of Waitangi*, Government Print 1890; 'Wednesday, February 5th.'

125 Ibid.

126 Ibid.

127 Ibid.

128 Orange, p. 56.

129 William Colenso, The *Authentic and Genuine History of the Signing of the Treaty of Waitangi*, 'Wednesday, February 5th.'

130 Ibid.

131 WTu MS Papers 1983 Busby, James Papers, 'Three documents by or relating to James Busby, 1840'.

132 Orange, p. 53; see also MS Papers 1983 Busby, James Papers, 'Three documents by or relating to James Busby, 1840'.

133 King, *The Penguin History of New Zealand*, p. 163.

134 WTu MS Papers 1983, Busby, James Papers, 'Three documents by or relating to James Busby, 1840'.

135 Vaggioli, p. 115.

136 WTu MS-Papers-1611, Colenso, William Papers, 'Memoranda of the Arrival of Lieut. Governor Hobson in New Zealand'. This is the 'first draft' of Colenso's later 'Authentic and Genuine History' and its emendations suggest it was written at or soon after the meeting. Compare 'Authentic', Thursday February 6th.

137 William Colenso, *The Authentic and Genuine History of the Signing of the Treaty of Waitangi*, 'Thursday, February 6th.'

138 Orange, p. 71.

139 Wilson, *History of Hawke's Bay*, p. 140.

140 The Waitangi Tribunal were asked by Ahuriri claimants in 1994 to rule that Ngati Kahungunu had signed the Treaty of Waitangi, but were unable to do so because most Ngati Kahungunu had not been signatories. Wai 55 p. 32.

141 William Colenso, 'Wednesday, February 5th.'

142 Argued by Paul Moon, *Hone Heke*, David Ling, Auckland, 2001, p. 18.

143 Maning, p. 247.

144 William Colenso, 'Wednesday, February 5th.'

145 Cited in Vaggioli, p. 96.

146 Maning, p. 247.

147 Orange, p. 66.

148 Ibid., p. 67.

149 Maning, p. 243.

150 Ibid.

151 Cited in Wright, *Town and Country*, p. 23.

Chapter 3: Shadows of Empire

1 Philip Temple, *A Sort of Conscience – The Wakefields*, Auckland University Press, Auckland, 2002, p. 4.

2 Temple, pp. 537–39.

3 *New Zealand Gazette*, 13 June 1840.

4 John Ward, *Information Relative to New Zealand Compiled for the Use of the Colonists*, John W. Parker, London, 1840; Capper Press reprint, Christchurch 1975, p. 105.

5 *New Zealand Gazette*, 13 June 1840.

6 Burns, p. 41.

7 Ibid., pp. 19–21.

8 Cited in ibid., p. 44.

9 John Ward, *Information Relative to New Zealand Compiled for the Use of the Colonists*, John W. Parker, London, 1840; Capper Press reprint, Christchurch 1975.

10 Temple, pp. 226–27.

11 *New Zealand Gazette*, 21 August 1839. Ward, p. 147, cites £400,000.

12 Ward, p. 149.

13 *New Zealand Gazette*, 21 August 1839.

14 Quoted in Burns, p. 110.

15 Ward, p. 136.

16 Temple, pp. 231–32.

17 Ibid., pp. 242–46.

18 Michael King, *Moriori – A People Rediscovered*, Penguin, Auckland, revised edition 2001.

19 Argued by Belich, *Making Peoples*, p. 197.

20 Temple, p. 248.

21 Cited in Ward, pp. 118–19.

22 Ibid., p. 120.

23 Angela Caughey, *The Interpreter – The Biography of Richard 'Dicky' Barrett*, David Bateman, Auckland, 1998, p. 107; Temple, pp. 249–50.

24 Wakefield, p. 34, footnote.

25 Burns, p. 115.

26 Ward, p. 122.

27 Wakefield, p. 35.

28 Temple, p. 252.

29 Ibid., p. 253.

30 Edward Hopper, cited in Burns, p. 132.

31 Wakefield, p. 26.

32 Cited in Caughey, p. 140. See also Belich, *Making Peoples*, p. 201.

33 Caughey, pp. 140–43.

34 *New Zealand Gazette*, 21 August 1839.

35 Ibid.

36 Caughey, pp. 33, 48, 50.

37 McKinnon, *The New Zealand Historical Atlas*, Plate 31.

38 Burns, p. 226–27.

39 *New Zealand Gazette*, 13 June 1840.

40 Ibid.

41 Ibid.

42 Burns, pp. 137–43.

43 Ibid., p. 155.

44 Cited in the Waitangi Tribunal *Ngai Tahu Report 1991*, p. 257; see also Adams, p. 180.

45 Cited in Adams, p. 184.

46 W.P. Morrell, *The Provincial System in New Zealand, 1852–76*, Whitcombe and Tombs, Wellington, 1964, pp. 32–33.

47 T.L. Buick, *New Zealand's First War*,

the Rebellion of Hone Heke, Capper Press, reprint, Christchurch, 1976.

48 See, e.g., James Belich, *The New Zealand Wars*, Penguin, Auckland, 1985, pp. 31–36.

49 Paul Moon, *Hone Heke*, p. 33.

50 Maning, p. 249.

51 Ibid.

52 Argued by Belich, *The New Zealand Wars*, pp. 31–33.

53 Maning, p. 250.

54 Buick, p. 49.

55 Vaggioli, p. 116.

56 Maning, pp. 252–53.

57 Ibid.

58 Buick, p. 74.

59 Vaggioli, p. 122.

60 Buick, p. 79, footnote.

61 Belich, *The New Zealand Wars*, p. 79 cites 140; Buick, p. 117, cites 300.

62 Cited in Buick, p. 147.

63 Cited in Belich, *The New Zealand Wars*, p. 48.

64 Maning, p. 339.

65 Vaggioli, p. 129.

66 Maning, p. 343.

67 Chris Pugsley, 'Walking Heke's War', *Defence Quarterly*, No. 4, Autumn 1994, p. 32.

68 Maning, p. 348.

69 Buick, pp. 272.

70 See, e.g., Belich, *The New Zealand Wars*, p. 70; King, *The Penguin History of New Zealand*, p. 185.

71 Cited in Vaggioli, p. 124.

72 Maning, p. 338.

73 See, e.g., Tom Gibson, *The Maori Wars*, A.H. & A.W. Reed, Wellington, 1974; Belich, *The New Zealand Wars*, pp. 73–74.

74 WTu MS-Papers 1234, Donald McLean, Diary 11 November 1851. My italics.

75 Great Britain Parliamentary Papers Vol. 5, 1846–47, Earl Grey to Governor Grey, 23/12/1846, pp. 67–69.

76 *AJHR* 1890 G-1, Sir William Martin, Pamphlet of 1848, p. 3.

77 Great Britain Parliamentary Papers, Vol. 6, 1847–1850, Governor Grey to Earl Grey, 15/5/1848, p. 24.

78 Ibid.

79 WTu MS-Papers 1286, McLean Diary 8 April 1851.

80 See, e.g., *AJHR* 1886 G-1 'Reports from Officers in Native Districts'.

81 See, e.g., *AJHR* 1858 E-1 'Report of Ahuriri Native Industrial School 1856'.

82 *AJHR* 1862 E-4 'Report of Inspectors on Native Schools', 'Report on the Te Aute Native Industrial School in the Province of Hawke's Bay', 25 June 1862.

83 *AJHR* 1862 E-4, 'Report from W.R. Baker, esq, on the Waerengaahika (Turanga) School', 6th May 1862'.

84 Ann Parsonson, 'The Pursuit of Mana', in W.H. Oliver and B.R. Williams (eds), *The Oxford History of New Zealand*, Oxford University Press, Auckland, 1981, p. 153.

85 W.B. Sutch, *The Quest for Security in New Zealand 1940 to 1966*, Oxford University Press, London, 1966, p. 39.

86 *AJHR* 1862 C-1 No. 74, 'Cooper to McLean 20th June 1861'.

87 *AJHR* 1861 E-9 'Minutes of Proceedings of the Kohimarama Conference', p. 25.

88 A. McKirdy, 'Maori-Pakeha Land Transactions in Hawke's Bay 1848–1864', MA Thesis, Victoria University Press, 1994, pp. 82–83.

89 Cited in Ross, 'Te Tiriti o Waitangi', in Judith Binney (ed.), *The Shaping of History*, p. 101.

90 Hawke's Bay Museum, Resident Magistrate's Letterbook, Domett to Harawera 1 October 1855.

91 WTu MS 1234, McLean Journal, 30 March 1851.

92 *AJHR* 1890 G-1 'Opinions of various authorities on native tenure'.

93 See, e.g., Joan Metge and P. Kinloch, *Talking Past Each Other: Problems in Cross-Cultural Communication*, Victoria University Press, Wellington, 1984.

94 See, e.g., M.P.K. Sorrenson, 'Maori and Pakeha' in W.H. Oliver and B.R. Williams (eds), *The Oxford History of New Zealand*, Oxford University Press, Auckland, 1981, pp. 168–96.

95 R.D. Hill, 'Pastoralism in the Wairarapa, 1844–53', in R.F. Watters (ed.), *Land and Society in New Zealand*, A.H. & A.W. Reed, Wellington, 1965, reprint 1967, p. 29; also A.G. Bagnall, *Wairarapa: An Historical Excursion*, Masterton, 1976, pp. 23–24.

96 Bagnall, p. 48.

97 Hill, pp. 33–34.

98 Bagnall, p. 84.

99 *Government Gazette of the Province of New Munster*, 9 October 1847.

100 See, e.g., Sorrenson, 'Maori and Pakeha', p. 175.

101 Archives New Zealand NM 10/9 Series 10/9, 'Colonial Secretary's Inwards Correspondence, 28 Apr 1848–4 Sep 1848', Domett to Native Secretary 26 September 1848; Domett to Kemp, 12 October 1848.

102 Archives New Zealand NM 10/9 Series 10/9, 'Colonial Secretary's Inwards Correspondence, 28 Apr 1848–4 Sep 1848' Domett to Kemp, 12 October 1848.

103 Archives New Zealand, NM 8/35, 1849/39, 'Colonial Secretary's Inwards Correspondence, 1849', Colenso to Domett, 23 December 1848.

104 Archives New Zealand NM 10/9 Series 10/9, 'Colonial Secretary's Inwards Correspondence, 28 Apr 1848–4 Sep 1848', Domett to Colenso, 17 January 1849.

105 Colenso Journal entry October 4th 1847, quoted in Wilson (ed.), *History of Hawke's Bay*, p. 247.

106 Archives New Zealand G7/6/61, Te Pohipi, Na Hou and Hoani Waikau to Governor Grey, 12 April 1849, translation and transcript.

107 Hawke's Bay Museum, McLean Inwards Letterbook Vol. 24, Eyre to McLean, 24 September 1849.

108 Hawke's Bay Museum, McLean Inwards Letterbook, transcript, Vol. 24, Fox to Domett, 3 July 1850.

109 Op. cit., McLean to Domett [n.d.].

110 Archives New Zealand, Series 2/4 'Inwards Despatches from Governor-In-Chief, 24 Jan–23 Dec 1850', Grey to Eyre, 14 September 1850.

111 Archives New Zealand, Series 10/10, 1850/746 'Colonial Secretary's Outwards Correspondence, 1850', S.E. Grimstone to McLean 7 October 1850.

112 Op. cit., 14 November 1850.

113 Hawke's Bay Museum McLean Inwards Letterbook Vol. 28, Journal 14 October 1850. This line was omitted from the version published by the Waitangi Tribunal.

114 *AJHR* 1862 C-1, Enclosure No. 1 in No. 6, Te Hapuku to Grey, 3 May 1851.

115 *AJHR* 1862 C-1.

116 This differs from the assertion in a 1994 background report commissioned by the Waitangi

Tribunal. Angela Ballara and Gary Scott, 'Crown Purchases of Land in Early Provincial Hawke's Bay', Waitangi Tribunal Wai 201, January 1994, p. 81.

117 McKirdy, p. 90.

118 Ibid., pp. 4, 90–91.

119 Keith Sinclair, *A History of New Zealand*, pp. 119–22.

120 *AJHR* 1858 C-1 Native Land Purchases; Summary of Purchases Effected from 1st March 1856 to 30th June 1856 and 1st July 1856 to 31st March 1858.

121 Noted in Parsonson, p. 153.

122 Ibid.

Chapter 4: The road to Erewhon

1 David Thorns and Charles Sedgwick, *Understanding Aotearoa/New Zealand: Historical Statistics*, Dunmore Press, Palmerston North, 1997, p. 32.

2 John Ralston Saul, *Voltaire's Bastards*, Penguin, Canada, 1992, pp. 38–76; Eric Hobsbawm, *The Age of Revolution, Abacus, London*, 1977.

3 Matthew Wright, *New Zealand's Engineering Heritage*, Reed, Auckland, 1999, pp. 2–4.

4 W. Cooke Taylor, 'Notes of a Tour in the Manufacturing Districts of Lancashire', 1842, in B.I. Coleman (ed.), *The Idea of the City in Nineteenth Century Britain*, Routledge and Kegan Paul, London, 1973, p. 81.

5 Edwin Chadwick, 'Report on the Sanitary Conditions of the Labouring Population of Great Britain', in B.I. Coleman (ed.), *The Idea of the City in Nineteenth Century Britain*, pp. 77–81.

6 Tony Simpson, *A Distant Feast*, Godwit, Auckland, 1999, pp. 39, 49.

7 Eric Hobsbawm, *On History*, Abacus, London, 1998, p. 155.

8 McNab, Vol. I, n.d., pp. 41–42; McLintock, *Crown Colony Government in New Zealand*, p. 8.

9 Fagan, pp. 174–80.

10 R. Vaughan, 'The Age of Great Cities', p. 89.

11 Smith referred to 'an', not 'the'. Quoted in Bruce Jesson, *Only Their Purpose is Mad*, Dunmore Press, Palmerston North, 1999, pp. 26–29.

12 Keith Rankin, 'Approach is orthodox but so is burning witches', *New Zealand Herald*, 2 March 2000.

13 Hobsbawm, *On History*, p. 179.

14 Cited in Tony Simpson, *The Immigrants*, Godwit, Auckland, 1997, p. 40.

15 David Thomson, *England in the Nineteenth Century*, Penguin, London, 1950, p. 77.

16 Fagan, p. 179.

17 Argued by Thomson, pp. 80–81.

18 Ian Tattersall, *The Fossil Trail*, Oxford University Press, Oxford, 1995, pp. 18–19; also Steven Jay Gould, *Ever Since Darwin*, Penguin, London, 1991, pp. 21–45.

19 Cited in David Taylor, *Poverty*, Heinemann Educational, Oxford, 1990.

20 Eric Hobsbawm, *On History*, p. 130.

21 G.R. Hawke, *Railways and Economic Growth in England and Wales 1840–1870*, Clarendon Press, Oxford, 1970, pp. 363–66.

22 See Mark Blaug, *Great Economists Before Keynes*, Wheatsheaf Books, Brighton, 1986.

23 See, e.g., David Ward, 'The Victorian Slum: An enduring myth', *Annals of the Association of American Geographers*, Vol. 66, 1976, pp. 323–30; A.A. MacLaren, 'Class Formation and Class Fractions, the Aberdeen bourgeoise 1830–1850', in G. Gordon and B. Dicks (eds), *Scottish Urban History*, Aberdeen University Press, Aberdeen, 1983.

24 Simpson, *The Immigrants*, pp. 41–43.

25 Miles Fairburn, *The Ideal Society and Its Enemies*, Auckland University Press, Auckland, 1989, pp. 26–27.

26 Rodger D. Win, *Who Ploughed So Well,* private publication, Nelson, 1996.

27 Thorns and Sedgwick, p. 33.

28 Ibid., p. 37.

29 *AJHR* 1863, D-6 'The Otago Gold Fields', p. 10.

30 Rollo Arnold, *The Farthest Promised Land*, Victoria University Press and Price Milburn, Wellington, 1981, pp. 18–19.

31 McKinnon, *The New Zealand Historical Atlas*, Plate 49.

32 Ibid.

33 F.W. Campbell, 'Early Days in New Zealand', Noble-Campbell Papers.

34 WTU MS-Papers-3779-1/2, Hay Family: Papers, Letters from William and Mary Hay, William Hay to his mother, August 13, 1865.

35 F.W. Campbell, 'Early Days in New Zealand', Noble-Campbell Papers.

36 Matthew Wright, *Havelock North — The History of a Village*, HDC, Hastings, 1996, p. 44.

37 Simpson, *A Distant Feast*, p. 66.

38 WTu MS-Papers-4328, Hamilton, Francis William, 1840–1901: Outward letters, letter to Mr J. Morton, 7 January 1862.

39 Havelock North Public Library, A/397/1879, William Rainbow, diary, 2 January 1880, typescript.

40 Charlotte Godley, Letters from Early New Zealand, Whitcombe and Tombs, Auckland, 1951, p. 8.

41 Havelock North Public Library, A/397/1879, William Rainbow, diary, 6 January 1880.

42 Ibid., 11 January 1880.

43 Godley, p. 1.

44 Havelock North Public Library, A/397/1879, William Rainbow, diary, 8 January 1880.

45 Ibid., 12 January 1880.

46 Ibid., 6 February 1880.

47 Godley, p. 7.

48 WTu MS-0667, Davie, Cyrus Papers, 'Journal of a voyage on board the *Sir George Seynour* and *Randolph* of 850 tons from Plymouth to Port Victoria, New Zealand'.

49 Godley, p. 8.

50 Cited in Simpson, *A Distant Feast*, p. 65.

51 Havelock North Public Library, A/397/1879, William Rainbow, diary, 31 December 1879.

52 Godley, p. 3.

53 Ibid.

54 Ibid., p. 13.

55 Godley, p. 61. Godley was referring to a railway magnate.

56 Alison Drummond and L.R. Drummond, *At Home in New Zealand — an Illustrated History of Everyday Things Before 1865*, Blackwood and Janet Paul, Auckland, 1967, p. 127.

57 Notably Sir Keith Holyoake, see Ken Comber, 'Personal reflections on my father-in-law', in Margaret Clark (ed.), *Sir Keith Holyoake, Towards a Political Biography*, Dunmore Press, Palmerston North, 1997, esp. pp. 21, 23.

58 *Hawke's Bay Herald*, 10 and 12 March 1868.

59 Stevan Eldred-Grigg, *A Southern*

Gentry, A.H. & A.W. Reed, Wellington, 1980, pp. 119–20; see also David Thomson, *A World Without Welfare, New Zealand's Colonial Experiment*, Auckland University Press/Bridget Williams Books, Wellington, 1998, p. 69.

60 *Hawke's Bay Herald*, 30 December 1892.

61 Ibid.

62 Hawke's Bay Museum, *D.P. Balfour, His Life, By Himself*, typescript.

63 Calculated from M.F. Lloyd Prichard, *An Economic History of New Zealand to 1939*, Collins, Auckland, 1970, p. 60.

64 Lloyd Prichard, p. 63.

65 Charlotte Macdonald, *A Woman of Good Character*, Allen and Unwin/Historical Branch, Wellington, 1990, table p. 49.

66 Thorns and Sedgwick, pp. 61–62. See also Lloyd Prichard, p. 100.

67 Cited in Alison Drummond and L.R. Drummond, *At Home in New Zealand*, p. 32.

68 Frances Porter, *Born to New Zealand, a Biography of Jane Maria Atkinson*, Bridget Williams Books, Wellington, 1995, p 173.

69 Macdonald, p. 124.

70 Cited in Drummond, p. 158.

71 See, e.g., ibid., pp. 376–78.

72 Claire Toynbee, 'Class and Social Structure in Nineteenth Century New Zealand' and Tom Brooking, 'Commentaries', in D.A. Hamer (ed.), *New Zealand Social History*, Papers from the Turnbull Conference on New Zealand Social History, 1978, University of Auckland, Auckland, 1978.

73 Erik Olssen, *Building the New World, Work, Politics and Society in Caversham, 1880s–1920s*, Auckland University Press, Auckland, 1995, pp. 8–11.

74 Wright, *Town and Country*, p. 241, also Balfour, 'His Life, By Himself'.

75 Wright, *Hawke's Bay – The History of a Province*, esp. chs 4–5.

76 Eldred-Grigg, *A Southern Gentry*, p. 105.

77 Noted in John. E. Martin, *The Forgotten Worker*, Allen and Unwin, Wellington, 1990, p. 10.

78 Cited in King, *The Penguin History of New Zealand*, p. 225.

79 Hill, p. 34.

80 Ibid., p. 41.

81 Ibid., p. 43.

82 WTu MS-Papers-3520, Smith, Hector William Pope, 1837–1878, Extracts from journal.

83 Belich, *Making Peoples*, p. 401.

84 A.H. McLintock (ed.), *An Encyclopedia of New Zealand*, Government Print, Wellington, 1966, Vol. 3, p. 113.

85 Cited in Cherry A. Hankin, *Life in a Young Colony*, Whitcoulls, Christchurch, 1981, p. 78.

86 Ibid., p. 81.

87 Lloyd Prichard, p. 84.

88 Thorns and Sedgwick, p. 61.

89 Cited in Martin, p. 12.

90 Ibid., p. 101.

91 *Hawke's Bay Herald*, 11 April 1876.

92 Martin, p. 13.

93 McLintock (ed.), *An Encyclopedia of New Zealand*, Vol. 2, p. 716.

94 Belich, *Making Peoples*, p. 397.

95 Cited in Drummond, p. 150.

96 Argued by Belich, *Making Peoples*, p. 397.

97 Eldred-Grigg, *A Southern Gentry*, pp. 87–88.

98 *Hawke's Bay Herald*, 27 October 1876.

99 Wright, *Town and Country*, pp. 178–79.

100 Eldred-Grigg, *A Southern Gentry*, p. 85.

101 For a description of the British ethos see Leonore Davidoff and Catherine Hall, 'The architecture of public and private life, English middle class society in a provincial town, 1780 to 1850', in Derek Fraser and A. Sutcliffe (eds), *The Pursuit of Urban History*, Edward Arnold, London, 1983.

102 Eldred-Grigg, *A Southern Gentry*, p. 98.

103 F.W. Campbell, 'Early Days in New Zealand', Noble-Campbell Papers, p. 15.

104 Eldred-Grigg, *A Southern Gentry*, p. 99.

105 A.H. McLintock, *An Encyclopaedia of New Zealand*, Vol. 1, p. 322. Belich, *Making Peoples*, p. 397 cites a fortune of £230,000.

106 McLintock (ed.), *An Encyclopedia of New Zealand*, Vol. 1, p. 688.

107 Cited in Hankin, pp. 132–33.

108 *Hawke's Bay Herald*, 19 December 1892.

109 Eldred-Grigg, *A Southern Gentry*, p. 104.

110 Wright, *Hawke's Bay – The History of a Province*, p. 42.

111 Wright, *Town and Country*, p. 92.

112 WTu MS Papers 1635-05 Monro, David (Sir), Papers. Statements of assets and monies owing.

113 David Thomson, *A World Without Welfare*, New Zealand's Colonial Experiment, p. 69.

114 *Hawke's Bay Herald*, 27 October 1876.

115 Guthrie-Smith, p. 139.

116 Guy H. Scholefield (ed.), The Richmond-Atkinson Papers, II, p. 341.

117 Ibid., p. 141.

118 P.R. Stephens, 'The Age of the Great Sheep Runs', in R.F. Watters (ed.), *Land and Society in New Zealand*, A.H. & A.W. Reed, Wellington, 1965, reprint 1967, p. 58.

119 *Hawke's Bay Herald*, 17 September 1880.

120 Stephens, p. 56

121 WTu MS-Papers-4328, Hamilton, Francis William, 1840–1901: Outward letters, letter to Mr J. Morton, 13 November 1861.

122 Guthrie-Smith, p. 157.

123 Ibid.

124 WTu MS-Papers-4328, Hamilton, Francis William, 1840–1901: Outward letters, letter to his sister 30 January 1862. £65 in 1861 money translates to about $13,000 in early twenty-first-century dollars.

125 *Daily Telegraph*, 15 March 1877.

126 Belich, *Making Peoples*, p. 377.

127 Wright, *Town and Country*, pp. 59, 98.

128 McLintock (ed.), *An Encyclopedia of New Zealand*, Vol. 2, p. 27.

129 Cited in Hankin, p. 228.

130 Cited in Martin, p. 12.

131 Wright, *Town and Country*, p. 235.

132 *Hawke's Bay Herald*, 2 May 1876.

133 Martin, p. 21.

134 Lloyd Prichard, p. 63

135 WTu MS-Papers-3895-06 Haslam family: family papers, Typed transcripts of the letters from Sarah Ann Self, (Haslam), letter 26 January 1863.

136 Ibid., 4 February 1864.

137 Lloyd Prichard, p. 60.

138 Martin, p. 15.

139 Wright, *Havelock North – The History of a Village*, p. 45.

140 Martin, p. 144.

141 Martin, *The Forgotten Worker*, p. 99 provides a useful diagram.

142 See, e.g., R.J. Morris, 'The Middle Class and British Towns and Cities of the Industrial Revolution, 1780–1870', in Derek Fraser and A. Sutcliffe (eds), *The Pursuit of Urban History*, Edward Arnold, London, 1983.

143 Cited in W.H. Oliver and B.R. Williams (eds), *The Oxford History of New Zealand*, Oxford University Press, Auckland, 1981, reprint 1991, p. 136.

144 Thorns and Sedgwick, p. 54.

145 Martin, p. 21.

146 Cited in Hankin, p. 113.

147 Eldred-Grigg, *A Southern Gentry*, p. 101.

148 *Hawke's Bay Herald*, 31 May 1889.

149 Hamer, pp. 16–17.

150 Giselle Byrnes, *Boundary Markers*, Bridget Williams Books, Wellington, 2001, p. 50.

151 Cited in ibid., p. 55.

152 See Asa Briggs, *Victorian Cities*, Pelican, London, 1968, p. 135 for a discussion of middle-class association between dirt, poor and nature.

153 Wright, *Town and Country – The History of Hastings and District*, p. 189.

154 Cited in Briggs, p. 26.

155 Byrnes, pp. 55–56.

156 Archives New Zealand, LS Misc 2044 Samuel Cobham Wellington street plan.

157 Byrnes, p. 82.

158 Wright, *Havelock North – The History of a Village*, p. 22.

159 Simpson, A Distant Feast, pp. 70–71.

160 See Wright, *Havelock North – The History of a Village*.

161 Miles Fairburn, 'Local Community or Atomized Society', in Judith Binney (ed.), *The Shaping of History*. This chapter reprinted Fairburn's article from the New Zealand Journal of History, Vol. 16, No. 2 (1982), pp. 146–65; Miles Fairburn, *The Ideal Society and Its Enemies*, Auckland University Press, Auckland, 1989.

162 Fairburn, 'Local Community or Atomized Society', p. 243.

163 Noted by Belich, *Making Peoples*, p. 425.

164 Caroline Daley, 'Taradale Meets the Ideal Society and its Enemies', in Binney (ed.), pp. 267–82.

165 Calculated from Thorns and Sedgwick, p. 40.

166 Eldred-Grigg, *Pleasures of the Flesh*, A.H. & A.W. Reed, Wellington, 1984, p. 24.

167 Population Census 1891, Part V, Conjugal Condition of the People.

168 Population Census 1881, Part III, Conjugal Condition of the People.

169 Eldred-Grigg, *Pleasures of the Flesh*, p. 12.

170 Macdonald, Table 1.1, p. 21.

171 Ibid.

172 Eldred-Grigg, *Pleasures of the Flesh*, p. 24.

173 Macdonald, Table 2.8, p. 68.

174 Cited in Hankin, p. 225.

175 Cited in Macdonald, p. 140.

176 *New Zealand Times*, 5 July 1877; also cited in Fairburn, *The Ideal Society and Its Enemies*, p. 217.

177 Duncan Mackay, 'The Orderly Frontier', in Binney (ed.), pp. 257–65.

178 Belich, *Making Peoples*, pp. 424–28.

179 Hawke's Bay Museum, Extracts from the Diary of C.C. Weston, 10–30 April 1888.

180 Balfour, *His Life, by Himself*, typescript.

181 Ibid.

Chapter 5: Desperate times

1 Hawke's Bay Museum, McLean Papers, typescript Vol. 15, A. Alexander to McLean, 7 January 1858.

2 Ibid., Vol. 12, Domett to McLean, 12 July 1854.

3 Ibid., T.H. Fitzgerald to McLean, 14 December 1858.

4 Sinclair, *A History of New Zealand*, p. 109.

5 Wright, *New Zealand's Engineering Heritage*, pp. 12–14.

6 Wright, *Hawke's Bay – The History of a Province*, pp. 72–73.

7 Sorrenson, 'Maori and Pakeha', p. 180.

8 *AJHR* C-1, 1862, The District Commissioner to the Chief Commissioner, 29 November 1856.

9 Sorrenson, 'Maori and Pakeha', p. 180.

10 Parsonson, p. 156.

11 *AJHR* 1862 C-1 No. 43, Cooper to McLean, 29th July 1858.

12 Vaggioli, p. 169.

13 *AJHR* 1862 C-1 Nol. 67, Cooper to McLean, 12th March 1860.

14 Belich, *The New Zealand Wars*, pp. 76–77.

15 *AJHR* 1860 E-2 Extract from Sub-Protector Clarke's Report to the Chief Protector, 29 June 1844, p. 11.

16 Op. cit., 'Report from District Commissioner Cooper, 8th August 1854'.

17 Op. cit., 'Report from Native Secretary, 27th January 1855'.

18 Op. cit., 'Proclamation by the Governor, 12th February 1858'.

19 Sinclair, *A History of New Zealand*, p. 124.

20 Ibid., p. 125.

21 See, e.g., Gibson, *The Maori Wars*, also Belich, *The New Zealand Wars*.

22 Belich, *The New Zealand Wars*, esp. p. 298.

23 As argued below; see also Pugsley, 'Walking Heke's War', *Defence Quarterly*, No. 4, Autumn 1994, and subsequent articles in his series.

24 Pugsley, p. 33.

25 Nigel Prickett, *Landscapes of Conflict – A Field Guide to the New Zealand Wars*, Random House, Auckland, 2001, pp. 60–65.

26 Tim Ryan and Bill Parham, *The Colonial New Zealand Wars*, Grantham House, Wellington, 1986, pp. 39–48; Belich, *The New Zealand Wars*, pp. 109–12.

27 Belich, *The New Zealand Wars*, pp. 124–26.

28 Ryan and Parham, pp. 53–57; Belich, *The New Zealand Wars*, pp. 134–38.

29 Ryan and Parham, pp. 65–68; Belich, *The New Zealand Wars*, pp. 145–57.

30 Prickett, *Landscapes of Conflict*, pp. 81–84; Belich, *The New Zealand Wars*, pp. 160–65.

31 *New Zealand Herald*, 6 April 1864; also Ryan and Parham, pp. 82–84; Belich, *The New Zealand Wars*, pp. 166–75.

32 Belich, *The New Zealand Wars*, p. 199.

33 Cited in ibid., p. 200.

34 Ibid., p. 100.

35 *New Zealand Herald*, 2 May 1864.

36 Noted in Belich, *The New Zealand Wars*, p. 124.

37 Byron Farwell, *Queen Victoria's Little Wars*, Allen Lane, London, 1973, p. 163.

38 Ibid., p. 170–71.

39 *AJHR* 1864 E-3 'Further Papers Relative to the Native Insurrection', Enclosure in No. 24, 'Account of Wiremu Nero's Visit to Maungatautari'.

40 See, e.g., Farwell, pp. 160–61.

41 *New Zealand Herald*, 2 May 1864.

42 *AJHR* 1874 E-2, 'Further Papers relative to peace and confiscation of native lands', Te Waharoa Tamihana to Pompallier, Enclosure in No. 1 and Memorandum by the Governor. Two different translations of the letter were published.

43 *New Zealand Herald*, 6 April 1864.

44 *AJHR* 1864 E-3 'Further Papers Relative to the Native Insurrection', Lieutenant-General Cameron to His Excellency Sir George Grey, 5 May 1864.

45 *New Zealand Herald*, 2 May 1864.

46 Prickett, *Landscapes of Conflict*, pp. 90–91. See also *AJHR* 1864 E-3 'Further Papers Relative to the Native Insurrection', Colonel Greer to the Deputy Adjutant-General, 1st May 1864.

47 *New Zealand Herald*, 2 May 1864.

48 Cited in Lloyd Prichard, p. 109.

49 Lloyd Prichard p. 87.

50 Ibid., p. 119.

51 Wright, *Town and Country*, p. 178.

52 Thomson, *A World Without Welfare*, p. 69.

53 P.R. Stephens, p. 60.

54 Cited in Lloyd Prichard, p. 77.

55 Ibid., p. 108.

56 Ibid., p. 101.

57 Ibid., p. 102.

58 Ibid., p. 108.

59 Ibid., p. 113.

60 James Belich, *Paradise Reforged*, Allen Lane, Auckland, 2001, pp. 54–55.

61 *AJHR* 1863, D-6 'The Otago Gold Fields', p. 8.

62 Cited in Lloyd Prichard, p. 116.

63 Ibid., p. 115.

64 James Forrest, 'Otago During the Goldrushes', in Watters (ed.), *Land and Society in New Zealand*, p. 83.

65 *AJHR* 1863, D-6 'The Otago Gold Fields', Vincent Pyke, esq. to the Superintendent of Otago, p. 2.

66 Ibid.

67 Ibid.

68 Ibid., citing Read to Richardson, 4 June 1861.

69 Ibid.

70 *AJHR* 1863, D-6 'The Otago Gold Fields', p. 10. See also Forrest, Table 1, p. 86.

71 Op. cit., Vincent Pyke, esq. to the Superintendent of Otago, p. 3.

72 Op. cit., pp. 10–11. See also Forrest, Table 1, p. 86.

73 Ibid., p. 84.

74 Sinclair, *A History of New Zealand*, p. 107.

75 Cited in Lloyd Prichard, p. 84.

76 Forrest, p. 98.

77 *AJHR* 1863, D-6 'The Otago Gold Fields', p. 13.

78 Ibid., p. 8.

79 *AJHR* 1866, D-11 'Return showing the amount of gold exported from the various ports in the colony for the year commencing on 1st April 1865, and ending the 31st March 1866.

80 See W.B. Sutch, *Colony or Nation?*, Sydney University Press, Sydney, 1966, second edition 1968, pp. 3–34; W.J. Gardner, 'A Colonial Economy', in W.H. Oliver and B.R. Williams (eds), *The Oxford History of New Zealand*, pp. 57–86; and Brian Easton, 'Three New Zealand Depressions', in W.E. Willmot (ed.), *New Zealand and the World*, University of Canterbury, Christchurch, 1980.

81 *Hawke's Bay Herald*, 24 March 1868.

82 WTu Micro-MS-0425, Maunder, George, Letters written from Hawke's Bay to his sister Jane, and to his mother.

83 Elsmore, esp. pp. 87–90.

84 See, e.g., Paul Clark, *Hauhau, The Pai Marire Search for Maori Identity*, Auckland University Press, Auckland, 1975.

85 *AJHR* 1864 E-6 'Papers Relative to the Pai Marire Religion, etc', Lieutenant-Colonel Logan to the Assistant Military Secretary, 2 July 1864, and enclosures.

86 *AJHR* 1865 E-5 'Papers Relative to the murder of the Rev. Carl Sylvius Volkner by the Hau Hau Fanatics', Extract of a letter from Miss Wallace, 21 February 1865.

87 Prickett, *Landscapes of Conflict*, p. 114.

88 Wright, *Town and Country*, pp. 71–72.

89 Belich, *The New Zealand Wars*, p. 210; also Richard Boast, 'Esk Forest Claim: Report on the Mohaka-Waikare confiscation', Waitangi Tribunal, Wellington, p. 43.

90 Wright, *Town and Country*, pp. 71–72.

91 *AJHR* 1867 A-1a, sub-enclosure 1 to Enclosure in No. 30, McLean to Stafford, 9 October 1866.

92 Ibid.

93 Belich, *The New Zealand Wars*, pp. 254–55.

94 Ryan and Parham, p. 185.

95 Maurice Gee's novel *Season of the Jew* gives an excellent, if fictionalised, account of Te Kooti.

96 For more details see Wright, *Hawke's Bay*, ch. 6.

97 *Balfour, His Life*, By Himself, typescript, p. 84.

98 Reported in the *Hawke's Bay Herald*, 16 September 1868.

99 *Hawke's Bay Herald*, December 1868.

100 Cited by Colonel G.S. Whitmore, *The Last Maori War in New Zealand*, Sampson, Low, Marston & Co., London, 1902, p. 76.

101 Ibid., p. 84.

102 WTu MS-Papers-MS-Papers-0069-049, Copy of journal of the capture of the Ngatapa by A. Kempthorne. See also Matthew Wright 'Pressure on Whitmore for victory in the east', *Daily Telegraph*, 3 September 1998.

103 For further details see Whitmore, pp. 79–88, Belich, *The New Zealand Wars*, pp. 258–67.

104 *Balfour, His Life*, By Himself, typescript.

105 Judith Binney, *Redemption Songs*, Bridget Williams Books, Wellington, 1995, p. 160.

106 Whitmore p. 187.

107 Quoted in W.H. Oliver and Claudia Orange (eds), *The Dictionary of New Zealand Biography*, Vol. I, BWB, Wellington, 1997, p. 325.

108 *Hawke's Bay Herald*, 12 October 1869.

109 Whitmore, p. 189.

110 Ibid., p. 191.

111 Sinclair, *A History of New Zealand*, p. 153.

112 Ibid., p. 153, citing R.M. Burdon.

113 *AJHR* 1867 F4 'Railway Gauge Committee'.

114 *AJHR* 1885 D6 'The North Island Trunk Railway' p. 3; Matthew Wright, *New Zealand's Engineering Heritage*, p. 38.

115 Supplement to the *New Zealand Gazette*, No. 48, 'The Railways Act 1870', 13 September 1870.

116 *AJHR* 1874 E-8 Appendices to the Public Works Statement 1874, Appendix A.

117 *AJHR* 1879 E-1 Appendix M, 'Annual Report on Working Railways by the Commissioner of Railways for the Middle Island'.

118 *AJHR* 1879 E-1 Appendix L, 'Annual Report on Working Railways by the Commissioner of Railways, North Island'.

119 Calculated from *AJHR* 1879 E-1 Appendix L, 'Annual Report on Working Railways by the Commissioner of Railways, North Island', Tables 1 and 2.

120 Thorns and Sedgwick, p. 33.

121 Ibid., p. 37.

122 Arnold, *The Farthest Promised Land*, p. 18.

123 Ibid., p. 103.

124 M. Wynn Papers, 'Pratly, Pratley and Prattley Reunion, Timaru, 15 May 1993'. See also Arnold, *The Farthest Promised Land*, p. 128. Pratley family records indicate these events took place in 1873, not 1874 as implied by Arnold.

125 M. Wynn Papers, 'Pratly, Pratley and Prattley Reunion, Timaru, 15 May 1993'. See also Arnold, *The Farthest Promised Land*, p. 128.

126 Arnold, p. 162.

127 Ibid., p. 220–23.

128 *AJHR* 1874 D-2 'Immigration to New Zealand', Hon. J. Vogel to the Agent General, 22 October 1873.

129 Op. cit., Commissioner's Report on ship *Salisbury*, 26 January 1874.

130 Op. cit., Commissioner's Report on ship *St. Leonards*, 28 September 1873.

131 Op. cit., Commissioner's Report on ship *Brerar*, 4 September 1873.

132 Op. cit., Commissioner's Report on ship *Helen Denny*, 27 November 1873.

133 Op. cit., Memorandum by Mr Diver for Mr Haughton, enclosure in Hon. J. Vogel to Agent-General, 6 February 1874.

134 Op. cit., Commissioner's Report on ship *Columbus*, 18 September 1873.

135 Op. cit., His Honor J.D. Ormond to the Hon. J. Vogel, 9 December 1873.

136 Op. cit., Commissioner's Report on ship *Star of India*, enclosure in Hon. J. Vogel to Agent-General, 6 February 1874.

137 Op. cit., Hon. J. Vogel to Agent-General, 6 February 1874.

138 Op. cit., Report by Immigration Commissioners on ship *Woodlark*, 6 April 1874.

139 Op. cit., Hon. J. Vogel to His Honor the Superintendent, Otago, 12 March 1874, and enclosures.

140 Wright, *Hawke's Bay*, p. 106.

141 G.C. Petersen, 'Pioneering the North Island Bush', in Watters (ed.), *Land and Society in New Zealand*, p. 66.

142 Scholefield, 1904, cited in Petersen, p. 73.

143 Ibid., p. 73.

144 J.G. Wilson, *The History of Umutaoroa 1896–1956*, Dannevirke Publishing Company Ltd, Dannevirke, 1956.

145 Petersen, p. 77.

146 *AJHR* 1884, D-1 'Return of immigration from 1st July 1883 to 30th June 1884, Nationalities of Immigrants'.

Chapter 6: Prelude to a century

1 Sinclair, *A History of New Zealand*, p. 172.

2 See, e.g., Ray Knox (ed.), *New Zealand's Heritage*, Paul Hamlyn, Wellington, 1971–73, Vol. 5., Part 56, Introduction. Sinclair, *A History of New Zealand*, p. 172.

3 Lloyd Prichard, p. 156.

4 Ibid., Table 11 (Appendix), p. 408.

5 Thorns and Sedgwick, p. 64.

6 Ibid.

7 Ibid., p. 113.

8 Ibid., p. 108.

9 *New Zealand Herald*, 3 January 1884.

10 Wright, *Town and Country*, pp. 178–80.

11 Thomson, *A World Without Welfare, New Zealand's Colonial Experiment*, p. 22.

12 See, e.g., R.J. Morris, 'Voluntary Societies and British Urban Elites, 1780–1850', *Historical Journal*, Vol. 26, No. 1, March 1983.

13 Thomson, *A World Without Welfare, New Zealand's Colonial Experiment*, pp. 21–28.

14 Ibid., pp. 29–31.

15 Judith Basset, 'The Exodus', in *New Zealand's Heritage*, Part 54, p. 1506.

16 Cited in Martin, p. 44.

17 Hawke's Bay Museum, Extracts from the Diary of E.C. Weston, 10–30 April 1888.

18 Thomson, *A World Without Welfare, New Zealand's Colonial Experiment*, p. 85.

19 Wright, *Hawke's Bay*, p. 120.

20 Thomson, *A World Without Welfare, New Zealand's Colonial Experiment*, p. 94.

21 *AJHR* 1885 D-6 'The North Island Trunk Railway', p. 3.

22 *Hawke's Bay Herald*, 15 and 16 June 1882.

23 *AJHR* 1883 D-1 p. 38. Te Kooti had taken refuge in the King Country in the early 1870s.

24 *AJHR* 1885, D-6 'The North Island Trunk Railway', p. 2.

25 Ibid.

26 G.S. Cooper to Donald McLean, 12 March 1860, *AJHR* 1862 C-1.

27 King, *The Penguin History of New Zealand*, pp. 251–56.

28 New Zealand Parliamentary Debates (NZPD) 1885.

29 *AJHR* 1871 A-2a, 'Memorandum on the Operation of the Native Lands Court by Sir William Martin'.

30 *AJHR* 1873 G-7, 'Report of the Hawke's Bay Native Lands Alienation Commission', p. 18.

31 *Hawke's Bay Herald*, 15 January 1877.

32 Wright, *Town and Country*, pp. 50–53.

33 *AJHR* 1867 A-15, 'Report by Mr G.S. Cooper on the subject of native lands in the province of Hawke's Bay', G.S. Cooper to J.C. Richmond, 14 August 1867.

34 Matthew Wright, 'Hawke's Bay was home of land rings', *Daily Telegraph*, 18 June 1994.

35 *AJHR* 1873 G-7 'Report of the Hawke's Bay Native Lands Alienation Commission', p. 18.

36 Ibid.

37 Ibid., p. 19.

38 *AJHR* 1874, G-2 Resident Magistrate Richard Woon to Native Under-Secretary, 16 June 1874.

39 Wright, *Town and Country*, pp. 84–86, 91–95.

40 *AJHR* 1878 G-1 'Reports from Officers in Native Districts', RM Richard Woon to Native Under-Secretary, 28 May 1878.

41 *AJHR* 1879, G-1 'Reports from Officers in Native Districts', RM Richard Woon to Native Under-Secretary, 24 May 1879.

42 For example, see the expenses account of Te Meihana Takihi in *AJHR* 1873 G-7, Appendix 3, p. 162.

43 Phil Briggs, *Looking at the Numbers, a View of New Zealand's Economic History*, New Zealand Institute of Economic Research, Wellington, 2003, p. 43.

44 See, e.g., Keith Sinclair, 'The Liberals Come to Power', in *New Zealand's Heritage*, Vol. 5, Part 56; Sinclair, *A History of New Zealand*, pp. 172–88.

45 Len Richardson, 'Parties and political change', in W.H. Oliver and B.R. Williams, (eds), *The Oxford History of New Zealand*, p. 205.

46 *New Zealand Herald*, 6 October 1890.

47 Ibid.

48 *New Zealand Herald*, 4 September 1893.

49 Lloyd Prichard, pp. 175–77.

50 King, *The Penguin History of New Zealand*, p. 265.

51 See Patricia Grimshaw, *Women's Suffrage in New Zealand*, second edition, Auckland University Press, Auckland, 1987, Introduction.

52 *New Zealand Herald*, 6 October 1890.

53 Micro-MS-0425, George Maunder, Letters written from Hawke's Bay to his sister Jane, and to his mother.

54 Noted in Grimshaw, p. 37.

55 Quoted in ibid., p. 42.

56 Ibid., pp. 41–44.

57 Quoted in Grimshaw, p. 46.

58 *New Zealand Herald*, 4 September 1893.

59 *New Zealand Herald*, 11 September 1893.

60 *New Zealand Herald*, 20 September 1893.

61 *New Zealand Herald*, 11 September 1893.

62 *New Zealand Herald*, 20 September 1893.

63 Matthew Wright, *Town and Country*, pp. 255–56.

64 Reproduced in Ray Knox (ed.), *New Zealand's Heritage*, Vol. 58, pp. 1608–9.

65 See note 3, p. 325..

66 Sinclair, *A History of New Zealand*, p. 171.

67 *Hawke's Bay Herald*, 4 July 1891.

68 Richardson, 'Parties and Political Change', p. 201.

69 Eldred-Grigg, *A Southern Gentry*, pp. 132–33.

70 Len Richardson and W. David McIntyre (eds), *Provincial Perspectives*, University of Canterbury, Christchurch 1980, p. 200.

71 Richardson, 'Parties and Political Change', pp. 200–201.

72 £60,000 was equivalent to around $11 million in early twenty-first-century money.

73 Lloyd Prichard, p. 138.

74 Ibid., p. 194.

75 Ibid.

76 Ibid.

77 Tom Brooking, '"Bursting up" the Greatest Estate of All' in Binney (ed.), *The Shaping of History*, Bridget Williams Books, Wellington, 2001, p. 167.

78 Ibid., p. 213.

79 Guthrie-Smith, p. 401.

80 Author collection, Lands and Survey Auction Map, 12 October 1905.

81 Lloyd Prichard, p. 146.

82 Ibid.

83 Joan Burnett, 'The Impact of Dairying on the Landscape of Lowland Taranaki', in R.F. Watters (ed.), *Land and Society in New Zealand*, pp. 101–19, esp. p. 104.

84 Michael King, *Nga Iwi o Te Motu*, p. 61.

85 Eldred-Grigg, *A Southern Gentry*, p. 115.

86 Douglas MacLean changed the spelling of his surname; his father was Donald McLean.

87 Eldred-Grigg, *A Southern Gentry*, p. 115.

88 *Hawke's Bay Herald*, 4 April 1894.

89 Eldred-Grigg, p. 161.

90 Ibid., p. 171.

91 Wright, *New Zealand's Engineering Heritage*, pp. 57–59; *Hawke's Bay Herald*, 29 December 1892.

92 Wright, *Town and Country*, p. 307.

93 Cited in ibid., p. 308.

94 Eldred-Grigg, *A Southern Gentry*, p. 162.

95 *Hawke's Bay Herald*, 19 December 1892.

96 *Hawke's Bay Herald*, 17 March 1897.

97 Eldred-Grigg, *A Southern Gentry*, p. 151.

98 Ibid., p. 167.

99 WTu MS Cha 1911, letter from John Chambers to directors of the *Hawke's Bay Tribune* 23/1/1911.

100 Ibid.

101 Ibid.

102 Ibid.

103 Wright, *Town and Country*, p. 285.

104 *New Zealand Herald*, 22 September 1890.

105 Olssen, *Building the New World*, p. 257.

106 *New Zealand Herald*, 4 November 1890.

107 Not to be confused with his son John Chambers (1854–1946).

108 Quoted in S. Grant, *In Other Days – A History of the Chambers Family of Te Mata*, Havelock North, CHB Printers, Waipukurau, 1980, p. 54.

109 *Hawke's Bay Herald*, 7 September 1885.

110 Lloyd Prichard, pp. 162–63.

111 *Hawke's Bay Herald*, 2 September 1882 and 20 October 1882.

112 W. Nelson, 'The Tomoana Freezing Works' in Cliff, E.S. & Co., *Hastings, The Hub of Hawke's Bay, New Zealand*, E.S. Cliff & Co., c 1918.

113 Ibid.

114 Wright, *New Zealand's Engineering Heritage*, p. 73.

115 Ibid., p. 132.

116 Burnett, 'The Impact of Dairying on the Landscape of Lowland Taranaki', pp. 101–19, esp. p. 104.

117 Cited in Lloyd Prichard, p. 113.

118 *New Zealand Herald*, 4 November 1890.

119 See figures in Lloyd Prichard, p. 204.

120 See figures in ibid., p. 209. The term 'trend' excludes atypical data spikes.

121 See figures in ibid., p. 204.

122 See figures in ibid., p. 291.

123 See figures in ibid., p. 293.

124 Matthew Wright, 'Australia, New Zealand and Imperial Naval Defence', MA Thesis, Massey University, 1986.

125 See, e.g., F.L.W. Wood, *New Zealand In the World*, Department of Internal Affairs, Wellington, 1940, p. 91.

126 Brian Easton, 'Beyond the Cringe', *New Zealand Listener*, 20 October 2001.

127 Belich, *Paradise Reforged*, p. 30.

128 Wright, 'Australia, New Zealand and Imperial Naval Defence'; Matthew Wright, 'Sir Joseph Ward and New Zealand Naval Defence, 1907–13', *Political Science*, Vol. 41, No. 1, July 1989. See also Wright, *Blue Water Kiwis*, Reed, Auckland, 2001, esp. ch 1. This material has been cited (and used uncited) by other historians.

129 See, e.g., James Morris, *Pax Britannica*, Faber and Faber, London, 1968, p. 404.

130 Cited in Morris, p. 118.

131 Morris, p. 404.

132 Farwell, pp. 339–53.

133 John Crawford and Ellen Ellis, *To Fight for the Empire: An Illustrated History of New Zealand and the South African War, 1899–1902*, Reed, Auckland, 1999, p. 14.

134 Ibid., p. 14.

135 Laurie Barber, *A Short History of New Zealand*, Century Hutchinson, Auckland, 1981, p. 79.

136 Barber, p. 81.

137 See, e.g., Farwell.

138 Morris, p. 115.

139 Glynn Barratt, *Russophobia in New Zealand*, Dunmore Press, Palmerston North, 1981, p. 78.

140 Wright, *Blue Water Kiwis*, pp. 11–12.

141 *New Zealand Herald*, 17 March 1885.

142 *AJHR* 1885 A-6 'Naval Defence of the Colony'.

143 *New Zealand Statutes 1887*, 51 Vict, pp. 129–31.

144 *NZPD* 1909, Vol. 148, p. 809.

145 Wood, *New Zealand in the World*, p. 85.

146 Ibid., p. 91.

147 Wright, *Blue Water Kiwis*, p. 19.

148 F.L.W. Wood, 'Why did New Zealand not join the Australian Commonwealth in 1900–1901?', *New Zealand Journal of History*, Vol. 2, No. 2, October 1968, pp. 115–29.

149 Belich, *Paradise Reforged*, p. 49.

150 Argued by Wood, 'Why did New Zealand not join the Australian Commonwealth in 1900–1901?', p. 127.

151 Belich, *Paradise Reforged*, p. 52.

152 R.M. Burdon, *The New Dominion*, A.H. & A.W. Reed, Auckland, 1965, p. 3.

153 A.R. Barclay, 'The Premier and his troubles', Pamphlet, S. Lister, Printer, Dunedin, 1909, p. 11.

154 Neville Meaney, *The Search for Security in the Pacific I*, Sydney University Press, Sydney, 1976, p. 177.

155 Wood, *New Zealand In the World*, pp. 82–85.

156 R.A. Loughmann, *Life of Sir Joseph Ward*, New Century Press, Wellington, 1929, pp. 50, 145–46.

157 CD 3523 'Minutes of the Proceedings of the Colonial Conference, 1907', pp. 134–36, 153–55.

158 Ibid., p. 134.

159 CD 4325 'Correspondence Relating to the Naval Defence of Australia and New Zealand', p. 40.

160 Archives New Zealand G2/17 'Confidential Inwards despatches from the Secretary of State, 29 Jun 1909–22 Feb 1910', 'Dominions No. 5', p. 176.

161 Archives New Zealand G2/16 'Confidential Outwards despatches from the Secretary of State, 29 Jun 1909–22 Feb 1910', Despatch No. 696/09, pp. 4–7.

162 Archives New Zealand G2/17 'Confidential Inwards despatches from the Secretary of State, 29 Jun 1909–22 Feb 1910', 'Dominions No. 7', pp. 70, 175–78.

163 Peter Padfield, *The Great Naval Race*, Hart-Davis, London, 1974, pp. 194–232; W.S. Churchill, *The World Crisis, 1911–1918*, Four Square, London, 1960, p. 31.

164 NZPD, Vol. 146, 1909, pp. 154–69, *AJHR*, 1909 A-5 'Imperial Naval Conference – proceedings of informal meeting of members of the House of Representatives on the Question of the representation of New Zealand at the.' p. 20; Archives New Zealand Series 1, 22/6/9, 'Naval Defence', from the file 'Naval Defence – Policy and Agreement, NZ Prior 1914, 1905–1914', statement by Massey.

165 Archives New Zealand G2/16 'Confidential Outwards despatches from the Secretary of State, 29 Jun 1909–22 Feb 1910', 'Governor-General's Secret Quarterly Report', May 1909, p. 6.

166 *Evening Post*, 18–22 March 1909.

167 Argued in Wright, *Blue Water Kiwis*, pp. 26–28.

168 *Evening Post*, 22–27 March 1909; CD 4948 p. 3.

169 Archives New Zealand G2/16 'Confidential Outwards despatches from the Secretary of State, 29 Jun 1909–22 Feb 1910', Despatch No. 696/09 'Dominions No. 16', pp. 7–8.

170 Archives New Zealand G2/16 'Confidential Outwards despatches from the Secretary of State, 29 Jun 1909–22 Feb 1910', 'Dominions No. 17', p. 30.

171 CD 4949 'Conference', p. 26.

172 Wright, *Blue Water Kiwis*, pp. 28–30.

173 Ibid., pp. 34–37.

174 Eric Hobsbawm, *Age of Extremes: The Short Twentieth Century 1941–1991*, Abacus, London, 1994, pp. 54–60; David Thomson, *Europe Since Napoleon*, Pelican, London, 1966, pp. 370–75, 391–408.

175 Barber, p. 89.

176 Oliver, p. 161.

177 Barber, p. 78.

178 Guthrie-Smith, p. 411.

Chapter 7: God's Own Country

1 Hobsbawm, *Age of Extremes – The Short Twentieth Century 1914–1991*, pp. 2–11.

2 Ibid., pp. 8–10.

3 Churchill, *The World Crisis*, p. 7.

4 A.J.P. Taylor, *How Wars Begin*, Book Club Associates, London, 1979, pp. 99–122; Churchill, *The World Crisis*, pp. 113–45.

5 Belich, *The New Zealand Wars*, pp. 295–98, 317–18.

6 Ian V. Hogg, *The Machine Gun*, Phoebus, London, 1976, pp. 14, 20, 24–26.

7 See, e.g., Leon Wolff, *In Flanders Fields*, Longmans, Green & Co, London, 1959, p. 24.

8 Lloyd Prichard, p. 266. Various figures have been given; see, e.g., *AJHR* 1921–22, H-19 'Defence Forces of New Zealand', report of General Officer Commanding, for period from 1st July 1920, to 30th June 1921', p. 2.

9 Lloyd Prichard, p. 266.

10 *AJHR* 1921–22, H-19, p. 2.

11 Lloyd Prichard, p. 266.

12 WTu MS Papers 2392, 'A Soldier's Book of Life' by Aubrey Tronson.

13 Wright, *Blue Water Kiwis*, p. 41.

14 R.L. Weitzel, 'Pacifists and anti-militarists in New Zealand, 1909–1914', *New Zealand Journal of History*, Vol. 7, No. 2, October 1973, p. 129.

15 Wright, *Blue Water Kiwis*, pp. 42.

16 WTu MS Papers 2477-2, Diary of Louisa Higginson, typescript.

17 Churchill, *The World Crisis*, pp. 399–407, esp. pp. 400–401.

18 WTu MS-Papers-2350, Bollinger, George Wallace 1890–1917, Diary and letters.

19 MS-Papers-2393, Tronson, Aubrey de Coudrey 1892–1957, A soldier's book of life.

20 Nicholas Boyack, *Behind the Lines*,

Allen & Unwin, Wellington, 1989, pp. 19–22.

21 WTu MS-Papers-2350, Bollinger, George Wallace 1890–1917, Diary and letters.

22 WTu MS-Papers-2477-2, Higginson, Louisa 1885–1978, Diaries/transcribed by Mrs R.L. Wilson.

23 Churchill, *The World Crisis*, pp. 403–04.

24 WTu MS-Papers-2477-2, Higginson, Louisa 1885–1978, Diaries/transcribed by Mrs R.L. Wilson.

25 King, *Nga Iwi o Te Motu*, p. 89.

26 WTu MS-Papers 2481, Bourke, Henry O'Donel, Diary 1917–1918.

27 Matthew Wright, *Italian Odyssey*, Reed, Auckland, 2003, pp. 107–09, and supporting documentation.

28 Lloyd Clark, *World War I: An Illustrated History*, Helicon, Oxford, 2001, pp. 199–200.

29 For a personal account of their genesis see Churchill, *The World Crisis*, pp. 350–53.

30 Belich, *Paradise Reforged*, p. 100.

31 See, e.g., King, *Nga Iwi o Te Motu*, p. 71; Belich, *Paradise Reforged*, p. 196.

32 Lloyd Prichard, p. 251.

33 Wright, *Town and Country*, p. 340.

34 King, *The Penguin History of New Zealand*, pp. 315–16.

35 *AJHR* 1920 H-37, 'No License Districts'.

36 *AJHR* 1920 H-37b, 'No License Districts'.

37 *AJHR* 1920 H-37a, 'No License Districts', Table V.

38 Poster reproduced in R.M. Burdon, *The New Dominion*, A.H. & A.W. Reed, Wellington, 1965, facing p. 119.

39 Burdon, p. 21.

40 *The Press*, 3 September 1928.

41 *AJHR* 1919 H-31, Appendix A, 'Influenza Pandemic – report on the epidemic in New Zealand by Dr H.H. Mackgill, District Health Officer, Auckland'.

42 Ibid.

43 Ibid.

44 Ibid.

45 Belich, *Paradise Reforged*, p. 193.

46 *AJHR* 1919 H-31, Appendix A, 'Influenza Pandemic – report on the epidemic in New Zealand by Dr H.H. Mackgill, District Health Officer, Auckland'.

47 *AJHR* 1919 H-31a, 'Report of the Influenza Epidemic Commission'.

48 *AJHR* 1919 H-31, Appendix A, 'Influenza Pandemic – report on the epidemic in New Zealand by Dr H.H. Mackgill, District Health Officer, Auckland'.

49 *AJHR* 1919 H-31a, 'Report of the Influenza Epidemic Commission'.

50 *AJHR* 1919 H-31, Appendix A, 'Influenza Pandemic – report on the epidemic in New Zealand by Dr H.H. Mackgill, District Health Officer, Auckland'.

51 Reproduced in *AJHR* 1919 H-31a, 'Report of the Influenza Epidemic Commission'; see also Hastings District Council archive HN 103 New Zealand Public Health Department Bulletin No. 2a "Protect Yourself Against Influenza", 5 June 1919.

52 *The Press*, 13 September 1928.

53 *Daily Telegraph*, 10 September 1921.

54 Ibid.

55 *AJHR* 1919 H-31a, 'Report of the Influenza Epidemic Commission'.

56 Cited in Wright, *Town and Country*, p. 350.

57 Sinclair, *A History of New Zealand*, p. 241.

58 Brian Easton, *The Nationbuilders*, Auckland University Press, Auckland, 2001, pp. 8–9.

59 *Daily Telegraph*, 10 September 1921.

60 Ibid.

61 King, *The Penguin History of New Zealand*, pp. 315–16; Belich, *Paradise Reforged*, pp. 114–16.

62 Lloyd Prichard, p. 291.

63 Ibid., p. 280.

64 Ibid., p. 336.

65 *Dominion*, 3 January 1919.

66 Calculated from Lloyd Prichard, p. 279.

67 Ibid., p. 291.

68 *AJHR* 1920, C-9 'Discharged Soldiers Settlement', p. 3.

69 Ibid., p. 6.

70 Burdon, pp. 104–5.

71 Ibid., p. 105.

72 Duncan Waterson, 'Transport in New Zealand 1900–1930', in Watters (ed.), pp. 120–138, p. 121. Conversion using Statistics New Zealand figures.

73 Burdon, p. 114. Wright, *New Zealand's Engineering Heritage*, pp. 74–75.

74 Conversion using Statistics New Zealand figures.

75 Wright, *New Zealand's Engineering Heritage*, pp. 75–76.

76 Sinclair, *A History of New Zealand*, p. 246.

77 Cited in W.D. McIntyre, 'Peter Fraser's Commonwealth: New Zealand and the Origins of the New Commonwealth in the 1940s', in Alastair McIntosh (ed.), *New Zealand in World Affairs*, Vol. 1, Price Milburn for the New Zealand Institute of International Affairs, Wellington, 1977, p. 39.

78 *Evening Post*, 29 April 1924.

79 Archives New Zealand Series 1, 6/1/4, 'Addition of Third Cruiser' from the file 'H.M. Ships attached to N.Z. Division, addition of third cruiser, 1935–42', *Evening Post* clipping 24 September 1925.

80 Op. cit., *New Zealand Times* clipping 17 July 1926.

81 *AJHR* 1927 A-7 'Singapore and Naval Defence', p. 2.

82 *AJHR* 1927 A-6 'Imperial Conference 1926: Summary of Proceedings', p. 21.

83 *AJHR* 1927 A-7 'Singapore and Naval Defence', p. 2. Conversion using Statistics New Zealand figures.

84 Michael Bassett, *Coates of Kaipara*, Auckland University Press, Auckland, 1995, pp. 94–95.

85 *AJHR* 1920 H-38 'Department of Imperial Government Supplies', p. 1. Conversion using Statistics New Zealand figures.

86 Ibid., p. 3.

87 Ibid., p. 4.

88 Ibid., p. 7.

89 Brian Easton, *In Stormy Seas*, University of Otago Press, Dunedin, 1997, p. 68.

90 Wright, *New Zealand's Engineering Heritage*, pp. 85–89.

91 Thorns and Sedgwick, p. 108.

92 Ibid., p. 113.

93 Calculated from ibid., p. 103.

94 Burdon, pp. 120–21.

95 Ibid., p. 124.

96 Simon Chapple, *The Economic Effects of the 1931 Hawke's Bay Earthquake*, New Zealand Institute of Economic Research (Inc), Working Paper 97/7, Wellington, August 1997, p. 5 notes that the general consensus is that the depression bottomed in 1933.

97 Matthew Bradbury (ed.), *A History of the Garden in New Zealand*, Viking, Auckland, 1995, pp. 135–36.

98 Davidoff and Hall, p. 325.

99 McLintock (ed.), *The Encyclopedia of New Zealand*, Vol. 3, p. 19.

100 Ibid., pp. 19–20.

101 Mulgan, *Report on Experience*, pp. 11–12.

102 Jeremy Salmond, *Old New Zealand Houses 1800–1940*, Reed, Auckland, 1986, reprint 1991, pp. 189–211, 212–15.

103 Bradbury (ed.), pp. 135–36.

104 Jeremy Salmond, pp. 200, 211.

105 Belich, *Paradise Reforged*, p. 248.

106 *The Press*, 12 September 1928.

107 Conversion using Statistics New Zealand figures.

108 *The Press*, 12 September 1928.

109 *Dominion*, 16 November 1935.

110 Lloyd Prichard, p. 298.

111 Jeremy Salmond, pp. 206–7.

112 *The Press*, 12 September 1928.

113 Quoted in Wright, *Town and Country*, p. 509.

114 *The Press*, 12 September 1928.

115 Lloyd Prichard, p. 299.

116 Cited in David McGill, *Guardians at the Gate*, Silver Owl Press, Wellington, 1991, pp. 122–23.

117 Hastings District Council Archive, HN 102, Minister of Internal Affairs Circular Letter, 4 May 1917.

118 Ibid., p. 123.

119 McLintock (ed.), *An Encyclopedia of New Zealand*, Vol. 3., p. 144.

120 Ibid., Vol. 1., pp. 573–604.

121 Ibid., Vol. 1, pp. 575, 604.

122 Antony Alpers, *The Life of Katherine Mansfield*, Oxford University Press, Oxford, reprint 1983; esp. pp. 87–106, 148–49.

123 Mulgan, *Report on Experience*, p. 12.

124 Nikolai Dmitrievich Kondratieff (1892–1931) theorised that the capitalist system was subject to very long cycles of prosperity and depression, a theory rejected by conventional economists and accepted by some historians. See Blaug, pp. 113–15; Hobsbawm, *Age of Extremes*, p. 87. The theory is far from certain, in part because it assumes economic constants over time.

125 Andrew Tylecote, *The Long Wave in the World Economy, The Present Crisis in Historical Perspective*, Routledge, London, 1991, pp. 9–12, 242–47.

126 Hobsbawm, *Age of Extremes*, p. 97. See also Tylecote, p. 236.

127 Lloyd Prichard, p. 354.

128 Ibid., p. 436.

129 Guthrie-Smith, p. 414.

130 Burdon, p. 129.

131 Ibid., pp. 127, 132.

132 Tony Simpson, *The Road to Erewhon*, Beaux Arts, Auckland, 1976, p. 86.

133 Guthrie-Smith, p. 414.

134 Mulgan, *Report on Experience*, p. 10.

135 Wright, *Wings Over New Zealand*, Whitcoulls, Auckland, 2002, p. 128.

136 'Hawke's Bay – Before and After', *Daily Telegraph*, Napier 1931, reprint 1981, p. 66.

137 'The Full Story of the Great Earthquake Disaster', *The Weekender*, third overseas edition.

138 Wilson (ed.), *History of Hawke's Bay*, p. 451 cited 246 casualties, possibly a typographical error for 256. McLintock (ed.), *An Encyclopedia of New Zealand*, Vol. 1, p. 475 cited 256 casualties: 161 in Napier, 93 in Hastings and 2 in Wairoa. This is the official tally. Geoff Conly, *The Shock of '31*, A.H. & A.W. Reed, Wellington, 1980, pp. 232–235 listed 258 names comprising 140 in Napier and 22 unidentified, 87 in Hastings and 6 unidentified, and 3 in Wairoa.

139 *Hawke's Bay – Before and After*, p. 69.

140 Ibid., p. 74.

141 *New Zealand Herald*, 5 February 1931.

142 Quoted in Matthew Wright, *Quake – Hawke's Bay 1931*, Reed, Auckland 2001, p. 102.

143 Wright, *Hawke's Bay – Before and After*, p. 78.

144 Quoted in Wright, *Quake – Hawke's Bay 1931*, p. 102.

145 Ibid., p. 82.

146 Ibid., p. 93.

147 Wright, *Hawke's Bay – Before and After*, p. 100.

148 *New Zealand Herald*, 6 February 1931.

149 WTu MS-Papers-5814, Campbell, Dorothy Beatrice, 1903–1975, Letter.

150 Wright, *Hawke's Bay – Before and After*, p. 77.

151 Quoted in Wright, *Quake – Hawke's Bay 1931*, p. 98.

152 Chapple, p. 12. About 100 vehicles were destroyed in the earthquake.

153 Wright, *Hawke's Bay – Before and After*, p. 118.

154 Chapple, p. 50.

155 Ibid., p. 26.

156 Comment by H.M. Campbell, MP for Hawke's Bay, quoted in Conly, *The Shock of '31*, p. 182.

157 Chapple, pp. 37–38, citing New Zealand Yearbooks.

158 Both Boyd and Chapple provided estimates only.

159 Boyd, p. 270.

160 Chapple, p. 44.

161 Figures from Chapple, p. 44. This interpretation differs from Chapple.

162 Burdon, p. 133.

163 Noted by Simpson, *The Road to Erewhon*, p. 89.

164 Lloyd Prichard, p. 354.

165 Tony Simpson, *The Sugarbag Years*, Hodder & Stoughton, Auckland, 1974, revised edition 1984, p. 13.

166 Barber, p. 131.

167 Guthrie-Smith, p. 414.

168 Bradbury (ed.), pp. 145–46.

169 *New Zealand Herald*, 2 February 1932.

170 Ibid.

171 Tylecote, p. 243.

172 See also Simpson, *The Slump: The 1930s Depression, Its Origins and Aftermath*, Penguin, Auckland, 1990, p. 28.

173 Lloyd Prichard, p. 380.

174 Simpson, *The Sugarbag Years*, pp. 14–15.

175 Lloyd Prichard, p. 380.

176 C.G. Scrimgeour, John A. Lee and Tony Simpson, *The Scrim-Lee Papers*, A.H. & A.W. Reed, Wellington 1976, p. 26.

177 Cited in Burdon, p. 140.

178 Summarised in Belich, *Paradise Reforged*, p. 255.

179 Lloyd Prichard, p. 385.

180 Ibid, p. 384.

181 Mulgan, pp. 11–12.

182 Bradbury (ed.), pp. 150–51, 156.

183 Mulgan, p. 12.

184 Burdon, p. 145.

185 Scrimgeour, Lee and Simpson, p. 32.

186 Simpson, *The Road to Erewhon*, p. 85.

187 King, *The Penguin History of New Zealand*, p. 348.

188 Burdon, p. 142.

189 Thorns and Sedgwick, p. 74; Lloyd Prichard, p. 379.

190 Simpson, *The Sugarbag Years* is illustrative, also Laurie Barber, pp. 124–32.

191 Hobsbawm, *Age of Extremes*, p. 247 suggested that this was still the case in the 1980s.

192 Lloyd Prichard, p. 383.

193 Thorns and Sedgwick, pp. 131–32.

194 Ibid.

195 Cited in Burdon, p. 147.

196 *Dominion*, Editorial, 'A Labour Government', 27 November 1935.

197 For description see Sinclair, *The History of New Zealand*, p. 266.

198 Scrimgeour, Lee and Simpson, pp. 48–49.

199 Ibid, p. 39.

Chapter 8: The quest for security

1 Scrimgeour, Lee and Simpson, p. 55.

2 Ibid., p. 59.

3 Argued by Simpson, *The Road to Erewhon*, p. 99; also Sinclair, *A History of New Zealand*, p. 289.

4 Labour election manifesto reproduced in Simpson, *The Road to Erewhon*, p. 93.

5 Easton, *The Nationbuilders*, p. 93.

6 Lloyd Prichard, p. 333.

7 Ibid., p. 349.

8 Wright, *New Zealand's Engineering Heritage*, pp. 86–87.

9 Ibid., p. 85.

10 Oliver, p. 189.

11 Sinclair, *A History of New Zealand*, p. 289.

12 Lloyd Prichard, p. 378.

13 Burdon, p. 225.

14 Easton, *The Nationbuilders*, p. 93.

15 Ibid., p. 126.

16 Burdon, p. 215.

17 Ibid., p. 218.

18 Oliver, p. 190.

19 Cited in Belich, *Paradise Reforged*, p. 260.

20 Matthew Wright, *Rails Across New Zealand*, Whitcoulls, Auckland, 2003, pp. 69, 78–79.

21 Thorns and Sedgwick, p. 70.

22 Burdon, pp. 223–24.

23 Easton, *The Nationbuilders*, pp. 91–97.

24 *New Zealand Herald*, 9 March 1937.

25 Lloyd Prichard, p. 379.

26 King, *The Penguin History of New Zealand*, p. 354.

27 Figures in Thorns and Sedgwick, p. 115.

28 Cited in Belich, *Paradise Reforged*, p. 261.

29 *New Zealand Herald*, 2 March 1937.

30 Wright, *Town and Country*, p. 507.

31 *New Zealand Herald*, 2 March 1937.

32 *Dominion*, 8 November 1935.

33 *New Zealand Herald*, 2 March 1937.

34 Wright, *Town and Country*, p. 509.

35 Thorns and Sedgwick, pp. 32–33.

36 Distinctions were drawn by jingo society, see, e.g., *Daily Telegraph*, 7 September 1921.

37 Belich, *Paradise Reforged*, p. 207.

38 *Daily Telegraph*, 8 September 1921.

39 *Daily Telegraph*, 9 September 1921.

40 *Daily Telegraph*, 10 September 1921.

41 *Daily Telegraph*, 7 September 1921.

42 King, *The Penguin History of New Zealand*, p. 328.

43 Ibid., p. 329.

44 Ranginui Walker, *Struggle Without End*, Penguin, Auckland 1990, pp. 180–81.

45 Wright, *Quake – Hawke's Bay 1931*, p. 124.

46 Ranginui Walker, *Struggle Without End*, Penguin, Auckland, 1990, p. 191.

47 Belich, *The New Zealand Wars*, p. 309.

48 See, e.g., *Daily Telegraph*, 27 July 1921.

49 Argued by King, *Nga Iwi o Te Motu*, p. 77.

50 Ranginui Walker, pp. 195–96.

51 Sinclair, *A History of New Zealand*, p. 277.

52 Belich, *Paradise Reforged*, pp. 265–66.

53 Sinclair, *A History of New Zealand*, p. 277.

54 Lloyd Prichard, pp. 354, 358.

55 Cited in Wright, *Pacific War*, Reed, Auckland, 2003, p. 36.

56 NZPD, Vol. 246, p. 539.

57 Wright, *Kiwi Air Power*, Reed, Auckland, 1998, p. 24.

58 Archives New Zealand G5/111, Series 5/111 'Inwards telegrams and acknowledgements of telegrams received, 1 Aug 1936 (1282)–19 Nov. 1937 (1827)', SSDA to Governor-General, 5 August 1937.

59 Archives New Zealand 'R.A. Cochrane: Report on the Air Aspect of the Defence Problems of New Zealand, including the suggested duties, strength and organisation of the New Zealand Air Force' from the file 'Pubs and Docs: RNZAF His. 1 w/c Cochrane 1937'.

60 Ibid.

61 Wright, *Pacific War*, pp. 14–16.

62 Archives New Zealand, 'R.A. Cochrane: Report on the Air Aspect of the Defence Problems of New Zealand, including the suggested duties, strength and organisation of the New Zealand Air Force' from the file 'Pubs and Docs: RNZAF His. 1 w/c Cochrane 1937'.

63 Kippenberger, H.K. (ed.), *Documents Relating to New Zealand's Participation in the Second World War*, War History Branch, Department of Internal Affairs, Wellington, 1949, Vol. I, No. 9, Governor-General of New Zealand to the Secretary of State for Dominion Affairs, 4 September 1939 (1.55 a.m.), pp. 6–7. Hereafter referred to as *Documents*.

64 Cited in Wright, *Desert Duel*, Reed, Auckland, 2002, p. 11.

65 Ibid., p. 22.

66 Wright, *Pacific War*, p.156.

67 George Clifton, *The Happy Hunted*, Cassell & Co., London, 1952, p. 225.

68 Ibid.

69 Cited in Easton, *The Nationbuilders*, p. 48.

70 Wright, *Kiwi Air Power*, pp. 31, 46.

71 See Wright, *Blue Water Kiwis*, pp. 91–98.

72 Documents, III, No. 191, Governor-General of New Zealand to the SSDA, 4 December 1940.

73 F.L.W. Wood, *Political and External Affairs*, War Histories Branch, Wellington, 1958, p. 198.

74 Documents, III, SSDA to the High Commissioner for the United Kingdom (Wellington), 14 July 1940, p. 1.

75 Op. cit., Governor-General of New Zealand to the SSDA, 30 July 1940, p. 14.

76 Op. cit., Governor-General of New Zealand to the SSDA, 5 August 1940, pp. 207–8.

77 Op. cit., SSDA to the High Commissioner for the United Kingdom (Wellington), 11 August 1940, pp. 18–19.

78 W.S. Churchill, *The Second World War, Vol. III*, Clarendon Press, London, 1950, pp. 157–58.

79 See, e.g., Michael Ashby, 'Fraser's Foreign Policy', in Margaret Clark (ed.), *Peter Fraser, Master Politician*, Dunmore Press, Palmerston North, 1998, p. 169.

80 S.D. Waters, *The Royal New Zealand Navy*, War Histories Branch, Wellington, 1956, pp. 223–24.

81 Documents, III, No. 193, Acting Prime Minister of New Zealand to the SSDA, 4 September 1941.

82 Wright, *Rails Across New Zealand*, p. 79.

83 *New Zealand Herald*, 9 December 1941.

84 Ibid.

85 *New Zealand Herald*, 15 December 1941.

86 Wright, *Desert Duel*, pp. 67–68.

87 Waters, p. 212.

88 *Southern Cross*, 26 July 1949.

89 *Evening Post*, 27 July 1942.

90 Documents, III, No. 209, Prime Minister to the New Zealand Minister, Washington, 13 March 1942, p. 236.

91 Op. cit., Prime Minister of New Zealand to the Prime Minister of the United Kingdom, 28 February 1942.

92 *New Zealand Herald*, 9 March 1942.

93 Documents, III, Fraser to Nash, 13 March 1942, Section IV, p. 241.

94 Op. cit., Chief of the General Staff to General Freyberg, GOC 2nd NZEF (Egypt), 2 January 1942, pp. 217–18.

95 *Auckland Star*, 11 March 1942.

96 Ibid.

97 Documents, III, Prime Minister of New Zealand to the SSDA, 19 February 1942, p. 228.

98 Op. cit., Prime Minister of New Zealand to the SSDA, 30 January 1942, p. 218.

99 Op. cit., SSDA to the Prime Minister of New Zealand, 3 February 1942, p. 219–20.

100 Op. cit., Prime Minister of New Zealand to the SSDA, 4 February 1942, pp. 220–21.

101 Op. cit., SSDA to the Prime Minister of New Zealand, 14 February 1942, p. 222–23.

102 Documents, III, SSDA to the Prime Minister of New Zealand, 23 March 1942, enclosures, p. 180.

103 Op. cit., New Zealand Minister, Washington, to the Prime Minister, 24 March 1942, p. 249.

104 Belich, *Paradise Reforged*, p. 290.

105 M. Wynn, pers. comm.

106 Cited in Oliver A. Gillespie, *The Pacific*, War History Branch, Department of Internal Affairs, Wellington, 1952, p. 107.

107 Documents, II, letter from the Hon. W. Nash, New Zealand Minister at Washington, to President Roosevelt, 24 January 1944, p. 333.

108 F.L.W. Wood, *Political and External Affairs*, Historical Publications Branch, Wellington, 1958, title of chapter 26.

109 Documents, III, Prime Minister of the United Kingdom to the Prime Minister of New Zealand, 15 August 1945, p. 508.

110 W.D. McIntyre, pp. 9–36; Wood, pp. 370–84; Ashby.

111 Cited in McIntyre, p. 39.

112 Wright, *Desert Duel*, pp. 18–19.

113 Wright, *The Battle for Crete*, Reed, Auckland, 1999, reprint 2003, pp. 112–14.

114 See ibid., esp. chs 2–4.

115 Documents, I, No. 444, Nash to Fraser, 5 June 1941.

116 Ibid., No. 447, Fraser to Nash 7 June 1941.

117 Wright, *Italian Odyssey*, pp. 16–24.

118 Ibid., pp. 116–18, 157–58.

119 David Cannadine (ed.), *The Speeches of Winston S. Churchill*, Penguin, London, 1989, p. 165.

120 Cited in Gillespie, p. 103.

121 M.P. Lissington, *New Zealand and the United States*, Government Print, Wellington, 1972, p. 84.

122 Cited in McIntyre, p. 40.

123 Cited in ibid., p. 39.

124 Mulgan, p. 15.

125 Wright, *Pacific War*, pp. 155, 160.

126 Ibid., p. 57.

127 Wright, *Kiwi Air Power,* Reed, Auckland, 1998, pp. 111–14.

128 Mulgan, p. 14.

129 Wright, *Pacific War*, p. 159.

130 Archives New Zealand AIR 118/8 'Information Concerning New Zealand's Air Effort during the Second World War, Section A: Statistics relating to New Zealand's Air Effort' from the file 'NZ Air Effort during the Second World War'.

131 Cited in Wright, *Kiwi Air Power,* p. 63.

132 Martyn Uren, *Kiwi Saga*, Anglo-Egyptian Bookshop, Cairo, 1943, p. 9.

133 Andrew Roberts, 'Prime Minister Halifax', in Robert Cowley (ed.), *What If? 2*, Berkley, New York, 2001, pp. 281–90; Heinz Magnenheimer, Hitler's War, Cassell, London, 1997, argues pp. 277–83 that Germany only moved away from political solutions after 1941–42.

134 Wright, *Blue Water Kiwis*, pp. 88, 90.

135 WTu MS-Papers-2446, Miller, Henry G, d 1940, Outward letters.

136 See, e.g., John McLeod, *Myth and Reality, The New Zealand Soldier in World War II*, Heinemann Reed, Auckland, 1986, esp. pp. 6–7, 190–91.

137 Wright, *Kiwi Air Power,* pp. 47–48.

138 MS-Papers-2183-09, Royal New Zealand Air Force – Review for the Hon. Minister of Defence, secret 1943 report.

139 Wright, *Kiwi Air Power,* p. 108.

140 Cited in Paul Freyberg, *Bernard Freyberg VC – Soldier of Two Nations*, Hodder & Stoughton, London, 1991, p. 328.

141 Basil Liddell-Hart (ed.), *The Rommel Papers*, Collins, London, 1953, trans. Paul Findlay. (German original written by Erwin Rommel and edited by Fritz Bayerlein, Lucie-Maria Rommel and Manfred Rommel), p. 240.

142 Cited in Sir John White, 'Hard Lessons Learned from another war', *Dominion*, 20 April 2000.

143 Archives New Zealand, WAII, 11/7, 'R. Walker's Notes, Minqar Qaim, Ruweisat etc; correspondence on the Minqar Qaim period: extracts from cables USAFIME to General Marshall', from the file 'R. Walker's Notes; Battle for Egypt, Syria, Minqar Qaim'; Maxwell to Marshall (II), 27 June 1942.

144 Sir John White Papers, 'The New Zealand Division in Egypt and Libya, Operations Lightfoot and Supercharge', Foreword.

145 Sir John White Papers, 'Message from the Army Commander to All Ranks 2nd New Zealand Expeditionary Force, 21 July 1943'.

146 See, e.g., Wright, *Desert Duel*, pp. 94–99.

147 Wright, *Italian Odyssey*, pp. 169–70.

148 Wright, *Desert Duel*, p. 18.

149 See summary in, e.g., Wright, *The Battle for Crete*, pp. 110–11.

150 See, e.g., Wright, *Desert Duel*, pp. 169–70; Freyberg; Laurie Barber and John Tonkin-Covell, *Freyberg: Churchill's Salamander*, Century Hutchinson, Auckland, 1989.

151 Cited in Fred Madjalany, *Cassino, Portrait of a Battle*, Longmans, Green & Co., London, 1957, p. 102.

152 Argued by Wright, *Desert Duel*, pp. 168–170; Wright, *Italian Odyssey*, pp. 169–70.

153 Wright, *Desert Duel*, pp. 168–70.
154 Cited in ibid., p. 170.
155 Wright, *Italian Odyssey*, p. 151.
156 Ibid., p. 170.
157 Mulgan, p. 138.
158 Ibid., p. 139.
159 Wright, *Italian Odyssey*, p. 27.
160 Barry Gustafson, *His Way, A Biography of Robert Muldoon*, Auckland University Press, Auckland, 2000, paperback edition 2001, pp. 37–38.

Chapter 9: Slices of heaven

1 Austin Mitchell, *The Quarter-Acre, Half-Gallon, Pavlova Paradise*, Whitcombe and Tombs, Christchurch, 1972.
2 Gordon McLauchlan, *The Passionless People*, Cassell, Auckland, 1976.
3 Organisation for National Development, 'Interim Report on Post-war Reconstruction and National Development', July 1944, p. 34.
4 Thorns and Sedgwick, p. 104.
5 Archives New Zealand, Series 11, 11/6 'Papers on Economic Stabilisation: memorandum of future stabilisation policy' from the file 'Correspondence of Maj. Gen. H. Kippenberger, 1947–55'.
6 Organisation for National Development.
7 Archives New Zealand, Series 11, 11/6 'Papers on Economic Stabilisation: memorandum of future stabilisation policy' from the file 'Correspondence of Maj. Gen. H. Kippenberger, 1947–55', F.P. Walsh, 'Economic Stabilisation in the Post-War Years.'
8 W.B. Sutch, *The Quest for Security in New Zealand 1940 to 1966*, Oxford University Press, London, 1966, p. 409.
9 Sutch, p. 411.
10 Thorns and Sedgwick, p. 64.
11 Wright, *Wings Over New Zealand*, p. 94.
12 Kenneth B. Cumberland and J.W. Fox, *New Zealand: A Regional View*, Whitcombe and Tombs, Auckland, 1958, second printing 1959, p. 23.
13 Ibid., pp. 24–25.
14 Ibid., p. 29.
15 Sinclair, *A History of New Zealand*, p. 288.
16 Sutch, p. 440.

17 Thorns and Sedgwick, pp. 113–14.
18 Ibid., p. 108.
19 Organisation for National Development, p. 30.
20 Wright, *New Zealand's Engineering Heritage*, pp. 104–38.
21 Ibid., pp. 121–22.
22 Ibid., pp. 136–38.
23 Wright, *Italian Odyssey*, p. 163.
24 King, *The Penguin History of New Zealand*, p. 420.
25 Organisation for National Development, p. 4.
26 See, e.g., Hastings District Council Archive, HBC 46/64 Transit Camp Temporary Housing Windsor Park 1946, Rainbow to Jones 04/09/1945.
27 Reproduced in Knox (ed.), *New Zealand's Heritage*, p. 3528.
28 Gael Ferguson, *Building the New Zealand Dream*, Dunmore Press, Palmerston North, 1994, p. 178.
29 Sinclair, *The History of New Zealand*, p. 287.
30 Ibid., p. 293.
31 Martin Walker, *The Cold War*, Viking, London, 1993, pp. 230–51.
32 Thorns and Sedgwick, p. 175.
33 Ibid., p. 41.
34 Ferguson, pp. 177–79.
35 Ibid., p. 181.
36 Ibid.
37 Cumberland and Fox, p. 32.
38 See, e.g., King, *Nga Iwi o Te Motu*, p. 102.
39 Noted in Ferguson, p. 204.
40 Cited in Wright, *Town and Country*, p. 648.
41 Mulgan, p. 15.
42 King, *The Penguin History of New Zealand*, p. 426.
43 Organisation for National Development, p. 39.
44 Sales figures from Knox (ed.), *New Zealand's Heritage*, pp. 2701–5.
45 *Edmonds Cookery Book*, Bluebird Foods, Auckland, 38th edition, 1995.
46 *Evening Post*, 11 February 1957.
47 Sutch, p. 419.
48 Graham Howard and Wright, 'The Reserve Bank Inflation Calculator', *Reserve Bank Bulletin*, Vol. 66, No. 4, December 2003.
49 *Evening Post*, 5 February 1957.
50 *Evening Post*, 3 February 1957.
51 *The Press*, 21 February 1972.
52 Peter Davis, 'Stratification and Class', in Paul Soonley, David Pearson and Ian Shirley (eds), *New Zealand*

Sociological Perspectives, Dunmore Press, Palmerston North, 1972, p. 127.
53 Ibid.
54 Graeme Hunt, *The Rich List*, Reed, Auckland, 1999, p. 173.
55 Ibid., p. 194.
56 Noted in Hunt, *The Rich List*, p. 197.
57 Comber, p. 22.
58 Author observation. See also James Marshall and Dominique Marshall, *Discipline and Punishment in New Zealand Education*, Dunmore Press, Palmerston North, 1997, p. 106.
59 Marshall and Marshall, p. 108.
60 King, *The Penguin History of New Zealand*, p. 431.
61 Belich, *Paradise Reforged*, pp. 505–6.
62 Sinclair, *A History of New Zealand*, esp. pp. 310–11; Oliver, p. 227.
63 See, e.g., W.B. Sutch, *Colony or Nation?*.
64 Easton, *The Nationbuilders*, p. 169.
65 See, e.g., Colin S. Gray, *The Geopolitics of the Nuclear Era*, Crane, Russak & Co. Inc., 1977, esp. pp. 14–32.
66 McIntyre, p. 81.
67 Wright, *Kiwi Air Power*, p. 120.
68 Wright, *Blue Water Kiwis*, pp. 156–58.
69 Sinclair, *A History of New Zealand*, p. 304.
70 NZ Foreign Policy Statements and Documents 1943–57, Foreign Affairs, Government Print, Wellington 1972, Doc 106, p. 391.
71 Ibid., Doc 86, pp. 336–37.
72 Ibid., p. 382.
73 Easton, *The Nationbuilders*, p. 184.
74 See, e.g., Robert J. Lieber, *Theory and World Politics*, Winthrop Publishers, 1972, esp. pp. 38–67, 120–45.
75 Geoffrey Kemp, 'The New Strategic Map', from Uri Ra'anan, *Arms Transfers to the Third World*, Westview Press, 1978, pp. 3–18.
76 R.D. Muldoon, *The Rise and Fall of a Young Turk*, A.H. & A.W. Reed, Wellington, 1972, p. 195.
77 Bruce Brown, 'Foreign Policy is Trade: Trade is Foreign Policy', in Ann Trotter (ed.), *Fifty Years of New Zealand Foreign Policy Making*, University of Otago Press, Dunedin, 1993, pp. 59–60.
78 Brian Easton, *In Stormy Seas*, University of Otago Press, Dunedin, 1997, Table 9.2, p. 142.
79 Brown, p. 65, note 24.

80 Ibid., p. 68.
81 See, e.g., Sutch, *Colony or Nation?*, esp. pp. 181–82.
82 Easton, *In Stormy Seas*, p. 102.
83 *The Post*, 21 February 1972.
84 See, e.g., Easton, *The Nationbuilders*, pp. 184–86.
85 Jesson, p. 74.
86 Geoff Conly, *Wattie's – The First Fifty Years*, J. Wattie Canneries Ltd, Hastings, 1984, p. 145.
87 Gustafson, p. 238.
88 Easton, *The Nationbuilders*, pp. 250–52; see also Gustafson, p. 469.
89 Noted in Gustafson, p. 267.
90 Easton, *The Nationbuilders*, p. 250.
91 Gustafson, p. 470.
92 Ibid., pp. 6–7. See also Easton, *The Nationbuilders*, p. 249.
93 Easton, *In Stormy Seas*, p. 102.
94 Thorns and Sedgwick, p. 64.
95 Ibid., p. 119.
96 R.D. Muldoon, *The New Zealand Economy, a Personal View*, Endeavour Press, Auckland, 1985, p. 105.
97 Wright, *Rails Across New Zealand*, pp. 122–23.
98 Wright, *Town and Country*, p. 663.
99 Ibid., p. 119.
100 Gustafson, p. 274.
101 Paul Stumpf, *The Music's All That Matters*, Quartet, London, 1997, pp. 197–99.
102 Wright, *Blue Water Kiwis*, p. 172.
103 Thorns and Sedgwick, p. 54.
104 Noted by, e.g., King, *Nga Iwi o Te Motu*, p. 96.
105 Sutch, *Colony or Nation?*, p. 157.
106 Thorns and Sedgwick, pp. 40–41.
107 Wright, *Italian Odyssey*, pp. 73–77.
108 E.g., at Minqar Qaim, see Wright, *Desert Duel*, p. 83.
109 Wright, *Pacific War*, pp. 65–66.
110 Thorns and Sedgwick, p. 54.
111 King, *Nga Iwi o Te Motu*, pp. 103–4.
112 Sutch, *Colony or Nation?*, p. 157.
113 King, *The Penguin History of New Zealand*, p. 473.
114 Ibid., pp. 470–72.
115 Simpson, *The Road to Erewhon*, pp. 141–42.
116 Calculated from Table XLI in Sutch, *Colony or Nation?* p. 159.
117 Argued by Michael King, *Being Pakeha Now*, Penguin, Auckland, 1999, p. 116.

118 Ranginui Walker, p. 212.
119 King, *The Penguin History of New Zealand*, p. 476.
120 Ranginui Walker, p. 222.
121 Ibid., p. 221.
122 Orange, p. 250.
123 Belich, *Paradise Reforged*, p. 479.
124 W.H. Oliver, 'The Future Behind Us', pp. 10, 12, 27, 29; also Paul Moon, *The Path to the Treaty of Waitangi*, David Ling Publishing, Auckland, 2002; Sharp, 'Recent Juridical and Constitutional Histories of Maori', p. 31.
125 Argued in Sharp, 'Recent Juridical and Constitutional Histories of Maori', p. 32.
126 King, *Being Pakeha* Now, pp. 206–7. See also Moon, *The Path to the Treaty of Waitangi*, p. 11. See also Sharp, 'Recent Juridical and Constitutional Histories of Maori', esp. pp. 30–36.

Chapter 10: Extreme decades

1 Gustafson, p. 278.
2 For background, see, e.g., Mike Patterson, *The Point At Issue*, HarperCollins, Auckland, 1991, pp. 110–16.
3 Wright, *New Zealand's Engineering Heritage*, pp. 138–40, 148–49.
4 Gustafson, p. 311.
5 This was watched by the author. Also cited in Gustafson, p. 312.
6 Author observation.
7 Gustafson, p. 319.
8 Muldoon, *The New Zealand Economy*, p. 118.
9 Stephen Stratford, *The Dirty Decade – New Zealand in the 80s*, Tandem Press, Auckland, 2002, p. 16.
10 Stratford, p. 37.
11 Gustafson, p. 335.
12 Ruth Richardson, *Making a Difference*, Shoal Bay Press, Christchurch 1995, pp. 31–32.
13 Thorns and Sedgwick, p. 104.
14 The 1983 figure was $3168.7 million in 1976 dollars.
15 Noted in Donald Brash, 'Economy', in George Bryant (ed.), *New Zealand 2001*, Cassell New Zealand, Auckland, 1981, pp. 33–34.
16 Richardson, pp. 24–27.
17 Jesson, p. 12.
18 Muldoon, *The New Zealand Economy*, p. 119.
19 See Jesson, p. 31.

20 Muldoon, *The New Zealand Economy*, p. 125.
21 Gustafson, pp. 372–73.
22 Sinclair, *A History of New Zealand*, p. 320.
23 The Treasury, *Economic Management*, The Treasury, Wellington, 1984.
24 Sinclair, *A History of New Zealand*, p. 322.
25 King, *The Penguin History of New Zealand*, p. 488.
26 Marcia Russell, *Revolution*, Hodder Moa Beckett, Auckland, 1996, p. 119.
27 For commentary see also Jesson, pp. 34–36.
28 Russell, p. 127.
29 Interviewed by the author.
30 Cited in Stratford, p. 77.
31 Stratford, p. 7.
32 Jesson, p. 104.
33 Stratford, p. 77.
34 Jesson, p. 126.
35 Belich, *Paradise Reforged*, pp. 406–7.
36 Hunt, *Hustlers, Rogues and Bubble Boys*, List, p. 63.
37 Roger Douglas, *Unfinished Business*, Random House, Auckland, 1993, reprint 1994, p. 222.
38 Russell, p. 212.
39 Ibid.
40 I was at *The Press* conference.
41 Richardson, pp. 74–76.
42 Ibid., pp. 94–95.
43 Briggs, p. 89.
44 Thorns and Sedgwick, p. 119. Briggs, Figure 54, p. 111 is illustrative.
45 Thorns and Sedgwick, p. 74.
46 Thorns and Sedgwick, p. 104.
47 Richardson, p. 99.
48 King, *The Penguin History of New Zealand*, p. 490.
49 Thorns and Sedgwick, p 74.
50 Author observation.
51 Thorns and Sedgwick, pp. 131–32. Traffic offences contributed to the 1994 rate. Hobsbawm, *Age of Extremes*, especially pp. 49–51, 336–43, 565, argued that the twentieth century brought general degradation of standards worldwide.
52 Thorns and Sedgwick, p. 132.
53 Wright, *New Zealand's Engineering Heritage*, p. 149.
54 See, e.g., *Wanganui Chronicle*, 22 December 1999; Tracey Lowndes, 'Economy a case of "minor adjustment"', *Otago Daily Times*, 4 January 2000; *Hawke's Bay Today*, 21 December 1999.

55 Ray Lilley, 'Labour-Alliance prepares for great tax leap backward', *National Business Review*, 10 December 1999; see also *Hawke's Bay Today*, 21 December 1999; 'Government delivers on Super promise', *New Zealand Herald*, 28 January 2000.

56 Jeff Gamlin, 'Treasury's white paper implies country is at a crossroads', *National Business Review*, 28 January 2000. See also Ruth Laugesen, 'Clark finds new energy', *Sunday Star-Times*, 23 January 2000.

57 Gordon McLauchlan, *The Big Con*, Government Print, Wellington, 1992.

58 Peter Lyons, 'Purity could be costly', *Southland Times*, 1 December 2003.

59 John Quiggin, 'Change long overdue in New Zealand', *Australian Financial Review*, 2 December 1999.

60 Graeme Peters, 'Time to ask if reform pain brought gain', *Evening Post*, 3 July 1999.

61 Jesson, pp. 77–78.

62 See, e.g., The Treasury, 'Government Management', (2 Vols), The Treasury, Wellington, 1987 especially Annex 1.

63 Jesson, p. 22.

64 Jesson, p. 22.

65 Belich, *Paradise Reforged*, p. 411.

66 Jesson, p. 13; Belich, *Paradise Reforged*, p. 411.

67 Gustafson, p. 8.

68 See, e.g., Paul Harris and Linda Twiname, *First Knights*, Howling at the Moon Press, Auckland, 1998, p. 201.

69 'Kiwis turn their backs on failed reforms – academic', *Evening Post*, 5 December 1999.

70 See, e.g., 'By The Numbers', *New Zealand Herald*, 19 July 2003.

71 Simon Collins, 'Good, but could be better', *New Zealand Herald*, 18 February 2003.

72 Frank Zappa/Moon Zappa, 'Valley Girl' (1982).

73 See, e.g., 'By The Numbers', *New Zealand Herald*, 19 July 2003.

74 'Fewer eggs in house basket', *New Zealand Herald*, 11 September 2002.

75 'Police may want a word with Greer', *Dominion Post*, 25 August 2003.

Glossary

ariki	chief or noble-born person
baby-boomer	generation born between the Second World War and mid-1960s
Brown Bess	nickname for the Tower musket, an eighteenth-century British weapon built to a particular quality standard
CMS	Church Missionary Society, the Anglican organisation responsible for setting up missions in British territories and protectorates, among other places
Generation X	children of the baby-boomers
hapu	a key Maori social grouping usually comprising of several whanau
heke	migration
iwi	grouping of hapu
kaumatua	elder, possibly under 40 in pre-European times
kupapa	Maori who sided with the government in the wars of the nineteenth century
mana	authority, influence, power or prestige
muru	part of a system of exchange
Nappy Valley	specific nickname for Wainuiomata; generic term for any post-war 'baby boomer' suburb
pukaea	conch-horn trumpet or wooden trumpet
rangatira	chief, person of noble rank
regiment	the main organisational unit of the nineteenth-century British army, with a social dimension
rohe	margin, territory
sap	a trench, usually dug so as to advance towards the enemy
tangata whenua	host tribe or people, original inhabitants, local people, indigenous people
taua	war party
toa	warrior
tohunga	expert, priest, artist
tutua	person of low birth
utu	reciprocal debt
VOC	Vereenigde Oostinsche Compagnie – Dutch East India Company
waka	canoe, vehicle
whanau	extended family in Maori society

Bibliography

Primary sources

UNPUBLISHED

Alexander Turnbull Library (WTu)

Micro-MS-0425, George Maunder, Letters written from Hawke's Bay to his sister Jane, and to his mother.

MS Cha 1911, letter from John Chambers to directors of the Hawke's Bay Tribune.

MS Papers 1635-05, Monro, David (Sir), Papers. Statements of assets and monies owing.

MS-1194-1214, McLean, Donald (Sir) 1820–77, Diaries.

MS-1215-1282, McLean, Donald (Sir) 1820–77, Diaries and notebooks.

MS-1284-1287, McLean, Donald (Sir) 1820–77, Journal (typescript of selected diaries and notebooks).

MS-Group-0556, Cordery, Eric Leofwin, 1910–, Papers.

MS-Papers f-76-048, Colenso, William, 1811–99: letter from James Busby to William Colenso and other papers, letter by Waka Nene and others (fragment).

MS-Papers-0032, McLean, Donald (Sir), 1820–77, Papers.

MS-Papers-0069-049, Copy of journal of the capture of the Ngatapa by A. Kempthorne.

MS-Papers-0667, Davie, Cyrus Papers, 'Journal of a voyage on board the Sir George Seymour and Randolph of 850 tons from Plymouth to Port Victoria, New Zealand.'

MS-Papers-1346, Bennett, Agnes Elizabeth Lloyd, 1872–1960, Papers.

MS-Papers-1611, Colenso, William Papers, Memoranda of the Arrival of Lieut. Governor Hobson in New Zealand.

MS-Papers-1983, Busby, James, 'Three documents by or relating to James Busby, 1840'.

MS-Papers-2183-09, Royal New Zealand Air Force – Review for the Hon Minister of Defence.

MS-Papers-2350, Bollinger, George Wallace 1890–1917, Diary and letters.

MS-Papers-2393, Tronson, Aubrey de Coudrey 1892–1957, A soldier's book of life.

MS-Papers-2418, Folder 4, W.J. Ashcroft writing of the quake in 'The Apiarist' in The New Zealand Smallholder, 16 March 1931.

MS-Papers 2481, Bourke, Henry O'Donel, Diary 1917–18.

MS-Papers-2446, Miller, Henry G., d 1940, Outward letters.

MS-Papers-2477, Higginson, Louisa 1885–1978, Diaries/transcribed by Mrs R.L. Wilson.

MS-Papers-3520, Smith, Hector William Pope, 1837–78, Extracts from journal.

MS-Papers-3779-1/2, Hay Family: Papers, Letters from William and Mary Hay.

MS-Papers-3895-06, Haslam family: family papers, Typed transcripts of the letters from Sarah Ann Self (Haslam).

MS-Papers-3975, Chapman, Leslie Walter, 1913–85, Papers.

MS-Papers-4328, Hamilton, Francis William, 1840–1901, Outward letters.

MS-Papers-5814, Campbell, Dorothy Beatrice, 1903–75, Letter.

Archives New Zealand/Te Whare Tohu Tuhituhinga O Aotearoa, Wellington Office

AIR DEPARTMENT (AIR)

Series 1, 102/4/1 'R.A. Cochrane: Report on the Air Aspect of the Defence Problems of New Zealand, including the suggested duties, strength and organisation of the New Zealand Air Force' from the file 'Pubs and Docs: RNZAF His. 1 w/c Cochrane 1937'.

Series 118/8 'Information Concerning New Zealand's Air Effort during the Second World War, Section A: Statistics relating to New Zealand's Air Effort' from the file 'NZ Air Effort during the Second World War'.

NAVY DEPARTMENT (N)

Series 1, 6/1/4 'Addition of Third Cruiser' from the file 'H.M. Ships attached to N.Z. Division, addition of third cruiser, 1935–42'.

Series 1, 22/6/9 'Naval Defence', from the file 'Naval Defence – Policy and Agreement, NZ Prior 1914, 1905–1914'.

WAR ARCHIVES, WORLD WAR TWO (WAII)

Series 11, 11/7 'R. Walker's Notes, Minqar Qaim, Ruweisat etc; correspondence on the Minqar Qaim period: extracts from cables USAFIME to General Marshall', from the file 'R. Walker's Notes; Battle for Egypt, Syria, Minqar Qaim'.

Series 11, 11/6 'Papers on Economic Stabilisation: memorandum of future stabilisation policy' from the file 'Correspondence of Maj. Gen. H. Kippenberger, 1947–55'.

NEW MUNSTER PROVINCE (NM)

Series 2/4 'Inwards Despatches from Governor-In-Chief, 24 Jan–23 Dec 1850'.

Series 8/35, 1849/39 'Colonial Secretary's Inwards Correspondence, 1849'.

Series 10/10, 1850/746 'Colonial Secretary's Outwards Correspondence, 1850'.

Series 10/9 'Colonial Secretary's Inwards Correspondence, 28 Apr 1848–4 Sep 1848'.

GOVERNOR (G)

Series 2/17 'Confidential Inwards despatches from the Secretary of State, 29 Jun 1909–22 Feb 1910'.

Series 5/111 'Inwards telegrams and acknowledgements of telegrams received, 1 Aug 1936 (1282)–19 Nov 1937 (1827)'.

Series 7/6,61 'Inwards despatches from Lieutenant-Governor Eyre, New Munster, 2 June–11 July 1849'.

Communicate New Zealand, Series 6401 and 6403

Hawke's Bay Museum

Resident Magistrate's Letterbook.

Donald McLean Inwards Letterbook.

Donald McLean Papers, typescript volumes.
Extracts from the diary of E.C. Weston, 10–30 April 1888.

Havelock North Public Library
A/397/1879, William Rainbow diary, typescript.

Hastings District Council archive
HN 102
HBC 46/64 Transit Camp Temporary Housing Windsor Park 1946.
HNL 98/1100 'The Hawke's Bay Master Builders Assn. In Conjunction with the Hastings City Council presents Flaxmere Parade of Homes'.
HCC577 Finance 'A Financial Report, Flaxmere 1963–1987'.

PUBLISHED
Appendices to the Journal of the House of Representatives (AJHR)
1858 C-1 Native Land Purchases.
1858 E-1 Report of Ahuriri Native Industrial School 1856.
1860 E-2 Extract from Sub-Protector Clarke's Report to the Chief Protector, 29 June 1844.
1861 E-9 Minutes of Proceedings of the Kohimarama Conference.
1862 C-1 Correspondence.
1862 E-4 Report of Inspectors on Native Schools, 'Report on the Te Aute Native Industrial School in the Province of Hawke's Bay'.
1862 E-4 Report from W.R. Baker, esq, on the Waerengaahika (Turanga) School, 6th May 1862.
1863 D-6 'The Otago Gold Fields'.
1864 E-2 'Further Papers relative to peace and confiscation of native lands'.
1864 E-3 'Further Papers Relative to the Native Insurrection'.
1864 E-6 'Papers Relative to the Pai Marire Religion, etc'.
1865 E-5 'Papers Relative to the murder of the Rev. Carl Sylvius Volkner by the Hau Hau Fanatics'.
1866 D-11 'Return showing the amount of gold exported from the various ports in the colony for the year commencing on 1st April 1865, and ending the 31st March 1866'.
1867 A-1a.
1867 A-15 'Report by Mr G.S. Cooper on the subject of native lands in the province of Hawke's Bay'.
1867 F-4 'Railway Gauge Committee'.
1871 A-2a 'Memorandum on the Operation of the Native Lands Court by Sir William Martin'.
1873 G-7 'Report of the Hawke's Bay Native Lands Alienation Commission'.
1874 D-2 'Immigration to New Zealand'.
1874 E-8 Appendices to the Public Works Statement 1874.
1874 G-2.
1878 G-1 'Reports from Officers in Native Districts'.
1879 E-1 Appendix M 'Annual Report on Working Railways by the Commissioner of Railways for the Middle Island'.
1879 E-1 Appendix L, 'Annual Report on Working Railways by the Commissioner of Railways, North Island'.
1879, G-1 'Reports from Officers in Native Districts'.
1884, D-1 'Return of immigration from 1st July 1883 to 30th June 1884, Nationalities of Immigrants'.
1885 A-6 'Naval Defence of the Colony'.
1885 D-6 'The North Island Trunk Railway'.

1886 G-1 'Reports from Officers in Native Districts'.
1890 G-1 'Opinions of various authorities on native tenure'.
1890 G-1 'Sir William Martin, Pamphlet of 1848'.
1909 A-5 'Imperial Naval Conference – proceedings of informal meeting of members of the House of Representatives on the Question of the representation of New Zealand at the'.
1921-22 H-19 'Defence forces of New Zealand, report of General Officer Commanding for period from 1st July 1920, to 30th June 1921'.
1919 H-31, Appendix A, 'Influenza Pandemic report on the epidemic in New Zealand by Dr H.H. Mackgill, District Health Officer, Auckland'.
1919 H-31a 'Report of the Influenza Epidemic Commission'.
1920 C-9, 'Discharged Soldiers Settlement'.
1920 H-19a 'War Expenses Account'.
1920 H-37a 'No License Districts'.
1920 H-37b 'No License District'.
1920 H-38 'Department of Imperial Government Supplies.
1921–22 H-19 '23rd Annual Report of the Pensions Department'.
1927 A-7 'Singapore and Naval Defence'.
1927 A-6 'Imperial Conference 1926: Summary of Proceedings'.

Other government publications
Command Papers.
Government Gazette of the Province of New Munster.
New Zealand Parliamentary Debates.
New Zealand Statutes.
Population Census.
Supplement to the New Zealand Gazette.
The New Zealand Gazette.

Newspapers
Evening Post
Hawke's Bay Herald
National Business Review
New Zealand Herald
New Zealand Times
Southern Cross
The Daily Telegraph
The Dominion
The Dominion Post
The New Zealand Gazette and Port Nicholson Advertiser
The Press
The Weekender

Private papers and collections
Noble-Campbell Papers.
Sir John White Papers.
M. Wynn Papers.

Author collection
Cunningham, Ashley, 'The Indigenous Forests of East Coast – Poverty Bay, Hawke's Bay'.
Elder, N.L., 'Maori Cultivation and the Retreat of Forest', talk given 9 October 1956.
'Gereduceedre Kaart vant Zuid-Land, print
'Mar di India', print of c1630 map.
Lands and Survey Auction Map, 12 October 1905.
Letter and newspaper files.

Secondary sources

Adams, Peter, *A Fatal Necessity*, Auckland University Press, Auckland, 1977.

Aitken, Jefley J., *Rocked and Ruptured, Geological Faults in New Zealand*, Reed, Auckland, 1999.

Alpers, Antony, *The Life of Katherine Mansfield*, Oxford University Press, Oxford, reprint 1983.

Anderson, Atholl, 'Canterbury and Marlborough', in Nigel Prickett (ed.), *The First Thousand Years*, Dunmore Press, Palmerston North, 1982.

——, 'North and Central Otago', in Nigel Prickett (ed.), *The First Thousand Years*, Dunmore Press, Palmerston North, 1982.

——, *Prodigious Birds – Moas and Moa Hunting in Prehistoric New Zealand*, Cambridge University Press, Melbourne, 1989.

Anderson, Grahame, *The Merchant of the Zeehaen – Isaac Gilsemans and the Voyages of Abel Tasman*, Te Papa Press, Wellington, 2001.

Arnold, Rollo, The *Farthest Promised Land*, Victoria University Press and Price Milburn, Wellington, 1981.

Ashby, Michael, 'Fraser's Foreign Policy', in Margaret Clark (ed.), *Peter Fraser, Master Politician*, Dunmore Press, Palmerston North, 1998.

Ashton, Robert, 'Aristocracy in Transition', *Economic History Review*, Vol. 22, 1969.

Bagnall, A.G., *Wairarapa: An Historical Excursion*, Hedleys, Masterton, 1976.

Ballara, Angela, *Taua*, Penguin, Auckland, 2003.

Ballara, Angela, and Scott, Gary, 'Crown Purchases of Land in Early Provincial Hawke's Bay', Waitangi Tribunal Wai 201, Wellington, 1994.

Barber, Laurie, *A Short History of New Zealand*, Century Hutchinson, Auckland, 1981.

Barber, Laurie, and Tonkin-Covell, John, *Freyberg: Churchill's Salamander*, Century Hutchinson, Auckland, 1989.

Barclay, A.R., 'The Premier and his troubles', Pamphlet, S. Lister, Printer, Dunedin, 1909.

Barratt, Glynn, *Russophobia in New Zealand*, Dunmore Press, Palmerston North, 1981.

Bassett, Judith, 'The Exodus', in Ray Knox (ed.), *New Zealand's Heritage*, Paul Hamlyn, Wellington, 1971–73, Part 54.

Bassett, Michael, *Coates of Kaipara*, Auckland University Press, Auckland, 1995.

Beaglehole, J.C., (ed.), *The Journals of Captain James Cook on his Voyages of Discovery*, Vol. 1: 'The Voyage of the *Endeavour*', Cambridge University Press, London, 1968.

Beckham, A.J. (ed.), *The Discovery of the Maori*, Pemaka Press, Whitcombe and Tombs, Wellington, 1969.

Belich, James, *The New Zealand Wars*, Penguin, Auckland, 1985.

——, *Making Peoples*, Penguin, Auckland, 1996.

——, *Paradise Reforged*, Allen Lane, Auckland, 2001.

Biggs, Bruce, 'Does Maori have a closest relative?', in Douglas G. Sutton (ed.), *The Origins of the First New Zealanders*, Auckland University Press, Auckland, 1994.

Binney, Judith, 'The Expansion of the Missions', in Ray Knox (ed.), *New Zealand's Heritage,* Paul Hamlyn, Wellington, 1971–73.

——, 'The Expansion of a Competitive Society', in David Hamer, 'Towns in Nineteenth Century New Zealand', in D.A. Hamer (ed.), *New Zealand Social History, Papers from the Turnbull Conference on New Zealand Social History, 1978*, University of Auckland, Auckland, 1978.

——, *Redemption Songs*, Bridget Williams Books, Wellington, 1995.

Blaug, Mark, *Great Economists Before Keynes*, Wheatsheaf Books, Brighton, 1986.

Boast, Richard, 'Esk Forest Claim: Report on the Mohaka-Waikare confiscation', Waitangi Tribunal, Wellington.

Boyack, Nicholas, *Behind the Lines*, Allen & Unwin, Wellington, 1989.

Boyd, Mary, *City of the Plains*, Hastings City Council, Hastings, 1984.

Bradbury, Matthew (ed.), *A History of the Garden in New Zealand*, Viking, Auckland, 1995.

Brash, Donald, 'Economy', in George Bryant (ed.), *New Zealand 2001*, Cassell New Zealand, Auckland, 1981.

Briggs, Asa, *Victorian Cities*, Pelican, London, 1968.

Briggs, Phil, *Looking at the Numbers, a View of New Zealand's Economic History*, New Zealand Institute of Economic Research, Wellington, 2003.

Brooking, Tom, 'Commentaries', in D.A. Hamer (ed.), *New Zealand Social History*, Papers from the Turnbull Conference on New Zealand Social History, 1978, University of Auckland, Auckland, 1978.

——, '"Bursting up" the Greatest Estate of All' in Judith Binney (ed.), *The Shaping of History*, Bridget Williams Books, Wellington, 2001.

Brown, Bruce, 'Foreign Policy is Trade: Trade is Foreign Policy', in Ann Trotter (ed.), *Fifty Years of New Zealand Foreign Policy Making*, University of Otago Press, Dunedin, 1993.

Buchanan, J.D.H. (D.R. Simmons ed.), *The Maori History and Place Names of Hawke's Bay*, A.H. & A.W. Reed, Wellington, 1973.

Buick, T.L., *New Zealand's First War, the Rebellion of Hone Heke*, Capper Press, reprint, Christchurch, 1976.

Burdon, R.M., *The New Dominion*, A.H. & A.W. Reed, Auckland, 1965.

Burnett, Joan, 'The Impact of Dairying on the Landscape of Lowland Taranaki', in R.F. Watters (ed.), *Land and Society in New Zealand*, A.H. & A.W. Reed, Wellington, 1965, reprint 1967.

Burns, Patricia, *Fatal Success – A History of the New Zealand Company*, Heinemann Reed, Auckland, 1989.

Byrnes, Giselle, *Boundary Markers*, Bridget Williams Books, Wellington, 2001.

Cannadine, David (ed.), *The Speeches of Winston S. Churchill*, Penguin, London, 1989.

Caughey, Angela, *The Interpreter – The Biography of Richard 'Dicky' Barrett*, David Bateman, Auckland, 1998.

Chadwick, Edwin, 'Report on the Sanitary Conditions of the Labouring Population of Great Britain', in B.I. Coleman (ed.), *The Idea of the City in Nineteenth Century Britain*, Routledge and Kegan Paul, London, 1973.

Chapple, Simon, *The Economic Effects of the 1931 Hawke's Bay Earthquake*, New Zealand Institute of Economic Research (Inc), Working Paper 97/7, Wellington, August 1997.

Chrisp, Stephen, 'The Maori occupation of Wairarapa: orthodox and nonorthodox versions, *Journal of the Polynesian Society*, Vol. 102, No. 1, March 1993.

Churchill, W.S., *The Second World War* (6 vols), Clarendon Press, London, 1948–54.

——, *The World Crisis, 1911–1918*, Four Square, London, 1960.

Clark, Lloyd, *World War I: An Illustrated History*, Helicon, Oxford, 2001.

Clark, Paul, *Hauhau, The Pai Marire Search for Maori Identity*, Auckland, University Press, Auckland, 1975.

Cliff, E.S. & Co., *Hastings, The Hub of Hawke's Bay, New Zealand*, E.S. Cliff & Co., c 1918.

Clifton, George, *The Happy Hunted*, Cassell & Co., London, 1952.

Colenso, William, 'The Authentic and Genuine History of the Signing of the Treaty of Waitangi', Government Print, Wellington, 1890.

Comber, Ken, 'Personal reflections on my father-in-law', in Margaret Clark (ed.), *Sir Keith Holyoake, Towards a Political Biography*, Dunmore Press, Palmerston North, 1997.

Conly, Geoff, *The Shock of '31*, A.H. & A.W. Reed, Wellington, 1980.

——, *Wattie's – The First Fifty Years*, J. Wattie Canneries Ltd, Hastings, 1984.

Cook, Gary J., and Brown, Thomas J., *The Secret Land: People Before*, StonePrint Press, Christchurch, 1999.

Cooke Taylor, W., 'Notes of a Tour in the Manufacturing Districts of Lancashire', 1842, in B.I. Coleman (ed.), *The Idea of the City in Nineteenth Century Britain*, Routledge and Kegan Paul, London, 1973.

Crawford, John, and Ellis, Ellen, *To Fight for the Empire: An Illustrated History of New Zealand and the South African War, 1899–1902*, Reed, Auckland, 1999.

Crosby, R.O., *The Musket Wars*, Reed, Auckland, 2000.

Cullen, Michael, 'Lawrence Stone, the Manors and other ruins', *Historical News*, March 1969.

Cumberland, Kenneth B., and Fox, J.W., *New Zealand: A Regional View*, Whitcombe and Tombs, Auckland, 1958, second printing 1959.

Czerkas, Sylvia A., and Czerkas, Stephen A., *Dinosaurs: A Global View*, Dragons World, London, 1990.

Daley, Caroline, 'Taradale Meets the Ideal Society and its Enemies', in Judith Binney (ed.), *The Shaping of History*, Bridget Williams Books, Wellington, 2001.

Davidoff, Leonore, and Hall, Catherine, 'The architecture of public and private life, English middle class society in a provincial town, 1780 to 1850', in Derek Fraser and A. Sutcliffe (eds), *The Pursuit of Urban History*, Edward Arnold, London, 1983.

Davidson, Janet, 'Auckland', in Nigel Prickett (ed.), *The First Thousand Years*, Dunmore Press, Palmerston North, 1982.

——, *The Prehistory of New Zealand*, Longman Paul, Auckland, 1984.

Davis, Peter, 'Stratification and Class', in Paul Soonley, David Pearson and Ian Shirley (eds), *New Zealand Sociological Perspectives*, Dunmore Press, Palmerston North, 1972.

Diamond, Jared, *Guns, Germs and Steel*, Vintage, London, 1998.

Douglas, Roger, *Unfinished Business*, Random House, Auckland, 1993, reprint 1994.

Dowrick, David, 'Damage and Intensities in the Magnitude 7.8 1931 Hawke's Bay, New Zealand earthquake', *Bulletin of the New Zealand National Society for Earthquake Engineering*, Vol. 31, No. 3, September 1998.

Drummond, Alison, and Drummond, L.R., *At Home in New Zealand – an Illustrated History of Everyday Things Before 1865*, Blackwood and Janet Paul, Auckland, 1967.

Easton, Brian, 'Three New Zealand Depressions', from W.E. Willmot (ed.), *New Zealand and the World*, University of Canterbury, Christchurch, 1980.

——, *In Stormy Seas*, University of Otago Press, Dunedin, 1997.

——, 'Beyond the Cringe', *New Zealand Listener*, 20 October 2001.

——, *The Nationbuilders*, Auckland University Press, Auckland, 2001.

Economic Management, The Treasury, Wellington, 14 July 1984.

Edmonds Cookery Book, Bluebird Foods, Auckland, 38th Edition, 1995.

Edwards, Philip (ed.), *The Journals of Captain Cook: Prepared from original manuscripts by J.C. Beaglehole for the Haklyut Society, 1955–1967*, Penguin, London, 1999.

Elder, N.L., *Vegetation of the Ruahine Range: An Introduction*, Royal Society of New Zealand, Wellington, 1965.

Eldred-Grigg, Stevan, *A Southern Gentry*, A.H. & A.W. Reed, Wellington, 1980.

——, *Pleasures of the Flesh*, A.H. & A.W. Reed, Wellington, 1984.

Elliott, H.B., Striewski, B., Flenley, J.R., Kirkman, J.H., and Sutton, D.G., 'A 4300 year palynological and sedimentological record of environmental change and human impact from Wharau road swamp, Northland, New Zealand', *Journal of the Royal Society of New Zealand*, Vol. 27, No. 4, December 1997.

Elsmore, Bronwyn, *Like Them That Dream*, Reed, Auckland, 2000.

Enting, Brian, and Molloy, Les, *The Ancient Islands*, Port Nicholson Press, Wellington, 1982.

Evans, Jeff, *The Discovery of Aotearoa*, Reed, Auckland, 1998.

Fagan, Brian, *The Little Ice Age – How the Climate Made History*, Basic Books, New York, 2000.

Fairburn, Miles, *The Ideal Society and Its Enemies*, Auckland University Press, Auckland, 1989.

——, 'Local Community or Atomized Society', in Judith Binney (ed.), *The Shaping of History*, Bridget Williams Books, Wellington, 2001.

Farwell, Byron, *Queen Victoria's Little Wars*, Allen Lane, London, 1973.

Ferguson, Gael, *Building the New Zealand Dream*, Dunmore Press, Palmerston North, 1994.

Finney, Ben, 'Experimental Voyaging and Maori Settlement', in Douglas G. Sutton (ed.), *The Origins of the First New Zealanders*, Auckland University Press, Auckland, 1994.

Forrest, James, 'Otago During the Goldrushes', in R.F. Watters (ed.), *Land and Society in New Zealand*, A.H. & A.W. Reed, Wellington, 1965, reprint 1967.

Fox, Aileen, 'Hawke's Bay', in *The First Thousand Years*, Dunmore Press, Palmerston North, 1982.

Freyberg, Paul, *Bernard Freyberg VC – Soldier of Two Nations*, Hodder & Stoughton, London, 1991.

Gamlin, Jeff, 'Treasury's white paper implies country is at a crossroads', *National Business Review*, 28 January 2000.

Gardner, W.J., 'A Colonial Economy', from W.H. Oliver and B.R. Williams (eds), *The Oxford History of New Zealand*, OUP, Auckland, 1981.

Gibson, Tom, *The Maori Wars*, A.H. & A.W. Reed, Wellington, 1974.

Gillespie, Oliver A., *The Pacific*, War History Branch, Department of Internal Affairs, Wellington, 1952.

Godley, Charlotte, *Letters from Early New Zealand*, Whitcombe and Tombs, Auckland, 1951.

Goff, James R., and McFadgen, Bruce G., 'Nationwide tsunami during prehistoric Maori occupation, New Zealand', ITS 2001 Proceedings, Session 3, No. 3-1.

Gould, Steven Jay, *Ever Since Darwin*, Penguin, London, 1991.

Government Management, Briefing to the Incoming Government, vols I and II, The Treasury, Wellington, 1987.

Grant, Patrick J., 'Climate, Geomorphology and Vegetation', in Douglas G. Sutton (ed.), *The Origins of the First New Zealanders*, Auckland University Press, Auckland, 1994.

——, *Hawke's Bay Forests of Yesterday*, CHB Print, Waipukurau, 1996.

Grant, S., *In Other Days – A History of the Chambers Family of Te Mata*, Havelock North, CHB Printers, Waipukurau, 1980.

Gray, Colin S., *The Geopolitics of the Nuclear Era*, Crane, Russak & Co. Inc., 1977.

Grimshaw, Patricia, *Women's Suffrage in New Zealand*, second edition, Auckland University Press, Auckland, 1987.

Gustafson, Barry, *His Way, A Biography of Robert Muldoon*, Auckland University Press, Auckland, 2000, paperback edition 2001.

Guthrie-Smith, H., *Tutira*, third edition, William Blackwood & Sons, London 1951.

Hamer, David, 'Towns in Nineteenth Century New Zealand', in D.A. Hamer (ed.), *New Zealand Social History*, Papers from the Turnbull Conference on *New Zealand Social History*, 1978, University of Auckland, Auckland, 1978.

Hankin, Cherry A., *Life in a Young Colony*, Whitcoulls, Christchurch, 1981.

Harris, Paul, and Twiname, Linda, *First Knights*, Howling at the Moon Press, Auckland, 1998.

Hastings, *The Hub of Hawke's Bay*, New Zealand, Hastings Borough Council, n.d.

Hawke, G.R., *Railways and Economic Growth in England and Wales 1840–1870*, Clarendon Press, Oxford, 1970.

Hawke's Bay – Before and After, Daily Telegraph, Napier, 1931, reprint 1981.

Hesselberg, Erik, *Kon Tiki and I*, Allen and Unwin, London, 1949.

Hexter, Robert, 'The English Aristocracy, its Crises, and the English Revolution, 1558–1660', *Journal of British Studies*, Vol. VIII, 1968.

Hill, R.D., 'Pastoralism in the Wairarapa, 1844–53', in R.F. Watters (ed.), *Land and Society in New Zealand*, A.H. & A.W. Reed, Wellington, 1965, reprint 1967.

Hobsbawm, Eric, *The Age of Revolution*, Abacus, London, 1977.

——, *Age of Extremes; The Short Twentieth Century 1941–1991*, Abacus, London, 1994.

——, *On History*, Abacus, London, 1998.

Hogg, Ian V., *The Machine Gun*, Phoebus, London, 1976.

Holdaway, Richard N., 'A spatio-temporal model for the invasion of the New Zealand archipelago by the Pacific rat Rattus exulans', *Journal of the Royal Society of New Zealand*, Vol. 29, No. 2, June 1999.

Holdaway, Richard N., Roberts, Richard G., Beavan-Athfield, Nancy R., Olley, John M., and Worthy, Trevor H., 'Optical dating of quartz sediments and accelerator mass spectrometry 14C dating of bone gelatin and moa eggshell: a comparison of age estimates for non-archaeological deposits in New Zealand', *Journal of the Royal Society of New Zealand*, Vol. 32, No. 3, September 2002.

Holdaway, R.N., and Worthy, T.H., 'A reappraisal of the later Quaternary fossil vertebrates of Pyramid Valley swamp, North Canterbury, New Zealand', *New Zealand Journal of Zoology*, Vol. 24, 1997.

Houghton, Philip, 'A Vigorous People', in John Wilson (ed.), *From the Beginning, the Archaeology of the Maori*, Penguin, Auckland, 1987.

——, *The First New Zealanders*, Hodder & Stoughton, Auckland, 1980.

Howard, Graham, and Wright, Matthew, 'The Reserve Bank Inflation Calculator', *Reserve Bank Bulletin*, Wellington, Vol. 66, No. 4, December 2003.

Howe, K.R., *The Quest for Origins*, Penguin, Auckland, 2003.

Hunt, Graeme, *The Rich List*, Reed, Auckland, 1999.

——, 'Ignorance lets Tuia spread her poisoned gospel', *National Business Review*, 8 September 2000.

Irwin, Geoffrey, *The Prehistoric Exploration and Colonisation of the Pacific*, Cambridge University Press, Cambridge, 1992.

Jesson, Bruce, *Only Their Purpose Is Mad*, Dunmore Press, Palmerston North, 1999.

Jones, Kevin, 'Skill with Stone and Wood', in John Wilson (ed.), *From the Beginning, the Archaeology of the Maori*, Penguin, Auckland, 1987.

Kemp, Geoffrey, 'The New Strategic Map', from Uri Ra'anan, *Arms Transfers to the Third World*, Westview Press, 1978.

King, Michael, *Being Pakeha Now*, Penguin, Auckland, 1999.

——, *Moriori – A People Rediscovered*, Penguin, Auckland, revised edition 2001.

——, *Nga Iwi o Te Motu*, revised edition, Reed, Auckland, 2001.

——, *The Penguin History of New Zealand*, Penguin, Auckland, 2003.

Kippenberger, H.K. (ed.), *Documents Relating to New Zealand's Participation in the Second World War*, War History Branch, Department of Internal Affairs, 3 vols, Wellington, 1949, 1951 and 1963.

Knox, Ray (ed.), *New Zealand's Heritage*, Paul Hamlyn, Wellington, 1971-73.

Law, Garry, 'Coromandel Peninsula and Great Barrier Island', in Nigel Prickett (ed.), *The First Thousand Years*, Dunmore Press, Palmerston North, 1982.

Law, R. Garry, 'Multiple settlement in Eastern Polynesia', in Douglas G. Sutton (ed.), *The Origins of the First New Zealanders*, Auckland University Press, Auckland, 1994.

Lee, Jack, *The Old Land Claims in New Zealand*, NHPS, Kerikeri, 1993.

Lees, C.M., Neall, V.E., and Palmer, A.S., 'Forest persistence at coastal Waikato, 24,000 b.p. to present', *Journal of the Royal Society of New Zealand*, Vol. 28, No. 1, March 1998.

Lewis, David, and Forman, Werner, *The Maori: Heirs of Tane*, Orbis, London, 1982.

Liddell-Hart, Basil (ed.), *The Rommel Papers*, Collins, London, 1953, trans. Paul Findlay (German original written by Erwin Rommel and edited by Fritz Bayerlein, Lucie-Maria Rommel and Manfred Rommel).

Lieber, Robert J., *Theory and World Politics*, Winthrop Publishers, 1972.

Lilley, Ray, 'Labour-Alliance prepares for great tax leap backward', *National Business Review*, 10 December 1999.

Lissington, M.P., *New Zealand and the United States*, Government Print, Wellington, 1972.

Lloyd Prichard, M.F., *An Economic History of New Zealand to 1939*, Collins, Auckland, 1970.

Loughmann, R.A., *Life of Sir Joseph Ward*, New Century Press, Wellington, 1929.

Macdonald, Charlotte, *A Woman of Good Character*, Allen and Unwin/Historical Branch, Wellington, 1990.

Mackay, Duncan, 'The Orderly Frontier', in Judith Binney (ed.), *The Shaping of History*, Bridget Williams Books, Wellington, 2001.

MacLaren, A.A., 'Class Formation and Class Fractions, the Aberdeen bourgeoise 1830–1850', in G. Gordon and B. Dicks (eds), *Scottish Urban History*, Aberdeen University Press, Aberdeen, 1983.

MacNab, Robert, *Historical Records of New Zealand*, vols I and II, Government Printer, Wellington, 1908 and 1914.

Madjalany, Fred, *Cassino, Portrait of a Battle*, Longmans, Green & Co., London, 1957.

Magnenheimer, Heinz, *Hitler's War*, Cassell, London, 1997.

Maning, F.E., *Old New Zealand*, Golden Press reprint, Auckland, 1987.

Marshall, James, and Marshall, Dominique, *Discipline and Punishment in New Zealand Education*, Dunmore Press, Palmerston North, 1997.

Martin, John E., *The Forgotten Worker*, Allen and Unwin, Wellington, 1990.

McCulloch, Beverley, illus. Geoffrey Cox, *Moas – Lost Giants of New Zealand*, HarperCollins, Auckland, 1992.

McCulloch, Beverley, and Trotter, Michael, *Digging Up the Past, New Zealand's Archaeological History*, revised edition, Penguin, Middlesex, 1997.

McGill, David, *Guardians at the Gate*, Silver Owl Press, Wellington, 1991.

McGlone, H.S., Anderson, A., and Holdaway, R.N., 'An ecological approach', in Douglas G. Sutton (ed.), *The Origins of the First New Zealanders*, Auckland University Press, Auckland, 1994.

McGlone, H.S., Mark, A.F., and Bell, D., 'Late Pleistocene and Holocene vegetation history, Central Otago, South Island, New Zealand', *Journal of the Royal Society of New Zealand*, Vol. 25, No. 1, March 1995.

McIntyre, W.D., 'Peter Fraser's Commonwealth: New Zealand and the origins of the New Commonwealth in the 1940s', in

Alistair McIntosh (ed.), *New Zealand in World Affairs*, Vol. 1, Price, Milburn for the New Zealand Institute of Internal Affairs, Wellington, 1977.

McKinnon, Malcolm (ed.), *The New Zealand Historical Atlas*, Bateman, Auckland, 1997.

McKirdy, A., 'Maori-Pakeha Land Transactions in Hawke's Bay 1848–1864,' MA Thesis, VUW, 1994.

McLauchlan, Gordon, *The Passionless People*, Cassell, Auckland, 1976.

——, *The Big Con*, Government Print, Wellington, 1992.

McLeod, John, *Myth and Reality, The New Zealand Soldier in World War II*, Heinemann Reed, Auckland, 1986.

McLintock, A.H., *Crown Colony Government in New Zealand*, Government Print, Wellington, 1958.

——, (ed.), *A Descriptive Atlas of New Zealand*, Government Printer, Wellington, 1959, second edition 1960.

——, *An Encyclopedia of New Zealand*, Government Print, Wellington, 1966.

Meaney, Neville, *The Search for Security in the Pacific I*, Sydney University Press, Sydney, 1976.

Metge, Joan, and Kinloch, P., *Talking Past Each Other: Problems in Cross-Cultural Communication*, VUW Press, Wellington, 1984.

Mitchell, Austin, The *Quarter-Acre, Half-Gallon, Pavlova Paradise*, Whitcombe and Tombs, Christchurch, 1972.

Moon, Paul, *Hone Heke*, David Ling, Auckland, 2001.

——, *The Path to the Treaty of Waitangi*, David Ling Publishing, Auckland, 2002.

Moorhead, Alan, *The Fatal Impact*, Hamish Hamilton, London, 1966.

Morrell, W.P., *The Provincial System in New Zealand, 1852–76*, Whitcombe and Tombs, Wellington, 1964.

Morris, James, *Pax Britannica*, Faber and Faber, London, 1968.

Morris, R.J., 'The Middle Class and British Towns and Cities of the Industrial Revolution, 1780–1870', in Derek Fraser and A. Sutcliffe (eds), *The Pursuit of Urban History*, Edward Arnold, London, 1983.

——, 'Voluntary Societies and British Urban Elites, 1780–1850', *Historical Journal*, Vol. 26, No. 1, March 1983.

Muldoon, R.D., *The Rise and Fall of a Young Turk*, A.H. & A.W. Reed, Wellington, 1972.

——, *The New Zealand Economy, A Personal View*, Endeavour Press, Auckland, 1985.

New Zealand Foreign Policy Statements and Documents 1943–57, Foreign Affairs, Government Print, Wellington, 1972.

Mulgan, John, *Report on Experience*, Oxford University Press, London, 1947.

O'Malley, Vincent, *The Ahuriri Purchase*, Crown Forestry Rental Trust, Wellington, 1995.

Oliver, W.H., *The Story of New Zealand*, Faber and Faber, London, 1960.

Oliver, W.H., and Orange, Claudia (eds), *The Dictionary of New Zealand Biography*, Vol. I, BWB, Wellington, 1997.

——, 'The Future Behind Us', in Andrew Sharp and P.G. McHugh (eds), *Histories, Power and Loss*, BWB, Wellington, 2001.

Oliver, W.H., and Williams, B.R. (eds), *The Oxford History of New Zealand*, Oxford University Press, Auckland, 1981, reprint 1991.

Olssen, Erik, *Building the New World: Work, Politics and Society in Caversham, 1880s–1920s*, Auckland University Press, Auckland, 1995.

Orange, Claudia, *The Treaty of Waitangi*, Bridget Williams Books, Wellington, 1987.

Orbell, Margaret, *Hawaiki – A New Approach to Maori Tradition*, University of Canterbury, Christchurch, 1985.

Organisation for National Development, 'Interim Report on Post-war Reconstruction and National Development', July 1944.

Padfield, Peter, *The Great Naval Race*, Hart-Davis, London, 1974.

Parsonson, Ann, 'The Pursuit of Mana', in W.H. Oliver and B.R. Williams (eds), *The Oxford History of New Zealand*, Oxford University Press, Auckland, 1981.

Patterson, Mike, *The Point At Issue*, HarperCollins, Auckland, 1991.

Petersen, G.C., 'Pioneering the North Island Bush', in R.F. Watters (ed.), *Land and Society in New Zealand*, A.H. & A.W. Reed, Wellington, 1965, reprint 1967.

Porter, Frances, *Born to New Zealand, a Biography of Jane Maria Atkinson*, Bridget Williams Books, Wellington, 1995.

Prickett, Nigel, *Landscapes of Conflict – A Field Guide to the New Zealand Wars*, Random House, Auckland, 2001.

——, *Maori Origins – from Asia to Aotearoa*, David Bateman, Auckland, 2001.

Pugsley, Chris, 'Walking Heke's War', *Defence Quarterly*, No. 4, Autumn 1994.

Quiggan, John, 'Change long overdue in New Zealand', *Australian Financial Review*, 2 December 1999.

Rabb, Theodore K., *The Struggle for Stability in Early Modern Europe*, Oxford University Press, New York, 1975.

Richards, Rhys, 'Rongotute, Stivers and "Other Visitors" to New Zealand', *Journal of the Polynesian Society*, Vol. 102, No. 1, March 1993.

Richardson, Len, 'Parties and political change', in W.H. Oliver and B.R. Williams (eds), *The Oxford History of New Zealand*, Oxford University Press, Auckland, 1981, reprinted 1991.

Richardson, Len, and McIntyre, W. David, (eds), *Provincial Perspectives*, University of Canterbury, Christchurch, 1980.

Richardson, Ruth, *Making a Difference*, Shoal Bay Press, Christchurch, 1995.

Roberts, Andrew, 'Prime Minister Halifax', in Robert Cowley (ed.), *What If? 2*, Berkley, New York, 2001.

Ross, R.M., 'Te Tiriti o Waitangi', in Judith Binney (ed.), *The Shaping of History*, Bridget Williams Books, Wellington, 2001.

Russell, Marcia, *Revolution*, Hodder Moa Beckett, Auckland, 1996.

Ryan, Tim, and Parham, Bill, *The Colonial New Zealand Wars*, Grantham House, Wellington, 1986.

Salmond, Anne, *Two Worlds*, Viking, Auckland, 1991.

——, *Between Worlds*, Viking, Auckland, 1997.

Salmond, Jeremy, *Old New Zealand Houses 1800–1940*, Reed, Auckland, 1986, reprint 1991.

Saul, John Ralston, *Voltaire's Bastards*, Penguin, Canada, 1992.

Schwimmer, Eric, 'The Maori Hapu: A generative model', in *Journal of Polynesian Studies,* Vol. 99, No. 3, September 1990.

Scrimgeour, C.G., Lee, John A., and Simpson, Tony, *The Scrim-Lee Papers*, A.H. & A.W. Reed, Wellington, 1976.

Sharp, Andrew, 'More blood out of Stone; what was the crisis of the aristocracy?', *Historical News*, March 1969.

——, 'Recent Juridical and Constitutional Histories of Maori', in Andrew Sharp and Paul McHugh (eds), *Histories, Power and Loss*, Bridget Williams Books, Wellington, 2001.

Simmons, David, *The Great New Zealand Myth*, A.H. & A.W. Reed, Wellington, 1976.

Simpson, Tony *The Sugarbag Years*, Hodder & Stoughton, Auckland, 1974, new edition 1984.

——, *The Road to Erewhon*, Beaux Arts, Auckland, 1976.

——, *The Slump: The 1930s Depression, Its Origins and Aftermath*, Penguin, Auckland, 1990.

——, *The Immigrants*, Godwit, Auckland, 1997.

——, *A Distant Feast*, Godwit, Auckland, 1999.

Sinclair, Keith, 'The Liberals Come to Power', in Ray Knox (ed.), *New Zealand's Heritage*, Paul Hamlyn, Wellington, 1971–73, Part 56.

——, *A History of New Zealand*, Penguin, Auckland, 1959, revised Pelican edition 1988.

Smith, H. Guthrie, *Tutira*, third edition, William Blackwood & Sons, London, 1951.

Sorrenson, M.P.K., *Maori Origins and Migrations*, Auckland University Press, Auckland, 1979.

——, 'Maori and Pakeha', in W.H. Oliver and B.R. Williams (eds), *The Oxford History of New Zealand*, Oxford University Press, Auckland, 1981, reprint 1991.

Stephens, P.R., 'The Age of the Great Sheep Runs', in R.F. Watters (ed.), *Land and Society in New Zealand*, A.H. & A.W. Reed, Wellington, 1965, reprint 1967.

Stevens, Graeme, and McGlone, Matt, and McCulloch, Beverley, *Prehistoric New Zealand*, Heinemann Reed, Auckland, 1988.

Stone, R.C.J., *From Tamaki-Makau-Rau to Auckland*, Auckland University Press, Auckland, 2001.

Stratford, Stephen, *The Dirty Decade – New Zealand in the 80s*, Tandem Press, Auckland, 2002.

Stumpf, Paul, *The Music's All That Matters*, Quartet, London, 1997.

Suggate, R.P. (ed.), *The Geology of New Zealand*, Government Printer, Wellington, 1978.

Sutch, W.B., *The Quest for Security in New Zealand 1940 to 1966*, Oxford University Press, London, 1966.

——, *Colony or Nation?,* Sydney University Press, Sydney, 1966, second edition 1968.

Sutton, Douglas G. (ed.), *The Archaeology of the Kainga*, Auckland University Press, Auckland, 1990, second edition 1994.

Tasker, John, *Myth and Mystery*, Tandem Press, Auckland, 1997.

——, *Secret Landscape*, Kanuka Press, Hastings, 2000.

Tattersall, Ian, *The Fossil Trail*, Oxford University Press, Oxford, 1995.

Taylor, A.J.P., *How Wars Begin*, Book Club Associates, London, 1979.

Taylor, David, *Poverty*, Heinemann Educational, Oxford, 1990.

Temple, Philip, *A Sort of Conscience – The Wakefields*, Auckland University Press, Auckland, 2002.

Thomson, David, *A World Without Welfare, New Zealand's*

Colonial Experiment, Auckland University Press/Bridget Williams Books, Wellington, 1998.

Thomson, David, *England in the Nineteenth Century*, Penguin, London, 1950.

——, *Europe Since Napoleon*, Pelican, London, 1966.

Thorns, David, and Sedgwick, Charles, *Understanding Aotearoa/New Zealand: Historical Statistics*, Dunmore Press, Palmerston North, 1997.

Toynbee, Claire, 'Class and Social Structure in Nineteenth Century New Zealand', in D.A. Hamer (ed.), *New Zealand Social History*, Papers from the Turnbull Conference on *New Zealand Social History*, 1978, University of Auckland, Auckland, 1978.

Treasury, The, *Economic Management*, The Treasury, Wellington, 1984.

——, *Government Management* (2 vols), The Treasury, Wellington, 1987.

Trevor-Roper, H.R., 'The General Crisis of the Seventeenth Century', *Past and Present,* No. 16, 1959.

Trotter, Michael and McCulloch, Beverley, *Digging up the Past, New Zealand's Archaeological History,* revised edition, Penguin, Middlesex, 1997.

Tylecote, Andrew, *The Long Wave in the World Economy, The Present Crisis in Historical Perspective*, Routledge, London, 1991.

Uren, Martyn, *Kiwi Saga*, Anglo-Egyptian Bookshop, Cairo, 1943.

Vaggioli, Dom Felice, *History of New Zealand and its Inhabitants*, trans. John Crockett, Otago University Press, Dunedin, 2000.

Vandergoes, Marcus J., Fitzsimons, Sean J., and Newnham, Rewi M., 'Late glacial to Holocene vegetation change in the eastern Takitimu mountains, western Southland, New Zealand', *Journal of the Royal Society of New Zealand*, Vol. 27, No. 1, March 1997.

Vaughan, R., 'The Age of Great Cities', 1843, in B.I. Coleman (ed.), *The Idea of the City in Nineteenth Century Britain*, Routledge and Kegan Paul, London, 1973.

Waitangi Tribunal, *Ngai Tahu Report 1991*, Wellington, 1991.

——, *Muriwhenua Land Report*, Wellington, 1997.

Wakefield, E. Jerningham, *Adventure in New Zealand*, ed. Joan Stevens, Golden Press, Auckland, 1975

Walker, Martin, *The Cold War*, Viking, London, 1993.

Walker, Ranginui, *Struggle Without End*, Penguin, Auckland, 1990.

Ward, Alan, *A Show of Justice*, ANU Press, 1974.

Ward, David, 'The Victorian Slum: An enduring myth', *Annals of the Association of American Geographers*, Vol. 66, 1976.

Ward, John, *Information Relative to New Zealand Compiled for the Use of the Colonists*, John W. Parker, London, 1840; Capper Press reprint, Christchurch 1975.

Waters, S.D., *The Royal New Zealand Navy*, War Histories Branch, Wellington, 1956.

Waterson, Duncan, 'Transport in New Zealand 1900–1930', in R.F. Watters (ed.), *Land and Society in New Zealand*, A.H. & A.W. Reed, Wellington, 1965, reprint 1967.

Weitzel, R.L., 'Pacifists and anti-militarists in New Zealand, 1909–1914', *New Zealand Journal of History*, Vol. 7, No. 2, October 1973.

Wells, Andrew, Stewart, Glenn H., and Duncan, Richard P., 'Evidence of widespread, synchronous, disturbance-initiated forest establishment in Westland, New Zealand', *Journal of the Royal Society of New Zealand*, Vol. 28, No. 2, June 1998.

Whitmore, Col. G.S., *The Last Maori War in New Zealand*, Sampson, Low, Marston & Co., London, 1902.

Wilson, J.G. (ed.), *History of Hawke's Bay*, A.H. & A.W. Reed, Wellington, 1939.

——, *The History of Umutaoroa 1896–1956*, Dannevirke Publishing Company Ltd, Dannevirke, 1956.

Win, Roger D., *Who Ploughed So Well*, private publication, Nelson, 1996.

Wolff, Leon, *In Flanders Fields*, Longmans, Green & Co, London, 1959.

Wood, F.L.W., *New Zealand in the World*, Department of Internal Affairs, Wellington, 1940.

——, *Political and External Affairs*, War Histories Branch, Wellington, 1958.

——, 'Why did New Zealand not join the Australian Commonwealth in 1900–1901?', *New Zealand Journal of History*, Vol. 2, No. 2, October 1968.

Wright, Matthew, 'Australia, New Zealand and Imperial Naval Defence', MA Thesis, Massey University, 1986.

——, 'Sir Joseph Ward and New Zealand Naval Defence, 1907–13', *Political Science*, Vol. 41, No. 1, July 1989.

——, *Hawke's Bay – The History of a Province*, Dunmore Press, Palmerston North, 1994.

——, *Havelock North – The History of a Village*, HDC, Hastings, 1996.

——, *Kiwi Air Power*, Reed, Auckland, 1998.

——, *New Zealand's Engineering Heritage*, Reed, Auckland, 1999.

——, *Battle for Crete*, Reed, Auckland, 1999, reprint 2003.

——, *Quake – Hawke's Bay 1931*, Reed, Auckland, 2001.

——, *Blue Water Kiwis*, Reed, Auckland, 2001.

——, *Town and Country – The History of Hastings and District*, Hastings District Council, Hastings, 2001.

——, *Desert Duel*, Reed, Auckland, 2002.

——, *Wings Over New Zealand*, Whitcoulls, Auckland, 2002.

——, *Italian Odyssey*, Reed, Auckland, 2003.

——, *Pacific War*, Reed, Auckland, 2003.

——, *Rails Across New Zealand*, Whitcoulls, Auckland, 2003.

Index

demographic change 379; European disease 33; European trade 32–33; impact on New Zealand 11–14; missionaries 34–36; muskets 38–48; origins 9–11; population growth 12; population recovery 423; post-war economic position 424–25; potato 46–47; re-assertion 422; response to settler expansion 197–200; tools 20; urbanisation 423; warfare 17

Marlborough 113, 115, 149, 163

Marsden, Samuel 34–35

Martin, Sir William 87, 199

Martinborough 142

Massey, William Ferguson 247, 249, 251, 252–53, 270, 274, 280, 283

Massey's Cossacks 254

Masterton 138, 445

Matamata 396

Mathew, Felton 140

Mazengarb, Oswald 404

McDonnell, Colonel Thomas 176

McIntosh, Alister 387

McIntyre, Peter 389

McKenzie, John 216

McKenzie, Thomas 253

McLean, Allan 113

McLean, Donald 65, 86–87, 89–90, 92–94, 109, 119, 128, 149, 151, 153, 170–71, 173–74, 176, 200, 215

Mercer, Henry 157

Meremere 157

Methodist Missionary Society 36

missionaries 46–47

Mixed-member Proportional Representation (MMP) 443

moa 12–14; extinction 13

modernism 330–33

Mohaka massacre 174

Monro, Sir David 121

Moore, G.H. 109, 120

Moorehouse, William 150

Morris 1000 385, 393

Mount Algidus 113

Mount Egmont/Taranaki 108, 229

Mount Ruapehu 367

Muldoon, Sir Robert 366, 411, 414–16, 418, 427, 429, 433, 435–36, 438, 441, 446

Mulgan, Alan 300

Mulgan, John 303, 305, 308–9, 311–12, 316, 357, 366

Munro, Donald 390

Murphy, Geoff 432

Mururoa Atoll 421

musket pa 48, 256

Nanto-Bordelaise Company 74, 76

Napier 89–90, 119, 123, 139, 141, 146, 176, 181, 184, 194–95, 199–200, 229, 249, 279; earthquake 305–8, 334, 381, 393, 403

Nash, Walter 318, 320–21, 350, 354, 369, 379, 403

National Airways Corporation (NAC) 375, 418

National Expenditure Adjustment Act 311

National Party founded 325; comparison with Labour 377–78, 414, 418, 427, 441, 443

Nelson Football Club 203

Nelson 72–73, 141, 149, 278

Nelson, William 228–29

Nene, Tamati Waka 58, 61, 77–82

Nepia, George 294

New Munster 76

New Plymouth 63, 83, 139, 143–144, 153, 229, 230, 313, 368

New Zealand and Australia Land Company 114

New Zealand Ballet 390

New Zealand Company 53, 55, 63, 74–75, 83, 92, 95–99, 141,152

New Zealand Farmers Union 251

New Zealand First Party 443

New Zealand Land Company 65

New Zealand Legion 316

New Zealand National Orchestra 399

New Zealand Permanent Air Force 341

New Zealand Railways 231

New Zealand, HMS 248

New Zealand agrarian revolution 274; and censorship 294; and missionaries 36; baby boom 379; 'big' government 273–74; cars 393–94; causes 304; colonial cringe 413; cultural cringe 232–34, 240; cultural cringe and try-hard ethos 232–33; cultural cringe and expatriates 300–3; defence 342–43; defence thinking 244–46; double patriotism 255, 408; dreadnought offer 246–47; early European explorers 21–26; early settlements 63–73; economic crisis 161–62; economic crisis 285; economic recovery 369–70; effects 446–47; egalitarian ideal 108–10; egalitarianism 402–4; European attitudes 34–35; flat tax 283; frozen meat trade 227–31, 233; generation gap 19; gentry life 112–14; gentry lifestyle 220–23; gold mining 166–69; government 74–77; growth 371; ideas of Dominion 244–45; irrelevance of Marx 111; jingoism 234–40; land purchases 86–94; Liberal thinking 244–48; literature 390; long depression 169; marriage 119; moral evangelism 210–11; motor camps 388; motorisation 292; new migration 179–85; oil crises 413, 427; part of British sphere 52; Pavlova society 384–92; Polynesian arrival 9–10; post-colonial thinking 420–21; public service 215; quarter-acre ideal 136; quarter-acre promotion 323; recovery 318–19; relief schemes 313; retirement 120; riots 315; rise of left 250–52; scale of settler movement 99; second agrarian revolution 369; shaped 9; Singapore defence 282–83; six o'clock closing 266, 268–69, 385; social complexity 206–9; social cost 311–12; social purity 287–90, 294; state restructuring 438, 440; superficially boring 385; technology 393; temperance 210; Think Big 428–29; traders 32–33; TV 394; unemployment 309; unemployment 371; union with Australia 243–44; upper class ideals 111; urban idealism 141–46; urban life 136–40; Vogelism 177–79; voyage to 104–7; war scares and defence 240–43; wartime commandeer 283; wartime social change 266–67; working classes 133–35; working life 126–27; youth lifestyles 291–92; yuppies 438

Nga Puhi 42–43, 46, 50, 78, 81–82

Ngai Tahu 51

Ngai te Rangi 159–60

Ngaruawahia 155, 157–58, 283, 339

Ngata, Sir Apirana Turupa 334–36, 338, 422

Ngati Hineuru 170

Ngati Kahungunu 10, 61, 89–90, 93, 94, 112, 156, 170, 174, 176

Ngati Mutunga 65, 68

Ngati Raukawa 41, 46, 66

Ngati Toa 42, 43, 65–66, 83, 84

Ngati Tumatakokiri 23

Ngati Whatua 43, 61

Niagara, SS 270–271

Normanby, Lord 54–55

Norsewood 277

North Island Main Trunk line 87–88, 194, 196–97, 376–77, 442

Northland 12

nuclear protests 436–37

Nugent, C.L. 152

OECD 447

Ohinemutu 334–35, 337

Old Age Pensions Act 1891 253

Oliver, W.H. 449

Onehunga 134, 211

Opotiki 170